Balloon Ace

Balloon Ace

The Life of an Early Airpower Visionary

Charles D. Dusch Jr.

UNIVERSITY PRESS OF KENTUCKY

Publication of this volume was made possible, in part, by a generous donation from James W. Holsinger Jr.

Copyright © 2025 by The University Press of Kentucky

Scholarly publisher for the Commonwealth,
serving Bellarmine University, Berea College,
Centre College of Kentucky, Eastern Kentucky University,
The Filson Historical Society, Georgetown College,
Kentucky Historical Society, Kentucky State University,
Morehead State University, Murray State University,
Northern Kentucky University, Spalding University,
Transylvania University, University of Kentucky,
University of Louisville, University of Pikeville,
and Western Kentucky University.
All rights reserved.

Editorial and Sales Offices: The University Press of Kentucky
663 South Limestone Street, Lexington, Kentucky 40508-4008
www.kentuckypress.com

Frontispiece: Lieutenant Louis Bennett Jr. and a friend's dog stand in front of a Sopwith Pup prior to departing for France. (West Virginia and Regional History Center, WVU Libraries.)

Cataloging-in-Publication data is available from the Library of Congress.

ISBN 978-1-9859-0161-2 (hardcover : alk. paper)
ISBN 978-1-9859-0160-5 (pbk. : alk. paper)
ISBN 978-1-9859-0163-6 (pdf)
ISBN 978-1-9859-0164-3 (epub)

This book is printed on acid-free paper meeting the requirements of the American National Standard for Permanence in Paper for Printed Library Materials.

Manufactured in the United States of America.

Member of the Association of University Presses

To Kate, Conner, and Kyle. Thank you for your many sacrifices . . .

Contents

Introduction. I'll Never Forget: The Impact of Commemoration on Generations   1

1. In Stonewall's Shadow: Shaping a Generation for Total War   12
2. The War to End All Wars through the Lens of College Boys   18
3. Aerial Militia: Americans Prepare for War beyond the Borders   32
4. "A More Distinguished Way of Doing Greater Good": Americans Lurch toward War   55
5. Unusual Courage: Becoming a Pursuit Pilot   78
6. Most Remarkable Work: "A Son to Be Proud of Indeed"   100
7. To Die a Fiery "Miserable Death": Air Combat on the Western Front, 1918   113
8. Mothers of Heroes: Waiting for News on the Home Front   135
9. A Job So Sacred: Women, Governments, and Care for the Fallen   164
10. The Gratitude of All Those Present: Commemoration on the World Stage   190

Conclusion. Ready to Serve: The Monument as Exemplar   215

Acknowledgments   229
Notes   231
Index   261
About the Author   271

Illustrations follow page 134

Introduction

I'll Never Forget: The Impact of Commemoration on Generations

Usually each August, eight-year-old "Bud" Dusch was impatiently awaiting another birthday, but on the morning of August 4, 1927, he and the entire Upper Ohio Valley were expecting the arrival of "Lucky Lindy," Charles A. Lindbergh—America's newest hero who stunned the world by flying his Ryan monoplane, the *Spirit of St. Louis*, nonstop from New York to Paris the preceding May. This unprecedented achievement catapulted "Lindy" into mega-celebrity status. Beginning with his welcome at Le Bourget airfield in Paris, huge crowds greeted him everywhere. Bud hoped to see Lindbergh when he arrived in Wheeling, West Virginia, as part of his celebratory cross-country tour of the United States.

Bud was in his yard restlessly anticipating Lindbergh's visit when the throaty roar of a powerful motor caused him to look up. Instead of seeing Lindbergh's *Spirit of St. Louis*, he saw a US Army pursuit plane cruising at about 150 knots (172 miles per hour) above the National Road flying below the hills, so low that the boy could clearly see the pilot's features. When the aircraft came over the family home, the wheels of the fixed landing gear clipped some branches off one of the trees. The plane curved to the right following the road and valley, where the pilot spotted a foursome of golfers on a nearby golf course. He pulled up in a rapid climb, rolled over, and dove in a mock attack on the men. The golfers hit the dirt. The pilot then aggressively pulled up so that vapors came off the wings, steered west toward the Ohio River, and was soon out of sight. Young Bud stood motionless throughout, thrilled with the aerial display, which lasted only seconds. The pilot of the aircraft was one of the best in the Army, Lieutenant James "Jimmy" Doolittle, who came to Wheeling in the vanguard of Charles A. Lindbergh and would later command the Tokyo Raid in World War II.[1]

Lindbergh's conquest of the Atlantic Ocean symbolized peoples' confidence in the new technologies of the "modern" twentieth century. Lindbergh and the *Spirit* were making a triumphal tour of seventy-five US cities across the continent to promote aviation, sponsored by Daniel Guggenheim. It began in New York City on July 20 and ended in October. While Doolittle "beat up" Langin Army Airfield, the Valley's only airport located south of Wheeling in nearby Moundsville, Lindbergh was preparing to take off from Pittsburgh. After a short stay in historic Wheeling overnight, he would proceed to Dayton, Ohio.[2]

About 1349 hours that August afternoon, the *Spirit of St. Louis* appeared over Wheeling from the north. Lindbergh circled the city five times before turning south to land at Langin Field. Over twenty West Virginia State Police kept the crowd of twenty thousand back from the aircraft. After taxiing to a stop, Lindbergh did a quick postflight inspection of his ship, greeted the reception committee and photographers, and stood quietly while the *Spirit* was secured in the field's hangar. He was then whisked away with a police motorcycle escort.[3]

Hours before Lindbergh's arrival, traffic jammed the streets and highways within a ten-mile radius of Wheeling. Crowds were so thick that it took the official party one hour to travel the thirteen miles from Langin Field to Wheeling Island. The *Wheeling Intelligencer* estimated that one hundred thousand people came out to see the aviation icon. Bud's father had promised to take him to the state fairgrounds on Wheeling Island where Lindbergh was to speak at three that afternoon. However, by the time he came home from work, the roads and bridges to the city were clogged with onlookers.[4]

Bud feared that he wouldn't get to see his hero, when his mother came home from her doctor's appointment bearing good news. The doctor's son went to school at nearby Linsly Institute and learned that Lindbergh was visiting the military school after his speech on Wheeling Island. At Linsly, he would lay a wreath at the foot of *The Aviator* statue, which was erected by Sallie Maxwell Bennett and bore the likeness of her son, Louis Bennett Jr., West Virginia's only World War I ace. She dedicated that monument to honor her son as well as all Americans who died in the Great War, the "gift of *one* mother for *all* mothers."[5] It was one of some twelve memorials she initiated in her son's honor. Since Linsly planned a small and intimate ceremony, it was the best place for Bud to see his hero.

Bud and his father climbed into the family Chevrolet and drove the eight miles from their home along National Road to Thedah Place, the site of the new Linsly campus. The trip took about twelve minutes. Only about twenty cadets were there, along with the dean of the school, Guy Holden, and a few of the Linsly Board of Trustees. Bud was able to stand near *The Aviator* statue where he could be close to Lindbergh. It wasn't long before he heard the police escort sirens and the official party consisting of Lindbergh, Doolittle, and Wheeling city officials drove into view along the National Pike. Lindbergh had spoken for fewer than three minutes at Wheeling Island before departing for Linsly. As he approached the statue, Bud could hardly believe what was happening. Some eighty years later, he still recalled that "Lindbergh [walked] over to the Aviator statue to lay a wreath. I never forgot that. He had a beat up old jacket on, and I stood right alongside of him. I'll never forget that—I stood alongside of him!" After the brief ceremony, Lindbergh departed for his quarters at the distinguished Fort Henry Club and a banquet that evening at the Scottish Rite Cathedral.[6]

For young Bud Dusch, this was a cherished, forever remembered "life moment," carried into his nineties as clearly as if it were yesterday. Yet it is a typical story from the "Golden Age" of aviation in America, a time when aviation was a new, modern technology and its masters were the pop stars of that era—an era in which people saw not only an airplane for the first time but also saw another human being *fly* for the first time in their lives. Though multiple new technologies contributed to the concept of this new, "modern" age, aviation was foremost among them and came to symbolize the so-called American Century.

And first among aviators was Charles Lindbergh. One might wonder why Wheeling was one of his tour stops or why he dedicated the majority of his visit to a small military school laying a wreath at *The Aviator* instead of speaking at the main event. When one considers other sites along the Lindbergh tour, its meaning comes into focus. On his return from Paris, Lindbergh first visited Arlington National Cemetery outside Washington, DC, accompanied by his mother. There, he paid his respects by placing a wreath at the Tomb of the Unknown Soldier. After leaving Wheeling, his next destination was Dayton, Ohio, where he placed a wreath at the grave of Wilbur

Wright, one of the founders of heavier-than-air flight.[7] Clearly, Lindbergh in part linked his conquest of the Atlantic with those who had paved the way for him, both in the Great War and in aviation. By going to Wheeling, America's newest aviation hero honored this seemingly obscure Great War pilot from West Virginia memorialized in *The Aviator* statue.

But Louis Bennett Jr. is only obscure to us in the twenty-first century. In 1927, the aviation community was still relatively small, and the masters of the sky knew one another as well as the reputations of their peers. They kept tabs on aviation developments around the world as well as the distinguished aviators in the Great War. In the United States, a core of these aviators came from Ivy League schools, in those days small, insulated, elitist societies in their own right, and their connections to the rich and powerful, the "movers and shakers" of industry and government, spread the fame of the small aviation community further afield.

Since Lindbergh served as a Reserve Army aviator, there is little doubt that he would have been acquainted with Louis Bennett Jr.

Bennett was a gifted young pilot who demonstrated his skill—or "hands" in fighter pilot jargon—early in his flight training. In many ways, he was typical of his generation of air warriors: he was a product of the Ivy League and competed in several intercollegiate sports, he was adventurous and lived life to the full, and machines interested him. In an age when many questioned mechanization, which seemed to strip away the dignity of workers by taking their jobs and thus their "manhood," Bennett's generation embraced it—especially the new air weapon. He took to the sky with an aggressiveness and abandon one saw especially in the foremost aces of the war.[8]

Nonetheless, Bennett was very much a product of his American heritage and upbringing. He was born into a Southern family that was prominent in their state. His father, a Confederate veteran, was related by marriage to one of the most able and notable commanders of the Confederate Army during the American Civil War, Thomas J. "Stonewall" Jackson. Jackson was eventually elevated to the pantheon of Confederate heroes after the war in the narrative of Lost Cause mythology, which justified the war and spread during the Reconstruction period. Bennett's mother embraced this Lost Cause narrative and sought to indoctrinate her son in its importance.[9] As a child, Louis Bennett Jr. was taught that he had big shoes to fill.

Young Bennett was not alone in this pedagogy. By the time war erupted in Europe in 1914, Americans were immersed in the myths of their Civil

War heritage. They both celebrated and commemorated the fiftieth anniversary of that war, hosting reunions for the veterans as well as erecting numerous monuments in their honor among the various battlefields. Civil War commemoration peaked in the United States between 1903 and 1914, with a number of monuments unveiled during the First World War.[10] In 1915, D. W. Griffith's silent movie *The Birth of a Nation* was released. As the fiftieth anniversary events came to a close, many young Americans were left with Griffith's interpretation of the war and Reconstruction, which perpetuated Civil War myths and glorified the Ku Klux Klan.

When the United States declared war on Germany in 1917, many Americans looked backward to frame the context of the war in Europe in which they were about to engage within the national narrative of Civil War mythology. Newspaper articles repeatedly drew on Civil War themes. Communities invited Civil War veterans—including those maimed in the war—to places of honor at rallies as a demonstration of reconciliation and unity. Marching together, the veterans from the Grand Army of the Republic and the United Confederate Veterans served two purposes: first, they represented the solidarity of patriotism; second, they reminded American youth of the courage and commitment of their ancestors—those who had fought and those who were "sacrificed on the altar of the nation." The newspapers of the era described these ancient veterans as "an inspiring sight" for members of Bennett's generation on the eve of war. In this way, the myth as much as the history of the Civil War shaped American attitudes toward the Great War by presenting a romantic and adventurous view of the Civil War. Thus, many Americans approached the war in Europe as something akin to a religious crusade.[11]

On the eve of American entry into the Great War, Louis Bennett Jr. was a student at Yale University in New Haven, Connecticut. From his letters, it is clear that he intended to be very much "his own man" and make his own way in the world apart from his Civil War heritage. Perhaps this determination came about because of it. Bennett's interest in machines led him to the field of aviation. But unlike many of his peers who were merely enticed by the thrill of flying and became good pilots in the war, Bennett was much, much more. He clearly thought about aviation keenly and its impact on the war in larger terms.

Bennett was strategically positioned as an undergraduate at Yale University at a critical time in history. Yale was among the first schools to offer a course in aeronautics, stimulating ideas and possibilities. Bennett's concepts reflected those ideas. They were far-reaching and would eventually shape airpower development in the United States. First, they influenced his classmates, many of whom were the sons of wealthy industrialists and politicians who were destined to become America's future leaders. Next, they inspired other aviation-minded students at Yale who imitated Bennett's ideas about military aviation units. After the war, his former classmates became the leaders who carried those ideas into the future.

As early as 1915, Bennett announced to the president of the Aero Club of America that he wanted to establish a volunteer aviation unit in his home state that would be "ready to serve" in time of war, not unlike the volunteer units his Southern forebears founded in the so-called "War of Secession." He began to discuss the idea with other distinguished members of the Aero Club. He took a job in an aircraft factory to learn all he could about how aircraft worked as well as how aircraft were produced. He learned to fly. He shared his ideas with his classmates at Yale, many of whom caught his enthusiasm and joined him. His ideas spread around campus and likely influenced Frederick Trubee Davison to form his own volunteer aviation unit, the First Yale Unit, dubbed by the press as "the Millionaires' Unit."[12]

In the spring semester of Bennett's senior year at Yale, Imperial Germany's program of unrestricted submarine warfare intensified. Bennett purchased an aircraft and outlined his plans for a "West Virginia Reserve Aerial Unit" composed of volunteers. He promoted it as an archetype of the Escadrille Lafayette—a famous French pursuit squadron composed of American volunteers. He enrolled pilots, ground crew, and support personnel on his own initiative, financing most of it.[13] He established an airfield, aviation school, and maintenance facilities for the unit in addition to recruiting instructor pilots. He eventually convinced both the governor and legislature to financially support the West Virginia Flying Corps (WVFC), and the governor issued Bennett a state commission as the unit's captain and permitted him to enlist men as soldiers. As the idea came to fruition, it had the hallmarks of an aerial militia—a state volunteer unit similar to the volunteer units of the American Civil War. However, as a modern man and product of the Industrial Revolution, Bennett also partnered with his father and brother-in-law to begin aircraft manufacture in his home state. Bennett understood that the new air weapon needed a steady industrial and financial base, and his aircraft factory would supply his unit, maintain it logistically, and provide aircraft and parts for the Army's war effort. He built the West Virginia Aircraft Factory a few miles south of his airfield, and he persuaded investors from the nearby industrial city of Wheeling to help finance it. Years before noted aviation theorists Giulio Douhet and William "Billy" Mitchell wrote about this relationship of public and private financing to aviation's industrial base, Louis Bennett Jr. was putting it into practice.[14]

Immediately after the United States declared war on Imperial Germany, Bennett contacted the Signal Corps' aviation section to determine the Army's standards for aviation training so he could offer it a credible combat unit. At that time, the Army's aviation section was woefully unprepared for combat on the Western Front. By some accounts, it only had 131 officers, of whom 65 were aviators. Only 26 of them were fully trained. Its enlisted force consisted of 1,087 men. None of its aircraft were capable of flying in combat in Europe and were only good for training. This lack of readiness in the aviation section reflected the War Department's overall unpreparedness.[15] One senior US Army Air Service (USAAS) officer remarked that prior to American entry into the war, the War Department "made no plans as to what it would do in case we were suddenly called upon to become one of the great military nations of the world."[16] The sudden expansion, lack of organization, and bureaucratic red tape created congestion and confusion that disrupted the mobilization process. Young Bennett quickly learned he was on his own if he wanted to make his dream a reality.

By the summer of 1917, Bennett's unit acquired additional aircraft and was actively training. As his worldview expanded, Bennett foresaw the need for a national aviation reserve with flying units in every state and major city, postured to support both military and commercial aviation. Each unit was to have a supporting airfield, aviation schools, skilled personnel, and a factory. They would be funded by the state and federal governments as well as private and corporate investors. Therefore, in addition to his West Virginia Flying Corps, he acquired aviation schools in New Jersey and Florida and sought to expand even further. In August 1917, Bennett lobbied giant businesses like the DuPont Corporation in Delaware to support his idea for a national aviation reserve system. Bennett continued to lobby the War Department for acceptance of his WVFC. Even were the War Department inclined—or capable—of helping him, the Wilson administration prohibited the Army from accepting volunteer units, fearing the resurgence of former president and political rival Theodore Roosevelt. Secretary of War Newton Baker declined numerous requests from other volunteer groups, including those formed by both Bennett and Davison.[17]

Baker recommended that Bennett and his pilots apply for Army aviation training through the Signal Officers' Reserve Corps aviation section as the best means of obtaining a commission as an Army pilot, emphasizing he would not accept a state volunteer organization. Bennett was equally as persistent as the intractable Wilson administration, insisting that the War Department grant conscription exemptions to the unit's personnel and allow it to represent his beloved home state. The War Department held all the cards, however, and when the draft began, the West Virginia Flying Corps lost both pilots and mechanics to the Army. Its future as a military unit was precarious.[18]

At this point, the frustrated Bennett made a fateful decision. Placing the future of the unit and his idea for a national aviation reserve with his brother-in-law, a successful businessman who was neither an aviator nor familiar with the aviation industry, Bennett went to Canada to join the Royal Flying Corps (RFC). He knew from his Yale colleagues in the USAAS that the Army training program was rife with interminable delays. Struggling to expedite training, the Air Service sent its brightest cadet ground school graduates to France for accelerated flight school, only to have them languish in purgatory waiting for training to begin. Many waited so long that their classmates who were trained back in the United States by a fumbling USAAS arrived as rated pilots and commissioned officers, while they remained aviation cadets. Morale plummeted.[19]

Bennett's conclusion that going to Canada to join the RFC was the fastest means of getting into the war for any American pilot was also shared by the director of aeronautical training for the Air Service, due to the "slow grinding machinery" of the training bureaucracy. In fact, the director himself was sent to Canada in May 1917 to learn firsthand from the RFC how to put together the training program for the USAAS.[20]

When Bennett joined the RFC in 1917, his narrative merged into the larger, global story of the Great War. Indeed, in many ways the account of Bennett and his family mirrors that of the larger narrative of the West, writ small: Bennett completed his training, served on the Western Front with distinction, was shot down in flames, died in hospital, and was obscurely buried in a military cemetery in France.

Bennett's ideas about a national aviation system did not die with him, however. During the 1920s, when Bennett's Yale brethren entered government service and industry, they became the "movers and shakers" and put Bennett's ideas into practice, refined from both their own Great War experiences and those of the Allies. They threw their support behind airpower advocates like Brigadier General William "Billy" Mitchell or Major General Mason Patrick and set the vector of American airpower through aviation's Golden Age and World War II. One of these elites, F. Trubee Davison, became the first assistant secretary of war for air in 1926 when congressional legislation established the Army Air Corps.[21]

This study seeks to place Louis Bennett Jr. in the context of the development of American military aviation and the Preparedness Movement by examining the way he merged traditional and modern approaches toward American war readiness. It follows the evolution and refinement of his thinking as well as the practical applications he chose in order to tackle those obstacles to his plans. His choices, like those of his contemporaries, mattered to many: to his peers who fought the same fight, embraced his passionate ideas for aviation, and carried them forward; to Charles Lindbergh, who fulfilled Bennett's dream of a nonstop transatlantic flight; and to his family, who lost a son and heir. Bennett's concepts reached far into the future and influenced those of us who also became aviators. Finally, the United States was shaped by the transnational scope of the Great War.

After the war, the Bennett family's narrative also amalgamated into the larger story of Great War commemoration. After Bennett was reported missing "over the lines," his mother waited in agony with the unknown. Her world came "crashing down" when she received the fateful telegram that announced his death. From this point the Bennett story veers somewhat from the collective narrative and conjoins the grieving and commemorative experiences of Great War families with those of the American Civil War. Like many family members of the fallen, in both the American Civil War and the Great War, Sallie Bennett sought to recover her son's body, bring him home, commemorate his memory, and convey to future generations her account of what her son's life and death truly meant.[22]

When his mother arrived in France and found his remains, she learned that she was prohibited from removing them. So she conspired with the local parish priest to have them secretly exhumed and smuggled to the United States in defiance of French law. Grateful to the local village for its help, she built a chapel there to commemorate her son. For the next six years, she actively sought to memorialize her son across borders and continents. Besides the church in France, she commissioned a wreath at the Cenotaph in London and a window in Britain's Westminster Abbey. At home in the United States, she dedicated an airport and a library. She donated a tapestry and sponsored a parachute contest in her son's memory. Her crowning achievement was to commission *The Aviator* statue by a noted Southern sculptor and place it in Wheeling, the city where her son's dream of an aviation militia became reality—in all, some twelve memorials to him.[23]

But she often had to battle governments to get her way, whether it was building monuments to her son or bringing him home. She was a tenacious advocate that the US government honor its promise on the disposition of American war dead, insisting that families be allowed to bring their soldier dead home for burial, contrary to the desires of the Army and the Wilson administration.

Today, there is a robust body of literature on memory and commemoration of both the American Civil War and the Great War, but there are fewer accounts that compare the American experience of that first total war of the Industrial Revolution with the American experience of the Great War, which belatedly joined in Europe's first total war of the Industrial Revolution, which of course was a much more transnational experience. After the First World War, human behaviors, responses, monuments, cemeteries, and memorials strongly follow those of Americans after their Civil War. Sallie Maxwell Bennett's story is particularly compelling, especially her advocacy that the US government submit to the desires of the families of the fallen. This one woman made a lasting impact. Today, America's fallen service members are repatriated for burial in the United States rather than interred overseas. She championed the cause of private memorials for the fallen alongside official government-sponsored monuments. Through her example, one sees that American Civil War and World War I commemoration are largely inseparable, and therefore, an analysis of their linkage makes this study unique.

Bud's recollection, though typical of the so-called Golden Age of aviation, is also a fleeting memory of the era. Sallie Maxwell Bennett sought a more permanent and pedagogical commemoration of her son, one in which mega-celebrities like Charles A. Lindbergh would come to pay their respects.

At the end of the day, this is a narrative about the life and commemoration of a very driven, thoughtful, brave, and resourceful young man who died before his potential was fully realized. It is both an account of a remarkable individual and the saga of a generation. From the American perspective, it is rooted in that country's Civil War; became part of a larger transnational narrative; and returned again to its post–Civil War heritage through the commemorative efforts of his very tenacious mother, who was a force in her own right. This, then, is their story.

1

In Stonewall's Shadow

Shaping a Generation for Total War

West Virginia's only Great War ace, Louis Bennett Jr., was born in Weston, Lewis County, West Virginia, on September 22, 1894, the youngest of three children. Weston sits in the heart of central West Virginia, the only state completely nestled within the region of Appalachia. His mother, Sallie Maxwell Bennett, was a persistent influence on the young man. Her father, James Maxwell, was a successful merchant, entrepreneur, and philanthropist.[1] Although Wheeling was the hub of Unionist activity in western Virginia during the American Civil War and eventually became the first capital of the new state of West Virginia, the Maxwell family was labeled one of the "Traitors in Wheeling" by the *Wheeling Intelligencer* for siding with Richmond on the issue of secession. Sallie Maxwell Bennett married Weston attorney Louis Bennett and gave birth to three children: James, who died as an infant; Agra, who was born in Denver and later married noted Wheeling industrialist Johnson C. McKinley; and Louis Bennett Jr., known to his friends as "Lou" or "Ben."

The Bennett family came to America from Scotland before the Revolutionary War and settled in Virginia. Their wealth originated from their large landholdings. Lou's father was from Weston and served as a midshipman in the Confederate Navy during what his family called the "War of Secession." Later, he became president of Glenville College and the Lewis County Bank, and he served as the Democratic speaker of the West Virginia House of Delegates. In 1908, he unsuccessfully ran for governor. He was a Mason, Knight Templar, and member of the Episcopal Church. Young Lou's grandfather Jonathan M. Bennett was auditor of Virginia when the American Civil War began and remained with the South. However, his influence on Southern military capabilities was far-reaching.[2]

In the summer of 1842, Constable Tom Jackson came to Jonathan Bennett with a request. Having learned that another young local man had resigned from the US Military Academy at West Point after being there only a few days, Jackson intended to petition Congressman Samuel Hayes for an appointment there. Jackson asked Bennett if he and his prominent Lewis County colleagues would help him. Jonathan Bennett had previously loaned Jackson books or offered him advice. He knew that the young constable was an avid reader but had no formal education. Bennett asked him if he thought he would be able to succeed in such a rigorous academic environment like West Point. Jackson acknowledged his limitations but was resolved to compensate for them through hard work and study, stating, "I know I have the energy and I think I have the intellect."[3]

Bennett, who was related to Jackson through marriage, agreed to support him and gathered letters of recommendation and petitions to the local congressman and the secretary of war from as many influential people as he could. Bennett wrote that these signatories "recommend to his Excellency, the Secretary of War, Thomas J. Jackson as a fit and proper person to receive the appointment of cadet in the military academy at West Point." Jackson eventually finished seventeenth out of fifty-nine in his class. During the American Civil War, he joined the Confederate Army, and at the first Battle of Manassas, he earned the nickname "Stonewall" Jackson through his tenacity. He achieved remarkable success as one of Robert E. Lee's corps commanders, and his campaign in the Shenandoah Valley is still considered one of the most brilliant campaigns in military history. He was an important role model for young Lou, whose "boyhood days were spent in and around the home of Thomas Jonothan [sic] 'Stonewall' Jackson." As a child growing up in the shadow of "Stonewall" Jackson, young Louis regarded the Confederate icon as his favorite historical figure. Much of that influence was because Sallie accentuated the family's Confederate identity and relation to Jackson. She formidably impressed this upon her son.[4]

Despite this immersion in family history, Lou was very interested in machines. As he got older, he owned a motorcycle, and by the time he was fourteen, he had built a jalopy from motorcycle and automobile parts. Thrilled with his achievement and the speed it generated, young Louis dashed over the dirt roads in Lewis County kicking up dust with his friends. His exploits around Weston were captured in the local newspaper, the *Weston Democrat*. His mechanical inclination and fascination with machines was very common for young men of his generation, and certainly it was a common trait of many early pilots. Aviation pioneer Charles A. Lindbergh had a motorcycle that he drove cross-country to Florida. Quentin Roosevelt, the youngest son of former president Theodore Roosevelt, liked to buy "broken-down" motorcycles and automobiles, "fix them up, and drive them until they broke down again." He, too, became a combat aviator in the Great War. Other future World War I aviators enjoyed rebuilding various types of engines and racing the cars they built. America's Great War "ace of aces," Eddie Rickenbacker, was himself a famous automobile racer before the war and later sought to raise a squadron comprised of his racing partners for military service.[5]

Like most children of wealthy parents, Lou went to boarding school, first attending a preparatory school in New Jersey and later in Pennsylvania. In 1912, he took the entrance examination to Yale University. Although Louis scored well in Cicero, Latin Grammar, Algebra A and B, Geometry, French A, and English B, he was not accepted in Virgil, Latin Composition, English and German A, Plane Trigonometry, and French B. Having been rebuffed by Yale, Louis, as captain of the prep school football team for the 1912 season, took a solemn oath with his teammates "not to smoke or eat or drink harmful things during the 1912 football season." Lou maintained this abstention from tobacco and alcohol throughout his time at Yale.[6]

Admission to an Ivy League school such as Yale was crucial to upper class parents who had aspirations for their children. The doors to corporate America as well as American government were always open to Ivy League graduates. It must have been a great relief for the Bennett family when young Louis received a "second colloquy appointment" into Yale in the fall of 1913. Lou packed up his desk, clothing, and books and left St. Luke's with his mother on the New York, New Haven and Hartford Railroad on September 17, 1913. He arrived at Yale and roomed at 551 Pierson Hall.[7]

The Yale of 1913 more closely resembled the English public school tradition, and in many ways desperately emulated its rituals. Freshmen began campus life with a beating—literally. During freshman rush, they ran a gauntlet of upperclassmen who lashed out at them with punches or kicks. Supervised by the Yale senior class, the freshmen chose champions from among their ranks to wrestle the best of the sophomore class. Later during the year came the "cane rush," where sophomores, who stood by the College Fence that ran along the inner roadway of the Old Campus, used bamboo canes or poles to hold off charges by surging freshman. Students who came away from this melee with injuries, black eyes, or cuts as badges of honor were said to have "sand." That was the name Yale students gave to the unique quality they found in their "best" classmates. Like the sand that the engineer spread beneath the great wheels of a locomotive in order for it to grip the rails on a steep grade, the sand of a Yale student was supposedly a public manifestation of his character. Students were expected to do their duty "for God, for country and for Yale." The very best proved their sand by doing something significant for Yale, such as managing the prestigious crew team; being elected editor of the *Yale Daily News*; touring the country as one of Yale's "gentlemen songsters," the Whiffenpoofs; forming a club; or playing any sport that brought victory over Harvard. Sports were by far the most important means of proving sand. Teamwork and competition groomed Ivy League graduates for the boardroom and the battlefield. Academics, on the other hand, were seen as "a wasted pursuit." In a student culture that emphasized everything but study, President Arthur Twining Hadley lamented to a gathering of alumni in 1915 that "we need to elevate study to the level of an extra-curriculum activity." Most Yale students believed they had gathered enough book knowledge during their long years at boarding school before coming to Yale. Academic success at Yale could bring mockery or alienation. The lucky ones combined athleticism with good grades or made classwork seem so effortless that their peers disregarded their academic achievements.[8]

Aspiring freshmen, like Lou, trying to prove their sand were known as "heelers," a campus term for "competitors," who pursued election to campus leadership positions and ultimately admittance into one of the three secret, closed-door, seniors-only societies—Wolf's Head, Scroll and Key, and Skull and Bones. These elite forty-five classmates were perceived as the cream of the crop most likely to lead America in the future. Selection gave them a substantial advantage over their equally privileged peers, when they were chosen on Tap Day, held the second Tuesday in May at five o'clock in the afternoon. Under the branches of the century-old Tap Day Oak, fifteen graduating seniors from each of the secret societies chose their own successors from the ranks of the junior class by tapping them firmly on the shoulders and commanding, "Go to your room!" Publicly recognized for "proving" his sand, the honored junior would march off to his room to await whatever orders his society dictated in order to begin the rites of initiation. Those not selected might be publicly shamed or humiliated. Stung, some resolved to still prove their sand after Yale and eclipse their "tapped" classmates.[9]

Lou fit naturally into this environment with his active, energetic nature and love of sports. He was among the first of the Class of 1917 to distinguish himself at the opening day of school during freshman rush. Shortly after his class assembled in front of Osborn Hall, the seniors approached and ordered them to "fall in" behind the ranks of the upper classes that were already formed up. Seemingly dignified, the authoritative, quiet seniors—with pipes in mouths—drove the freshmen in lines of eight and ten and marched them to the center of the campus. As they marched, the upper classes began to sound cheers, with each class ending its cheer with its respective class year until it was time for the neophyte Class of 1917 to offer up its own cheer, which was answered by the upper classmen. Lou and his classmates found themselves swept forward behind the great mass of the cheering, singing college.[10]

Reaching the center of the campus, the neat lines were broken, and the seniors divided the classes by year, forming a circle around a small clearing. Seniors wearing the letterman's Y varsity sweaters directed the freshmen in the front rank to sit, as their comrades in the rear "took a knee" just behind them. Situated directly opposite the Class of 1917 were the members of the sophomore Class of 1916. Satisfied that the college was properly deployed, the seniors next commanded, "Call out the lightweights," and the sophomore class erupted with shouting. Into the ring stepped the lightweight champion for their class. The seniors then called for a candidate from the freshman class. Without hesitation, "Louie" Bennett stepped into the ring to "be the first man in the class to publicly admit" he was a member or the Class of 1917.

Lou "earned his drawer" by winning the wrestling match, and he was followed by his classmates in victories over the Class of 1916. The campus exploded with cheering, and one freshman brazenly shouted, "Down with 1916!" The rush was on, and Lou celebrated joyfully with his classmates. The sophomores, stung by their reversal of fortune, spent the night roaming the campus and hazing any freshman they happened upon. The Class of 1917 complained that they slept that night to the tune of "Wake, Freshman, Wake."[11]

Encouraged by his initial combat, Lou went out for football, wrestling, lacrosse, and track, as well as the prestigious crew team. He became a member of the Yale wrestling and lacrosse teams, through which he distinguished himself. When he came to Yale, Lou stood five feet seven inches tall and weighed about 139 pounds; he had wavy dark-brown hair and blue eyes.[12] Despite his slight frame, he set out to prove his sand on the playing fields.

Sport was not the only discriminating factor to advancement in the Ivy League, and at Yale, proving one's sand was a more complex and intricate process. After 1912, freshmen, like Lou, found clues for successfully navigating Yale's social ladder by consulting a best-selling novel written by Yale alumnus Owen Johnson, Class of 1901. Entitled *Stover at Yale*, the novel describes the travails of John Humperdink "Dink" Stover, who arrived at Yale from prep school and learned that if he wished to succeed, he must work for his class, be discreet, choose his friends wisely, avoid "fooling around women," and be a leader. Admittance to sophomore and junior fraternities also mattered. An upper classman ominously admonished Stover, "Remember, you're going to be watched from now on."[13]

Competition in the Ivy League was stiff, especially for a lawyer's son from a small Appalachian town. Although Lou came from a prominent family, he was surrounded by the sons of the very powerful—imposingly rich, famous, and prominent. Classmate and close friend Frederick Weyerhaeuser was one of the heirs to the Weyerhaeuser Company, started by his father, the great lumber magnate also named Frederick Weyerhaeuser, and classmate Prescott Bush was the son of one of America's top industrialists. Fellow Great War pilot F. Trubee Davison from the Class of 1918 was the son of a managing partner of one of the world's most dominant bankers.[14] These sons of the Gilded Age's wealthiest American families included in their circles the world's most rich and famous. For them, money was no object, and they spent it freely at Yale. To be admitted to those circles and make a name at Yale, one had to both prove one's sand and likewise participate in the "right" social events. This could be an impediment for those coming from a traditional Southern family, where spending money frivolously was seen as lacking sense. In the case of Louis Bennett Jr., having enough money to stay in those circles proved a serious challenge during his four years at Yale.

2

The War to End All Wars through the Lens of College Boys

Lou's freshman year appears to have passed uneventfully. He took his language courses' anticipatory exams to later make room in his class schedule for law courses in the spring semester of his sophomore year, which proved to be a very eventful academic year for the young man.[1]

It began in his typically adventurous fashion by touring the United States "from the Atlantic to the Pacific and return" in his Cadillac. This was a daunting task in the summer of 1914, since most American roads were unpaved and gasoline stations, garages, and repair facilities were scarce, restricted to larger towns and cities. Parts inventories and distribution were problematic. Early automobiles broke down frequently enough that one needed to have basic mechanical knowledge and skills—as well as one's own repair and tool kit—before attempting such an endeavor. The journey was risky in 1914. Just the sort of adventure that would appeal to a young Yale student intent on proving his sand.[2]

It was during this trip out West that Lou's mother developed "painful spots," which turned out to be cancer. She needed surgery, and already tense relations with her husband manifested. Sallie accused him of infidelity and gave him an ultimatum. Meanwhile, she had the surgery and recovered alone in her hotel room. When the deadline for her ultimatum passed with no response from her husband, Sallie moved to New York City, informing him that "his outraged and mistreated wife" expected nothing more from him and he should expect nothing from her. They were now, she declared, married in name only, and she no longer cared what the neighbors thought. As Lou began his sophomore year at Yale, his family was falling apart.[3]

Lou moved into 268 Durfee Hall and began his coursework in chemistry, logic, and English. Once he was safely off to college, Sallie left New York in the fall to continue her recovery with a tour of South America. She kept close watch on his affairs, however. It was apparent that having the "right" financial obligations as a Yale student was having an adverse impact on Lou economically. He kept writing to his parents that he was "broke" or close to it. He needed to buy a typewriter for class. He needed new clothing, or his car needed repairs. His father's parsimonious responses led the younger Bennett to conclude that his father was "hard up" and that Lou's choices were to finish Yale quickly or quit and take a job so that he could help his father. Although the elder Bennett was only trying to teach the young man lessons about budgeting and fiscal responsibility, his estranged wife sent him a scolding letter. From Panama, she wrote that he should give young Louis an allowance and not be "so stingy to account for every dollar he spends."[4] This contentious family issue continued for most of Lou's time at Yale.

Of course, 1914 was a contentious year for many people across the globe, for the Western world was also falling apart. The Great War erupted in Europe during Lou's adventurous summer of 1914. It was a war that almost everyone believed would be short, but with no decisive battles and many unintended consequences, the war dragged on for 1,500 days. Its human toll reached across oceans and its impact was felt across the planet long after hostilities ended on the Western Front on November 11, 1918. Of the over seventy million soldiers from all the combatant nations or their colonies, over nine million were killed or died while on active duty. Five million civilians died. Three million women were widowed, and ten million children were orphaned.[5] It was mass slaughter on a cataclysmic scale befitting the mass production assembly lines of the Industrial Revolution that fed its arsenals. Its scars linger to this day.

None of this was clear in the late summer and early autumn of 1914, however. Americans commemorated the fiftieth anniversaries of Kennesaw Mountain and other Civil War battles, such as Cold Harbor and the siege of Petersburg. Appropriately, these battles had more in common with the trench warfare of World War I than they did with the newspapers' romantic recollections of the so-called Great War Between the States. With distant fascination, Americans read newspapers or watched newsreels of events in Europe as the populations of the Great Powers mobilized for war. From across the European continent, young men rallied to their nations' colors and volunteered for military service, soon to be joined by young men from all over these nations' empires in a truly global, transnational conflict. The announcement of the declaration of war was often met with joyous cheering and patriotic songs, although many reservists simply accepted military service as part of their patriotic duty. Marching soldiers were showered with cascades of flowers on their way to the local train stations, from which points they would begin the formal mobilization process. Railroads were essential to the armies of the Great War.

European military strategists were fascinated by the Americans' use of railroads during the American Civil War and sought to emulate the audacity and speed of "Stonewall" Jackson's Shenandoah Valley Campaign in 1862. They hoped that a speedy mobilization coupled with the use of railroads would give their side an edge against the enemy. Railroads were crucial to moving these massive armies with their millions of troops and horses and tons of war matériel to the frontier. Therefore, European war plans placed great emphasis on railroads, timetables, and speed. To meet these timetables, historian Jay Winter remarked, "German commanders were willing to pay in lives."[6]

These ornate plans for a modern, industrialized army—like the German Army's Schlieffen Plan—depended on a precise schedule of trains, cargo, and personnel in order to meet the war plan timetable. All other rail traffic was stopped so that troops and matériel could be rushed to the frontier. The Schlieffen Plan was designed with a two-front war in mind to enable Germany to fight and win against both France and Russia. Count Alfred von Schlieffen, its author, predicted that Russia, with its vast distances and poor railroad system, would need approximately six weeks to mobilize for war. He therefore conceived of a great encircling attack through Belgium, the Netherlands, and northern France, sweeping as far north as the English Channel to swing around behind Paris and capture the French capital from its more vulnerable rear, thus ending the war. Reserve troops would defend East Prussia and Alsace-Lorraine should attacks by Russian or French troops occur before the plan was complete. By virtue of their central position, the victorious Germans would then reverse the process and send their two-million-man army by rail back across Germany's interior lines of communication to crush the Russian Army. The Schlieffen Plan was bold and ambitious with monumental requirements. German troops needed to march about thirty-two kilometers (twenty miles) in a day carrying a twenty-five-kilogram (fifty-five-pound) pack to keep to its timetable, and the right wing of the German Army had to remain very strong throughout the attack. The plan was meticulously detailed down to the minute through the first twenty days of the campaign, employing 20,800 trains with fifty cars each to move the two million troops, 118,000 horses, and 400 tons of war matériel to reach the frontier of Belgium and France. It was a logistical nightmare that required years of preparation and training to bring it to maturity. Like most works of genius, it also had elements that bordered on the insane. Besides fighting the French and Russians, the German Army was also fighting the clock. To stay on schedule, it had a mere thirty-nine days to capture Paris before turning east to engage the Russians. Germany's military leaders were counting on the speed of new technologies like railroads, "wireless" radios, telephones, and motor vehicles to accelerate the pace of war.[7]

By August 1914, while Lou was touring the western United States in his motor car, European diplomacy failed, mobilization was in full swing, and the German Army put its Schlieffen Plan into execution. On August 4, German cavalry moved into Belgium and hostilities commenced. The Belgian Army resisted, but Belgium quickly fell to the Germans. In response, Britain declared war on Germany and sent its British Expeditionary Force to the Continent to join France and Russia in fighting the Germans. Most Americans agreed with President Woodrow Wilson's declaration of neutrality, but many of Lou's classmates were outraged by accounts of *Schrecklichkeit*, or terror tactics, used by the German Army against Belgian civilians to prevent any form of guerrilla warfare behind their lines. They agreed with former president Theodore Roosevelt, who urged the United States to join the other "civilized nations" in the fight against these German "barbarians" and defend "Poor Little Belgium."[8] News of the war crossed oceans and continents very quickly through newspapers and wire services. Mass media had a global impact during the Great War.

Besides mass media, a classmate—Robert Paul Pflieger from Ghent, Belgium—kept Lou and the Class of 1917 informed about the war. He was a former Belgian Army officer and later captain of the Yale fencing team his senior year. From Pflieger, the Class of 1917 learned of Belgium's plight while the country suffered from German atrocities in 1914.[9]

By September, the great First Battle of the Marne had begun. Having underestimated the impact of technologies like the machine gun and heavy artillery, French and British forces retreated before the seemingly unstoppable onslaught of the German Army, which closed to within twenty-five miles of Paris. In panic, wealthy Parisians joined the French government in evacuating the city. It seemed only a matter of time before the big Krupp guns of the German Army pounded Paris to dust. The Germans, however, were exhausted, too, and they were to be stopped by the so-called miracle at the Marne, when French general Joseph Jacques Césaire "Papa" Joffre used French railways to transfer soldiers from the Alsace-Lorraine front to Paris. Sensational headlines trumpeted the heroism of Parisian taxicabs, which seemingly in the nick of time rushed some six thousand French poilus through the streets of Paris from *la Gare de l'Est* to the Marne battlefield as they returned from the front in Alsace-Lorraine. The journalists' extravagant accounts left the faculty and students of Yale bemused that autumn, wondering at the French Army's desperation.[10]

Their attack blunted, German commanders sought to encircle the flanks of their French and British adversaries, who countered with flanking maneuvers of their own. Each side began the so-called Race to the Sea in an effort to encircle the enemy without being encircled themselves. At the English Channel, all maneuver stopped. Each army began "digging in" so as to hold its ground and avert further casualties. In a very short space of time, a labyrinthine trench system evolved that stretched from the Channel to the Swiss border. Just as in the American Civil War, the maneuver phase of battle was superseded by murderous trench warfare. Cold Harbor and Petersburg were to be echoed by Verdun and the Somme. The staggering casualties that the world had already seen in the first phase of the war only escalated with trench warfare.[11]

Still, Lou and his classmates who followed the dramatic newspaper accounts of the European war found a new source of inspiration emerging above the slaughter of the trenches. Among the unsung heroes of the First Battle of the Marne were British and French aviators, who observed gaps in the German Armies and quickly reported these to their commanders. Thus, the Allies were able to act first, blunting the German offensive and forcing them to react to the Allies' maneuvers instead, giving allied armies a distinct maneuver advantage. By the end of September, aircraft had evolved from being an auxiliary source of intelligence to become the primary means of operational reconnaissance by which armies gathered information about their foe.[12] The new air weapon was about to move into the limelight on the Western Front.

Although these early aircraft were still immature compared to those produced later in the war, they had an immediate impact on the Great War battlefield, which was demonstrated during the First Battle of the Marne. Because early aircraft engines had limited horsepower, aircraft construction required the use of materials that were as lightweight as practicable. Linen was a lightweight material that could be stretched over the surface of the aircraft and then covered with a gluelike substance known as "dope" that protected the material from moisture and made it more aerodynamic, thus reducing drag on the surface of the aircraft. Early motors were small, with low horsepower, and could only do about 90–100 kilometers per hour (50–60 miles per hour) and climb to a service ceiling of only 900–3,500 meters (3,000–12,000 feet) in altitude. They were not very maneuverable. Most were unarmed and could carry only the pilot and perhaps an observer. In addition, they were few in number. Some sources claim that France had only 138 aircraft at the commencement of hostilities in 1914; Germany, 295 aircraft; Great Britain, 48 aircraft; and the United States, a paltry 6 aircraft. If most military leaders gave aircraft any consideration, they were generally regarded as having only limited utility and were mainly seen as a sport of the rich. General Ferdinand Foch, destined to play a key role in the Great War remarked, "Aviation is good sport, but for the army it is useless." Considering the aircraft available for military use in 1914, one can hardly blame them for their opinions, though the French Army had the foresight to incorporate aircraft into its reconnaissance system during autumn maneuvers beginning in 1910, which served it well at First Marne. These early machines were comparable in capability to ultralight aircraft of today.[13]

However, after the First Battle of the Marne, the importance of aviation grew. Aircraft reconnaissance reports changed the speed at which Army commanders received intelligence, allowing them to react faster, and thereby denied huge armies the strategic surprise necessary to maneuver and outflank their foe in the Race to the Sea. Intelligence reports that in the past took a day to reach commanders were in their hands within an hour or two because of aircraft. And as each side entrenched across northern Europe, the space between opposing trenches became killing fields, known as no-man's-land, where soldiers were exposed to lethal machine gun and artillery fire. An army's traditional eyes and ears, the cavalry, could no longer conduct reconnaissance of enemy positions because moving into no-man's-land proved fatal to both horse and rider. Since the trenches were bounded by the English Channel to the north and the Swiss border on the south, cavalry could no longer maneuver around to the enemy's rear or flanks to scout its formations. Cavalrymen found themselves relegated to carrying messages in the rear, while aircraft crossed the lines routinely and brought back vital information concerning enemy forces. Once the camera was mated to aircraft, the value of these machines to their respective armies increased exponentially, since generals and soldiers on the ground could see the aviator's view of the battlefield.[14]

At first, unarmed allied and German aviators might wave or gesture to each other in passing. However, as casualties on the ground increased, commanders sought to deny enemy aerial observation, and airmen on both sides tried to frustrate their opponents' reconnaissance. Some attempted to drop bricks or grenades on enemy aircraft. Others began to carry pistols or rifles in an effort to stop the enemy. Although largely ineffectual, these initial efforts portended the evolution of an aerial arms race that became especially lethal when the machine gun was joined with the aircraft. It did not take long, however, for aircraft to become still more deadly. The Germans were quick to use aircraft to strike enemy cities. The first aerial bombardment of Paris occurred on August 30, 1914, when *Leutnant* Ferdinand von Hiddessen flew his Taube monoplane over Paris and dropped small bombs and leaflets on the French capital. In another German air raid on September 28, 1914, *Leutnant* G. von Detten dropped several more bombs on Paris, killing one man and injuring a girl in the vicinity of the US embassy on the Rue de Chaillot, nearly killing Ambassador Myron T. Herrick. On October 6, 1914, a French Voisin two-seater flown by Joseph Frantz and armed with a machine gun manned by observer Sergeant Quénault shot down a German Aviatik in aerial combat. Although it was only eleven years old, the "aeroplane" was rapidly evolving into a true war machine. Nationalistic journalists and air service recruiters captured these exploits and cast World War I aviators in the image of medieval knights, jousting high above the clouds in glorious combat.[15]

Such romantic depictions captured the imaginations of Lou and his classmates, who only recently devoured newspaper accounts of the "romance" and adventure of the American Civil War during the fiftieth anniversary celebrations and reunions. The speed and glamour of the new air weapon appealed to Yale students like Bob Lovett, Jarvis Offutt, and Louis Bennett Jr., as well as many others. In 1915, his sophomore year, Lou became a member of the Aero Club of America, which was formed to promote the cause of aviation in the United States. Its members included aviation pioneers like Alberto Santos-Dumont and Lieutenant Frank P. Lahm, US Army, who won the first international balloon race in 1906 and was the world's first airplane passenger. Its ranks also included famous explorers like Rear Admiral Robert E. Peary, businessmen like Albert B. Lambert, and industrialist and philanthropist Godfrey L. Cabot, elites with whom Lou identified and with whom he fit in.[16]

The Aero Club became an active partner with Yale in developing a course in aeronautics in collaboration with the Sheffield Scientific School. In April 1914, Professor of Engineering Lester Page Breckenridge met with Aero Club president Alan R. Hawley to secure Aero Club support. Breckenridge announced that Yale "had committed itself to a liberal policy in support of aviation and had made plans to open a course in aeronautics." President Hawley expressed his "delight" that one of America's foremost universities had committed itself to aviation. Hawley encouraged engineering students to consider aircraft design and manufacture as "an important industry," since in the previous three years there were "10,000 aeroplanes in use, representing an investment of $100,000,000." Distinguished members of the Aero Club lectured at the Sheffield Scientific School. One of these was the former president of the Aero Club and one of its most recognized governors, Henry Woodhouse. Woodhouse was an Italian immigrant who anglicized his name in 1910 when he began writing aviation articles in periodicals. When war broke out in Europe, Woodhouse became a strong supporter of military preparedness, particularly government support of American military aviation. He criticized President Wilson's neutrality policy, claiming that the government was failing to adequately finance military aviation. Knowing that well-prepared aviators required a long training period, Aero Club members like Woodhouse and Bennett became increasingly concerned with government inertia while the air war in Europe escalated.[17]

Woodhouse later recalled that after one of his lectures at the Sheffield Scientific School, "when the entire U.S. Air Service consisted of six planes and twice as many pilots," Lou came to the Aero Club in New York City and met with Woodhouse in his office. With the new air war clearly on his mind, Bennett introduced himself and said, "I am from West Virginia. I am going through Yale and have read the address you delivered at the Sheffield Scientific School. I'd like to get into aviation. I think I can serve better in aviation than elsewhere. I'd like to learn to fly and to organize a reserve flying corp[s] for West Virginia and train men so we'll be ready to serve if we are needed. Otherwise, we'll make ourselves useful by developing aviation." Woodhouse acknowledged that the conditions in 1915 were "not at all promising for such a project," but with war potentially on the horizon, the young Yale man demonstrated a spirit of persistence that was to prove fruitful.[18]

It appears that Lou was the first Yale man to plan a reserve flying corps for American military service, but he wasn't the only Yale student who thought about the war. For most of them, it was more of an exercise in fun—cheering for a particular side akin to a school sporting event. Some debated American participation in the war. A few left Yale to join one of the combatant armies. Most favored the Allies. Joining a growing Preparedness Movement, many Yale students enlisted in the Connecticut National Guard and sought to establish Yale's own unit, which became the Yale Battery. Initially, the battery had its own aero corps, which enticed Lou to join.[19]

While war raged across the seas, college life at Yale went on. In May, Yale resurrected its lacrosse team after a dormancy of three decades. Lou started as its third defenseman. On a rainy spring day in the Yale Bowl, they lost a tight match with Harvard.[20] Sports were among the many activities Americans considered a necessary part of national preparedness. Elsewhere in the United States, other Americans sought ways to prepare the nation for the eventuality of war.

By the summer of 1915, there was a new sense of urgency concerning war preparations. In May, a German submarine sank one of the world's largest and fastest ocean liners, the Cunard steamship *Lusitania*, drowning approximately 1,200 civilians, including 128 Americans. This was only the most spectacular of the many German attacks on civilian or neutral shipping. While allied propagandists had a field day with this latest example of German "barbarism," the American public was horrified by what seemed to them blatant murder of noncombatants. Coming only a month after the Germans introduced poison gas on the Western Front, the sinking of the *Lusitania* unleashed a barrage of protests. As if to emphasize Imperial Germany's savagery toward civilians, at the end of May 1915, a German military airship, the LZ 38 successfully bombed London. Afterward, the Imperial German naval airship service took up the challenge and began a systematic onslaught of the city. On September 8, zeppelins started numerous fires and destroyed about £500,000 worth of property. By January 1916, they completed 21 raids, dropped 1,900 bombs comprising 36 tons, killed 277, and wounded 645.[21]

With each example of German "barbarism," Wilson's rival—former president Theodore Roosevelt and his small group of supporters—became increasingly more vocal, shifting the tide of public opinion slowly toward the allied cause.[22]

Although few Americans wanted war, most—like Wilson—recognized that the escalation of the German submarine campaign was a challenge that the president had to answer. The majority applauded Wilson's tough stance toward the German government and approved of his declaration that "there is such a thing as a man being too proud to fight." On May 13, 1915, Wilson took the high ground in his response to the Imperial German government, citing incidents in the submarine campaign up to the sinking of *Lusitania*. He effectively demanded that Germany abandon submarine warfare against unarmed merchantmen altogether, to which the German government gave an evasive response. Wilson appealed to the German people to respect "the rights of humanity, which every Government honors itself in respecting." His tough, moralistic stance toward Germany without an equally balanced position against the British blockade was much too strong for Secretary of State William Jennings Bryan, who resigned rather than endorse Wilson's position, which Bryan argued moved the United States from neutrality toward siding with the Allies. When the Imperial German government again gave what Wilson considered an unsatisfactory response, Wilson warned them that to continue a ruthless and merciless submarine campaign would be "deliberately unfriendly" toward the United States, and potentially might result in a breach in diplomatic relations and ultimately war.[23]

While Wilson worked his diplomacy during the summer of 1915, the nation took its first hesitant steps toward war preparation. Building on its experiences in 1913 with the three student military training camps established after the reunion of the Battle of Gettysburg, the US Army in 1915 provided instructors, tents, horses, and guns to students who participated in voluntary military summer training camps at Plattsburgh, New York; Gettysburg and Tobyhanna, Pennsylvania; and Burlington, Vermont. These camps were popularly known as "millionaires' camps" because of the pedigree of many of its participants, several of whom were wealthy businessmen. However, only a fraction were actually millionaires, but because the participants paid their own expenses and bought their own uniforms, the camps were attended by men who not only wanted to go but could also afford the expense. These camps became the foundation of the Plattsburg Movement, and those who attended them, a corps of reserve officers for the Army. The Army supervised the training.[24] America's colleges and their graduates, led by Harvard and Yale, provided the raw manpower.

Addressing the Western Association of Yale Alumni Clubs in May, Yale president Arthur Hadley argued that America's lack of preparedness was "inviting war." Hadley declared that America's "unpreparedness is a standing invitation to the stronger powers of the world to come and help themselves to whatever plunder of ours they may desire." He argued, "There are two ways for a nation to become involved in an international controversy. One is to be too much prepared for war; the other is to be too little prepared. I believe we are in the latter boat."[25]

Harvard president A. Lawrence Lowell agreed, citing Great Britain's experience and its need for officers to lead its army of volunteers. He believed that the United States needed more officers "than our regular army and the militia can possibly supply." Both Harvard and Yale decided to establish their own National Guard regiments in order to prepare their students as military leaders. Harvard students formed the 8th Regiment of the Massachusetts National Guard in Cambridge, while the Yale Battery was formed in New Haven. The State of Connecticut hoped that it could enroll at least 135 students. However, 950 Yale students showed up the first day. Surprised by such numbers, the state could not provide adequate equipment, and those on the waiting list had to drill with broomsticks or lumber, while their counterparts, who were formally "mustered in," practiced artillery drills on the Yale athletic fields. The battery members did calisthenics and took classes in military theory, tactics, and weapons. They were celebrated by the residents of New Haven when they periodically paraded through the town.[26]

Preparations continued throughout the tense summer of 1915. War hysteria remained high while William Jennings Bryan embarked on his national "peace campaign." In June, Major General Leonard Wood visited the Yale campus as the semester was coming to a close, hoping to recruit eager Yale "heelers" for the Army's summer student military training camps. Choosing self-sacrifice as his theme, Wood addressed 2,500 students in Woolsey Hall during a preparedness rally. He warned that the nation was, at present, unprepared to defend against attack from any of the major powers, and Americans should not rely solely on the professional Army and Navy for national defense. Appealing to the students' democratic idealism as well as their sense of duty, Wood argued that "the obligation to defend the country rests on everyone. The foundation stone of this democracy is equality of opportunity and privilege, and this equality enjoins also equality of obligation." He stressed that because of their status, the Yale men had an obligation to national service and that Americans looked to them as members of their class "to produce the officers necessary to make any body of troops efficient." Stressing this theme at a later speech at the Harvard Club in New York, Wood quoted President Wilson, who in December 1914 told Congress, "We must depend in every time of national peril . . . not upon a standing army, nor yet upon a reserve army, but upon a citizenry trained to arms. It will be right enough, right American policy, based upon our accustomed principles and practices, to provide a system by which every citizen who will volunteer for the training may be made familiar with the use of modern arms, the rudiments of drill and maneuver, and the maintenance and sanitation of the camps."[27] His use of Wilson's address to Congress seemed to imply official administration approval for the camps and was met with enthusiasm by the audience.

Wood, who played football in his youth, often compared military training to athletic training, which had a particular appeal to young college men like Lou. Wood finally brought the crowd to its feet with a roar of approval as he shouted, "Have you nothing to defend! Surely those who believe in the defense of liberty, so dearly bought by our forefathers, in defense of religion, of principles and of family, cannot have any but one opinion on the subject." The former physician, Rough Rider, and recipient of the Congressional Medal of Honor was so inspirational that he moved one of the Yale faculty to jump up on stage and offer an engraved silver loving cup worth about one hundred dollars to the Yale class that enrolled the most members in military training.[28] Though Lou never mentions these events in his letters, his reserve flying corps idea as well as his later actions place him squarely in the context of the Preparedness Movement.

International events reinforced Wood's sense of urgency. The next day, June 2, 1915, President Woodrow Wilson issued a warning to the leaders of the warring factions of the Mexican Revolution to stop fighting or face military intervention by the United States. One of these, Venustiano Carranza, rejected Wilson's warning and indicated that American intervention would lead to open war with Mexico. Since 1910, American interest groups argued for and against intervention in the Mexican Revolution, with some business groups desiring military occupation of Mexico while anti-imperialists insisted that Mexicans be allowed to settle their own affairs. Wilson acted when his agents in Mexico reported that a humanitarian crisis was unfolding. Mexican society, industry, and agriculture were collapsing from the fighting, and the Mexican people were near starvation. Neither faction was strong enough to take control and restore order. To Wilson, the situation appeared hopeless and only American arms could stop the fighting, stabilize the situation, and avert a human tragedy on a grand scale.[29]

With the prospect of war in Europe, Mexico, or both on the horizon, many young Ivy Leaguers flooded the Army training camps. There, they stayed up-to-date with the latest international news. Camps were carefully selected with access to rail lines and roads as a major consideration. The Plattsburg camp was also accessible by ferry. It was a modern town with adequate facilities where the volunteers could easily get the latest metropolitan newspapers. In the summer and fall of 1915, these papers reported that Carranza was slowly growing stronger in his bid for power in Mexico, and the German Navy was still attacking unarmed passenger ships, such as the White Star Line's *Arabic*, torpedoed on August 19, 1915, while sailing westbound for New York. The extensive loss of life included two Americans, and Wilson was forced to act, demanding "full satisfaction" from the German government or risk severed relations with the United States. Although Wilson did not intend to go to war, the seriousness of the crisis persuaded the Imperial German government to retreat from its previous position. On August 25, 1915, the German chancellor made the astonishing announcement that the submarine captain had exceeded his instructions in attacking the *Arabic* and that the Imperial German government would give Wilson "complete satisfaction" should their investigation of the incident reveal that he had done so. On August 26, the German kaiser ordered his navy to abandon unrestricted submarine warfare against all passenger liners.[30]

The tension between the two powers eased. Wilson had achieved a major diplomatic victory and preserved the peace, laying a major cornerstone of his reelection campaign in 1916 with the slogan "He kept us out of war." However, Wilson recognized that it was a near-term victory. Many of the issues that sprang from the *Lusitania* sinking remained unresolved, as was the status of merchant vessels. Wilson no longer had confidence that the German government was acting with good faith toward the United States. German agents in the United States and Mexico became especially active during the fall of 1915. While the possibility of war with Germany remained, Wilson acknowledged that it was imperative for the United States to avoid a second war with Mexico. He adjusted his diplomacy with his Southern neighbor accordingly, and on October 19, the United States recognized the Carranza government.[31]

Lou and his classmates returned to Yale in the fall of his junior year. He faced courses in Russian and the law as part of his coursework. To all, it appeared that American life had returned to normal, but events beyond the nation's borders, in Mexico and Europe, would once again disrupt their idyllic collegiate life and draw the nation ever closer to war.

3

Aerial Militia

Americans Prepare for War beyond the Borders

Lou returned to a different Yale in the fall semester of his junior year—uniforms were ubiquitous on campus. Although the crises with Germany and Mexico the previous spring and summer had passed, the members of the Yale Battery continued training and military instruction. As a member of Battery C, Louis donned his uniform, drilled, performed calisthenics, and attended classes.

Lou had changed too. He had matured and put on weight. As a wrestler, he weighed in at 149 pounds, so he had to move up to the next weight class. He settled into his room at 498 Haughton Hall. Lou's main circle of friends were members of the Yale Battery or shared interests in preparedness and aviation. Lou exchanged his ideas about an aviation reserve with his good friend, William "Tommy" Kent Jr. from Kentfield, California, who also lived in Haughton Hall, as well as with classmate Frederick K. "Fred" Weyerhaeuser from St. Paul, Minnesota, one of his closest friends.[1]

Another Westerner and very close friend with whom Lou shared his ideas was Jarvis "Jarve" Offutt of Omaha, Nebraska, who lived in Fayerweather Hall among some distinguished company. Of the forty-five classmates of the Class of 1917 who were "tapped" for one of the prestigious secret societies, ten were Jarve's neighbors, including Jarve's immediate neighbor Robert Paul Pflieger, the former Belgian Army officer, and Prescott Bush, member of the Yale Battery who served in the field artillery in World War I. Room proximity created a network of young men who kept up with the latest news on world events and preparedness, so Lou could share his interest and ideas with other like-minded members of the Yale Class of 1917. Cord Meyer of the crew team and his roommate Frank Browne Turner became Great War pilots—Turner with the Air Service and Meyer as a naval aviator in F. Trubee Davison's Millionaires' Unit. Meyer's other roommate, Al Sturtevant from the football squad, also joined that unit. Both Sturtevant and Turner were killed in the Great War.[2]

Despite the interests in war, aviation, and the Yale Battery—which required frequent trips to Hartford for training and cost Lou extra train fare—the Yale Class of 1917 settled into the 1915–16 school year. College life returned to something more or less normal. As juniors, the class prepared for the main event of the Yale social calendar: the Junior Prom. As hosts for the prom, the junior class sought to outdo last year's class and ensure that their prom went off without a hitch. Through the social scene and dances, Lou indulged in his other passions—women and cars. Lou attended parties in Wheeling; dances at Yale, at Lehigh, and in New York; and went to dinner and the theater with the girl he planned to take to the Junior Prom. He teased his father that he might take the elder Bennett's girls away, because he had just traded his Cadillac for a used Harmon Speedster sports car, which he described as "hot as an oven to ride in." But although it was fast and made "a great noise," he assured his dad he wouldn't fall out of it (!).[3]

More importantly, Lou carefully searched for a suitable flying school to begin his training and took his time deciding. He wrote to his father that he was considering the Curtiss school in Newport News and another school located in Marblehead, Massachusetts. He also began looking ahead for a summer job as a source of income.[4]

The allowance issue and lack of funds became very acute during Lou's junior year. Besides his tuition of $179.49, he paid $39.34 to keep his car in a garage, $40.00 for an Oliver Number 5 typewriter, $5.00 and $5.15 for his law courses, and $4.00 for his class books. He confessed he was spending on average about $5.00–$10.00 per month on books for the pleasure of just reading. Having a job, Lou argued, would provide him with an income for school and also "take some of the work off of my father's shoulders." Lou was especially enthusiastic about opportunities in South America, with its "unopened land, forests, and mines." His father warned him that he was spending too much, which Lou readily agreed. He decided not to go to the Junior Prom "because of the cost." Pressure from his mother and sister Agra, who was to chaperone prom dates for both Lou and his friend Fred Weyerhaeuser, plus a timely check from his father, changed his mind. After thanking him, Lou complained about the prom's expense. He and Fred paid by the dance—all forty-eight of them.[5]

While Lou and his classmates were consumed with the Junior Prom, a political battle in Washington, DC, pitted those supporting preparedness against the administration. Underlying this clash were broader differences regarding the changing relationships between local and national authority, state and citizen, and government and business. These differences involved customary American notions of states' rights, isolationism, and the role of the militia, as well as current issues of policy—pacifism versus militarism (i.e., "modernizing" the Army with a national reserve like Europe). Should the United States follow its traditions like the militia or mirror the more "modern" approaches of Western Europe? These issues were intensified, in part, by the Preparedness Movement, and culminated in the National Defense Act of 1916. Although Lou did not know this at the time, this struggle's outcome would directly impact his desire "to organize a reserve flying corp[s] for West Virginia and train men so we'll be ready to serve if we are needed."[6]

In his annual message in December, President Wilson made preparedness one of his key issues, specifically the formation of the Continental Army. This Continental Army was to act as a reserve force for the Regular Army of about 400,000 men and was more akin to European reserves than the National Guard. In fact, the intent was to replace the National Guard with the Continental Army as the nation's first line of defense. Secretary of War Lindley M. Garrison supported this measure based on reports from American military observers in Europe, such as George Squier. Garrison ordered the Army chief of staff, Major General Hugh Scott, to have the Army War College review American military policy and make recommendations. Their proposal, titled *A Proper Military Policy for the United States*, was released in the spring of 1915. It recommended that the administration expand the Regular Army, restrict the National Guard to "traditional home guard and local defense missions," and create a national reserve of volunteers who would enlist for six years and undergo annual training, following the European model described in those observers' reports.[7]

Having made his annual address, the newly married president left for his honeymoon on December 18. He was gone for several weeks, leaving the issue with Garrison, who found himself at odds with the House Military Affairs Committee over the issue of the Continental Army. In past dealings with Garrison, committee leadership thought he was dictatorial and interested only in the Army's point of view. Although the idea of the Continental Army had support from citizens' groups such as the Plattsburg Movement, many members of Congress vehemently opposed the measure, believing it threatened state and local control of the militia, thus changing the relationship between the states and the federal government.[8]

Supporters of the National Guard and states' rights were not the only ones opposed to the Continental Army. Progressives and rural Democrats feared that such an organization, under absolute control of the War Department, would be tainted with the kind of unrestrained European militarism that pulled Europe into the Great War. Other opponents included more conservative elements, like former president Theodore Roosevelt and former chief of staff Leonard Wood. They opposed the measure because it relied on volunteers instead of universal conscription. Garrison argued that any plan for a modern army that relied on the National Guard as the centerpiece of the reserves was dangerous and ineffective. The War College argued that the Constitution limited federal control of state forces and, therefore, by law, the National Guard could not be placed under presidential or War Department control. During congressional hearings, both Garrison and Scott conceded that a lack of volunteers would require the War Department to ask for peacetime conscription, which raised a few eyebrows among progressive and rural Democratic congressmen. When other proposals calling for universal peacetime conscription were eventually attached to the Continental Army plan, it entered the national debate with both issues permanently linked in the public eye.[9]

Congressman James Hay of Virginia, a states' rights Democrat and chairman of the House Military Affairs Committee, disagreed with the assertion that the Constitution limited federal control of the National Guard. Rather, Hay and other members of the committee argued that under the Constitution, congressional authority over the militia was practically unlimited, and he authored a bill designed to "federalize" the militia. This gave the War Department responsibility over the training, equipment, and manning of the National Guard. Daily control of the National Guard remained with the states, but in time of national emergency, it could come under federal control and be paid by the War Department. House Democrats rallied behind the Hay plan. Secretary Garrison would not compromise, and President Wilson found he had lost control of the House. After sampling public opinion, Wilson opted to support the Hay plan, and on February 10, Garrison resigned.

Two weeks later the US attorney general submitted a memorandum to Wilson that agreed with Hay's interpretation of congressional authority over the militia under the Constitution, and the Continental Army was a dead issue.[10]

To heal the rift between the War Department and the Congress, Wilson nominated Newton D. Baker, mayor of Cleveland, Ohio, for the post of secretary of war. Baker was an outspoken preparedness opponent agreeable to Progressives and states' rights Democrats. He was not a champion of a powerful, centralized War Department and preferred to make suggestions rather than dictate policy, believing multiple interests involved in national defense policy could best be served through cooperation and consultation. Working closely with President Wilson and the Congress, Baker suggested the creation of a Council of National Defense and was responsible for implementing the measures of the National Defense Act of 1916. Under its provisions, the authorized peacetime strength of the Regular Army doubled from 5,029 officers and 100,000 men to 11,327 officers and 208,338 men. The National Guard was integrated into the national defense establishment, and its authorized strength rose to 17,000 officers and 440,000 troops over the next five years. A Reserve Officers Training Corps would train additional officers at the nation's colleges, especially the Land Grant institutions founded by the Morrill Act of 1862. The National Defense Act of 1916 authorized the War Department to continue the very successful voluntary military summer training camps, such as Plattsburg. Finally, Congress authorized the War Department to build and operate a nitrate plant to build munitions. It was apparent to Baker that Congress adamantly supported the National Guard and would not allow any secretary of war to threaten it. Baker also knew, should the United States be drawn into the Great War, that Wilson did not want any volunteer celebrity units either, like the Spanish-American War's Rough Riders.[11] Any potential celebrity or state volunteer proposal would die on Baker's desk.

At Yale, Lou Bennett was concerned with another kind of mobilization. Wrestling season had arrived, and he was in "rotten condition" from lack of exercise. He wrote to his father that he was busy training and didn't like feeling tired every day, but, he continued, "Once you start something like that you can't leave it." Unsurprisingly, Lou did not make the first string at the beginning of the season, and competition was stiff. His hard work and training paid off later, when he won the New England Intercollegiate tournament in his weight class.[12] His pace never slowed down.

No sooner had wrestling season ended than Lou was back playing lacrosse for Yale. After a match at Lehigh, he attended their prom and noted which of his dance partners lived nearest to New York. Lou became secretary of his Alpha Delta Phi fraternity chapter in his junior year. Of course, money was a constant topic in his correspondence. He pleaded again with his father for an allowance since his expenses were mounting. He was "hard-pressed" from his tailor bills and costs for his car. The car's engine required an overhaul. He planned a trip to Philadelphia for the christening of his godson that spring. When the Yale Battery made more trips to Hartford, Lou's extra train fare further stressed his finances.[13]

As the spring semester began, international events created a new sense of urgency for military training at Yale. In January, after the Wilson administration recognized Venustiano Carranza as the legitimate president of Mexico, his rival Francisco "Pancho" Villa stopped a Mexico Northwestern train and killed sixteen of seventeen American citizens on board. Villa hoped to thereby discredit Carranza and force the United States to send its military to intervene in Mexico. When that did not bring about American intervention, Villa conducted a more desperate operation. On March 9, 1916, Villa raided Columbus, New Mexico, burning the town and killing nineteen Americans. The surprise attack had the desired effect, and President Wilson alerted his Army commanders in the Southwest to prepare for a punitive expedition into Mexico. Concurrently, Secretary of State Lansing began negotiations with the Mexican government that would allow either country to cross the border in pursuit of bandits. Once the protocol was signed but before the Mexican government ratified it, Wilson authorized General John J. "Blackjack" Pershing to lead the Punitive Expedition to hunt down Villa.[14]

Pershing led one of the most technologically advanced US Army operations up to that time, since his forces included motorized trucks and aircraft of the First Aero Squadron. Despite the technology, Pershing never caught Villa and only penetrated deeper into Mexico. Although advanced by US Army standards, his aero squadron lagged far behind its European counterparts. The First Aero Squadron was the Army's *only* aviation unit. Commanded by Captain Benjamin Foulois, it consisted of eleven officers, eighty-four enlisted men, and one civilian mechanic. They had eight Curtiss JN-3 aircraft that were already well-worn before arriving at the border on March 15, 1916. The unit also had twelve trucks, six motorcycles, and an automobile. New JN-3 aircraft had a service ceiling of about 2,000 meters (roughly 6,000 feet), and the rough terrain in northern Mexico dotted with mountain peaks of 2,400 meters proved hard on the weary aircraft. By the end of April 1916, all eight of the original aircraft were destroyed. Villa eluded capture. About this same time, Europeans were battling at Verdun, and the French introduced their superb Nieuport 17 fighter that carried its pilot and two machine guns to a service ceiling of over 5,000 meters (roughly 17,000 feet).[15]

Both governments had stumbled into a very dangerous situation. Mexican public opinion was openly hostile to the Punitive Expedition and President Carranza had to act or face losing power. Neither side wanted war, but after Mexican soldiers fired on American troops at the town of Parral, relations deteriorated further.[16]

Members of the Yale Battery kept up with Pershing's progress through American newspapers that maintained daily coverage of the expedition's travails. Despite the frequent drill and the Mexican crisis, life at Yale continued with relative normalcy. Tap Day for the Class of 1917 arrived on May 18, 1916. Neither Lou, his roommates, nor his friends Fred Weyerhaeuser or Jarve Offutt were "tapped" for any of the secret senior societies, though Lou was elected president of his Alpha Delta Phi fraternity chapter. A week later, he left for Boston and a lacrosse rematch with Harvard. Lou took a side trip to Marblehead, Massachusetts, where he secured a summer job at the aircraft factory there. He wrote to his father that "we have an unsuccessful aero corps here in connection with the Battery, so I thought it might be of good knowledge to learn how [aircraft] are put to-gether [sic]. I found it was quite a science and will be a good healthy job." With the lacrosse season over, Lou felt "like loafing physically for awhile" and began looking at various aircraft for sale. He still hoped to go out west sometime that summer with Fred Weyerhaeuser.[17]

But in early May, Villa's raiders struck Glen Springs, Texas, in a surprise attack across the border, similar to the Columbus, New Mexico, raid. Americans were outraged at Villa's brazen audacity and the Mexican government's impotence at curbing the northern bandits. Wilson dispatched troops to the border, calling up National Guard units from Arizona, New Mexico, and Texas. Hundreds of American men enrolled in the Plattsburg camps, while 150,000 marched through New York City on May 13 carrying small American flags in the "Great Preparedness Parade." Interventionists insisted President Wilson invade northern Mexico and secure the border, while anti-imperialists demanded that Mexicans be allowed to sort out their own affairs. Wilson faced a difficult decision; 1916 was an election year, and his action or inaction had to stand up under public scrutiny. As if to make the point, the student body conducted a mock presidential election when the semester came to an end at Yale, and the results overwhelmingly favored former president Theodore Roosevelt, "934 of 1,923." Only 401 undergraduates cast their ballots for Wilson, however, as the remainder preferred either Charles Evans Hughes (365) or Elihu Root (133). These Yale numbers did not reflect the national mood but the background of the student body, who largely came from eastern elite Republican families, with their interventionist bent. Their ranks dominated the Preparedness Movement and the Plattsburg camps.[18] Still, this latest Mexican crisis elevated the debate on intervention.

Unfazed by the political climate, Lou departed for Marblehead and a job at the aircraft factory at the end of his junior year. The enthusiastic young man "had a great time" and "stood in strong with everyone." Lou so impressed his foreman that he was given a pay raise, but Lou "could not figure out why." While working at Marblehead, he also began his initial flight training at the nearby flying school. Sallie wrote to him from the Brown Palace Hotel in Denver. She was accompanying the elder Bennett on a business trip out West. Sallie hoped that Lou was enjoying his work at Marblehead and told him not to get excited about the "Mexican business," expecting it to pass. Rather, she complained to him that she did not enjoy train travel, even in a sleeper car, "give me ocean travel—this wide West is too much for me." Sallie admonished her son to write to her more often and scolded Lou, "Keep at your trade and then if the worst comes to worst you will have some available knowledge."[19] However, the "Mexican business" was rapidly deteriorating into a serious crisis.

On June 15, Villa's bandits again crossed the border, this time just south of Laredo, and killed four US soldiers at San Ignacio, Texas. The next day Army Chief of Staff General Hugh Scott asked the Army War College to prepare plans for an invasion of Mexico along the railway lines from the north. On June 18, President Wilson called up 100,000 National Guardsmen to protect the border and ordered the US Navy to send additional warships to Mexico. Two days later, sailors from the USS *Annapolis* attempting to come ashore at Mazatlán found themselves in a fight with Mexican troops. The following day, at Carrizal, US and Mexican soldiers fought. American troops were expecting to surprise and ambush Villa, but instead found themselves engaged with the Mexican National Army. A de facto war between the United States and Mexico seemed to be underway. President Carranza accused the

Wilson administration of acting in bad faith. Tensions mounted. While the Massachusetts and Connecticut National Guard units were called to active service, Harvard and Yale students including the Yale Battery anticipated orders sending them to the border immediately. The *New York Tribune* commented that the Yale campus resembled "an armed camp" and that "the spirit of 1860 stalked on the Yale campus today." Many graduating seniors expected to receive their diplomas and depart for military service. Newspapers noted the numbers of graduating seniors in uniform, and remarked that not since the American Civil War had military uniforms so dominated a Yale commencement. Ninety-one members of the Yale Class of 1916, members of the Yale Battery, attended their commencement in uniform.[20]

Even the annual Harvard-Yale Boat Race was threatened with cancellation in 1916 because of the war hysteria. Simply known as "The Race," this competition between the two crew teams marked the final event of the academic year for both universities, and symbolized the beginning of summer vacation. Once Massachusetts and Connecticut called up their National Guard units, it appeared the annual competition might be scratched or postponed. Nonetheless, the crew teams were isolated in their respective training facilities preparing for "The Race."[21]

Lou's membership in the Yale Battery now interrupted his flight training with the Burgess Aeroplane Company in Marblehead. While the crew team geared up for the showdown with Harvard, members of the Yale Battery answered the call-up. Lou hoped to finish his flight training before reporting for active duty with the battery or perhaps to receive permission to revive the battery's aviation unit, so he asked his battery commander, Captain Alden, if he could have a furlough until his flight training was complete. In reply, Alden sent Lou a telegram on June 28 informing him that the call-up was not negotiable. Individuals who refused to respond to the activation order were "liable to trial by court martial." Lou needed to rejoin his unit immediately and did so. He did not, however, abandon his goal of learning to fly. After reporting for duty, Lou again requested a furlough from the battery in order to continue his flight training and also investigated the process for dismissal from the unit should that be necessary to continue flying. He had to be pragmatic, however, since after graduation the Yale Battery was now undermanned and was asking for additional manpower. Realizing he might not be released, Lou also inquired into flying schools in Texas, which agreed to take him should he be sent there.[22]

The day of "The Race," American sailors were in a fight with Mexicans. National Guard units were entering training camps or were en route to the border. American refugees in Mexico reached the coast but due to the crowds could not find shelter while they waited for transportation home to the United States. The Connecticut National Guard was expected to follow New Jersey and Massachusetts and leave on June 29. Harvard crushed the Eli rowers by three and a half lengths. Tensions eased slightly after Mexican president Carranza ordered the release of US soldiers previously captured during the Carrizal fight. In response, President Wilson made an appeal for peace. With this momentary lull in the crisis, the rush to send troops to the border paused. Orders sending Maine infantry to the border were canceled, while the Yale Battery was diverted to camp at Tobyhanna, Pennsylvania. Carranza seized American Independence Day celebrations as an appropriate occasion to issue a plea for direct and friendly negotiations to avert a war that neither administration wanted. Lou took advantage of this thaw and received a furlough to continue flight training, joining Davison, Lovett, and other Yale students at the Curtiss School in Fort Washington.[23]

It was at this time that Trubee Davison formed the First Aerial Coast Patrol made up entirely of Yale students. Perhaps Lou encouraged him to do so. Undoubtedly Lou discussed his plans to form a West Virginia aerial militia with his fellow aviators, and he would have enthusiastically supported like ideas. Davison envisioned a unit that patrolled the shallow waters along the shore, prepared "for air service in case of war" while performing "general patrol work and life-saving in peace times."[24]

The school on Long Island had two Curtiss model F flying boats "equipped with eight cylinder stationary motors and push propellers," incorporating the Deperdussin (Dep) flight control system recently standardized by the US Army. These training aircraft belonged to the American Transoceanic Company, the eastern agent of the Curtiss Aeroplane Company, formed by Lewis Rodman Wanamaker, heir to the department store fortune. Until war began in Europe, Wanamaker hoped to sponsor the first transatlantic flight from Long Island. Its lone instructor, David McCullough, taught the students to fly and how to care for and maintain their machines. Students woke at 0530 hours in order to prepare for flights in the dual-control aircraft, which varied from ten minutes to an hour. Although he flew with his fellow Yale students, Lou did not join the Aerial Coastal Patrol. He was still part of the Yale Battery and a member of its Aero Corps and, as such, began searching for a land plane to use in conjunction with the battery. Flying was "steady work," and despite his family's urgings that he come home to visit, he wanted to "stick with flying while it's running well" and take advantage of good flying weather and few mechanical problems with the machines.[25]

His father, however, was concerned that Lou had "been fired or dishonorably discharged" from the battery. It was inconceivable to him that a son of the South and relative of "Stonewall" Jackson would shirk his duty. Lou reassured his father that he had only joined the battery "because of the Aero Corps," and following the advice of "an Army officer detailed with the aero corps, a man who has been flying since 1907 or thereabouts," Lou asked for a dismissal to learn to fly, after which he would join "the Federal Reserve" with a lieutenant's commission. Once Lou formed a state aerial reserve, he could also respond for duty "in case volunteers are called."[26]

For the rest of July, most martial activity was limited to the National Guard training camps or Plattsburg, where General Wood reviewed the participants. Problems along the border erupted at the end of the month, when Mexican officials protested that Massachusetts guardsmen crossed the border at El Paso and attacked the homes of Mexican citizens. Then on July 31, Villista bandits crossed onto American soil raiding Fort Hancock, Texas, killing two Americans. United States troops killed five of the bandits in what proved to be a very small engagement. However, it was significant in terms of American-Mexican relations because, "for the first time in the history of the present differences with Mexico, Carranza soldiers fought by the side of American soldiers in the effort to capture or exterminate the bandits," and they fought together on the American side of the border. Coming just prior to the meeting of the international commission set up to discuss border issues, this cooperation by Mexican authorities was viewed favorably by many Americans. Mexico's minister of war confirmed the improving atmosphere, affirming Mexico's "good faith" vis-à-vis the Americans. Although guardsmen and Plattsburgers continued to drill and practice war games, Mexican-American relations were finally showing tangible signs of improvement.[27]

Unfortunately for Lou Bennett, late summer thunderstorms arrived, which impeded his efforts to finish flight training. By the second week of August, poor weather was "preventing steady flying." He managed to secure another furlough from the battery to continue, but he worried that time was running out and he would be recalled to camp. Like most Americans, Lou was encouraged by the diffusion of the Mexican crisis and expected to try out for football if the battery were released early. And he complained to his father that his sports car was getting "his girls too dirty," so he ordered a new Cadillac. He was still trying to procure an airplane, even though the battery might no longer need it after demobilization. However, the mobilization process and flying experience gave Lou some ideas about the complexity involved in raising a state flying squadron, and he hinted to his dad that he wanted to share something with him that "really is fairly important."[28]

September signaled the return of good flying weather and the end of summer storms, but unfortunately for Lou, his furlough from the battery also ran out. He was directed to report to camp at Tobyhanna without completing his flight training. He arrived just in time to read Secretary Baker's National Guard demobilization order. The Yale Battery was ordered to be "mustered out" at the state encampment at Niantic, Connecticut. Lou expected to be there awhile, however. A "paratyphoid" scare delayed some National Guard units from demobilizing and some schools from opening. Newspapers reported that in addition to demobilizing the National Guard, the Wilson administration recalled General Pershing's expedition from Mexico to comply with "the prospective agreement of the American-Mexican International Commission."[29]

Two days before the fall semester started, the last members of the Yale football team who deployed with the Yale Battery reported for practice. The "Eli Eleven" had already been practicing for over two weeks when they returned. Lou settled into his new and final residence at 6 Vanderbilt Hall to begin his senior year and seems to have elected to skip the football team. When Lou began his senior year, he was president of his fraternity, Alpha Delta Phi, and he expected to go into either law or business upon graduation.[30]

As the college assembled on the first day of class in front of Osborne Hall for freshman rush, Lou had come a long way since his freshman year, when he first distinguished himself as a member of the Class of 1917. It was time for Lou and his fellow seniors to approach the mingling clusters of freshmen, order them to "fall in" behind the ranks of the upper classes, and calmly drive them toward the center of the campus, cheering and singing the respective class songs. Lou's yearbook records nothing ominous about the opening Yale ritual for 1916, but some of those present would soon be dead—killed fighting in the Great War or training to fight in it or falling ill during the global influenza pandemic. Rather, the fall semester of Lou's senior year seemed to be one of hope, because the Mexican crisis had abated, Germany had seemingly been brought to heel, and President Wilson had "kept us out of war," which his presidential campaign slogan trumpeted before the November presidential election. College seniors could look to their futures in business or law and focus their immediate attentions on pursuing their passions.[31]

The college prepared for the Yale Pageant in October. Ever the socialite, Sallie wanted to come over from New York for it, expecting her son to entertain her. On return from his deployment with the battery, Lou found he owed back taxes, which he could not pay. Sallie paid his debt. She expected repayment in the form of a little time with her son while participating in the Yale social scene. The elder Bennett asked if he too should come up for the pageant, but the young man responded it was not worth coming all the way from Weston. Lou wanted to "avoid the mob, but Mother seems to think it my duty to entertain her at all these things." Lou could chauffer his mother in his new car, but it was not the Cadillac he ordered. The great demand for the new model that introduced a modern ignition starter created a backlog, so it could not be delivered before December. He "naturally" canceled the order and instead bought the "prettiest little car imaginable," an Oliver Magnetic Car, an early hybrid.[32]

Lou's studies consumed most of his time during his senior year, so much so that he complained to his father that he rarely had time to eat. Nonetheless, the Aero Club of America invited him to attend their annual meeting in New York, and as the football contest between Yale and Harvard approached, Lou boasted to his father that he had asked "a wonder" to be his date for the game. Soon, both father and mother left on their annual western trip looking after their investments, attending a convention in Denver, traveling to Boise and San Francisco before returning home. Lou's mother and sister came to visit on Thanksgiving after Sallie's trip west. Lou's college life had certainly returned to a routine pattern. He purchased a "leather cape coat" as well as other winter clothing items with the forty-dollar check his dad had sent him. As December approached, Lou prepared for the Yale College semiannual examination, which he took in two parts.[33]

The semiannual examinations also signaled the approach of the Christmas break. Lou planned to bring his friend Harold de Ropp with him over the holiday, before venturing on to Washington, DC, and New York City for dances and other social fun. Lou's expenditures were up again, however. After the spending spree on clothes and chauffeuring his mother and sister around town, he had to take his car in for repairs.[34]

Much was happening outside the Yale campus in the fall of 1916, in addition to the November presidential election in which Woodrow Wilson's campaign boasted, "He kept us out of war!" On October 28, the British merchantman *Marina* was torpedoed without warning, followed by the ocean liner *Arabia* on November 6. It became clear that Germany was slowly intensifying its submarine campaign against the Allies. Wilson was not prepared to condemn the Germans yet, because he hoped to initiate a major peace campaign after his reelection. While Germany intensified its submarine campaign, the British redoubled their economic warfare campaign and blockade against Germany. To Wilson and his advisers, this escalation of maritime hostilities by the European powers presented the United States with a potentially dangerous confrontation. Wilson believed that his reelection bid was a mandate from the American people to continue on the course of neutrality, yet the international situation put this path in jeopardy. Indeed, between November 1916 and January 1917, tensions between Britain and the United States were at their highest level. Evidence of deteriorating relations appeared as early as September, when Britain's Secretary of State for War David Lloyd-George indicated that any peace movements by the United States (or other neutrals, such as the Vatican) were seen in Britain as unneutral or pro-German. For the first time in the war, British citizens were suspicious of American motives, concerned that President Wilson might "butt in for the purpose of stopping the European War." For his part, President Wilson directed his close adviser Colonel House to inform the British foreign minister that the Americans had grown impatient with the "intolerable conditions of neutrality, their feeling as hot against Great Britain as it was first against Germany," and that the longer the war continued, the worse Anglo-American relations would become.[35]

Meanwhile, the Imperial German chancellor Theobold von Bethmann Hollweg asked Wilson to take the initiative for ending the war. Wilson welcomed Imperial Germany's overture, even though by doing so he opened himself up to criticism. Many of his advisers had grave reservations about German sincerity or about the American image, fearing that the Allies might consider such a move as siding openly with Germany. When the German government deported some 300,000 Belgians into Germany to perform forced labor, however, Americans were incensed and Wilson decided to act. The president drafted a note to all the belligerents in which he expressed his frustration that the war had made the position of neutrals increasingly intolerable. He lectured them about war's futility and its effect upon civilization. Not only had the belligerents made the position of neutrals impossible, he scolded, but the neutrals also did not know what the war was about. Wilson ultimately demanded that the warring powers define their war objectives. As the head of the leading neutral power, Wilson earnestly believed he was in a position to help without favoring either side. His goal was to accomplish a just peace, a "peace without victory," and as Lou and his classmates struggled through the second half of their semiannual examinations, Wilson pored over his notes while he prepared to announce his ideas to the world.[36]

Lou and his Yale classmates returned to school on January 9 after an exciting break. Lou sampled the social life in Wheeling; Washington, DC; New York; and Baltimore. Lou wrote to his dad that Baltimore girls were "as fine as ever according to reputation." He had met with his father briefly in Washington, where Lou's friend Harold de Ropp developed jaundice. As a result, young Bennett and de Ropp stayed in Washington longer than planned before returning to Yale and found themselves chastised by a lady friend for not phoning her. Still unattached, Lou decided to go "stag" to the prom and found that he liked it. Having recovered from jaundice, de Ropp and "the members of Franklin Hall" invited Lou to a dance in New Haven. The dance card announced that it was to be held on Tuesday, February 6, 1917, at "one o'clock in the morning."[37]

Besides the dizzying social scene, school kept Lou very busy. He still had exams to complete, and he tried out for the wrestling team again. Having been beaten in the last attempt, he wanted another chance—even though that meant he would "miss a good dance" that his fraternity hosted in New York. He also posed for his senior yearbook pictures and wrote to his mother that he would send her the proofs so she could select the best for the yearbook.[38]

Additionally, Lou was still trying to purchase an airplane so he could complete his flight training. He also wanted to pursue his idea for a West Virginia aerial militia, even though the prevailing national mood toward preparedness in the wake of the last Mexican crisis was, as the Army chief of staff lamented, "to let somebody else do it." At first, Lou was interested in an aircraft for sale by aviator O. E. Williams. It was an older model and Lou decided against it, continuing his search and resuming his social engagements.[39]

Both Lou and his mother invited his cousin Amy Bennett in Washington, DC, to New York for a dance. She broke several engagements to do it but looked forward to a "beautiful time" visiting with them, and seeing New York was a "wonderful prospect." Although he'd hurt his face again wrestling and was very busy with exams, Lou enjoyed the social scene in his final semester in college.[40]

The war was still on the minds of the Yale student body that January. Yale had a Reserve Officer Training Corps detachment that was established as part of the National Defense Act of 1916. It assumed responsibility for the cadets in the Yale Battery, and military training and drill were still a regular part of the curriculum for most Yale students. Most students supported this. A straw poll conducted about mid-month found 1,112 to 288 in favor of some kind of national universal military service. The cadets conducted their training and drill in the newly constructed Yale Armory built near the Yale Bowl and studied military academics in their classrooms at school.[41]

Even though northeastern elites and their children maintained their vigilant focus on the war, most Americans were much more hopeful that President Wilson could achieve some kind of breakthrough between the belligerents. Optimism was certainly in the air. On January 22, President Wilson was on Capitol Hill and delivered his "Peace without Victory" speech. Wilson believed no other kind of peace would last. Only if peace terms were settled by equals where no side was humiliated would a lasting peace succeed, he argued. Wilson acknowledged that as a nonbelligerent, the United States would not determine the specific details of a peace treaty, but he asserted that the United States did have a right to lay the broader foundation of a lasting peace in the world.[42]

In addition, Wilson thought the nations of the world had a right to know just what kind of peace Americans would seek to guarantee. Wilson suggested that "American principles," such as equality among nations, freedom of the seas, the end to militarism and huge armies, as well as the right of self-government were just such principles. He concluded that he believed he was speaking for everyman, the "silent mass of mankind everywhere who have as yet had no place or opportunity to speak their real hearts out concerning the death and ruin they see to have come already upon the persons and homes they hold most dear." Wilson's idealistic rhetoric found a receptive audience among many Americans as well as with many people in the warring nations. In Russia, the foreign office endorsed the president's humanitarian principles. In France, some eighty-nine members of the Chamber of Deputies praised Wilson's speech. In Great Britain, the trade unions sanctioned Wilson's League of Nations proposal. To add to the growing sense of hope, the British government informed Wilson on January 26 that it was finally willing to enter into peace talks with the Germans. The only British stipulation to talks was that the German terms be reasonable. On January 27, while Lou was writing to his dad that he was not sleeping much because of his exams, the Pershing Expedition began to withdraw from Mexico. Finally, it seemed, Wilson had brought a peaceful end to America's foreign crises.[43]

Therefore, Wilson pressed on with his peace campaign despite some vitriolic criticism at home and overseas. He was certainly aware of the Imperial German government's evasiveness toward his disarmament proposals and Britain's lack of faith in the peace process. He did not know, however, that in early January German military and naval leaders had already rejected a negotiated peace in favor of a strategic campaign designed to break the will of Great Britain and bring the Allies to their knees. Despite Ambassador Bernstorff's pleas to the Imperial Foreign Office to wait until Wilson had a chance to complete his peace plan, the militarist rulers of Germany decided to initiate a thorough, unrestricted submarine warfare campaign against both hostile and neutral shipping. When the unfortunate Bernstorff delivered his government's decision on January 31, declaring that an unrestricted submarine warfare campaign would begin on February 1, 1917, Americans were stunned by the seemingly sudden about-face.[44]

Germany's military and naval leaders made this decision deliberately, conscious of the fact that such an indiscriminate campaign against both belligerent and neutral shipping meant war with the United States. The German Admiralty's strategic planning staff concluded that the timing of the campaign was propitious. Harvests had been poor that year and Britain's stores were at a critical point. They confidently believed that they would break Britain's will and compel its capitulation before the United States could have any impact on the outcome of the war. Eduard von Capelle, the Imperial German naval minister, declared that "from a military point of view, America is as nothing." Chief of the Admiralty Staff Admiral von Holtzendorff promised that the United States "can neither inflict material damage upon us, nor can it be of material benefit to our enemies." He guaranteed that unrestricted submarine warfare would bring victory to Imperial Germany.[45]

Americans patriotically rallied behind their president. Even former Republican president William Howard Taft, addressing the League to Enforce Peace, appealed to all Americans to support Wilson. Believing that war had come at last, Taft declared that "we are seeing an exhibition of patriotism that we have not seen since the days of the Civil War." Taft called on Congress to pass a conscription law in order to defend the country and "do everything that any country can do to vindicate its rights." Because Americans were a "moral people," Taft argued that they would be willing to accept conscription as "a sacrifice to establish a moral principle" since "military duty is part of every citizen's duty."[46]

Wilson was still not convinced about the inevitability of war or the necessity of resorting to a military option to meet the German challenge. He remained conscious of his popular "mandate" for peace after the election of 1916, and he received many heartfelt letters from citizens urging him to avoid entering the war. Wilson also did not want to give the Europeans the idea that the United States was mobilizing for war. In fact, in February the War Department announced the final demobilization of the National Guard from the Mexican crisis. Commanders did receive secret orders not to actually demobilize any more guardsmen. Both the Army's general staff and the Navy Department staff became very active with planning, and Wilson met with his secretaries of war and the navy to discuss preparations. Yet Wilson remained cautious and wanted to avoid any provocation. Secretary Baker even convinced the president to not call a meeting of the Council of National Defense, in order to avoid sending the wrong message to the Germans that the United States was preparing for war.[47]

Personally, Wilson was extremely disappointed and insulted, believing that the only real solution was a negotiated peace with no winners. Therefore, he delayed severing diplomatic ties with Imperial Germany, which again might signal America's entry into the war. After thoroughly discussing his options with the cabinet, however, Wilson appeared before a joint session of Congress on February 3 to announce that the United States would break relations with Germany. In his address, Wilson avoided any bellicose rhetoric or suggestions that war was inevitable. In fact, he stressed that America remained the friend of the German people and wished to remain at peace with the German government. Wilson further emphasized that his administration would not believe hostilities had commenced unless Imperial Germany acted and "we are obliged to believe it." Many hoped that Germany would not commit a hostile act against the United States that would lead to war. Pacifists, like William Jennings Bryan, renewed the campaign for peaceful neutrality. Interventionists, like the American Rights Committee, redoubled their efforts to involve the United States in the war.[48]

On February 5, the Pershing Expedition crossed the border and returned to the United States having failed to capture Pancho Villa. Also in early February, the Wilson administration declined to provide US Navy warships as convoy escorts for American merchant vessels, despite requests from shipping companies and concerned citizens. Although some ships took the chance and sailed for Europe, an ever increasing number remained in their berths while merchandise piled up at the docks and warehouses. Germany's announcement was beginning to make an impact, and more Americans demanded that the government take steps to protect American merchant ships. For the next three weeks of February, this was one of the most frequently discussed subjects in cabinet meetings, resulting in a very acrimonious session on February 23.[49]

The government did not remain completely passive during this interlude. It amended a naval appropriations bill to allow for the construction of more warships and to give the president the emergency authority to seize ordnance factories and shipyards in wartime. The Army War College also quietly worked on the draft of a conscription bill. On the surface, the administration did its best to maintain a very nonprovocative calm. While Lou sweated through his exams and searched around for the right airplane to purchase, world events accelerated America's entry into the war that would alter the young man's life.

On February 25, a telegram was intercepted from German foreign secretary Arthur Zimmermann to the German ambassador to Mexico. It contained the shocking suggestion that, should war commence between the United States and Germany, Mexico might add to its territory by joining with Imperial Germany against the United States—specifically by reclaiming "lost territory in Texas, New Mexico, and Arizona." Zimmermann also invited Mexican president Carranza to suggest to Japan that it join the coalition as well. To his credit, Wilson did not overreact, since no "overt act" had been committed. As a precaution, he went before a joint session of Congress the next day to ask for the authority to arm American merchant vessels so that they could defend themselves from attack. He also requested congressional authority to take "necessary and adequate" measures to protect American citizens and ships at sea. His speech was deliberately measured and nonprovocative, and Wilson emphasized his hope for peace. Were the Zimmermann telegram the work of British agents hoping to goad America into fighting, he might commit the nation to an unjustified war. To improve ties with his southern neighbor, Wilson also took steps to recognize the Carranza government in Mexico and establish formal diplomatic relations.[50]

Although Wilson's request was generally well received by the nation's newspapers, many in Congress had their doubts, and the president encountered stiff opposition. When his proposal stalled in the Senate, Wilson released the Zimmermann telegram to the Associated Press. The bombshell struck the unsuspecting American public like a thunderclap and left the country and Congress stunned. Zimmermann himself admitted the authenticity of the note on March 3, complaining about the "hostile attitude" of the American government. This further piqued the nation's rage and dispelled the notion it was a British ruse. Wilson got his armed ship bill. Then, Imperial Germany made good on its threats to attack American ships when German submarines sank three American ships with heavy loss of life on March 18. Americans were alarmed and public opinion turned more hostile to Germany. It seemed clear that America could no longer maintain its neutrality.[51]

While the United States began arming its merchant ships, Lou completed his purchase of a Curtiss airplane. Lou still wanted to form an aerial militia for West Virginia, although he was considering several other options of military service. With war potentially looming on the horizon, he wrote to both his father and his brother-in-law, Johnson McKinley, for advice. The elder Bennett took his time before he answered his son. He conceded that "we can hardly escape a war with Germany" and that the nation was unprepared for war. The former Confederate midshipman emphasized the importance of the Battle of the Atlantic on the war and American commerce as well as Germany's desire to "foment trouble between us and Mexico." While addressing his son's desire to enter the war, the elder Bennett revealed that he stood with the majority of Americans, who hoped yet for peace. He wrote,

> You know that I am much opposed to war where it can be possibly avoided with honor. And I have always been opposed to your joining the army except where it was a question of patriotism. Even then, I would have you consider well how far it would demand sacrifices from you, and of what kind they might be. If you should join the service, I would first by all means endeavor to get a commission. Your education, your evident qualities for leadership, and such experience as you have had would fit you for it, and make you entitled

to it. And this too in whatever branch you might enter, in case you entered the service, your own inclinations might serve to guide you as to what particular branch it might be. But it seems to me that aviation presents more hazard with less opportunity for distinction and rise in rank than any of them, though of course merit should govern all branches, and by merit, I do not include rashness or foolishness.

Still, the Civil War veteran offered supportive advice: "And so, my dear boy, if it comes to the worst, and we have war, and you feel it your duty to enter the service, do not do so rashly or hastily. Get if possible some position worthy of you, and then fill it worthily and with honor. But I pray that we will have no war, and that none of our sons will have to make the sacrifice of active participation in it."[52]

Lou's aunt Marie in Baltimore also did not approve of aviation for the younger Bennett and let him know it. Sallie had mixed feelings about her son flying in the war. She wrote to him about his plans for a West Virginia aviation squadron, having read in the *New York Times* that a fellow Yale student, Bob Lovett, was forming a second Yale aviation unit, and she wondered if Lovett had asked Lou to lead it. Sallie also asked Lou if he knew if Lovett had secured government sponsorship and funding for this unit. She concluded her letter by informing him that a close personal friend and prominent lawyer advised her to counsel Lou to stay out of the military and study law. Sallie characteristically took action to convince her son to steer away from the profession of arms. She wrote to the assistant secretary of state to see if the State Department had any postings for Louis in Petrograd, Russia. He studied Russian at Yale, and after his midyear exams, he certainly had recent experience with the language. The assistant secretary responded that such a posting might be possible and included applications both for the diplomatic service as well as for an appointment by the secretary.[53]

Ironically, on the back of the assistant secretary's envelope, Lou had sketched out an outline for the "West Virginia Aerial Reserve Unit." Its purpose was "to train [fifteen] aviators for [Air Service] Aerial Reserve Corps under the auspices of [the] State." Lou wanted the unit to be composed of volunteers. Once they completed training, the unit's "ultimate object [was] to establish aerial efficiency in this section of the country." Donors would provide the equipment, and instructors would provide training in military discipline, basic flying, and "tactics." The unit's members were to be "always ready for service [to their] country," and in time of war they would "keep their integrity as a unit" when they deployed for battle.[54]

Lou shared his idea with Johnson, who made inquiries on his brother-in-law's behalf, sending Lou a telegram in late March informing him that "I think it entirely feasible [to] raise one in West Virginia and I understand who ever raises unit would secure commissions and probably command it." Johnson wanted to know about practical matters, such as from which source would the unit obtain its machines, either from the government or private subscription. What would the cost be? Finally, he informed Lou that he was helping raise an infantry battalion in Wheeling and that he might be able to confer a lieutenant's commission for Louis, if he were interested.[55]

Lou avoided advising his father, who had fallen ill, until the elder Bennett asked him for specific information, telling him, "Remember, I am deeply interested in anything that might interest you." The young man was very busy with his plans. Lou's aircraft was finally assembled. He was searching for an instructor and hoping to start flying again if the weather cooperated. Writing from Yale's Vanderbilt Hall on March 28, 1917, Lou wrote,

> Now I am going to tell you my tentative plans. You may oppose them but I think it unlikely in the face of conditions, unless someone else has already done so. I want to organize an aero unit in [West Virginia]. As to the type it is not at all certain which is best. I do not think it would be feasible to connect up with the [US government]. What would be the best type of state organization? Would it not be best to make it a private one? This latter is my idea . . . to get enough [West Virginia] fellows together to procure machine[s] and instructor and call it a [West Virginia] unit.

Lou added,

> After the same is started it might be possible to interest other influential people in it to the extent of getting more equipment and more students to the corps. For instance, give the donor the privilage [sic] of appointing or suggesting some one whom he wishes trained—the size of the corps to be limited to some certain number. I do not see need of connecting with the [US government] at all until training is complete. Am already in communication with Johnson on the

subject. I may be able to (fairly sure of it) get some boys from here as a starter. Think it would call for say donations to the extent of $1000 to a man.

He concluded by telling his father, "Would not bother you with this at all but you might feel I am not taking you into my confidence. But there is absolutely no worry to be connected with it and I think this the very best thing for me personally."[56]

His father immediately cabled back: "Am giving you free hand will help all I can." A grateful son thanked his father by letter, aware that it "imposes more confidence than I deserve." He confided that he did not yet know what was "the best form of aviation corps" to assemble, but he was researching it. He also revealed that he now owned an airplane but that no test flight had yet been accomplished on it. Lou concluded that he was going to the annual Aero Club of America banquet on March 30, where he hoped to get advice and find the answers to his questions.[57]

The Aero Club banquet was a momentous encounter for him. The young aviator came away from it with a more ambitious plan than he originally intended. Instead of just an aerial militia for West Virginia, Lou envisioned a national aviation militia. He later wrote, "At the outbreak of this war, I conceived the idea of aiding our Government in training aviators, also to create interest in aviation in sections of the country that knew very little about heavier than air machines. My underlying idea was that the whole country should be developed, that planes should be able to travel and alight anywhere, and that fields and repair stations should be so scattered as to aid toward this convenience."[58]

While Lou made his plans, President Wilson had a solemn meeting with his cabinet. He put two questions to them: Should he call for a special session of the Congress? If yes, what should he propose to them? After the meeting, Wilson announced that he would indeed convene a special session of Congress on April 2 about "grave matters of national policy."[59]

4

"A More Distinguished Way of Doing Greater Good"

Americans Lurch toward War

President Wilson kept his thoughts to himself as his cabinet assembled on March 20, 1917. He put his questions to his advisers and then quietly sat back and allowed them to speak their minds—would there be peace or war? One by one, they opined that the United States should declare war on Imperial Germany at the earliest possible moment. Even Secretary of War Newton Baker, a pacifist, agreed. Baker had become Wilson's most loyal friend in the cabinet. When he spoke, he too argued for a declaration of war "with wonderful clearness" and then discussed the speedy buildup of the armed forces. When the president polled Secretary of the Navy Josephus Daniels, Daniels paused. Like Baker, Daniels had pacifist leanings and was a close friend of William Jennings Bryan, one of the leading pacifists in the party. Many of his fellow cabinet members did not believe Daniels, who had very deep convictions, would bring himself to advocate declaring war. For Daniels, this moment was the "supreme moment" in his life—one that he prayed would not come or, in his words, that "this cup would pass." His eyes filled with tears, and in a low voice that trembled with emotion, Daniels admitted that there was no other course of action left open to the nation. Franklin Lane was the last of Wilson's cabinet to speak. Incensed by the German government's actions, Lane conveyed his outrage by urging war.[1]

The opinion of the cabinet was unanimous—the president should convene a special session of Congress and ask for a declaration of war. It had been a long meeting, beginning at two o'clock in the afternoon and lasting until around five thirty. Wilson was cool and lacked expression, thanking his advisers and acknowledging, "There is no doubt as to what your advice is." As they filed out through the throng of reporters waiting outside the room, they remained silent and expressionless so as not to reveal what had transpired. Neither the press nor Wilson's cabinet knew what the president would decide. However, the press speculated what transpired in the meeting, with some newspapers declaring that the "Cabinet has decided on a state of war."[2]

Whereas Wilson's advisers were resolute and unanimous, those advising Louis Bennett Jr. were not. Lou had only two advisers: his father and his brother-in-law. His father willingly acknowledged that he did not "know enough about military conditions here to advise [Lou]," and since he had fallen ill, he "had no way to learn." Instead, he gave his son the benefit of his business sense as well as moral and financial support. Johnson was busy organizing the infantry unit for Wheeling as well as running his many business interests in the Northern Panhandle of West Virginia. Because Johnson was a leading businessman in Wheeling and knew the "right" people, Lou asked him to compile a list of what Lou called the "really prominent" men in the state who could recommend the young West Virginians "best suited" for membership in the Flying Corps. Lou wanted these important men to provide financial backing and influence, to convince the governor and members of the legislature to support the project.[3]

Lou confided to his father that his meeting with the leadership of the Aero Club of America at its annual banquet on Saturday, March 31, was disappointing. Lou went to the meeting full of optimism, counting on the Aero Club to give him insightful guidance as to the best way for him to proceed with his idea. First, it made front-page news. Rodman Wanamaker, the department store magnate, announced to the assemblage that he offered the government use of a "fully equipped aerial coast patrol station at Port Washington, New York, together with an air cruiser [seaplane] fitted with two 200 horsepower motors and an aeroplane gun." Lou certainly approved of such private preparedness initiatives by other influential Americans. This kind of private support of the militia was crucial during the Civil War but dated back to colonial times, when businessmen and "gentlemen" frequented the ranks of the militia and used such gifts to improve their social status in the community.[4]

A second reason for Lou's optimism was that during the preparedness hype, the Aero Club established the National Aeroplane Fund to raise money to do exactly what Lou had proposed—"to train and equip airmen for the state militias." Their proposal was supported by the chief signal officer of the Army. In 1915, the Aero Club purchased five aircraft, valued at $29,500, for the First Aero Company of the New York National Guard.[5] By the end of 1916, the Aero Club had raised $171,000 to buy planes and provide flight training for other National Guard units. The Glenn L. Martin and Curtiss aircraft companies each donated a plane, and Curtiss offered to train one guardsman per state. Building on the "Plattsburg Idea," the Aero Club helped convince Congress to include aviation as part of the National Defense Act of 1916. In addition to making aviation a part of the Signal Corps, Congress eventually authorized funds intended to form twelve aero squadrons for the National Guard. An "Air Plattsburg" was organized at New York's Governor's Island in June 1916, and the New York National Guard organized an aviation company under Raynal Bolling and Philip Carroll, who had participated in the Plattsburg camps, with aircraft purchased through private funds. Even though the press demanded more pilots and aviation units, both the Regular Army and the National Guard were hindered by a lack of trained aviators available to instruct a new cadre. Additionally, the Mexican crisis left many states without the ability or time to form aero squadrons, since guardsmen went to the border and were demobilized just before the declaration of war. Only New York, California, and Missouri had small aviation units as part of the state National Guard. The Regular Army's only aero squadron and most of its aviators were in Mexico with the Pershing Expedition.[6] The appropriated funds allowed for a gradual increase in training capabilities, but the system lacked the capacity demanded by the Great War.

A third reason Lou optimistically anticipated this meeting with the Aero Club was its leadership. The Aero Club boasted many aviation pioneers, pilots, aeronauts, explorers, and inventers, such as Rear Admiral Robert E. Peary, Alberto Santos-Dumont, Albert Lambert, Frank Lahm, and Augustus Post. Lou met with the club's president, Alan Hawley, the stockbroker and aeronaut; Henry Woodhouse, the club's outspoken and controversial governor and former president; and Augustus Post, club secretary and one of its founding members, who was an accomplished automobile racer before he became a balloon racer and the thirteenth American to fly an airplane. It was said of Post that he was an expert on aviation's major celebrities and events, but Lou dismissed him as "mostly a negligent advisor." Instead, from the three of them together Lou "got what information I could and mostly [it was] to the effect that the problem before me was one that had not been worked out [by anyone], that [it] was at present before the [government] and with no signs of being worked out, and that it was up to me to work it out in its own development."[7]

Lou emerged from this meeting convinced that the execution of his plan was squarely on his shoulders. The aviation section of the US Army was minuscule in April 1917. According to some sources, it consisted of only 131 officers, 65 of whom were flying officers and only 26 of these were fully trained. The enlisted force consisted of 1,087 men. It had 55 machines consisting only of training aircraft, by European standards. None were of the caliber of a modern European warplane. The First Aero Squadron's employment with the Pershing Expedition proved disappointing because the aircraft technology was not up to its tasking. Therefore, Lou's idea for a state aerial militia across the whole country as a de facto military aviation reserve made good practical sense, as the Aero Club's National Aeroplane Fund indicated. Under Lou's system, aircraft would be able to travel and land anywhere at airfields with repair stations, positioned so as to make it convenient. In 1925, William "Billy" Mitchell argued for a like national aviation system. Lou's airmen would elect their officers to serve for one year, much as the volunteer and militia units had done during the Civil War. Each training facility would incorporate one flight school machine and one "military type machine." In time of war, these aviation reserves could be called up as all American militias had been since colonial times. However, he needed a starting point, and that was the aerial reserve for West Virginia, which at the moment was, in his words, "temporarily at a standstill."[8]

Lou had expected a faster response from his brother-in-law and complained to his father that Johnson was "not forthcoming with proper information," including the list of prominent West Virginians or the type and amount of funds Lou could expect to collect for the Flying Corps. Lou repeatedly complained about Johnson's seeming lethargy to the elder Bennett over the next two months. Additionally, Lou believed it was important that he personally ask the most influential man of each section of West Virginia for assistance in order for his aerial reserve to succeed. He estimated that it would cost about $15,000 to start the unit, and he planned to put forward a part of the total sum. Once he'd received that commitment, he could keep subsequent subscription amounts lower, which would allow the unit to gradually expand and not be limited to any set size. This was important, because in peacetime the volunteer organization would have to be generally self-sustaining. Only in time of war would the government assume responsibility for its cost, since the unit would be called up to active duty. By providing for adequate moneys from the very beginning, Lou's aerial reserve of trained aviators would "always be ready in [time of] need." "If Johnson is not succeeding in getting preliminary funds," Lou fretted to his father, "how can it best be done[?]"[9]

Nonetheless, Lou was not deterred and busied himself coordinating other requirements for a successful training unit. Although he had an aircraft, he was neither qualified to fly it solo nor to teach others to fly. He needed an instructor. Lou used his contacts at the Aero Club of America to try and locate one. He found a candidate in the United States on leave from the Royal Flying Corps (RFC), Captain E. A. Kelly, who was at Governor's Island, New York harbor, the headquarters of the Eastern Department of the United States Army. Finding a reputable instructor was crucial, as Major Harold Hartney observed: "I found that our camp and almost every other military concentration spot in the United States was on the visiting list of numerous gentlemen, practically all dodging front line service, who were spreading an amazing flood of misinformation [about the war] among America's new soldiers. A few had been in action briefly, and had built themselves up into heroes of astounding accomplishments. Most of them, however, had never been near the front and some had never even been in France. But all of them posed as the last word in war experts with brilliant records when facing the foe."[10]

Hartney was a Canadian who had flown in combat on the Western Front with the RFC and was asked to enter the US Army Air Service (USAAS) to train the masses of American airmen just entering the war and lead them into battle in France. With Kelly, Lou had a credible instructor trained in proven British methods. Not only could Kelly teach the West Virginia Flying Corps (WVFC) how to fly, but he would also be able to teach modern combat tactics—something almost no US Army aviators were able to do.[11]

Aircraft of the day required a great deal of daily maintenance to keep them safely flying. This included many spare parts and replacement engines as well as linen cloth to cover the airframe. Lou made inquiries with various New York City textile firms, such as the McCreery Company; the Courtrai Manufacturing Company; and Robert McBratney & Company, Linen Importers, for samples and prices of "Government Standard Pure Irish Linen Aeroplane Fabrics." Lou quickly delegated the procurement of aircraft linen to his mother, who was still living in New York.[12] His aerial militia for West Virginia was finally moving forward and required his immediate attention. World events had changed, and he was in earnest.

On April 2, 1917, while Lou was diligently working out his plans for a state aerial reserve unit, Congress gathered for the extraordinary session. The House of Representatives spent much of the day organizing the legislative body, while Democrats enlisted the help of independents to elect Champ Clark as speaker for another term. President Wilson remained at the White House, departing for the Capitol around 2030 hours that evening. There, he mounted the rostrum and addressed the joint session. Declaring that the "world must be made safe for democracy" and that "civilization itself" seemed "to be in the balance," he asked Congress to declare war on Imperial Germany. His address was met with loud applause. By 2130, Wilson was back in the White House with his family.[13]

Newspapers from New York to San Francisco, Chicago to New Orleans expressed support for the president's call to arms. Echoing Wilson's speech, the *New York World* declared that the "hope of Mankind [is] in the Balance." The *New York Tribune* trumpeted that "no praise can be too high" for the president, whose delivery resounded with "a new and yet original spirit the great words of Lincoln." The Springfield, Massachusetts, *Republican* called it "the most momentous hour of our history since the Civil War" and likened Wilson's speech to "a new Battle Cry for Freedom." The *Saint Louis Republic* urged Congress to "uphold the President" while the *San Francisco Chronicle* opined that the United States "could resist war no longer." Urged by Governor Cornwell, citizens across West Virginia held rallies to support Wilson. Over fifty cities in the Mountain State displayed flags, held marches, or organized mass patriotic meetings. In Lou's hometown of Weston, a large crowd assembled in the high school auditorium. In Charleston, the state capital, seven thousand people rallied. In Wheeling, where Johnson was seeking patrons for Lou's aerial militia and helping to organize an infantry regiment, four thousand townspeople gathered at the Market Auditorium. They were led in procession by "the half hundred Union and Confederate veterans" of the community, some of whom were maimed in the Civil War but who still "marched arm in arm to the Auditorium." To the reporter for the *Wheeling Intelligencer* who covered the event, the present assemblage joined with the Civil War veterans in the "spirit of ancestors who sacrificed themselves upon the altar of war in desperate resistance to tyranny of all kinds." These Civil War heroes were an inspiring sight of reconciliation and represented the solidarity of patriotism of the Wheeling meeting.[14]

After the congregation recited the Lord's Prayer en masse, they sang patriotic songs and listened to fiery nationalistic speeches "that made their blood tingle with loyalty." A journalist wrote that it represented "the highest type of citizenship and Christian humanity." Representatives from the business and labor community, interrupted by spontaneous applause, voiced their support for patriotic solidarity. Even those opposed to war, like labor leader Harry Corcoran, allowed that if a peace-loving man like President Wilson recommended war, "then there is no other course" to pursue. Americans of German ancestry pledged their undying loyalty to the United States and exhorted their countrymen to not "be afraid of them. Caution your friends that they do not despise them . . . they have been taught to love liberty and freedom and they will take up arms to protect the country that gives it to them." The gathering was briefly interrupted by the reading of a telegram that announced the sinking of the steamship *Aztec* by a German submarine, in which many American lives were lost. This brought a sobering stillness to the throng. Some in the crowd saw this as proof that Germany was already at war with the United States. Senator Warren Harding of Ohio next gave a short speech to the assemblage. He was followed by the mustachioed Republican congressman from West Virginia, William P. Hubbard, a Civil War veteran of the Third West Virginia Cavalry, who read the president's address to Congress to the Wheeling body, which afterward erupted in patriotic fervor and pledged loyalty to the president and the government.[15]

Not everyone was enthusiastic about the outbreak of war. Many, like Lou's father, hoped yet for peace. Many progressives, trade unionists, pacifists, and socialists were opposed to American involvement in the war. Additionally, Wheeling had a large German population, many of whom did not want to see their adopted country and their native land at war. One of the large banks in the city was the German Bank. While the *Wheeling News Register* and *Wheeling Intelligencer* supported Wilson's position, the *Wheeling Daily News* was more guarded. Its headline read, "Lafollette Blocks War Resolution," and it reported that pacifists and Americans of German ancestry hissed at the president's statements. Although it held on to a desperate hope that Lafollette and other congressional opponents to war would ultimately win the day, the paper conceded that the resolution "is confidently expected to pass both houses" of Congress.[16]

Across the country, the debate sometimes resulted in violence. In Baltimore, a crowd of four thousand war supporters interrupted Dr. David Starr Jordan, when he spoke at a meeting of the American League Against Militarism at the Academy of Music. Led by city businessmen and university professors from Johns Hopkins and the University of Maryland, among others, the antipacifists pushed aside the cordon of police, broke into the theater, and rushed down the aisles waving American flags. Numerous fistfights broke out, injuries occurred, and Dr. Jordan was forced to flee. Newspapers called it "the greatest patriotic demonstration this city has seen since the Spanish American War."[17]

On April 3, the Senate adopted Wilson's resolution, followed by the House on April 6. The United States had officially declared war on Imperial Germany. Louis Bennett Jr. left Yale University midsemester of his senior year and boarded a train. He arrived in Wheeling on April 7 in order to organize, train, and equip an aerial militia in his home state, which he publicly announced was named the West Virginia Flying Corps. Many of Lou's classmates also left Yale prior to graduation in order to fight for their country.[18]

With the formal declaration of war, Lou's plans for an aerial militia for West Virginia gained momentum. The outburst of patriotism helped Johnson find major investors to enthusiastically back a state aviation unit to bring it to the Wheeling area. Wheeling residents H. B. Lockwood, H. O. Wells, and George P. Whitaker agreed to sponsor the unit with Johnson and Lou. Lou also searched around the state for a site suitable for flight training. He had learned much since he first took to the air. He knew, for instance, that the airfield—or aerodrome, as they were called at the time—required plenty of level ground for flight operations. This was especially true for training student pilots. Airfields needed to be large enough so that pilots could take off and land directly into the prevailing winds, because the underpowered, lightweight aircraft of the day were difficult to land in a crosswind, especially for fledgling aviation trainees. To attempt such a landing could have fatal results. In a rugged state like West Virginia, finding an adequate site with a large, flat field was a challenge. The floodplain in a large river valley was potentially such a site. On April 17, Lou wrote to his father that he had leased some land for an airfield and was securing estimates on lumber to build a hangar for his aircraft.[19]

Lou also knew from both his flight training experience and his work at the aircraft factory in Massachusetts that the new aviation technology required a sufficient and uninterrupted supply of spare parts, without which aircraft did not fly and the training would grind to a halt. The Army calculated that it costs $50,000 a year to keep a single aircraft airworthy (in a safe flying condition). As a member of the Aero Club of America, Lou was also aware how poorly American aviation was prepared for the European war. Over the coming months, while the US Air Service increased its strength to the levels required for modern industrial combat, the dozen or so American aircraft manufacturers struggled initially to keep up the supply of both completed aircraft and spare parts to keep them flying. The secretary of war estimated that these companies' manufacturing capacity could provide for a three-year program, producing "three thousand airplanes for the fiscal year of 1918, four thousand for 1919, and five thousand for 1920." Although the United States had been the first nation to contract for a military aircraft in 1907, and it produced more automobiles than the rest of the world, by 1917 its aviation industry was well behind European industry in terms of both quantity produced and quality of product—in 1916 the US aircraft industry had only delivered 64 of the 366 planes contracted by the government. Worse, neither the military staffs nor the industry had a plan as to how they would achieve mass production upon the outbreak of hostilities.[20]

This shortcoming of the American aviation industry was an opportunity for Lou. If West Virginia's aerial reserve had its own airplane factory, the unit would have a ready supply of spare parts for its machines and could potentially make a profit through government contracts to provide spare parts and completed aircraft. Thus, it could become self-sustaining. Such a factory required access to railroads, which were used to ship the parts and completed aircraft. It needed a skilled labor force that could readily learn and apply the new aviation technologies, and it also called for sufficient electric power to run the factory. In order to have ready access to spare parts, the West Virginia Flying Corps had to be close to its factory.[21] All of these requirements suggested the Wheeling area in the state's Northern Panhandle as the best location for the unit.

Wheeling is located on the Ohio River and is itself built (in part) along the flood plain, and the Upper Ohio Valley had numerous farms and flat areas that had potential as airfields. Wheeling was a major transportation center, boasting several railroads and its large station for the Baltimore and Ohio line. Railroads connected the city to Baltimore, Pittsburgh, Columbus, Cleveland, Chicago, and New York. Access was not a problem, since many

West Virginians frequently traveled across the country by rail at this time and were extremely mobile. The state boasted over four thousand miles of track. Known as the Nail City or the Stogie City, Wheeling was also connected to Baltimore and the Midwest via the National Road, and two streetcar lines connected the city in the north with Steubenville, Ohio, in the south with Benwood, West Virginia, and ran east to West Alexander, Pennsylvania. It was a bustling community.[22]

Additionally, the Wheeling area was home to a very large skilled labor force that manufactured tin plate, glass, brick and tile, coal and oil, textiles, steel, tools, nails, finished wood products, cigars, and various machines. An additional pool of skilled labor was available in Eastern Ohio and Western Pennsylvania. In nearby Beech Bottom, located about ten miles north of the city along its trolley line, a massive 200,000 kilowatt steam-electric plant was set to open in the summer of 1917. One of the largest coal-operated steam-electric plants in the world, the Windsor Plant near Beech Bottom was built next to its coal mine and allowed Wheeling to compete with other cities as the location for a new War Department nitrate plant. Secretary Baker came to Wheeling in March to investigate the city as a potential site for the plant. The Northern Panhandle dominated industry in West Virginia, with over half of the state's manufacturing jobs located there.[23]

Based on these criteria, Lou selected a field at Beech Bottom, West Virginia, as his airfield. On April 16, he, Johnson, and the other sponsors incorporated the West Virginia Flying Corps. West Virginia's secretary of state, Houston Young, certified the corporation on April 18. The corporation was authorized, among many things, to "manufacture, buy, sell, exchange and deal in Aeroplanes, Flying Machines, Hydroplanes . . . machines and vehicles of every description" as well as "the right to acquire, construct, maintain and conduct schools of instruction in the art of manufacturing, repairing or operating all or any of the devices, machines or vehicles aforesaid." Eventually, the duties of manufacturing aircraft and spare parts would be done by a dedicated aircraft factory, which was incorporated as the West Virginia Aircraft Factory. It was located just north of Wheeling in the small town of Warwood, along the Pennsylvania Railroad line between Wheeling and Beech Bottom.[24]

Until the unit's personnel were selected and the field developed, Lou needed a headquarters for his work. He selected an office in one of the most prominent buildings in Wheeling, the Schmulbach Building on Market Street, in room 411. This situated Lou's office near the office of his brother-in-law whose Richland Mining Company operated out of room 916. Lou's office was centrally located and close to many other important Wheeling businessmen and firms as well. The West Virginia Telephone Company installed his phone line on April 18. He designed an emblem for the Flying Corps, a shield with the state seal of West Virginia in the center sporting wings on either side of the crest. A scroll marked "WVFC" completed the design, which he had made into wings for his pilots to wear.[25]

His plan was coming together. He had an organization, an airplane (albeit still back at Sheepshead Bay, New York), a training field, a headquarters, an emblem, and a budget. He bought stationery with the unit name and address on the letterhead and his name in the upper-left-hand corner. He also initiated construction on hangars and workshops at the field.[26] Johnson came through with sponsors. Lou's mother was working to obtain aircraft linen for the company. Lou now turned to his father for help. Because his father had been active in state politics with many connections, Lou asked his dad if he could line up prominent West Virginians to assist him in making the right contacts for the unit. He wanted to enlist the governor's aid in raising and financing the organization. Including his own money, Lou had raised $30,000 and hoped the state could provide about $10,000 more. The governor, John J. Cornwell, had just taken office and was deluged by petitioners seeking patronage. In addition, the War Department's Central Department, based in Chicago, required governors of each state to provide information on roads, bridges, water sources, and so on. This information was being cataloged for wartime use. Businessmen in Wheeling were seeking a War Department nitrate plant, while in Charleston they were seeking an armor-plate factory for the Navy.[27] State governors had to oversee the progress of conscription boards as well as contend with daily state affairs. Having the right connections would give the young man vital access.

In order to ascertain the War Department's standard procedures for aviation training, Lou first wrote to General George Squier, the head of the Army Signal Corps in 1917. The Air Service was under the Signal Corps, and thus it was Squier's responsibility. Squier had inspired both aviators and the American people when he called on the nation to "put the Yankee punch in the war by building an army in the air, regiments and brigades of winged cavalry on gas driven flying horses." Although Squier was not an aviator, he was an aviation enthusiast. He had a brilliant mind and a reputation as a distinguished scientist. After graduating from West Point, Squier earned a doctorate in electrical engineering from Johns Hopkins University. He pioneered the use of radio and photography in the Army, and he introduced aeronautics into the Army educational system.[28] Lou reasoned that he was the right man to approach.

Squier advised him that the government was reluctant to "recognize individual units because it would thus be unable to station individual officers wherever it thought best." If West Virginia wanted its own unit, then its members should obtain their own equipment, training, and manpower. Once training was complete, the men could receive their commissions. No doubt Squier had in mind the example of the aviation section of the New York National Guard. However, both regiments of the West Virginia National Guard had already been activated. Governor Cornwell had an adjutant general, but no guardsmen for him to supervise since they had already departed to their assembly points. With their call-up, the governor was so uncertain regarding the future status of the National Guard that he thought it inadvisable for West Virginia to continue to rent armories. The Army was still going through a period of modernization after the Spanish-American War, and that reorganization had a major impact on National Guard units. The size of American combat divisions doubled. Many historic National Guard units, including the aviation units, were either broken up or eliminated and integrated into a new organizational structure of regiments and divisions.[29]

On the other hand, the Wilson administration was more than merely "reluctant" to recognize volunteer units and for several important reasons. First, Wilson understood that in a modern, total war, the nation had civilians in key industrial positions that were more valuable to national survival where they were than at the front carrying a rifle. The president argued that these positions would be exempted from service through use of national conscription, thus assigning men to the necessary labor of the country. His central idea was to "disturb the industrial and social structure of the country just as little as possible." Wilson was influenced by the ideas of modernists in the Army, like General Tasker Bliss, who had explained that modern war required more than just soldiers and arms. Many in Congress opposed conscription and anticipated bloodshed in the streets, predicting draft riots like those that occurred in New York during the Civil War. These opponents argued that the Militia Act of 1792 and the Dick Act of 1903 directed that all American male citizens were under universal obligation to serve. The United States traditionally relied on its volunteers to organize units at the local and state levels who then offered their services to the government, much as Lou was doing from Wheeling. Wilson argued that nothing had really changed since 1792. Conscription was merely a means to select "from a nation which has volunteered in mass" and was in no way "a conscription of the unwilling." However, administrative power had shifted from the traditional periphery of the states to the central authority of the federal government.[30]

Another important reason the administration opposed volunteer units was Theodore Roosevelt. The former president, veteran Rough Rider, mercurial Republican, and prolific writer was a constant critic of the Wilson administration and its reluctance (or what Roosevelt regarded as neglect) in preparing the nation for war. "Colonel" Roosevelt proposed to form a "Roosevelt Legion" of volunteers "representative of the whole Nation" that "should be sent to the fighting front at once to fill the gap until the great army to be raised by selective draft is ready."[31] Roosevelt had strong Republican backing for his proposed volunteer division, which he "envisioned as a kind of showcase specimen of American virility." Many of its officers would come from Ivy League schools, but the unit would also include a sampling of the nation's "melting pot." There would be an immigrant division, with German Americans bravely fighting for "Old Glory." It would include a regiment of African Americans (with white officers), and it would recruit descendants of famous Civil War generals to be given places of special distinction. Enthusiasm for the unit was such that it was later expanded from a division to a corps.[32]

Yet the Roosevelt Legion was politically dangerous to both Wilson and conscription. It ran the risk of blundering into a debacle in France, damaging American prestige, and inhibiting a trained, professional army from successfully achieving its mission. Alternatively, should Roosevelt meet with success, the Republicans would trumpet it as a "patriotic success" to bludgeon the administration. Other volunteer units, like the Yale Battery and the first Yale Aerial Coastal Patrol Unit Number One, also sought inclusion into the armed forces.[33] To prevent the possibility of Roosevelt using command in France as a springboard of political advantage, Wilson sought to suppress all volunteer units. Congressional Democrats defeated a Republican-sponsored amendment to the Selective Service conscription bill that directed Wilson to grant Roosevelt an independent command. The compromise wording simply permitted the president to do so without making the provision a requirement. Wilson signed the bill into law but declined to give Roosevelt a command.

The legislation did allow the Army, Navy, and National Guard to accept volunteer units but did not require them to do so. Trubee Davison, who formed the Yale Aerial Coast Patrol, lobbied Navy Secretary Josephus Daniels to accept his unit into the US Navy Reserve. Daniels marveled at the patriotism and "wonderful" offer and then courteously turned Davison down. Like Lou, Davison turned to private subscriptions for the unit, obtaining about $200,000. Since Davison was the son of a managing partner of one of the world's most dominant banks, J.P. Morgan and Company, the bank provided half, and private donors made up the rest. They set up operations at Robert Wanamaker's Trans-Oceanic Company flying school in Palm Beach, Florida, rapidly building up a squadron of aircraft that was larger than the entire aviation section of the US Navy. With such formidable backing, Daniels eventually relented, and the unit was accepted into the Navy.[34] The provisions of the Selective Service conscription bill and the Navy's first aerial reserve gave Lou hope for Army acceptance of the West Virginia Flying Corps.

Aside from rare instances such as this, the Wilson administration consciously broke with the American tradition that predated the Civil War of accepting state volunteer units for military service in wartime. Wilson wanted a respectable, modern army.[35]

Lou tackled the formidable challenges facing him with audacity, though it was almost impossible to meet with the secretary of war. The demands of mobilizing the Army rapidly filled Baker's schedule, and he had to make several trips away from Washington. His staff had "no personal feelings for West Virginia" and were not especially helpful toward arranging a meeting with Baker. Lou's father, however, used his political influence to try to break through the logjam. He contacted the US solicitor general John W. Davis of Clarksburg, West Virginia, a friend and the future Democratic candidate for president. Davis liked the idea of an aviation unit for the Mountain State and "promised to go with [the Bennetts]" to see Baker, but Davis was convinced that "he will not recognize civilian schools." The elder Bennett also telephoned Governor Cornwell to set up a meeting for Lou to ask for an appropriation to train the unit. With Baker unavailable, Lou's father counseled him to go to Charleston to see the governor where they at least had "a *chance*," because the legislature was meeting in a few days in an extra session.[36]

Cornwell was also intrigued by the idea of an aviation unit for West Virginia. He agreed to contact Baker on behalf of the WVFC. He wrote a personal cover letter to the secretary and enclosed Lou's letter explaining the goals and purpose of the unit, "to conduct an aviation school under requirements of the War Department" in order to train West Virginians for the Air Service, and "to create interest in this State in that branch of the service, and to advance aviation as much as possible in this State." Cornwell asked Baker to advise him immediately whether such a corps would be accepted by the War Department. Were it so, Cornwell continued, he was "inclined to ask the Legislature to appropriate sufficient money to enable [Bennett] to carry out his plans."[37]

Lou also asked the governor for permission to inform the newspapers so that he could recruit members with the "equivalent of a college education" before they enlisted in other branches of the armed forces. That way, young West Virginians would "know that a more distinguished way of doing greater good is open to them" should they wish to serve both their state and their country. Cornwell gave his permission, and Lou sent out his press release to state newspapers. While Lou conferred with the governor and state legislature in Charleston, he also continued his work finding equipment to train his men.[38]

After Lou obtained a second aircraft, he suffered a major setback. Although the details are sketchy, Lou confided to his father that both aircraft were damaged "in tests" in New York. As a result, one of his WVFC backers decided he didn't want his son to fly and pulled out. It seems Lou was happy with the decision, since the son who was involved in the mishap "lost his head" and gripped the rudder bar with his feet, which the pilot could not get away from him. Since they were low to the ground, he was unable to recover the aircraft and both wings were broken. What seemed to gall Lou the most was that they both left the scene, "leaving the machine in my hands." It also seems as though the young man's father may have threatened legal action, because in subsequent letters Lou solicited his father's legal advice, referred to the aircraft as the one with "legal difficulties," and forwarded details of the mishap to Johnson for his advice. Lou's mother, Sallie, feared more trouble as a result of the accident and shared those fears with her son.[39]

Not content to simply select linen samples for the unit, Sallie also weighed in on the governor, sending him a clipping from the May 15 *New York Times* announcing that in June, the Army and Navy would establish an aviation training camp at the flight school in Atwood, Delaware. Sallie opined that the government "should *not* overlook West Virginia" and exhorted Cornwell to support her son before the state legislature as well as to let the [Wilson] administration know that a flight school was a great thing for West Virginia too. She concluded by asking Cornwell to not mention her letter to anyone else since she did "not want 'to butt in.'"[40]

The War Department had indeed begun to enlist the help of aviation schools across the country. The Air Service had only three flying fields, and its tiny cadre of officers could not hope to meet the proposed expansion program that would increase it 150-fold. Additionally, the whole organizational structure of military aviation was a mess and not adequate for modern, total warfare. The Army relegated its aviation service to a relatively insignificant role in its mobilization plan. There were personnel shortages. Frequent organizational changes created confusion toward organizational responsibility. The chief signal officer, who was responsible for organizing and training aviation squadrons, had no voice in production or allocation of materials. Finally, some kind of training standard was needed in these civilian flying schools, which traditionally only operated on a highly personalized basis. General Squier turned to Yale history professor Hiram Bingham to establish the ground school and flight training program for the Army. Bingham traveled to Canada with a study group to examine the Canadian flight training system, including how the University of Toronto cooperated with the Royal Flying Corps to conduct ground school. Before Bingham left Washington, DC, for Canada, he remarked, "No one appeared to know exactly how the plan was to be worked out in this country." The Bingham group was largely responsible for developing the training standards that the Army would follow. However, in the spring of 1917 when Lou was seeking to learn the Army standards, the Bingham group was still in the process of collecting information.[41]

After his father helped him pay for the cost of repairs, Lou also arranged to bring one of his aircraft from New York to Wheeling, a distance of about four hundred miles. Captain Kelly intended to make the flight with Lou as his student, but Kelly was injured in one of the earlier crashes. Lou once again had to find a qualified instructor for the WVFC. He found William Frey of Long Island, New York. The twenty-five-year-old Frey claimed to have been a pilot with the famed Escadrille Lafayette, a squadron of Americans who volunteered to fight for France in the French *Aéronautique Militaire*. Standing at five feet, eleven inches tall with light hair and blue eyes, Frey cut a striking figure. Unlike the fairly reputable Kelly, however, Frey was one of three Americans who deserted from the *Aéronautique Militaire* and was a wanted man.[42] He was in fact one of those "gentlemen" Hartney described as "dodging front line service." One cannot imagine that Lou would have enlisted such a character had he known his background. Events proved that he was not the best choice of instructor for the West Virginia Flying Corps.

At 0630 hours on May 30, 1917, Frey and Bennett launched in a Curtiss JN-4D "Jenny." Over New Jersey, they became disoriented. Seeing what they thought was an airfield, they landed only to find that they had in fact put down at the Salem Driving Park. Once they had gotten their bearings, they again attempted to fly to West Virginia. It was eleven o'clock. During the takeoff attempt, the aircraft blew a tire and they crashed into a fence. The aircraft suffered too much damage to continue the flight, so they had it shipped to Beech Bottom by rail.[43] There, the WVFC finally had a base of operations with the facilities to make the aircraft airworthy again.

The buildings at the base were complete with a large hangar that measured 150 feet long by 35 feet wide. It was large enough to hold three aircraft. The workshop measured 80 feet by 50 feet, and it included a small office building. There were also sleeping quarters for the men. The wrecked Curtiss was put back into flying order, and Bennett acquired two more machines. Of these, only one was a Curtiss JN-4 used for flight training. The other was a nonflying machine that taught students the essentials of controlling the aircraft while taxiing along the ground. This was part of the old Curtiss method of training adapted by the French for their pursuit (fighter) pilots. These training machines were known as "grass cutters" or "penguins" because they had short wings and were not able to fly. After successfully mastering this craft, the students were placed in the dual-control Curtiss biplane with an instructor. The student had to demonstrate his ability to successfully taxi across the airfield before being allowed to fly. Initial training sorties were restricted to short "hops" around the field, but as students successfully demonstrated proficiency with each phase of training, they progressed to flying at higher altitudes, performing acrobatics, and flying cross-country.[44]

Lou left these remaining two machines unassembled until he finished screening the applicants and completed their enlistment in the squadron. This was not unusual. It was common practice that ground school students first learned to assemble and repair the aircraft long before they made their first flight. The purpose of this training went beyond simply giving the students an in-depth knowledge of the mechanical operation of their machine. It had a practical application as well. Should a mechanical problem force them to make a landing away from the airfield, they would have the knowledge to repair the aircraft and fly it home.[45]

Meanwhile, in response to the call for volunteers, candidates began to apply to the WVFC. Lou sent a telegram to those who expressed an interest in joining the unit asking them to send their applications immediately. He knew from experience that it took time to train men to fly. The Army estimated that it took something like a full six months to turn out a first-class pilot. Out of the first forty applicants, Lou selected a group of twelve who arrived in Wheeling for evaluation. From the original group, several were eliminated during the screening process. Two men failed to pass the aviator examination, and Lou asked the governor to enlist them as mechanics. Another had eye problems that were detected during the physical exam. Yet another failed the military examination. After the initial screening, Lou advised the governor that the application process had gone smoothly and sent him a list of fifteen names, including himself and Frey. His friend from Yale Tommy Kent from California was among them. The remainder were from West Virginia. Another close friend from Yale, Fred Weyerhaeuser, was initially one of the founding members, but he decided to join the USAAS because of the aforementioned delays.[46]

Once the buildings were completed, Lou started living at the field. During the screening process, he continued flying. He and Frey flew around Wheeling in early June. They intended to land at the West Virginia State Fair grounds on Wheeling Island, but the weather had been poor, so they flew around the city, along the river south to Bellaire, Ohio, and then returned to Beech Bottom. Next, Frey took Tom Kent up for a short flight around the field. During engine start, which was accomplished by placing one's fingertips over the edge of the propeller and pulling the propeller down rapidly until the motor caught, the unit's mechanic broke his arm. Lou then started the machine by "hand-propping" it himself. As his father had cautioned, aviation was a hazardous undertaking.[47]

While Lou was still waiting for the state council of defense to accept the WVFC into state service, on June 5, 1917, he registered for the draft with other American men between the ages of twenty-one and thirty.[48] He continued to look for sponsors to help fund the organization but was having difficulty raising money since the "wire edge," the initial fervor after the declaration of war, had "worn off." He again went to Washington, DC, in an attempt to see Secretary Baker. While there, he wrote the governor and again asked him to consider enrolling the men as a "special body under state control," in either the National Guard or as a state National Guard Reserve, which is what he believed the First Yale Unit had done. Lou was quite satisfied that everything at his airfield was ready to begin training. Many of the men were already there. All he needed was the official blessing of the West Virginia Council of National Defense. Cornwell remained unsure as to the status of the National Guard postbellum and felt that it had been abolished by federal law when it had been called up to active duty. As a result, when the adjutant general resigned his post, the governor did not fill it since "he would be a general without an army."[49]

While in Washington, Lou also met with members of the Aircraft Production Board. He wanted definitive information from them so he would know what type of combat aircraft the United States would produce for the war in Europe. That way, the West Virginia Aircraft Company could build the right combat aircraft, obtaining lucrative contracts from the Army for producing it. The WVFC would then train with the latest type of Air Service combat aircraft. Once again, Lou came away disappointed. He wrote to his father, "The Aircraft Production Board are still indefinite. They have not yet their appropriation. They are trying to standardize a motor and until they do so they do not know what plane will be suitable for the motor." However, Lou was characteristically optimistic, adding, "But they have a few motors of other types and they may give out orders on them and from what we could learn we have a fair chance of getting a sample order of 30 or 40 [airplanes] in a few days. As soon as they get their appropriation, I think they will give out orders right and left."[50]

Meanwhile, the USAAS welcomed its first combat squadron on the Western Front in France: the famed Escadrille Lafayette transferred from the French Army to the United States Army.[51] America's first operational combat squadron, like many of the Army's weapons, came from the French.

At last, on July 16, 1917, the state council of defense recognized the West Virginia Flying Corps and approved Lou's request for a $10,000 appropriation. Governor Cornwell commissioned Bennett as captain and commander of the West Virginia Flying Corps, while Tom Kent and William Frey were commissioned as lieutenants. Cornwell also signed the men's enlistment papers, and training finally commenced. The thirteen members and occupations of the WVFC were Tommy Kent (aviation student), William Wright (draftsman), George Dudley Jr. (lumber dealer), Jack Adams (balloon student), Bertram Gilles (clerk), Ralph Lohr (engineer), Harold Holloway (dairy farmer), Guy Simpson (roofer), Courtney Lambert (chauffeur), Louis Bussler (chemist), Earnest Gate (banker), Dan Burns (bank clerk), and Paul Pashby (mechanical engineer).[52]

The main building at the field was used for meals and sleeping quarters. Lou hired expert mechanics to supervise his shops as well as two African American cooks to prepare the meals. In Jim Crow America, some criticized Bennett for this, but he stood his ground and kept the cooks. Additionally, the Army provided a drill instructor, Sergeant Dean Snedeker, to oversee the unit's military training. Disciplinary regulations went into effect, and movement for the unit members was restricted according to military regulations. Although Beech Bottom was fairly well isolated with only a few houses near the camp, newspapermen as well as "hundreds of autos and wagons" passed by and stopped daily to watch the operations.[53] Captain Bennett posted the WVFC regulations:

West Virginia Flying Corps Regulations
MORNING HOURS
5:15—Revielle [sic].
5:30—Assembly.
5:30 to 6:00—Calisthenics.
6:00 to 7:00—Police.
7:00—Breakfast.
8:00—Inspection of quarters.
8:30—Drill; shop work.
12:00 noon—Dinner.

AFTERNOON HOURS
1:00—School and shop work.
5:15—Retreat.
5:30—Supper.
9:30—Call to quarters.
10:00—Taps.
Evening lectures, 6 to 10 o'clock[.][54]

Lou and Tom received most of the flight training at first. Since they already had some flight experience, they could become qualified to fly and instruct in the least amount of time. With only one aircraft available in the hot, muggy summer weather, flight training time was limited, so the priority was for these two young men to master the art of flying, while the unit assembled its other aircraft. Once these were judged airworthy, training could begin for the remaining students. Flight training was restricted to early morning and early evening, usually after four o'clock in the afternoon. The winds are generally calmer during these times, and therefore the air is less turbulent than at midday. Additionally, higher summer temperatures and humidity result in a higher-density altitude. These conditions reduced the Curtiss JN-4's aircraft performance in such a way as to challenge a skilled pilot, let alone a novice just learning to fly. During the middle period, the students spent their time assembling the additional aircraft and conducting their ground school training. The grass cutter was assembled approximately two weeks after the unit was officially formed, and students added this to their training regimen. Next, the students began work on the second Curtiss. When it was time for the evening flight schedule, the instructor blew his whistle, the men wheeled the machine out of the hangar, and the instructor reviewed the operation of the flight controls and "instrument board" with all the students. Then, Frey and his primary student started the engine and departed on their training flight.[55]

Lou's sister donated a player piano to the Flying Corps for recreation. The large airfield served an auxiliary purpose as a baseball or football field on which the young men could compete. Following the example of the Europeans, Lou considered athletics an essential part of aviation training at Beech Bottom. One Royal Air Force (RAF) flight surgeon commented that a "successful flier must be one who has power to coordinate his limb muscles with a beautiful degree of refinement." He went on to explain, "It is because of the importance of this delicately coordinated effector [sic] response that great importance is attached to a history of sport in the selection of aviators." General Squier went so far as to advise Harvard University's president that the Air Service wanted "athletes who are quick witted, punctual and reliable. Intelligent men accustomed to making quick decisions are highly desirable. Men who ride well, can sail a fast boat or handle a motorcycle usually make good air pilots." To do otherwise, Hiram Bingham declared, was to waste "the most expensive education in the world."[56]

Besides sports and music, Lou continued his pursuits of the "fairer sex." He began seeing a young lady by the name of Mary Hays. Her mother, Cordelia Hays, was recently widowed, and mother and daughter divided their time between Wheeling and Great Barrington, Massachusetts. Whenever Lou was off duty, he and Mary were often together driving around the area in his car. His aerial militia gained recognition in national periodicals, such as *Flying* and *Colliers* magazines. Local newspapers carried stories on the progress of their training, and the Upper Ohio Valley seemed to adopt the unit as its very own.[57] Lou invited the governor to Beech Bottom to inspect his newest charges.

Still, questions nagged at the commander of the West Virginia Flying Corps. Because the governor had reservations about the status of the National Guard, the WVFC did not have official status as a National Guard unit, and its members were not guardsmen. He needed to keep his mechanics and asked the governor to grant permission for Lou to enlist more into state service. Lou feared that without official status, his men would be drafted into the US Army and he would have no way of stopping this from happening. Additionally, although the legislature had approved the $10,000 appropriation to the WVFC, Lou had not received it and the unit was still operating from his monies.[58] Then, there was the issue of War Department recognition for the unit. Lou had not given up on that either. If the Army or Secretary Baker gave the unit official status, then the draft would not threaten the unit's integrity—and it might receive some kind of federal funding or equipment. The young man was maintaining a very aggressive itinerary: commander of the WVFC, student pilot, public relations man, administrator, lobbyist, suitor.

His commute from the airfield to his office in Wheeling was longer too. On one of his trips around the Valley, the axle to his car was damaged. The car was in the Flying Corps workshop in Beech Bottom, where one of his mechanics was attempting to repair it.[59] Fortunately, his airfield was on the main line of the Peninsula Traction Company, a subsidiary of the Wheeling Traction Company, so he could still get to his office for administrative duties, check mail, and return correspondence. Once he had finished, Lou left his office in the Schmulbach Building for the return trip and walked down to the streetcar company terminal at Tenth Street to catch the electric trolley north. These ran every fifteen minutes.[60] He boarded car Number Three, the Loveland, Warwood, Glenova car and started for Beech Bottom. After passing the North Wheeling Hospital, which had served as the US Army General Military Hospital during the Civil War, Lou found himself out of the city along the River Road. Here, the breeze from the river afforded some relief from the heat and humidity of high summer. The McKinley mine, owned by his brother-in-law, was dug into the nearby ridgeline to the east of the road. The trolley continued on toward Warwood, a small community named for the tool factory there founded by Englishman Henry Warwood.[61]

As he entered the town, which today is a suburb of Wheeling, Lou regarded the community with more than a passing interest. He and Johnson selected

"A More Distinguished Way of Doing Greater Good" 77

the community as the site of the West Virginia Aircraft Company, and with good reason.[62] Warwood was a tidy, growing neighborhood of factories, mines, churches, shops, homes, and an amusement park. The factories sat along the river and rail line, while neat rows of single-family homes swept eastward across the floodplain. Although the homes of workers and managers intermingled, the workmen's homes favored the river side of Warwood Avenue, a broad, tree-lined thoroughfare illuminated by electric streetlights, while the larger homes of managers lined the hills to the east that today is dominated by the heights of Warwood Terrace. At the south end of town, the Army Corps of Engineers had just constructed a new lock-and-dam system on the river. Two Tudor-style houses for the lockmaster and his assistant completed the complex which greeted the trolley as it trundled north from downtown Wheeling.[63]

Continuing along the line, Lou passed beyond the inviting green space of the Garden family, one of the town's founding families, which in summer was full of children playing baseball and running under the majestic oaks. New construction—especially new schools—dotted the landscape, adding credence to the town's motto, "Watch us grow." The Catholic parish of Corpus Christi built a new parochial school on the east side of Warwood Avenue across from the Garden family's oaks. Two blocks north and just opposite the Bank of Warwood near Seventeenth Street, a newly constructed public school, Center Warwood School, was preparing to open and receive its first class. Victorian mansions, like the Dowler-Schreyer House at 1900 Warwood Avenue on the corner of Nineteenth Street near the firemen's hose house, added its stateliness to the community. It was a thriving, bustling, industrious town—and it was only about eight miles from his airfield. To an experienced eye, Warwood was a very promising site for the factory.[64]

Passing north out of the community, Lou's trolley traveled along the river past coal mines and the massive new 200,000 kilowatt coal-fired Beech Bottom power plant of the American Gas and Electric Company before he at last arrived at Beech Bottom and the West Virginia Flying Corps airfield.[65] The trip took about an hour. It was a much easier and faster journey when his car was not in the shop. Lou could be pleased with himself and what he had accomplished in so short a time. Things were looking up. The area was ideal. Training was ready to speed up. Louis Bennett Jr. intended to show the War Department what he and the Flying Corps could do. But was there time?

5

Unusual Courage

Becoming a Pursuit Pilot

It rained almost constantly throughout June, but by the end of the month, the rains finally stopped. At last flight training got underway in earnest at the West Virginia Flying Corps (WVFC) air base in Beech Bottom. Training progressed steadily in the first three weeks of operations. While Bennett and Kent built up their flight time, the remaining students continued with ground school, including mechanical work with the aircraft and engines. The unit also kept up a public relations campaign. On Sunday, July 29, Lou and instructor Frey flew over the West Virginia State Fair and dropped messages from President Wilson, Governor Cornwell, and Congressman M. M. Neely. Frey later flew Lou's sister, Agra, as a passenger. By early August, most of the trainees had completed ground school and were ready to begin flight training. Frey was promoted to captain by Governor Cornwell. Captain Kelly had recovered from his injuries and was nearly ready to fly again, adding another instructor to the roster.[1]

Flying conditions on Friday, August 3, 1917, were ideal for the remaining students' initial flights. Breezes were light and the sky was clear, promising only sunshine. The standard flight training routine began without interruption. Training sorties started early in the morning and continued until the heat of the afternoon, when winds and turbulence increased or storms formed. Training resumed again in the evening when the air cooled and winds died. After languishing in ground school for three weeks, each student eagerly anticipated his turn in the Curtiss. The students rolled the airplane out of its hangar with the help of the ground crew. One of the students then climbed into the forward seat of the tandem-seat aircraft. In the Jenny model of the Curtiss that Lou had purchased, the cockpit was roomy and instrumentation was basic. It had only five instruments—a water temperature gauge for the cooling system, an altimeter, an airspeed indicator, an oil pressure gauge, and the tachometer.[2] Frey climbed into the rear cockpit, checked his controls, and then ordered the engine to be started. Starting the engine was a difficult procedure that required close coordination between pilot and mechanic. The pilot had to hand-pump air pressure into the gas tank and open the air and gas intake valves. He next checked that the ignition switch was set to "off." Meanwhile, his mechanic began to rotate the propeller by hand, and slowly the pilot shut his air valve down. Once his mechanic was sure that enough fuel had been primed into the pistons, he shouted, "Contact," and the pilot set the ignition switch on. His mechanic "cranked" the motor with a pull of the propeller, called a "hand-prop." Whereas a motorcar's driver turned a crank in front of the vehicle to start the motor, an airplane mechanic placed his fingertips carefully over the edge of the propeller and adjusted his balance so that his pulling motion would not cause him to fall into the spinning blade where he could be injured or killed. The mechanic gave the propeller an aggressive "final heave and jumped back for his life." If all worked as advertised, the engine caught and started.[3]

After conducting his post-start-up checks, Frey and the student taxied onto the airfield, making short "hops" as they climbed into the air a few feet and returned to earth, Frey demonstrated the maneuver, followed by the student's attempt to imitate him. If necessary, they would stop for ten or fifteen minutes while Frey explained a point or critiqued the student's performance. Satisfied that the student could safely handle the aircraft, Frey positioned the Jenny at the edge of the field pointing into the wind. He eased the throttle forward, and after a takeoff run of just over 250 feet, the Curtiss launched into the air for a trip around the airfield's traffic pattern, about 700–800 feet above the field and turning to a course parallel to the runway. The instructor handed the controls to the student and coached him through the pattern, landing, and subsequent takeoff. This procedure was repeated as necessary so the student learned by repetition. All morning, Frey duplicated this ritual with each student. When the morning sorties ended, eight members of the WVFC had "taken to the skies."[4]

Prior to the evening training period, Frey reviewed these procedures with the next student, Cadet Courtney B. Lambert of Welch, West Virginia. The twenty-five-year-old Lambert was a chauffeur before the war. He stood five feet, six inches tall with brown eyes and black hair. By six o'clock that evening, the breezes were light and it was cool enough to resume training. The airmen once again rolled a Jenny out—the one that Frey and Lou "cracked up" in New Jersey on their flight from New York to Beech Bottom. Startup and taxi all proceeded normally, with Lambert performing the "hops" to Frey's satisfaction. The chief flight instructor positioned the Curtiss on the north edge of the field, pointed it into the light southerly winds, and advanced the throttle on the right side of the bulkhead. The aircraft left the earth and Lambert had also at last "taken to the skies." They continued south to the Beech Bottom power plant, circled to the west over the calm Ohio River, and climbed to pattern altitude, rolling out on a northerly heading. When they flew parallel to the camp buildings, Lambert's classmates gave him a "great ovation" that was drowned out by the Jenny's motor. The aircraft circled east while Lambert and Frey prepared to land in a descending, right-hand turn. At 1826 hours, the aircraft shuddered, a wingtip "dipped," the nose pitched over, and the Curtiss plunged straight into the ground.[5]

Passengers waiting for the Wheeling trolley at the terminal stood in stunned silence for a moment, suddenly shaken out of their stupor when a woman screamed. Farmer David Cross was at supper with his family and boarders in his farmhouse about a hundred feet away from the crash site. They raced outside to find a smashed aircraft in his cornfield. Cross found Lambert dead at the scene, crushed by the weight of the machine and impaled by brake handles. Frey was alive but unconscious and choking on a piano wire. Cross cut him free with an ax. After first aid was administered to the airman, he was taken into the Cross home. Later, he was carried by stretcher to the nearby Allen Burt house, which was nearer the trolley station. Mrs. Burt had seen the crash and sent for a doctor who came quickly to their home.[6]

Lou and Tommy Kent arrived with the doctor, who stabilized the unconscious man and dressed his wounds. The three men accompanied Frey, who was placed on an "express car" of the Traction Company line and transported to the North Wheeling Hospital. There, he was treated for a compound fracture of his left leg, a fractured jaw, and lacerations, from which he recovered. A guard was posted around the crash site to keep the growing crowd of onlookers from disturbing it. Captain Kelly also left that evening for New York to acquire a replacement aircraft so that training could continue as planned.[7] At 2140 hours that night, Lou sent a telegram from Wheeling to Governor Cornwell in Charleston: "Sad duty to report that in school flight this evening machine fell seriously injuring Capt Frey and with fatal result to cadet Lambert son of C B Lambert Welch WVA [West Virginia][.] Will you also wire family expressing regrets that their son should be first West Virginian to lose his life in the service of his country?"[8]

It was not an auspicious beginning for the West Virginia Flying Corps. However, in aviation circles, it was not unusual. Lambert was the fifth aviator killed that week in the United States. Two flyers previously died in a crash at Great South Bay, New York. Another was killed in an accident at Los Angeles, while a fourth died in a training accident at Mineola, New York. Aviators accepted accidental death as part of early aviation, and training losses often exceeded combat fatalities. Twice as many American pilots died in training accidents as in combat. Americans training with the more experienced British, like John McGavock Grider, experienced similarly high losses. While Lou made the slow trip back to Beech Bottom to meet with reporters late that night to discuss the events of the day, he must have again recalled his father's warning: aviation was indeed a "hazardous undertaking."[9]

Nevertheless, training resumed at the airfield, although the members of the unit were clearly "laboring under a great strain and that each one keenly felt the loss of his comrade." There was much to do, and they were short one aircraft and one instructor. Yet they did continue to move forward. Students received new uniforms, which resembled those of the US Army but had Lou's WVFC insignia embroidered on their tunics.[10] Even with one instructor, they still could train.

Lou divided his time between training with the unit and his other projects. He still tried to obtain formal US Army recognition of the Flying Corps. On July 20, the first draft numbers were drawn and neither Governor Cornwell nor Lou had received War Department assurances that members of the WVFC would be exempt. Several members, including its mechanics, had their draft numbers selected. Unless Lou or the governor secured official War Department recognition for the unit, the draftees were required to report for duty. Key personnel such as mechanics were essential to the unit's success. Lou petitioned the draft board to exempt his mechanics "on industrial claims," since mechanics at the Curtiss and the Princeton school were exempted on this basis, recognizing the importance of skilled labor in total warfare.[11]

Lou feverishly attempted to resolve this issue with the Militia Bureau of the War Department and Governor Cornwell. Lou's frequent letters repeatedly urged the governor to name the unit as a National Guard Reserve, although he provided several pages of similar options. Cornwell still believed that he had no National Guard on which to base a reserve and did not know if there would ever be a National Guard after the war, so he was reluctant to designate the WVFC as part of the state's National Guard. However, he did write to the Militia Bureau explaining, "It is our intention to treat them as a part of our State Guards Reserve and I would be glad to be advised whether they will be recognized to the extent of being exempt from the draft." Unfortunately, the War Department did not recognize a "State Guards Reserve."[12]

The governor soon traveled to Beech Bottom to inspect the unit and was "very well satisfied." Lou flew over to the races in Uniontown, Pennsylvania, that morning since "it would be a good notoriety" and dropped placards in the governor's honor. Although the status of the unit was in doubt, Lou and Johnson moved forward with Lou's idea for a national aerial militia. To expand the national aerial militia and improve the acceptability of the WVFC for military service, Lou searched for other flight schools that the War Department recognized. American universities finally operated as US Army Air Service (USAAS) ground schools following the Canadian model, and several of these had primary flight schools. One that caught Bennett's attention was the School of Military Aeronautics at Princeton University. Using his own money as well as capital from his father and brother-in-law, Lou purchased the entire Princeton "Outfit," thus increasing his aerial militia to five machines and the grass cutter. The list included the mishap JN-4 that took cadet Lambert's life and the other machine with "legal difficulties" from its previous mishap as well as several spare motors.[13]

At last, he had the nucleus of his system in place. Having succeeded in interesting the state of West Virginia to invest in his unit, Lou sought to attract major American business groups too so the system could expand. He wanted support from industrial giants like the DuPont Corporation. As he explained to the company's aeronautical division, "I am endeavoring to get people interested in the manufacturing concern who are interested primarily in the future of aviation itself. I want them to take over and maintain as many flying fields as reasonable and to establish factories not only in one place but to spread out and grow into other localities." With that in mind, he asked for DuPont's support to sustain both his fields at Wheeling and Princeton, and to acquire the flight school at Holly Oak, Delaware.[14]

Additionally, Lou and Johnson went to New York and Washington, DC, to obtain government contracts. Johnson wrote to Lou's father that prospects for contracts for either aircraft or parts from the Aircraft Production Board were good. Lou concurred. He informed DuPont that he was capable of "half of the financing of any company of capitalization up to half a million dollars," though with the prospect of imminent orders from the government, "Three Hundred Thousand Dollars would be sufficient capitalization for starting." In return, he offered to let DuPont secure the general manager to run the factory, since he and Johnson had already hired a plant manager and department heads.[15]

Johnson had concerns, however. During the swell of patriotic fervor that accompanied the declaration of war, many Wheeling-area men volunteered for military service. As a result, there was a shortage of skilled labor that caused delays in establishing the aircraft factory. Johnson investigated alternate sites for a manufacturing concern, such as Cleveland, Ohio. Although a plant in Cleveland would have supported Lou's idea to expand a national aerial militia, it would put the factory farther away from his main base in Beech Bottom. Additionally, they had already begun manufacturing operations in Warwood. Lou became increasingly impatient about the delay, and Johnson cautioned him to be practical with so much money invested. Still, Johnson expressed admiration for his brother-in-law, who was single-handedly organizing, training, and equipping the West Virginia Flying Corps, attempting to establish a national aviation reserve and obtain its corporate and government support, and at the same time learning to fly—all during a world war. Additionally, Lou was still dating Mary Hays in his "off time." Johnson wrote to Lou's father that, he was "rather sorry that Louis did not go directly into the manufacturing end of [aviation] first." The elder Bennett reminded Johnson that he supported his son unconditionally, and his support of the West Virginia Aircraft Company was contingent upon Lou's involvement with it.[16]

Lou was coming to grips with the realization that getting started was the greatest difficulty. Fortunately, he was able to find some local skilled laborers to get the aircraft company up and running. Small business owners like T. G. Cupp, who owned a roofing and sheet metal business in Warwood, closed his shop to work at the aircraft factory. During World War I, the West Virginia Aircraft Company produced spare parts and JN-4D airframes for the Army, valued at about one million dollars. Marked with US Army aviation insignia, they were crated and shipped via rail without engines. Even though Lou did not secure DuPont financial support or add the Holly Oak facility to his national aviation reserve, he eventually obtained a site in Daytona, Florida, and worked out an agreement with his instructor at the Princeton school to shift operations there for the winter. It was not uncommon for Northern units to train in the Southern United States or maintain training facilities there in the winter months.[17]

Lou's friend Fred Weyerhaeuser visited the airfield at Beech Bottom. Fred had joined the Air Service and was finishing training with a cross-country flight before departing for the war. Fred thanked Lou for his abundant hospitality and offered to return the favor "after the big [war] is over" when Lou came to visit him out West. (As a practical joke, "someone" removed the wheel pins on Weyerhaeuser's aircraft, causing the wheels to fall off just after takeoff near Wellsburg. He chided Lou that he hoped they found them.) Weyerhaeuser accompanied New York congressman Fiorello LaGuardia to Italy to train on Caproni aircraft.[18]

There were problems, however. Lou's father was losing weight and suffering from painful bowel problems, including what were termed cholera symptoms. Most of the family attributed this condition to overwork. As part of his therapy, the elder Bennett traveled to Oakland, Maryland, to stay with a doctor to rest and recover. Although he felt better, he was not able to gain weight. The doctor recommended medical tests and X-rays in order to discover what mysterious ailment afflicted him.[19]

At last, Lou received the War Department's answer to the governor's September 1 appeal to recognize the WVFC. On September 7, Cornwell forwarded a War Department letter, on which the governor wrote, "I hand you, herewith, a letter from the War Department refusing to exempt members of your Flying Corps." Secretary Baker conceded that the unit might proceed as one of the Army's primary flight schools if they accepted students from across the country, much like the Princeton school, but it could not train and fight together as a state unit. The Army would not accept elite units, period—whether they were Theodore Roosevelt's Legion, the Yale Battery, racing champion Eddie Rickenbacker's proposed flying unit of race car drivers, or the West Virginia Flying Corps. In this regard, Lou was in good company. Although the city of Wheeling held a banquet for the unit's drafted men before they departed for the Army, the WVFC suddenly had a tenuous existence.[20]

Still clinging to his vision, Lou insisted that the unit remain a West Virginia organization comprised mainly of natives to the Mountain State, and he continued to press Cornwell to "fight it out and get the corps recognized as a State Guard Reserve" to set "a precedent for other corps" in states throughout the country. In good faith, the governor again took up the issue with the War Department but found he had little influence there or with the draft board. He tried to obtain industrial exemptions for the unit's mechanics from the War Department as well. Secretary Baker responded through the Army's Adjutant General's Office. Although Baker appreciated the patriotic efforts and resourcefulness of the West Virginia citizens in organizing and training a flying corps for use by the US government, the secretary could not exempt members of the WVFC within the draft ages. Baker thought it "very unlikely" that its members could be used by the Army without the regular course given to flying cadets because military aviation involved more than mere flying. It included "radio telegraphy, aerial combat, and reconnaissance, machine guns, topography, etc." Without this training, the secretary added, a pilot was "of no value, even though he be expert in handling of an airplane in the air." Baker recommended that any member of the West Virginia Flying Corps who wanted to join the USAAS should submit an application to take the regular course of training "prescribed for men obtaining commissions in the Aviation Section, Signal Officers' Reserve Corps."[21]

This recommendation from the secretary of war confirmed Lou's fears. He was discouraged but opted to make one last attempt to gain Army recognition. Lou took up the matter with Major General Squier of the Signal Corps, who confirmed his chief's position and recommended Lou disband the unit and have its members enroll in one of the Army's primary schools as the best opportunity to join the USAAS. It seemed there were no options left. Since the Princeton school was one of the primary schools in use, Lou decided to take his top six students to Princeton in order to finish their flight training and obtain their pilot's licenses. In late September, he reluctantly acknowledged the West Virginia Flying Corps had to be disbanded.[22]

All that was left was for the state to send him the $10,000 appropriation for the WVFC, which Lou had to battle the state council of defense to receive. At last, on October 5, Lou acknowledged receipt of the state appropriation for the WVFC. His total expenditures had amounted to about $50,000.[23]

Before disbanding the organization, Lou put together a fundraiser. He refused to completely give up on his idea of a West Virginia unit, so he planned to keep a machinist and assistant at the airfield for the winter just in case it was needed or should his idea be resurrected. First, Lou put on an air show for the city of Wheeling, making "some wonderful flights and loops" there. Next, he did something new in the area; the West Virginia Flying Corps took passengers up for flights around the Ohio Valley. The number of people who came to fly was so large and it became "so crowded that they had to draw lots to go as it got too dark [to fly]." It was a befitting final gesture that endeared him to the community and helped keep the field open just a bit longer.[24]

Lou disbanded the unit and left the operation of the aircraft company in his brother-in-law's care. Then, Lou and six others set off for Princeton to complete their training. In its short existence, the West Virginia Flying Corps completed roughly 113 hours of training in the air. After Lou, Tommy Kent had the most flying hours with just over 11.5 hours. Five other aviators had just over 10 flying hours. Although it had not achieved Lou's goal of being a state combat unit like the Escadrille Lafayette, it captured the imagination of the public. It was one of the first few attempts to establish a national aerial reserve, akin to today's Air Force Reserve. It was symbolic of the transition from traditional, volunteer-based units to the modern professional armies of the industrial age. Eight years before Brigadier General William "Billy" Mitchell, the outspoken air power theorist of the US Army Air Service advocated such a program, Louis Bennett Jr. had tried to make it a reality.[25]

Lou completed his "Expert Flying exams" at Princeton and certified as a licensed pilot, but ignored General Squier's advice to join the USAAS. Lou was still stung by the Army's refusal to accept the WVFC into its ranks. He was very much aware that even were he accepted into the Air Service, he would start at the bottom just like everyone else, and he had worked too hard and come too far for that. He corresponded with classmates like Fred Weyerhaeuser, Jarvis Offutt, and other USAAS aviators and was fully aware of Army delays and "growing pains" trying to expand the USAAS to a force of over eleven thousand aircraft and ten thousand pilots for the war.[26]

The original Air Service plan to train pilots in the United States in phases—ground school, primary flight school, advanced training and specialization—soon proved impractical. Lack of equipment, especially aircraft, impeded pilot production. Ground school graduates faced long delays before beginning flight training. The USAAS then sent some cadets to Europe for their training where the Allies offered equipment, airfields, and facilities for American use. Bureaucratic mismanagement and lapses in communication there also hindered pilot production—some students languished at their flight schools, performing parade drills, inspections, or, in the worst case for some Ivy League elites, performing manual labor (for example, building their own air stations before they could begin flight training). The shift of primary training to Europe both disrupted the orderly flow of pilot production at home and abroad, and interrupted the shipping schedule of American troops to Europe. However, all advanced training had to take place in Europe for two reasons: one, the United States had no advanced flight training aircraft or modern combat aircraft with which to conduct such training, and two, the USAAS had "no pilots qualified to give advanced instruction." American aviation was a mess.[27] Eventually, the USAAS worked through these issues but only after many costly delays.

But the British needed pilots. They recruited men from all over the empire, including Canada (and even the US). Additionally, the US Signal Corps and the Canadian arm of the Royal Flying Corps, RFC Canada, made a reciprocal training agreement after the United States entered the war. The Canadians gave the Americans a model for ground schools and aerial gunnery instruction; Canadian instructors taught American aviation cadets until the USAAS training program could get up to speed; and the Air Service constructed three airfields equipped with training aircraft in the southern United States for Canadian use, especially in the winter months.[28]

Lou decided that "the quickest and most direct route" to active combat aviation service "was through the British Royal Flying Corps" in Canada. Because of his previous flight experience and training, Lou hoped that he would have a shorter training period than other aviation cadets. Before leaving Wheeling, Lou said goodbye to Mary Hays. To ease her anguish at their parting, Lou gave her the use of his recently repaired car "for the war." Then he went out to Beech Bottom one last time. His sister Agra packed for him, and she and Johnson "took him to Wellsburg and saw him off." Lou stopped in Atlantic City, New Jersey, en route to Canada. His father was there undergoing tests and medical treatment for his mysterious ailment. Tests revealed a lump in his intestines, which the doctor felt was not serious. He was resting and seemed to be improving and gaining strength. Lou wanted to see his father before going off to war. They had infrequently corresponded over the last few months, and the elder Bennett was very upset over Lou's decision. He wrote to Sallie, "I am all at sea about Louis. No one has ever given me full details about his affairs or his going abroad." He was especially perplexed by Lou's decision to go to Canada, asking her, "But why the Canadian instead of the American service? Since the United States declared war I have never had any real objection to his entering the military service in any branch of it he preferred, but I cannot as yet fully understand why it should not be the U.S. service."[29]

Having said goodbye to his father, Lou departed for Canada on October 5, 1917, to join the RFC Cadet Wing, Camp Borden, Long Branch, Ontario. He was given cadet number 152374. To enhance his standing, Lou carried letters of introduction from British aviators he knew. Lou enlisted on October 9, but was able to go into Toronto the following Saturday for his "weekly wash up [and] to write some letters." He informed his father that he "cannot shorten course any so will probably be down again in a couple of months." He also thought his timing was poor. He wished he had gotten there in time to fly. Lou wrote, "If they keep us here long we shall hardly be at flying again before well in the New Year." Lou expected to start ground school at the nearby university soon. He was happy, though, because they were in barracks and not tents. He was also very impressed with the base itself, which had "fifteen hangars [and] everything is well laid out."[30]

Ground school taught theory of flight and included practical applications such as radio communications, gunnery, engine control, and airplane inspection. Lou underwent the battery of inoculations and slow-moving military initiations that new recruits suffer through in most modern armies.[31]

Lou also suffered a visit from his mother. Ever since he decided to enlist, Sallie aggressively opposed his decision and tried to convince him to quit. She bombarded her son with letters demanding that he stop what he was doing. Lou complained to his father that he received letter after letter demanding that he, "quit, quit while the quitting is good, stop, back out, leave it, drop it." She wanted him to come back with her. Lou made it clear to her that he was in the Army and sticking to it, sometimes answering her with "a rather nasty letter." Agra, too, chastised their mother for this approach, telling her that it was too late for Lou to get out, adding people would say things about him like other local men that someone called "all yellow."[32]

Lou's mother was not the only one encouraging him to quit. Unlike personnel in other military branches, aviators realized early that not every volunteer was suitable to fly or be a combat pilot. Military aviators, unlike other soldiers, faced additional fears beyond confronting the enemy and being killed in combat. These fears dealt with flying itself. Many young men were drawn to aviation because of newspaper stories describing the glamour and excitement. Others sought to escape the draft. Once up in the air, these fears manifested. Some discovered that they feared heights. Some succumbed to airsickness—or "manifestations of fear of flight," in modern Air Force parlance. Once aerial maneuvering and aerobatics began, more students became ill, timid, or fearful. Some students were so terrified that they would "freeze," doing nothing while the machine hurtled at the ground. The alert instructor yanked the controls away and recovered the aircraft. Instructors carefully screened aviation cadets. As historian Rebecca Cameron observed, "deciding who would become 'superb pilots and fighters' remained among the most important tasks of training officials."[33] One Great War aviator recalled his RFC training, when a decorated combat pilot addressed his class and encouraged them to quit:

> You men are starting on a long trip. It's a hard trip and will require a lot of courage. You'll all be frightened many times but most of you will be able to conquer your fear and carry on. But if you find that fear has gotten the best of you and you can't stick it and you are beyond bucking up, don't go on and cause the death of brave men [through] your failure. Quit where you are and try something else. Courage is needed above all else. If five of you meet five Huns and one of you is yellow and doesn't do his part and lets the others down, the four others will be killed [through] the failure of the one and maybe that one himself.[34]

The training staff, instructors, and medical team were vigilant for candidates whom they suspected were unsuitable for aviation. They were sent to the camp doctor, who put them in a swivel chair and "would obligingly spin them until they said they didn't think they cared about being in aviation." The training system ruthlessly sought any excuse to eliminate aviation candidates, yet attached no opprobrium for those it did. "Washout" rates thus remained very high—generally over 50 percent of a class was eliminated.[35]

Perhaps the system did not associate any shame with quitting the program, but Louis Bennett Jr. did. He was acutely aware of his family's Civil War heritage and their relationship to "Stonewall" Jackson and believed he was "cut from the same cloth." His Yale indoctrination demanded the utmost from him, as well. He had every intention of exceeding expectations and making his own distinctive, brave mark in the world. Lou resolutely informed his father that he intended to "stick to my guns." He was not alone. Indeed, when the United States entered World War I, most Americans still accepted the Civil War conception of courage—courage that required heroic action undertaken without fear. John McGavock Grider agreed. After about ten of his "Oxford Group" quit flying, he wrote, "They never should have enlisted if they didn't intend to see it [through] after they found out it was dangerous. [Geoffrey] Dwyer gets them jobs at Headquarters or puts them in charge of mechanics. But yellow is yellow whether you call it nerves or not. I'm just as scared sometimes as any of them."[36] Grider also "stuck."

Lou finished ground school in Canada and traveled to the Canadian flight training facilities collectively known as the Taliaferro fields near Fort Worth, Texas, to begin flight training. Each of the fields introduced cadets to different levels of flight training. Benbrook and Everman fields were used for primary training by both RFC Canada and the USAAS, while Hicks was solely Canadian and used for aerial gunnery training. Ironically, Lou received his flight training at Canadian schools built by the United States and equipped with the same type of aircraft, the JN-4D Jenny, that he mastered in Beech Bottom. He was back in his element, back in the air and flying in a familiar machine. He progressed rapidly through flight training. Cadets spent the first four to ten hours in dual instruction with their instructor pilot, who was responsible for a group of four or five cadets. During this phase, he flew with each of them twice a day in flights of about twenty to thirty minutes. The instructor demonstrated how controls worked and how to maneuver the aircraft, often using hand signals to be heard above the motor's din. Student pilots flew alone, or solo, as soon as the instructor determined they were ready. This phase required sixteen to twenty-one hours of flight time and included local flights, cross-country flights, aerobatics (stalls, loops, dives, spins, etc.), and formation flying. Before graduation, students also had to demonstrate the ability to land with a "dead" motor and land over an obstacle.[37]

By late 1917, about one-third of the Taliaferro Fields, Texas, had become the RFC Canada School of Aerial Gunnery, equipped with more advanced planes like the Avro 504 and experienced instructors, including a few American instructors trained in aerial gunnery in Canada. The integration of aerial gunnery into the US flight training curriculum was an immediate result of this cooperation. The United States provided RFC Canada with the docile Jenny training aircraft as more airplanes became available.[38]

The RFC Canada curriculum included classroom and practical work. Lectures included artillery observation, aerial fighting, bombs and bombing, cross-country and general flying, internal combustion engines, map reading, reconnaissance, meteorology, astronomy, photography, wireless (radio), signaling, and theory of flight. Finally, they studied the various types of machines and undercarriages (landing gear). In the finest traditions of the British Service, students also received a class on mess etiquette.

Wireless instruction at both Elementary and Higher Training Wings was especially rigorous. Students trained in "buzzing," wireless communication in which they had only six minutes to transmit and receive six words per minute in code. Other wireless training included a written examination of six questions with a passing score of 80 percent, artillery code, and "Artillery Picture Target," an exercise in which students ranged three targets correctly by sending map coordinates using both artillery code and ground signals without error. Finally, wireless training included "Panneau" (panel) signaling, in which students had to accurately read miniature panels from a distance of one hundred yards at the rate of four words per minute.[39] The practical portion of the curriculum comprised courses on "stationary engines," including carburetor and magneto; rotary engines; instruments; sail making and splicing; rigging; machine-gun operations; the miniature range; and tools.

Cadets were introduced to machine guns early in ground school, sighting and firing them during primary flight training on the firing range and at moving targets. The Aerial Gunnery course included mechanism study, stripping guns, drill, and gun care. Gunnery also continued at the Elementary and Higher Training Squadrons, but students required a final course at the School of Aerial Gunnery to be fully qualified aviators. At the Elementary Training Wing, Lou trained on both the Lewis and Vickers machine guns, with lectures on "Immediate Action" and stoppages, before going to the twenty-five-yard firing range.[40]

When the holiday season approached, Lou enjoyed numerous Christmas cards and telegrams from family and friends. Mary Hays sent him a Christmas card with a color drawing of a Curtiss JN-4D on an airfield blanketed with snow. She wrote, "Christmas comes but once a year, and then it goes away—My love for you is always here, Because it *came to stay*." Lou's mother sent her season's greetings and wishes for a "good dinner, good weather, good flying, and no accidents" as well as a small package with several "useful" articles, including a chess set.[41]

For his part, Lou sent Mary a very special gift. He asked his sister, Agra, to take his fur coat and give it to Mary on Christmas Eve. His mother found a "long card with an aeroplane carrying [a] Christmas greeting," and sent Lou's note to her: "Please wear my coat—until end of the war—Louis." Mary was thrilled with the gift and Lou's hopeful message to return to her and "claim" his coat. It was a great surprise, but Mary's mother did not initially give Mary her consent to accept so personal a gift. Sallie also informed her son that Johnson had a very satisfactory meeting at Princeton to complete the arrangements to set up the school in Daytona. They would send the instructor and two aircraft—one from Princeton and one from Beech Bottom—to Daytona for winter flight training.[42]

Lou completed training at Camp Everman just before the New Year, and had New Year's dinner with the family of a fraternity brother whose father was president of a Dallas bank. Lou began the last phase of training at Camp Hicks Field Number Two on Wednesday, January 2, 1918. Lou's training at Hicks Field exposed him to a higher level of airmanship, finally flying the Avro with its one-hundred-horsepower rotary engine, which was much more demanding than the American-build Jenny. It was Britain's primary training aircraft at their Central Flying School.[43]

Most students were enthusiastic about advanced gunnery training, calling it "great fun." Students again began the program with machine guns on a firing range, shooting at moving targets. Next, they began aerial gunnery by firing at ground targets. This was followed by firing at targets in the air that were towed by an aircraft or held aloft by balloons. Shooting accuracy was ascertained by a camera mounted to the gun. Although gunnery was one of the weaker phases of primary instruction, it did provide a basic foundation for the cadets upon which to build. That, combined with mastering the higher-performance Avro, prepared them for their follow-on training in Europe.[44]

Lou maintained his steady training pace and had hoped to finish by the end of the second week of January. However, bad weather delayed his class—snow, rain, freezing temperatures, and heavy winds. He pulled guard duty waiting for the weather to clear and resume flying. When it did, he completed his primary training in the minimal amount of time. A week later, on January 21, 1918, Louis Bennett Jr. was commissioned as a second lieutenant in the Imperial Royal Flying Corps. He took leave and wired his parents that he would depart for Wheeling that evening and stop in New York on the way back. A snowstorm delayed his train, but Lou got to Wheeling and New York City before sailing for Europe. Lou's father had stopped traveling unless absolutely necessary and had already canceled several important trips, including the annual meeting of Confederate Veterans, but he went to Wheeling to see his son off to war.[45]

Sallie procured numerous letters of introduction for Lou so that he would be "known" when he arrived in Europe. These included a letter to the Royal Aero Club from President Hawley of the Aero Club of America, which Sallie believed would put Lou *"inside* there—as an aero member here." She admonished her son to write Hawley a thank-you note. There was a letter to Mrs. Etta LeRougetel, a "great friend" of Sallie's whose son, Ian, was in the British Army. Sallie reminded Lou that he had Alice Williams's card, who was on His Majesty's Service. Sallie considered her very good company with propitious connections, because Williams "knows *all* the best people . . . half of her relations are among the nobility." Sallie promised her son a letter for him from Lady Atcheson, because "you can't have too many London letters. People over there look after strangers if they know them." She reminded her son to cable her when he arrived since she "worries."[46]

Having said his farewells, Lou sailed for Great Britain. Canadian troops sailing for Europe often departed from the Port of Halifax. There, transport ships anchored together awaiting camouflaged naval warships to escort them across the U-boat-infested Atlantic Ocean. These convoys took longer in transit than did the swift prewar luxury ocean liners, sometimes taking ten days to reach Britain, but proved to be the best method of neutralizing the German submarine threat.[47] Convoys left the harbor through two submarine nets that were stretched across its entry, departing after sunset so as not to be U-boat targets. One convoy departing Halifax carrying Americans and New Zealanders was met by British battle cruisers with bands playing patriotic music. One lone bugler played "The Star-Spangled Banner" and "God Save the King," while troops on the transports stood at attention. Lou wore his life belt continuously on the journey. Every day, the convoy ships practiced "boat drill," emergency procedures for abandoning ship. Soldiers participated in the "submarine watch," sentry duty for the telltale sign of a periscope and its wake. Ships altered formation periodically to deceive the U-boats. At night, no lights were permitted, including smoking on deck. The ships sailed in total darkness. Escorts, painted in "dazzle" camouflage patterns, steamed rapidly around and through the formation. Sometimes, they circled and maneuvered through the convoy to hunt submarines. Lou's voyage on the Canadian Pacific Ocean Services vessel was uneventful. There were two concerts on board, though Lou lamented that the nurses backed out from going with him and his mates. They did host a mixed dinner for Valentine's Day, however. Lou read five books on his journey, so time passed swiftly.[48]

Lou landed in Britain but had ten days to report to the Military Wing in Upavon, Wiltshire. He left for London and checked in at the Savoy Hotel. The Savoy was where RFC flyers stayed in London, especially when on leave from the front. It sat back off the Strand and welcomed Lou with a horseshoe-shaped driveway entrance. On the right hand of the entrance and just downstairs was the Savoy Theatre, which was famous for its Gilbert and Sullivan productions. The large entrance door led to an ample lobby with the reception desk on the right. On the left, Lou passed through a wide door to the very roomy lounge, and behind the lounge was a bar with two barmaids who were kept busy serving RFC officers from six to eight each evening, when the Savoy bar was open. In the back was a sizable dining room.[49]

In late February, Lou wrote to his father that he was "getting at home in London." He quickly became familiar with his surroundings, he added, since "in a strange city, I hoof it around trying to get lost until I am pretty well satisfied." Lou discovered London was much more expensive than he expected and hoped his father approved Lou's decision to put his money in a British bank account instead of purchasing stock.[50]

He reported to the Central Flying School at the Upavon Airfield for training and graduated a mere week later. His foundation in Beech Bottom and Texas served him well. The Central Flying School, established in 1912, was the primary RFC flight training facility in the Great War. Lou was subsequently promoted to full lieutenant. Unlike most training systems, the British introduced students to combat maneuvers almost immediately and were notorious for the high fatality rate in training. Air forces at the front suffered an attrition rate that mirrored the war of attrition on the ground; therefore, the RFC believed that flight training must replicate combat maneuvers as accurately as possible. Their Gosport system required completion in five weeks. Each student was assigned a single instructor pilot who gave them intensive, personal instruction. In flight, he issued instructions over the din of the motor through a one-way speaking tube—the Gosport. British students were "expected to undertake extremely complex and dangerous maneuvers very quickly, leading to 'recklessness in pilots,' in the minds of

Americans." Instructors often reflected this wildness.[51] The British system was alleged to kill more instructors than students.

One of the major problems with pilot training was that training airplanes were not compatible with frontline, operational combat aircraft. Once students completed primary training, they had to nearly start over again when in their next course on a new aircraft. This process of constantly relearning to fly—or "transition training," as it later became known—was repeated for each new aircraft. At each new station and beginning of each training block, instructors and commanders observed students so as to match them up with a given specialty, pursuit, observation, or bombardment training, based on their proficiency. It was imperative to select students as early as possible to avoid duplication and lost time in training, especially regarding pursuit, or scout, pilots.[52]

Appointed at last as a flying officer, on March 4, Lou reported to his new duty station at Beaulieu, Hants, on the southeastern edge of the New Forest National Park in Hampshire, England, for advanced training with Number 1 (No.1) Training Squadron. He joyfully wrote to his father that he had been accepted to "a Scout Wing, thank heaven." Because he faced "quite a list ahead of me," Lou had to wait before he could begin advanced flight training. He had not written much because they were billeted three miles from the airfield, and he found it difficult to write at the airfield mess because of "the noise and other fellows." Lou noted the privations of wartime Britain. He obtained a bicycle for transportation since it was difficult to obtain a permit for a privately owned car. There were only a very few privately owned cars in service, except special cases with permits or those in London using coal gas in large canopy bags on the top of the vehicle. Taxis were still available, he observed. Meat ration cards were "now in vogue," and one could get jam but not sugar. He wrote to Mary and his family and asked them to send him candy to satisfy his sweet tooth, along with all the news. He assured his father that he wanted to get home safely and that he was not overconfident but had a sort of feeling of certainty about his abilities.[53] He was able to take a few days of furlough to travel to London and stay at the Savoy. Sallie admonished her son to go to Easter Services to show those English lads that American boys were practiced in the Anglican religious service. She concluded, "*Please* [her emphasis] follow my good example [and] go me one better."[54]

Lou paid a visit to his mother's friend, Alice Williams. She was "down with a cold," and Lou brought roses that cheered her up. She wrote to her friend Elizabeth Perkins, who lived near Lou's airfield. Perkins invited the young man over for tea and tennis and to socialize with her friends and other ex-patriot Americans. Lou quickly became a favorite. Perkins wrote to Williams that Lou was a "dear" who gave her family more pleasure than anybody had given them before. She was "just ever so grateful to [Alice] for thinking of introducing him." Williams marveled to Sallie, "Talk about winning hearts indeed! *He* seems to have taken them by storm!" Occasionally, Lou brought along an American officer whose motorcycle shortened their journey.[55]

Lou waited almost three weeks before he could fly again, at the end of March. Despite the unpredictable spring weather, at last he was flying. Once more, Lou began his training by flying the reliable Avro. The British frequently used the two-seat Avro as a transition aircraft for the fledgling pursuit pilots before they moved on to combat aircraft. By 1918, when Lou reached the scout wing at Beaulieu, the combat-proven Sopwith Pup served as an additional transition aircraft between the Avro and current production combat aircraft. Lou was glad to have friends at Beaulieu with whom he had previously trained, including Orville A. "Tubby" Ralston and O. P. Johnson.[56]

Once the fledglings demonstrated proficiency on the Avro, they advanced to the Pup.[57] Pilots universally considered the Pup to be "a wonderful little bus." It had been a frontline combat aircraft beginning in the fall of 1916. Pilots found the Pup a thrill to fly—so quick and sensitive compared to the Avro that it allowed young pilots to get the feel of high-performance aircraft—but it was much more docile compared to the more advanced pursuit aircraft then in use by Britain, such as the Sopwith Camel and Dolphin. Once Lou completed five hours on Pups, he advanced to fly Camels and Dolphins.[58]

Powered by a rotary motor, "that damnable Camel" was known for its maneuverability and quick response to the pilot's control inputs. Sopwith achieved these characteristics by designing it to be very lightweight and unstable. The rotary motor produced a great deal of torque that added to the instability of the aircraft. In the hands of a good or very experienced pilot, it was extremely agile and lethal. However, its instability often proved treacherous, and Camels were notorious for killing new pilots, especially in a right-hand spin. Pilots either loved the Camel or hated it. The Dolphin was less maneuverable than the Camel and easier to fly but also considered very tricky. One of Lou's friends wrote that his squadron met with disaster from a Dolphin. One of their majors took off and climbed to 4,000 feet when the wing folded, and he crashed to earth. Another American took off in a

Dolphin, climbed to 1,000 feet when his left wing also folded up. He was killed instantly in the crash. The wings on the Dolphin were "staggered" in configuration, with the top wing located just aft of the lower wing. The pilot had uncanny visibility since his head sat up above wing and fuselage. However, if the aircraft flipped over on the ground, he was in a very vulnerable (if not fatal) position, because the entire aircraft would then settle on his exposed cranium. Lou didn't know yet which kind of aircraft he would be assigned, since "everyone wants the best machine out but it is hard to tell which is the best. Guess one can give a good account of oneself in any of them, however."[59]

Lou battled one of these Dolphins in a mock combat, or "dogfight," while he was flying a Sopwith Pup. He observed that, "from a maneuvering point of view [the Pup] had it all over [the Dolphin]. [It] could dive better and could run away from me but then the Pup is no longer a service machine." Nonetheless, Lou found the Dolphin, with its two-hundred-horsepower engine and four guns to be a stable and accurate gun platform. Since he had seen no one at the field stunt it, Lou decided to take one up and "throw it about" because he did not want a machine "that could not be thrown about in flight." He complained that the unobstructed visibility caused him to loop it poorly since he was used to an upper wing serving as an attitude reference, but he was beginning to enjoy flying a warplane. He wrote about one sortie where Lou and his comrades flew "a formation this morning in the mist. We flew just over the tree tops and would dive on various houses [and] other aerodromes and must have looked pretty good. There were five of us [and] we traveled on an average between 80 [and] 90 [knots]." When his Dolphin was down for repairs, Lou went to London to have dental work. He stayed at the Savoy, of course. He wrote to his mother that he did not want to fly the Camel while the Dolphin was in for repairs because he was concerned his superiors might assign him to a Camel squadron. He preferred the Dolphin's patrol mission against the Imperial German Air Service, which was flown at higher altitudes. Camels were then largely used in the "trench strafing" role at low altitude in support of the Army. It appeared his superiors were eyeing him for a Camel squadron, and he "personally fought to get off of Camels."[60]

Occasionally, Lou flew an aircraft over the Perkinses' house and put on a display for the family's five children.[61] However, his zigzags over their lawn frightened Mrs. Perkins, who thought "of his Mother away in Virginia [sic]" whenever he did that. Still, she conceded, he flew "so neatly and looks so safe." Lou enjoyed visiting the family and playing with the Perkins children, and he confided in his mother that he was "fairly welcome" with other local families, some of whom were friends of Sallie.[62]

His skills as a fighter pilot were becoming more refined. By the end of April, Lou completed his training at Beaulieu and was sent to the Finishing School of Aerial Gunnery at Turnberry, Scotland. He arrived at Number 2 School of Aerial Gunnery on May 4, 1918. Lou saw no real benefit in gunnery school but wrote that he could tolerate it since it lasted only a week or two. Still, it was just one more delay keeping him from seeing action. He wrote to his father from the comfort of the Savoy and reflected on his British scout training. He told his father, "I left Beaulieu with a good reputation and a fair amount of respect." This was due, he added, "from what is to most of them a surprising eagerness to get over [to France] and also to [my] apparent ability to handle a machine." He continued that he wasn't just boasting or trying to impress his father. Instead, both his instructors and his peers showed "confidence that I would soon be bringing down Huns." He assured his father that this would not "inspire me to take any more risks than on any account, but does give me the unusual courage to tell you as I think it will please you." Then for the first time, he signed off, "Affectionately, Louis."

The younger Bennett had not only achieved the respect of his instructors and his peers but also earned confidence in his fighting skills and in himself. He had flown four British aircraft, three of which were scouts and two of which were "service machines," or frontline combat aircraft. He had displayed the skill to do practically any stunt, adding the roll and half roll to his repertoire of loops, spins, and Immelmann turns. He had learned to "handle [his] machine more or less instinctively and by feel and thus know in whatever position [he found himself] while keeping [his] eye on [the] adversary." Despite a few warm days, April was mainly cool, rainy, and windy, delaying any flying and hence Lou's posting to a combat unit in France. He was extremely disappointed that he would arrive too late to participate in the "Great Battle on the front" and hoped that "it may still be going in a month's time."[63]

The "Great Battle" that Lou referred to was the massive Ludendorff offensive, Operation Michael, which began at 0440 on March 21, 1918. German general Erich Ludendorff hoped to capitalize on a fleeting advantage—the Bolshevik Revolution had knocked Russia out of the war, freeing forty-two divisions of German soldiers from combat in the East.[64] The German Army could at last infuse these "fresh" yet experienced combat troops into its weary lines on the Western Front. A timely, well-coordinated offensive with these reinforcements against the exhausted allied armies in the spring of 1918 was Imperial Germany's best hope for victory before the American Expeditionary Force massed in strength against them there. Germany's Allies, Austria-Hungary and Ottoman Turkey, were faltering. German civilians were suffering. Domestic and labor unrest coupled with political collapse undermined the war effort. It was clear to the German General Staff that time was running out.

Although the Allies had accurately predicted the day of the offensive, they were completely surprised by the immensity and concentrated violence of the assault. Ludendorff massed some six thousand guns for artillery preparations. Firing in orchestrated phases with a combined mixture of poison gas, tear gas, smoke, shrapnel, and high explosive shells, the German artillery unleashed a *Feuerwalze*, or "fire waltz," barrage against the Allies (also called a "hurricane barrage").[65] This enabled special "storm troopers" using new tactics to rapidly advance through allied lines into the rear areas, followed by regular German infantry to exploit their gains. Bad weather and fog greatly aided the German offensive. It hampered the numerically superior allied air forces and concealed the movement of German storm troopers from allied reconnaissance. The advancing German infantry seemed to be irresistible and quickly overwhelmed British defenses. According to one observer, the "British Fifth Army was a thing of the past, a running mass of fugitives, and a great gaping hole existed in the line" and by April 1918, the Germans again were shelling Paris with their long-range cannon. Admitting the gravity of the situation, British commander field marshal Sir Douglas Haig issued his "Backs to the Wall" message, declaring, "Every position must be held to the last man: there must be no retirement. With our backs to the wall, and believing in the justice of our cause, each one of us must fight on to the end."[66] It seemed to Lou that the war might be over before he ever saw combat. Many worried that the Allies could not stem the German assault.

6

Most Remarkable Work

"A Son to Be Proud of Indeed"

While British troops fought desperately on the Western Front to arrest Ludendorff's "Peace Offensives," Lou continued his combat training in Britain. There was good news for the Allies during a month dubbed by British fliers "another Bloody April." The war's most renowned fighter pilot, Baron Manfred von Richthofen, the "Red Baron," was dead. He was shot down and killed on Sunday, April 21, 1918, while Lou had been to tea at Mrs. Perkins's.[1] Captain A. Roy Brown, the "A" flight commander of No. 209 Squadron, was stunned to learn that the red Fokker Triplane he claimed to shoot down that day was Richthofen's aircraft, although Australian infantrymen also made the same claim. They had thrown up a hail of fire at the low-flying Fokker.[2]

Richthofen's passing was one of the many changes that came to the front during the spring of 1918. On Monday, April 1, the British Army's Royal Flying Corps and the Royal Naval Air Service combined into a new independent branch of service, the Royal Air Force (RAF). The transformation came without ceremony to the frontline units locked in violent combat with the Germans.[3] Lou was now part of the Royal Air Force, the world's first independent armed air branch. Another significant change was the appearance of American soldiers on the front lines. Before the spring of 1918, the American Expeditionary Force (AEF) was most notable for its absence along the allied lines. American airmen had made forays against the enemy, but soldiers of the AEF remained in the rear training. Pershing stubbornly fought with allied commanders who sought to amalgamate American troops into European armies as replacements. He insisted that the American Army would fight as a unified, national force. However, the allied situation had become so desperate from the German offensive that at last Pershing was forced to make some concessions. By mid-April, he had five infantry divisions available for combat, the 1st, 2nd, 26th, 32nd, and 42nd. Although these had not finished their training and still lacked proper equipment, Pershing agreed to put them in the line on quiet sectors of the front so as to release allied divisions for combat in the teeth of the German assault.[4]

The announcement that American forces had entered the lines was received joyously across the Western alliance. Etta LeRougetel expressed a combination of joy and relief, promptly picking up her pen to write to Sallie after the public announcement that the AEF had joined the Allies' fight "in this hour of crisis . . . [it] is grand [and] has called forth the admiration of the whole civilized world." She compared it to Lou's joining the RAF, adding "he must be a fine fellow! How splendid of him to do all he has done! And then to come over here [and] fall in with his English (or British) cousins!" She was thankful that both Lou and Etta's son, Ian, had missed the German offensive. Ian was an infantry officer. Like Lou, Ian was away undergoing training at a special course at a machine-gun depot when the Ludendorff offensives began. She expressed her hopes that he would take a week of leave and perhaps meet up with Lou before going back into the lines.[5]

Lou's frustration mounted. Instead of being sent to France to fight Germans after his training, Lou was sent to a "holding depot" in Britain at Marske-by-the-Sea. He was told it was only for six days. He'd been there eleven days when he dejectedly wrote to his father that there were no vacancies for Dolphin pilots at the front, nor were there any Dolphin aircraft available at Marske for him to fly.[6] Therefore, he had flown only two sorties, and these were in an aircraft that he had never before flown, the S.E. 5 (Scouting Experimental), a product of the British Royal Aircraft Factory.[7] The S.E. 5 at Marske and the Sopwith Dolphin shared the same motor, a 220-horsepower Hispano-Suiza liquid-cooled engine manufactured by Peugeots. The later S.E. 5a was powered by either a 180- or 200-horsepower British Viper engine. Pilots favored the reliability of the Wolsey over the Peugeots. Early variants of the S.E. 5 had frequent engine problems. Some pilots thought that the S.E. 5 was much more maneuverable and technologically advanced than the Dolphin.[8] Aviation historian Walter J. Boyne regarded the S.E. 5a as a "rugged" warplane and "an excellent gun platform."[9] It was well suited for combat on the Western Front, armed with two forward-firing machine guns, including the lethal Vickers gun mounted on the forward fuselage in front of the pilot. The S.E. 5's advanced Constantinesco hydraulic synchronizer coordinated firing of the gun with the position of the propeller blade better than any other corresponding technology of the day. With an eight-hundred-rounds-per-minute rate of fire, the Vickers gave its pilot instant massed firepower, putting rounds on target in the few seconds of opportunity air combat usually gave its combatants. One only had to take care that one did not waste ammunition, because this also meant the Vickers could expend its magazine of ammunition in just thirty seconds.[10]

Paired with a Lewis gun that was mounted on the top wing of the aircraft which fired over the propeller arc and held ninety-seven rounds of ammunition, the twin guns gave the scout pilot superb firepower. Both guns were canted upward at one degree to fire slightly above the aircraft centerline, which in a turning "dogfight" gave the pilot another advantage against a hostile machine because he did not have to pull his nose too far ahead of his target in order to hit it. Since the Lewis gun could be pulled down on its mounting track to the pilot, he could reload his ammunition by replacing the empty drum with a full one. This also gave the pilot the flexibility to carry different types of ammunition or to adjust the gun in flight.[11] He could fire upward at high-flying reconnaissance aircraft that cruised above his aircraft's maximum service ceiling of 22,000 feet, or he could fire the Lewis gun forward with the Vickers for more firepower, the usual arrangement.[12] Its sophisticated armament was not the S.E. 5's only advanced technology.

As Lou climbed into the unfamiliar S.E. 5 cockpit, he must have felt—as one American aviator had—that he had climbed "inside of a locomotive cab." In contrast to the simple instrumentation of most Great War aircraft, the S.E. 5 instrument panel included "a compass, airspeed indicator, radiator thermometer, oil gauge, compensator, two gun trigger controls, synchronized gear reservoir handle, hand pump, gas tank gauge, two switches, pressure control, altimeter, gas pipe shut-off cocks, [radiator] shutter control, thermometer, two cocking handles for the guns, booster magneto, spare ammunition drums, map case, throttle, joystick and rudder bar." Lou made good use of his sortie to "get used to the machine." He found it very stable and powerful. It flew "hands off," and he easily reached 130 miles per hour in level flight. Visibility was excellent. The aircraft was agile and responsive to the pilot's control inputs. It climbed rapidly. The S.E. 5 could reach 10,000 feet in twelve minutes. Loops, rolls, "zooms" and a "spinning tail slide" from high altitude could all be accomplished with confidence. It was an impressive aircraft that many believed was "the best plane of the war." The S.E. 5 could dogfight with the elite aircraft of its day. Its greatest weakness was at low altitude, where the radiator of the water-cooled engine was vulnerable to ground fire.[13]

When he returned from his agreeable morning flight in the S.E. 5, Lou wondered why the Camel pilots at Marske dominated the daily "scraps," or mock dogfights. He admitted to his father that the Camels were, "little light things and for quick turns and stunting near the ground [they] cannot be beaten," however, after handling the S.E. 5, he could not see why its pilots were "getting licked so badly" by the Camel pilots. A little later after Lou's sortie, one of the flight commanders came over to the group area and asked if any of the pilots "wished to scrap a Camel." Like he had done his first day at Yale, Lou immediately "hopped up" and accepted the challenge. The flight commander told Lou to take the S.E. 5 into the air and meet Captain Mattox in his Camel above the airfield at 2,000 feet. Lou's aircraft was being refueled, however, so Mattox, who was "*the* Camel pilot of this station," jumped in his aircraft, took off and began to put on an aerial demonstration, "doing stunts [and] fancy things as he always does," in order to intimidate his challenger and to use up some of the Camel's fuel, making his aircraft lighter in weight and more maneuverable. He would also be personally "warmed up" before the fight and ready to pounce on his latest victim. Lou would be meeting him in a fully fueled, much heavier (and thus less maneuverable) aircraft.[14]

The S.E. 5 was at last fully fueled and ready. Lou climbed in, started his engine, ran his checks, took off, and climbed to 2,000 feet. There, he and Mattox circled each other in a neutral position, and then the "fight" began. Since most airmen met each other head-on at the beginning of a dogfight, each pilot turned to aim his aircraft directly at the other one. When they passed each other "nose to nose," Mattox pulled hard on his aircraft, tightening his turn and taking advantage of the Camel's small turn radius. Lou immediately recognized the danger. Since the Camel could turn tighter than the S.E. 5, it was only a matter of time before Mattox was on Lou's tail—the most vulnerable position of a fighter aircraft—*if* he stayed in a turning fight with the Camel. Lou at last knew how the Camel pilots were able to do so well against the rest of the Marske pilots, and he did something about it. Taking firm advantage of the S.E. 5's lift and ability to "zoom fifteen hundred feet from the level," Lou stood his machine on its tail and soared above the Camel. Lou's aircraft quickly lost airspeed and stopped in mid-flight. It was a potentially vulnerable position should his adversary pull his nose up and bring his guns to bear, but Mattox was caught. Having committed himself to a turning fight, the experienced Camel pilot did not have enough airspeed or potential energy to do that. Helplessly he watched as Lou's machine gradually stalled above him. The plane shuddered as it approached the stall, and Lou neutralized his flight controls to avoid going into a spin. The nose of the S.E. 5 pitched down, the air began to rush over its wings again, and Lou was flying—strategically positioned on the Camel's tail. Lou had unlocked the secret of fighting in the new S.E. 5—he took the fight into the vertical, a maneuver usually performed only by more seasoned pilots. Mattox knew he had a real fight on his hands. Lou continued, "He quickly dodged and after that we had a pretty even go—one dodging [and then] the other dodging." Back and forth they went, until at last it was time to land. After dismounting from their aircraft, the other instructors surrounded the two pilots and "began kidding the [captain] for letting me get on his tail." Mattox was hot and "wanted to go right back up" and go at Lou again. "Nothing doing," Lou wrote his father. He wanted the lesson "to sink in as it was for the moral effect on these Camel pilots who were getting so *cocky*." Lou confessed to his father that his performance had "pleased me immensely."[15]

At last, the young man knew he was a fighter pilot. Lou had quickly learned the strengths of his new mount, "fought" an experienced opponent who had a clear advantage, and held his own. He had assessed the "battle" situation quickly and took the proper action. He had earned the respect of his instructors and his peers. The young man liked this and was pleased with himself. Lou had confidence in his flying skills, or in fighter pilot jargon, his "hands." He was eager to get to the fight on the Continent and felt he was "lucky enough to get up out of the rank [and] file of trench straffers [sic]." More than ever, Lou felt ready to go to war and he happily wrote to Mary about this "fight" at Marske.[16]

Although many lady friends made him the object of their attention, pursued him, and corresponded with him, Lou received the strongest support from Mary Hays. Mary was interested in everything he did and thought. She sent her "*own*, dearest Louis" a pressed rosebud after the two had exchanged professions of love. She rejoiced that Lou had written telling her "that you really love me," and she expressed her faith in him. The couple began discussing the possibility of marriage after the war, and Mary vented her frustration at Lou's absence, declaring, "Oh! If only the Germans would be all killed. Then you would come back and I will be perfectly [happy] forever and ever." She was sorry she wasn't more cheery and implored her beau to be her "comforter." Lou's sister, Agra, and her husband, Johnson, paid Mary and her mother a visit that summer. Agra teased her brother, complaining that "Mary got three letters from you this morning—I am jealous."[17]

There were nagging concerns, however. On May 22, he received two letters from his father that discussed the elder Bennett's illness. Although his father told Lou he was feeling better, Lou was deeply anxious and admonished his father "to quit work [and] stay well hereafter," adding, "Please do not get sick." There was good reason for his fears, though the family was hiding the details from him. Dr. Marvel in Atlantic City had conducted a series of tests on the elder Bennett and found an obstruction in his stomach that prevented food from passing through properly. Sallie quickly wrote to Dr. Marvel. She had a sense that his illness might be fatal and wanted to know the details. Yet she also chastised the doctor, declaring that she had once helped her husband recover from previous illnesses "by pure bluff." If an operation wouldn't help, she demanded her husband be told his condition so he could summon his great reserves of strength. She added that if the illness was "exactly the *worst*," she wanted the doctor to conceal it from her husband so his last days would not be unhappy. A family friend, Dr. Fleming Howell, followed Dr. Marvel's work carefully and believed it was impossible to know if improvement would ever come for the elder Bennett's feeble digestion.[18]

Sallie deliberately avoided telling Lou about his father's condition. Instead, she wrote to Lou when his father was "looking well," adding he only needed "rest [and] change." She sent her son a small chess set, and she sent him packages with sugar, tea, and chewing gum in response to his complaints about the lack of sweets. She voiced her disapproval of "stunting" the Dolphin, admonishing him to not "be brash."[19]

The sudden letter about his father's ill health surprised Lou. Then he received more bad news. Instead of being posted to a combat squadron in France, he received orders to report to Shotwick airfield, near Chester in Northwest England, to fly Sopwith Dolphins with a home defense unit, No. 90 Squadron. He reported for duty on May 31 and promptly requested a posting to the Western Front, which was refused. He was told that he must deploy with his squadron. It would be at least two months before No. 90 Squadron rotated to the front lines. Even then, Lou groused, units "take a couple of months getting settled before going over the lines." He had received no mail since he arrived in Flintshire and was understandably worried for his father. He spent more time in Chester than in the air, only flying "a bit each day," so he rented a bicycle to go into town two or three times a week "for a good bath" and tea. He complained that he could not live off his pay due to the wartime cost of living. On a recent sortie, he "just made the airfield on a dud machine" causing him to worry he might break a leg before he ever saw combat. He didn't think he would ever see a "real German" until Christmas and lamented that if he performed badly, maybe his squadron "will try to get rid of me." Dejected and feeling sorry for himself, he wrote to his father that the Allies would have to "get along without me." To his aunt Mary, Lou confided he felt "interned for the duration [of the war] and that is the final word."[20]

Additionally, he did not like his squadron. True, there were a few good officers. The commander was "very good," and so was Captain John Tudhope. Tudhope was an ace who transferred from one of the premier combat units, No. 40 Squadron, to become a flight commander in No. 90 Squadron. Some of the squadron's pilots were sons of the British rich and famous. They wore their parents' class and privilege on their sleeves without having done anything significant. As a Yale graduate and descendant of a Southern Civil War hero, Lou was not impressed. He judged their flying skills as mediocre, at best. He saw nothing "remarkable about them which always makes them more important in bearing, of course." One of the least likable pilots was "a son of the Vickers of gun and aeroplane fame." Fortunately, he was not in Lou's flight. Still, Lou complained, "there seems such a lack of anything that would make the squadron famous." He tried three times to transfer from No. 90 Squadron, and three times, he was stopped. For some sort of genial companionship, he got a dog which he ironically named "Ninety," after the squadron.[21]

Adding to Lou's misery, his friends from flight training Orville A. "Tubby" Ralston and Rowland "Bless" Blessley were on their way to France. "They are all beating me over after all," he grumbled to Sallie in a birthday letter to his mother. He had finished training first, only to see them posted to combat units first. He was well, he told his mother, but frustrated he "cannot get out." Yale classmate and friend Fred Weyerhaeuser was in Italy with Captain Fiorello La Guardia learning to fly Caproni bombers at the Italian Flying School in Milan. Fred's training seemed equally interminable, because the leisurely pace of Italian instruction was frustrating him as well. He asked Lou for news of the war, since "you see there are so damn few of us down here, that we are sort of isolated and only occassionally [sic] bits of dope drift through to us." The main benefit of his training post was "the Milanese girls! You *ought* to be here. We had a wild party the other night that you would have enjoyed, I believe. I managed to preserve my virtue intact as usual, but it's a hard job down here."[22]

While Fred shared Lou's frustration at not fighting and tried to entice his classmate with stories of "Milanese girls," Tubby's letters from the front lines kept Lou fighting hard to be transferred. From France, Ralston wrote, "Well here I am and here I have been for nearly [ten] days in one of the best squadrons in France." Tubby was picked up as a replacement pilot in No. 85 Squadron by one of Britain's top aces and combat leaders, Major Edward "Mick" Mannock. Mannock had a sterling reputation in his previous post as a flight commander in No. 40 Squadron, and he had no peer in his techniques that prepared his men for battle. He had great compassion for the infantry in the trenches and watched closely over his charges in the air. He had that rare gift of being able to lead, teach, and fight well. When he assumed command of No. 85 Squadron in July 1918 from Major William A. "Billy" Bishop, Britain's leading "ace," Mannock continued the "Bish" practice of personally selecting promising young fighter pilots chosen for their flying skills, enthusiasm, and élan. Ralston found himself in the company of other noted pursuit pilots, including Americans Lawrence K. Callahan, John McGavock Grider, and Elliott White Springs. Besides being an accomplished pilot, Springs wrote the classic account of the first air war, *Warbirds: The Diary of an Unknown Aviator*, in 1926, based in part on Grider's diary and Springs's war experiences.[23] Ralston found himself in some impressive company.

Ralston added, "Lou, old fellow, I wish you were here with me. They have the [biggest] times here. The Major and everybody raises [sic] hell every night. No formal mess. Everybody comes to all meals in shirt sleeves etc." Not only was the squadron easygoing, Tubby added, but also "nearly half of them have medals or from [one] to [five] Huns. The [Major] has [sixty-three] now" (Mannock had sixty-one confirmed victories at the time of his death). Ralston had not yet crossed the lines, because Mannock insisted that new pilots be given additional training to develop their "air eyes" for about two weeks on the allied side of the lines, "unless a big push comes and every man is needed."[24]

That "big push" was fast approaching for the Allies. Ludendorff continued his series of offensives, shattering the French Sixth Army along the

Aisne River, severing major rail lines. German storm troopers advanced to within forty miles of Paris. The Imperial German Army yet again scored a major tactical success and demonstrated their ability to outmuscle the allied armies along the front. However, Ludendorff had also exhausted his army. In March and April, the Germans suffered over 490,000 casualties. They captured scorched ground and were some ninety miles from their own rail depots and supplies. The strategic cities of Amiens and Paris were still firmly in allied hands and the Germans did not have the capability to reach Paris. Seduced by his successes along the Aisne River, Ludendorff reinforced troops in that sector. Thus, he stripped away resources from his original and most important strategic goals, Flanders and Amiens, and halted his offensive to regroup and reorganize before lashing out again at the Second Battle of the Marne. His actions led Marshal Ferdinand Foch, the recently appointed joint commander of the allied armies of the Western Front, to remark, "I wonder if Ludendorff knows his craft." The Germans were no longer capable of decisive victory. The tide of battle had at last turned. Tenacious fighting by the British, sound strategic leadership by Foch, and timely commitment of American forces into the battle helped avert the crisis by the early summer of 1918. Indeed, the élan and resolute determination of the green American forces earned the respect of both the Allies and the Germans. At the Battle of Belleau Wood, the ferocity of US Marines led German troops to dub them as "Devil Dogs." So stubbornly did the 3rd American Infantry Division defend its bend of the river against the attacking Germans that it earned the nickname the "Rock of the Marne" Division. The allied victory crushed Ludendorff's hopes of taking Paris or resuming the offensive in Flanders. Foch announced to his generals that the joint allied armies were to resume the offensive. The last "big push" of the war was on, and Louis Bennett was tired of waiting in Britain.[25]

His mother, however, admonished him not to be discouraged about waiting. It was "part of the training our characters *need*," she wrote. Sallie told Lou that the general consensus at home was that the next big battle would be in August. She was in no hurry to see her son in battle, and she reminded him that "your father [and] I have only you. We want you to do your duty—we *know* you will—[t]hat is the Great Comfort—in fact the only comfort I have these days that I can count on you." She did not directly comment on her husband's illness, but did disclose that her trips to Atlantic City took her "nerve" away. She concluded by allowing that she trusted Lou and his judgment, but "if anything happened to you it would break my poor heart, which is not too strong at the best. So do be careful—don't take unnecessary risks. Don't be disappointed if you don't get all the medals, crosses, etc., some fellows get."[26] Her letter did nothing to break his determination to fight in France.

Socially, Lou was doing much better. He went to tea and some shows with Alice Williams. She, in turn, introduced the young officer to Marquis John Frost, the mayor of Chester. Sir John and his wife, Dora, were quite impressed with Lou and enjoyed his company. Lady Frost wrote Sallie a letter: "Since your son has been living at Shotwick, I have had the pleasure of seeing him here and thought you might like to hear of him even if from a stranger!" She informed Sallie that Lou's unit was moving to another posting in England and she was sorry to see him go. "We liked him so much [and] you may like to know that he looks so brown [and] well, in splendid health, we had just got to know him well enough to tease him [and] feel quite at ease [and] friendly." Her words reassured Sallie, because Lady Frost commented on Lou's flying, declaring, "He is a wonderful airman, but *so* sensible [and] not foolhardy or rash. I was so pleased too, to see that he is an abstainer, it must be an advantage to him. You must be very proud of him [and] I am sure he is worthy of your pride, he will always make friends where ever he goes I am sure."[27]

Lou soon put his winning personality to good use. The squadron came under a new wing, Lou's "old division, in fact," when it changed stations from Shotwick to Brockworth, near Gloucester. Lou saw this move as "his chance." When his squadron arrived at its new posting, they had no aircraft and did not want the pilots "hanging about." All were given a week's leave, even though Lou didn't want to take it. He seized the opportunity to see the wing staff about "moving heaven [and] earth" for a transfer to a combat unit. On the morning of July 18, he "reported for overseas [duty] as if I had not already been posted here. That got me into the proper room with a pass. They were nice [and] sent me to see a Major. He was tracticable [*sic*] [and] phoned the Southern Division Headquarters. They did not care [and] I said I was ready *toute suite* [*sic*] (immediately) [and] so I report tomorrow with kit at London. I had to transfer to S.E. 5s to do it but I would have transferred to Curtisses to do it." Lou was thrilled at his success, "dancing around all day as if crazy. . . . Hooray."[28]

He rushed back to Gloucester to get his "kit" and ran into Captain Tudhope, who wrote letters of recommendation for Bennett. One letter was to

Major Keen of No. 40 Squadron, where Tudhope had previously been assigned, and the other was for Tudhope's good friend "Mick" Mannock in No. 85 Squadron. As a combat veteran, Tudhope challenged the young West Virginian's hurry to see combat, but wrote the letters anyway because Lou was so keen. Lou was thrilled because both squadrons had a reputation of being "Hun getters." Thus armed, Lou returned to London and stored his trunk and bicycle at the Savoy, as did many RAF pilots. The next day at "1700 hours," he reported to the Air Board in London for the official answer. His transfer was approved at last. He had fewer than twelve hours to report for overseas duty, since his train departed London at 0435 hours on Saturday, July 20. Lou made a quick phone call to Alice Williams and sent a note and photo of himself to Etta LeRougetel before departing for France. He was exuberant to at last be on his way to war. Etta immediately wrote to Sallie with the news: "Certainly he has gone out at a very opportune moment. Foch's counter attack has gone splendidly up to the present [and] the Americans have been doing [marvelous] things." She thought Lou looked splendid in the "snap," as Lou called it. He was, she added, "a son to be proud of indeed."[29]

Although it was "an opportune moment" for combat, it was not an opportune time for the family. At long last, Sallie received definitive news from Dr. Marvel. Her husband was dying and did not have long to live. She had kept the gravity of the news from Agra until July 7, "when Dr. Marvel said—it was only a question of time—that your father could not assimilate his food [and] an operation would do no good." Sallie did not want to alarm young Louis, but at long last, she grudgingly decided to break the news to him and ask her son to come home. Since it seemed to her that he was still languishing in Britain and "his services have not been urgently needed," Sallie wrote to the RAF liaison in New York requesting that they order Lou home on furlough. They replied that she needed to "cable your son to apply there." At Agra's urging,[30] Sallie cabled Lou at "90 Squadron, Shotwick": "Can you get immediate furlough or release for the dying cable Mother in Atlantic City. Bennett."[31] There was no immediate response. Lou had already changed stations and was in the process of going to France. That cable never caught up to him. Sallie hoped he had received her cable and was on his way home, but still she sat down and wrote her son a very long, imploring letter, not "to spoil your chances at advancement [and] glory, *but* you are more needed here than there."[32]

The elder Bennett was transferred to Dr. Marvel's Sanitarium and was bedridden. He was only able to take liquid nourishment, and even that rarely stayed down. Sallie confided that she was "nearly crazy with the anxiety for him," and that added to her worries for Lou in Europe. She felt "so helpless." Yet her husband urged the family to let young Louis stay in Europe, declaring "I'd want to [stay] if in his place." She conceded that he rallied occasionally, especially after receiving one of Lou's letters. Therefore, she acquiesced, "if you can't get away—don't worry" but reminded him to "be as careful as you can—you are all I have [and] I cannot give you both up at once." Sallie added that if he was in France, Lou might be able to transfer into the US Army Air Service (USAAS) of the AEF. Its commander was an old family friend, Major General Mason Patrick of Lewisburg, West Virginia. Patrick was the son of a Confederate surgeon and a classmate of General Pershing at West Point. Pershing had appointed Patrick, an engineer, to command the Air Service in the AEF and "bring order out of confusion" in that fledgling branch. Patrick would certainly approve a transfer or furlough, she reasoned. Lou's posting to France greatly lengthened the travel time of her letters. A letter she sent on July 7 was postmarked as received on July 27, 1918, in Britain, before it was forwarded to "40 Sqd. BEF France."[33]

Johnson suggested that Sallie cable her friend Alice Williams in Britain and ask her to "help cut red tape." Sallie immediately cabled her, "Please help Louis get furlough—Father Dying."[34] Alice Williams sent him a cable at his address at the Brockworth airfield, but it was returned to her the night of July 18. She did not know where he was. At last, she received a phone call. It was Lou, calling to tell her that he was departing directly for duty overseas and did not have time to meet with her. Williams knew she had to be cautious as to how she approached the topic of his father's health. She wrote to Sallie, "I did not actually use the word 'dying' to him, but said that his father was *most seriously* ill [and] that you wanted him to get furlough. He seemed surprised that he had heard nothing." She recognized that it was "impossible to do anything as the dear boy had been moving Heaven [and] Earth to get out." Lou promised her that he would send her his address the moment he got to his destination. Alice apologized to Sallie, wishing she could have been more help and "for better news."[35]

Lou immediately cabled his mother from London, "No word from you. Williams tells me serious but have just managed to be sent out so cheer up Bennett." Sallie was confused. Did "to be sent out" mean that he was coming home, or going to France? She cabled Alice Williams in London for clarification, adding, "If ordered to France let him go with courage. Father don't [sic] need him. Thanks for kindness. Have written." Williams, it appears, had gone on to Wales and apparently did not receive Sallie's latest cable. The elder Bennett told Sallie to let the boy "see it through—he is only doing what I would do if I were his age." Most of the family had now gathered at his bedside expecting the end at any time. Surprisingly, Lou's father rallied. Dr. Marvel was amazed at his strength.[36]

Agra also wrote to her brother. She gave Lou good news about the aircraft factory. Johnson had secured government orders for parts worth $360,000. The factory was adding three more buildings to accomplish the orders by the first of December. She sent Lou pictures of the Wheeling Independence Day Parade. The factory employees made an aircraft float and marched alongside in the parade. Wheeling saw a very large patriotic turnout despite the heat.[37] Agra also marveled at her father's tenacity in spite of his grave condition. He remained "sweet and patient" with the nurses and eagerly anticipated news from his son. The elder Bennett asked Agra to tell Lou he had "every confidence in his never doing anything to be a discredit to me or to himself."[38] Of course, the dying Civil War veteran understood that communications in wartime were difficult, at best, and chose his words to his son with care.

7

To Die a Fiery "Miserable Death"

Air Combat on the Western Front, 1918

Because of the recent moves, Lou hadn't received any mail from home for some time, and he gently chided his family about it. Nevertheless, he was thrilled to be in France at last. He arrived about July 21 and was posted to the pilot pool in Boulogne. Since he knew Tubby Ralston in No. 85 Squadron was nearby, Lou went over to see him and hoped they might be posted together. Tubby introduced him to the squadron members and Lou instantly made friends with several of them. Then, Tubby left on patrol and Lou waited around for him to return. In the meantime, Major Mannock arrived. They had an affable meeting and the major seemed to like Lou, even though he had not received Tudhope's letter of introduction. Mannock told the young West Virginian that he already had an extra pilot assigned to the squadron but "promised [him] the first vacancy." Back at the pool, Lou received a phone call, expecting Tubby to call after his patrol. However, it was the duty officer calling to inform Bennett that he was posted to No. 40 Squadron as their extra man, also known as the "supernumerary pilot." Lou replaced Lieutenant Indra Lal "Laddie" Roy, a No. 40 Squadron ace from India who was killed on July 22, 1918, and posthumously awarded the Distinguished Flying Cross.[1]

It rained the next day, so Mannock took the opportunity to visit the pilot pool in Boulogne and give the fledgling fighter pilots "a real lecture," as Lou explained, "as a man with 75 [sic] Huns feels free to express his opinion." Mannock recognized Bennett immediately and they chatted until the tender arrived to take him to his new squadron. Lou looked to this assignment with great anticipation. No. 40 Squadron was one of the two S.E. 5 (Scouting Experimental) squadrons to which he was hoping to be posted, the other being No. 85 Squadron. Both had solid reputations as combat units. During the Ludendorff offensives in the spring, they were part of the tenacious British defense, launching numerous strikes against German troops and ground targets. In fact, No. 40 Squadron finished the war as one of the outstanding Royal Air Force (RAF) units. It destroyed some 130 enemy aircraft and sent down another 144 out of control. It also destroyed thirty balloons and damaged another ten. The squadron was flying out of Bryas in northern France when Lou arrived.[2]

Within a week, Etta LeRougetel learned *exactly* where Lou was stationed, and told Sallie that Bryas "is located about [five] miles from St. Pol on the North. This is [northwest] of Arras." She added that she got this information "*unofficially* thro' a man who has come from France" and wrote to Sallie so she would know too. Etta informed her that "there is not much doing where he is" and that Lou was still "an extra man—so [he] has only been doing short flights yet." She had some better news too, adding that Lou's "Flight Commander is a first rate man—just the one he would have chosen."[3]

Lou's flight commander was Captain George E. H. "McIrish" McElroy, another of Britain's leading aces. He and his flight members were reputed for their "great determination, reckless bravery and abandonment."[4] Lou was delighted to be in McElroy's "C flight." He wrote, "Now let me tell you about Capt. McElroy. He has 47 or 50 Huns and it is his record that keeps the squadron up to [Number] 85 [Squadron]. Also one learns more from his flight commander than from his squadron commander and there is no better [flight commander] in all the S.E. [5] squadrons for results. After a week or two I hope to be getting real busy. But just now I am tickled to death at my luck." McElroy had been flight commander for another American pilot, William Lambert, in No. 24 Squadron in March. Lambert described McElroy as "one of the most fearless men I have ever met. He was also most considerate of the pilots under him and at all times tried to keep his pilots out of trouble. He would not allow me to go out until he felt I was ready and I think I owe my survival to his teaching."[5] From Lou's description of McElroy, Mary thought he "certainly must be a wonder to get up to Bishop and then some." She encouraged Lou to "keep up the squadron record and bring a lot of new laurels to it."[6]

Lou was not the first American to fly with the squadron. During the March offensive, the American 148th Aero Squadron equipped with Sopwith Camels shared the airfield with No. 40 Squadron, which was to shepherd them through their baptism of fire and flew with them until June. David

Wesley, R. R. Spafford, Ralph Donaldson, A. J. Anderson, and W. O. Archer were fellow Americans who, like Lou, commissioned as British officers and flew in the squadron. Robert Anderson, Paul V. Burwell, Michael F. Davis, William R. Everett, Reed Landis, Donald Poler, and Grady Touchstone were US Army Air Service (USAAS) officers flying in No. 40 Squadron until a vacancy occurred in an American squadron. Davis became commander of the 4th US Pursuit Group; Landis became commander of the 25th US Pursuit Squadron and brought Burwell and Poler along with him as pilots. Anderson and Touchstone became prisoners of war while flying with No. 40 Squadron. Everett left flying to become supply officer in the 148th US Pursuit Squadron. Lou knew A. J. Anderson from the training camps and, in a roundabout way, knew of Landis from Jarve Offutt.[7]

American troops on the Western Front were making an impact by mid-July 1918. After waiting for "the final spasm of the German Peace Offensive," the Second Battle of the Marne, which began on July 15, Marshall Foch, the joint allied commander, launched a major counterattack on July 18 committing fresh American divisions. Foch hoped to reverse the gains the Germans had made along the lines in March and turn the tide of battle. Allied air forces launched coordinated attacks against the German Army along the front that helped blunt the last of Ludendorff's offensives. Indeed air power played a major role to dampen the German Spring offensives. When Haig issued his "Backs to the Wall" order to stiffen the defensive resolve of the British Expeditionary Force, air force commanders issued an equally famous telegram to their pilots to "attack everything in sight." Squadrons launched determined, relentless low-altitude attacks against German troops and strong points of resistance. Their offensive spirit caught the numerically superior German Army and air services unprepared. In late June, the 1st US Pursuit Group joined the battle, flying obsolescent French-built Nieuport fighters. They were joined by another American unit, the I Corps Observation Group. They found themselves battling some of the best German air units on the front, including Richthofen's old fighter wing now commanded by Hermann Göring. Allied pursuit planes loaded with machine-gun ammunition and four twenty-pound bombs attacked ground targets. The "trench strafers" found themselves vulnerable to attack by prowling enemy patrols that pounced on them from higher altitude. Squadrons therefore placed patrols above the attacking formations to protect them from the Germans. An unintended consequence of these new tactics was that a fierce battle for command of the air ensued at low altitude. Previously, these battles occurred at higher altitudes and often involved protecting reconnaissance flights. Casualties rose substantially. Not only did allied airmen have to contend with enemy pursuit planes, but they also flew into the teeth of German antiaircraft cannon and machine guns. Pilots especially feared machine-gun fire from the ground because it was extremely lethal, even to the best aces.[8]

Ralston wrote to Lou describing the intensity of the fighting, reporting that "usually the machines come back with quite a few holes in them." One of the casualties was Quentin Roosevelt from the 95th US Pursuit Squadron. He was the youngest son of former president Theodore Roosevelt, and American ace Eddie Rickenbacker described him as "one of the most popular fellows in the group." When seven German fighters attacked his flight, Roosevelt became separated from them in the swirling dogfight. He was shot down and killed by one of the Richthofen Circus. The German High Command gloated over his death. In order to boost morale, they published picture postcards depicting his corpse next to the crumpled remains of his Nieuport. The propaganda backfired. One German soldier later admitted,

> It was whispered from ear to ear, from trench to trench. . . . In it one could see how in free America everybody was fighting. . . . The son of an American President, engaged in one of the most dangerous lines of service, was lying back of enemy lines, while their country had been at war three years and . . . neither the Kaiser, nor any of his sons were ever so much as scratched. . . . It gave the soldiers a vision of the democracy of America, and helped to deepen the feeling that they, the common soldiers, were only cannon fodder for the Kaiser.[9]

German morale continued to suffer. The Allies, and in particular American airmen, applied the hard lessons they had learned and helped turn the tide of the fighting. The chief of the USAAS I Corps at the time, then Colonel William "Billy" Mitchell, made a crucial decision. Rather than continue using his air forces piecemeal to strike bridges, roads, and troop emplacements, Mitchell organized a massed allied strike force, consisting of French and British bombers and American pursuit and observation aircraft, to attack the German headquarters, supply depot, and railhead located at Fere-en-Tardenois. As he predicted, the air attacks succeeded in disrupting the German offensive along the Marne and forced the German Air Service to go on the defensive. Thus, they surrendered the initiative to the allied air forces and German reconnaissance aircraft were unable to detect Foch's counterattack massing near Soissons. Although the air superiority fight continued to be bitterly contested, the American First Brigade commander jubilantly remarked, "We had . . . seized the initiative from the air. . . . It is the first case on record where we, with an inferior air force, were able to put the superior air force on the defensive and attack whenever we pleased, without the danger of the Germans sending great masses of the pursuit aviation over to our side of the line."[10] It also meant that allied airmen flew deep behind German lines in order to do battle, greatly increasing the number of allied casualties. American units began doing this in mass formations. Their Allies continued this practice. This was the situation along the Western Front when Lou began flying offensive patrols in late July 1918.

With the great allied counteroffensive in full swing, there was little time for Lou to develop his "air eyes," because every man was needed as soon as practicable. Lou's first sortie in France was a "target practice" sortie on July 25 in order to become familiar with his new aircraft and his area of operations. It also gave his squadron a chance to evaluate his ability to attack a target. These first flights were conducted on the allied side of the lines led by an experienced pilot, such as a flight commander, who shepherded the new pilot on the practice patrol and gave him "a look at the lines." Although these first sorties were often benign, flights were still at risk should hostile aircraft cross the lines and attack. Pilots who had not received all their training, such as gunnery, expected to receive additional training with their combat squadron before being permitted to go "over the lines." Lou's second sortie was a line patrol up north to see Tubby. Ralston returned from a patrol near Dunkirk and the two had just missed each other. Lou met Captain George "Dixie" Dixon, who was transferring from Ralston's No. 85 Squadron to Lou's No. 40 Squadron. Tubby wrote Lou that Dixon had led them on a July 24 patrol in which Ralston destroyed a German scout, which he attributed to "our leader's skill I know or we would probably have been in the Hun's place." Dixon was, Ralston added, "a prince of a fellow" and "likes you very much from what he told me."[11]

En route back to his airfield, Lou made a forced landing but flew again the next day when he undertook his first offensive bombing patrol over the lines. To support the great counteroffensive on the ground, Bennett's flight bombed east of Wancourt but met no enemy fighters during the two-hour-and-five-minute sortie. The battle tactics for industrial air war required formation flights consisting of at least six aircraft. Two streamers on the struts denoted the flight leader, positioned at the front of the formation with two "wingmen" on his right, behind and slightly above each aircraft. The wingman nearest the leader on the right was the second-in-command denoted by a single streamer. Two more wingmen were positioned on the left of the flight lead, again behind and slightly above with the "back corners high." The sixth man filled the gap in the formation between the trailing corners to form a triangle, the toughest position in the formation. The newest and least experienced pilots occupied one of the positions behind the leader.[12] Lou most likely flew in this position of the formation.

His second combat patrol on July 31 started well but proved disastrous. McElroy engaged and destroyed a German observation aircraft at around 0930 hours that morning near Laventie. However, the flight came under intense ground fire and McElroy's aircraft was hit. He was shot down and killed. Lou survived and was understandably upset by his leader's death. He sat down to share his grief with Mary Hays. The young man had a lot on his mind—the loss of his flight commander, his forced landing, and his initial combat experiences—all had affected him profoundly. He knew he had changed, and he worried that Mary would no longer know him. He also feared that she would not like the "new" Louis Bennett and would no longer want him. He thought his "disposition was beyond repair."[13] Stéphane Audoin-Rouzeau and Annette Becker explored how battle survivors were significantly changed by the violence of war and the loss of friends and comrades. Modern warfare itself is psychologically damaging for participants and often leaves the survivors with very strong feelings of guilt. This was especially true of the Great War but was also noted in the American Civil War.[14] Nor were elite units like pursuit squadrons spared the mental anguish of combat. Pilots at the front quickly learned the sobering reality of "wastage" from combat. One pilot opined that the average life expectancy of a combat pursuit pilot was three weeks. Even if he survived those three weeks, he could only take about six months of continuous fighting. Of the 210 American pilots who began flying with the British during the summer of 1918, 51 were killed, 30 were badly wounded, 14 became prisoners of war, and 20 were relieved due to mental stress, a total of 115 casualties or roughly 54 percent.[15] It was taboo to speak of one's fears, and the psychological damage inflicted by modern war was typically "hushed up."[16] It is indicative of the bond that Lou and

Mary shared that he entrusted her with these thoughts that caused him such disquiet.

For her part, Mary refused to believe that his feelings for her had changed and protested that she would not let him "say such things about yourself 'cause they aren't true." She had reread his letter several times and thought long and hard about what he wrote to her. She counseled him to "let all future developments take care of themselves" and to "keep on as usual and let the future time out as it may." She insisted that they knew each other better than Lou realized and that she would be "just the same when you come back."[17]

Air fighting reached its crescendo on August 1 while the RAF sought to win the battle for air superiority. They wanted to sweep the skies before Field Marshall Douglas Haig, commander of the British Expeditionary Force, launched a major attack in support of the French on August 8. Tubby Ralston's letters reflect the intensity of the August air battles:

> We had one terrible scrap and got away from [nine] Huns. There were [five] of us and we feel sure we met young Reichtofens [sic] circus for they were the most remarkable [and] daring pilots I ever hope to see, coming way over our lines.
>
> We were badly shot up but had consolation of helping to drive one down to the ground . . . we could not kill him he was so good at tricks. Watch out for them.[18]

As a supernumerary pilot, Lou did not have his own machine, or "bus," and only flew whenever one of the line pilots was given a rest and an aircraft was available. He flew his next sortie on August 2, when he brought a new machine to Bryas. On August 3, he flew another offensive patrol. Lou spotted a German observation balloon and attacked it, firing about fifty rounds of ammunition at the target during his attack, but he achieved no appreciable result. The weather deteriorated on August 4, which was a gloomy, rainy day with low clouds and poor visibility. He spent his downtime writing letters. Lou sent a letter to his friend Fred Weyerhaeuser in Italy "full of 'damns' about not enough flying." Fred cautioned his friend not to "get excited about that. . . . There will be plenty of opportunity for everybody yet." Still, Lou seethed to get back into the air, but he did not fly again until August 7, when he flew two sorties. The first was an uneventful one-hour observation patrol, and the second was a ten-minute practice bombing mission in mist and poor visibility.[19]

Lou's first patrols were typical of a new aviator. He had difficulty seeing other aircraft in the air. Although he had worn glasses to read since he was at Yale, his eyeglasses do not seem to have been a factor. He was still flying in formation with his flight commander, and Lou's new flight commander was "Dixie" Dixon, a seven-victory Canadian from Tubby's No. 85 Squadron who replaced McElroy.[20] It was imperative that a new pilot learn to divide his time between maintaining his formation position with his flight leader and watching for his signals. In addition, he had to learn how to scan around the formation for hostile aircraft. Unlike modern aircraft where the pilot sits in the nose of a jet fighter under a "bubble" canopy and can scan around his aircraft with few impediments, upper wings, struts, braces, and wires obstructed the vision of Great War aviators. To complete a good scan, one must study the skies above, below, in front, behind, and on each side of the aircraft—yet one must still be able to interrupt one's search so as not to miss the leader's signals. Then as now, developing a disciplined search technique took time and practice.[21] Another British S.E. 5 pilot, Cecil Lewis, described it thus: "But the fighting pilot's eyes are not on the ground, but roving endlessly through the lower and higher reaches of the sky, peering anxiously through fur-goggles to spot those black slow-moving specks against land or cloud which mean full throttle, tense muscles, held breath, and the headlong plunge with screaming wires—a Hun in the sights, and the tracers flashing."[22] Lou's own letters reflect his frustration. He wrote, "Have seen one or two Huns and that is all." Later, he wrote again, "Our flight dove on a two-seater the other day which I did not even see." As he flew more, Lou's scanning technique improved too. He wrote about the difficulties of discerning whether the "black slow-moving specks" he saw were friend or foe, "First, I saw a two-seater below me, but I was afraid to open fire on it as I could see no markings on it." He also began to notice where the Germans had located their observation balloons, such as the one he tried to destroy on August 3. When he could, he attacked these. Since he only carried conventional ammunition, his attacks were ineffective.[23]

Lou wasn't the only one having difficulty discerning friend from foe. His friend Rowland "Bless" Blessley wrote to him about an encounter he had with a German Fokker formation. Due to engine trouble, Blessley left his flight to return to base, but after making several adjustments, the problem cleared up, and he turned back to rejoin them. He saw a formation of scouts "just where I expected to pick up my patrol and without paying much attention to anything, I dropped into my place just behind the leader on the right. Then I turned around to wave my hand to the man following. Even before I turned my head completely around, I saw what was up." Bless had joined a patrol of German Fokkers. "Oh! that I had been a Bishop or a McCudden. I stayed there just long enough to consider shooting up the leader," but Bless decided that the better part of valor was discretion, so he "pulled my stick into the corner and 'skooted' [sic]. The fellow behind me started to follow . . . However, the rest of the formation apparently were sound asleep so he turned back."[24]

The British offensive on August 8 also caught the German forces "sound asleep" and launched Britain's most successful advance on the Western Front. There was no preparatory artillery bombardment, and aircraft were used to mask the engine noise of tanks moving forward to the lines. Following tactics developed by Australian general John Monash, massed formations of air and armor worked in concert with the infantry to overcome enemy defenses. Artillery used sophisticated techniques to counter enemy batteries and eliminate that threat to the attackers. It was so successful that Ludendorff called August 8 the "black day" of the German Army.[25]

Despite mist and fog in the early morning hours of August 8, allied squadrons were very active in supporting the offensive. They dropped down to strafe and dive-bomb retreating German infantry. They also attacked and knocked down any enemy observation balloons they encountered. American pilot Bill Lambert flew such a sortie that day and shot down a German balloon at 500 feet, while Lou brought another new machine to the squadron in the morning and flew an unremarkable two-hour offensive patrol in the afternoon. He did not fly again until August 10.[26]

Although weather improved during this time,[27] Lou found "the Huns are very scarce [and] never come around when I get on a patrol." Aware of his father's illness, he wrote, "I have wanted so badly to get a Hun so that I could cable [and] help cheer up father."[28] However, Lou eagerly anticipated the scheduled offensive patrols on August 10, because he was slated to fly Captain McElroy's former machine, C8869. Flying this S.E. 5 in combat from June 26 to July 25, "McIrish" had destroyed fourteen German aircraft and three balloons. Lou no doubt hoped it would bring him similar luck. Unfortunately, the tired engine was not up to the challenge, and twice Bennett returned to base with engine trouble after only being aloft a few minutes each time. He finally got airborne at about 0830 hours that morning in another aircraft for a two-hour offensive patrol that resulted in an "indecisive combat with [an] enemy [two]-seater near *Forêt de Nieppe*." He flew two more test flights in 8869 before launching on an offensive patrol, only to return after twenty minutes with engine trouble. After five fruitless attempts, a frustrated Louis Bennett took the aircraft up for one more engine test flight as evening came on.[29]

The next morning, Lou was again flying McElroy's former aircraft on an offensive patrol over the lines. Although he was up for almost two hours, he recorded no engagements.

Despite his frustrations, Lou was gaining more and more experience with each sortie and with experience came benefits. He brought another new machine to the airfield at Bryas on August 13.[30] The next day, Lou wrote home about it: "I have a *bus* of my own now however, [and] shall try not to miss many patrols—although these engines are awfully hard to keep going." His "bus" was a new H. P. Folland–designed S.E. 5a, serial number E3947 with a new two-hundred-horsepower Brasier Hispano engine. Having one's own aircraft also meant one's own ground crew. Two airmen, called colloquially "ak-emmas," were assigned to him to maintain and service his machine. *Ak-emma* is an obsolete term coming from the British phonetic alphabet for the letters *AM—aircraft mechanics*. Lou's rigger was William Reid, and his fitter was Charles Dredge. They were responsible for keeping the "bus" in fighting shape and arming the machine guns. The ground crews were perhaps the most important element of successful Great War air operations. They worked long hours, often overnight in harsh conditions with primitive tools to keep the cantankerous, battle-damaged machines fighting. One small slip or mistake on their part might be fatal to the pilot. Although the ground crews did not fly, they felt the joys of triumph when "their bus" returned with an aerial victory and shared the suffering of the squadron pilots when their ship and pilot "go west." Fellow American and RAF pilot Frederick Libby believed that "every combat pilot owes his life" to these fellows and believed each enlisted man deserved a medal similar to the Distinguished Service Order to recognize the importance of their service, which often went unheralded.[31]

Having one's own machine also meant that the pilot could configure the aircraft to his own personal preferences. He could give it a name and add a small box "for spare goggles, machine gun tools, cigarettes, etc." Lou added a special brass clip near his left hand to hold revolver cartridges. Meticulous pilots also personally synchronized the gun interrupter gear and swung the compass to ensure it indicated the correct heading. Lou could also carry a drum or two of flat-nosed "Buckingham ammunition," a special type of incendiary round that was especially effective against enemy observation balloons. Observation balloons were also called "kite balloons" or "captive balloons" because they were tethered with a cable to a powered winch that adjusted their elevation and quickly pulled them to the ground when danger appeared.[32]

Lou flew his first sortie in his new aircraft on an offensive patrol on August 14. Although aloft for two hours and twenty minutes, he recorded no engagements. Lou left on a midmorning patrol the next day, departing from Bryas at 0955 hours with his flight on a patrol behind the German lines. While scouting about ten kilometers (six miles) behind the German trenches near Brebières, just southwest of Douai in northern France, his flight observed a formation of five German Fokker D VII pursuit aircraft even though it was misty and cloudy. The Fokker D VII was one of the best fighter aircraft of the war and a dangerous adversary for pilots flying the S.E. 5a. As the formation dove on the German flight from 7,000 feet, Lou singled out one German who was "scooting East" and attacked. Because of the poor visibility, he thought it might have been a "two-seater." He dove to the left of his formation to prevent the German from escaping. He was approaching from his adversary's right front to avoid coming under fire from the observer guarding the tail with machine guns. This was the tactic favored by the famous British S.E. 5 ace Mick Mannock. As the distance closed between them, Lou recognized that the aircraft was not a two-seater but instead the dangerous Fokker D VII scout. He opened fire, but his Vickers gun jammed, and he was only able to fire his Lewis gun. Instead of diving under his adversary like Mannock had taught his pilots to do against a two-seater, Lou passed just over the top of the Fokker and began a climbing turn above him. As he merged, he noted that the Fokker D VII had a "beautifully streamlined fuselage of [a] red chocolate color." Bennett fired about half a drum of ammunition from the Lewis gun, beginning at a range of about eighty yards and closed to within a few feet. He observed that the pilot was slumped over "with his head inside the cockpit probably scared to death."[33] By skillfully climbing above and behind the German, Lou gained a position of advantage against the more maneuverable Fokker. Should the frightened pilot try to flee in the faster German scout, which Lou most likely expected him to do, Lou was in place to cut off his retreat to the east. Should the German turn and fight, Lou could use his perch above the enemy in a vertical fight like he had done against the Camel instructor at Marske and negate the enemy's turn advantage.

Instead, his opponent did something quite unexpected; as Lou turned, the German "went into a spin [and] disappeared through the clouds." His flight members saw the German spin down out of control into the clouds, but because of their distance behind enemy lines and dwindling fuel supplies, they did not dive down to confirm the kill. Rather, Lou received credit for getting "a Hun down out of control." Lou felt that the enemy pilot panicked and put his aircraft into a spin, or "vrille" to escape attack. He modestly told his family that he was "afraid he was just damaged or properly scared."[34] Although unlikely, it is certainly plausible that Bennett killed or injured his adversary when he made his attack. In subsequent combats, Lou proved that he was most expert in using the Lewis gun.

He flew two sorties in fair weather on August 16. His first was an inconclusive combat with three "enemy scouts" and a "[two]-seater," which he drove "down to 2,000 [feet]" but could not follow further because of the German pursuit planes. On his second sortie, he saw neither German aircraft nor balloons. Although Lou complained about the scarcity of enemy aircraft, the German Army found itself hard-pressed all along the front and dependent on its observation machines. Thus, German reconnaissance machines were frequently over allied lines. The ground fighting hung in the balance since the Germans were spent from their spring offensives and pressed by the advancing Allies. They were even more dependent upon quickly finding the enemy and blunting his thrusts with their superb artillery. Combats with three of these reconnaissance aircraft on August 17 taught Bennett that sometimes he needed to check his aggression. Lou found himself "too eager" in his attacks. When he dove on the enemy aircraft, he did not check his speed and was only able to get off a short, ineffective burst before he overshot his target. Sometimes, the German pilot was skilled and would twist, turn, and dive in such a way as to force Lou to overshoot. He was frustrated with himself, but he learned from the experience. At about 0740 hours on August 17, his patrol was scouting just east of Hénin-Liétard at about 13,000 feet when they spotted a German LVG two-seat observation aircraft. Lou reported, "When at 13000′ I saw [Lieutenant] Knobel diving on E.A. [enemy aircraft] 2-seater at 5000′. When at same height as E.A. I opened attack from all directions, firing bursts from close range whenever opportunity offered. In all I fired about 250 rounds into E.A. which crashed [south] of Henin Lietard."[35]

Knobel attached himself to the tail of the LVG and maneuvered with the well-piloted machine. He reported making "several good bursts with both guns" until it crashed. "C" and "E" antiaircraft batteries confirmed this action.[36] Although Lou felt he had been the one to destroy the aircraft, Bennett and Knobel shared credit for this victory, which Lou found frustrating.

On his return flight to base at Bryas, Lou again noted numerous German observation balloons, which they called *Drachen*, along the lines and resolved to destroy one. He landed without shutting his motor down and directed Reid and Dredge to give him a drum of the Buckingham ammunition that was so deadly to balloons. He launched with Lieutenant L. H. Sutton and flew east toward Lens. They noted a line of balloons to the north and turned to engage them. A number of allied warplanes flew overhead. Lou singled out a balloon at 2,000 feet southeast of Merville and flew just east of it. He turned west and made a diving attack on the target, holding his fire until he was very close. Lou found that the stable S.E. 5 made aiming guns and hitting the target much easier for a combat pilot once the target was sighted. He unloaded three-quarters of his ninety-seven round drum of incendiary ammunition, causing the balloon to burst into flames almost instantaneously. The balloon's observer parachuted to safety. Sutton confirmed the victory. On their return to Bryas, Bennett ran out of fuel and made a forced landing just outside the airfield.[37]

Lou flew an uneventful two-hour offensive patrol on the morning of August 18. His next combat occurred on August 19, when he was scheduled to fly an offensive patrol with his flight. His takeoff was delayed by an engine oil problem, so Lou departed the airfield alone. Bennett wrote in his combat report that he was unable to catch up or locate his squadron's patrol, but in fact, he did locate them. The lack of enemy air activity shaped his judgment, because he wrote home that "I saw them above me but was rather pessimistic about their finding anything and as there were some Hun balloons out I went after them instead." The sky that day was filled with clouds but the visibility was relatively good. Lou dove from 11,000 feet on the most easterly balloon of a group well east of Merville. His target was floating at about 2,000 feet. He closed rapidly and "fired about ¾ drum of flat nosed Buckingham into the balloon, which burst into flames, one observer making a parachute descent."

Ten minutes later, he targeted a second balloon nearer the German trenches at about 1,000 feet. Evading "heavy M.G. [machine-gun] fire," Bennett again closed and "fired [the] rest of [the] drum at very close range." The observer bailed out. Allied antiaircraft batteries confirmed both kills.[38]

Lou returned to base, where he learned that his flight "had a run in" with the Germans—and he missed it. Reed Landis from "C" flight destroyed both a Fokker D VII and a Triplane near Seclin. Lou decided to go out again immediately "to get even with them." Reid and Dredge refueled and rearmed his S.E. 5. He took off alone at 1205 hours, climbed above the clouds and again flew northeast toward Merville. At about 1340 hours, he spotted a single balloon at 2,000 feet and dove from the north through the broken cloud deck to attack. Bennett fired on his target from close range, using half a drum of incendiary ammunition. The observer jumped to safety, and the balloon went down in flames. Spotting a second balloon at 500 feet, Lou banked his fighter hard to attack it before it was hauled down. He fired the remainder of his incendiary drum from "very close range" when the gun jammed or expended its ammunition. Bennett observed the balloon on fire on the ground. Allied batteries again confirmed both kills. In just four hours, this young aviator from West Virginia had emulated British ace Mick Mannock by destroying four Germans in one day. Lou wrote his family to give them the news but was still smarting from having to share credit for the LVG. Two days later, Lou's combat was published in both the *London* and *Manchester Daily News*. Additionally, the squadron commander told him that "General [John] Salmond telephoned congratulation" for him. Salmond commanded RAF forces in the field. Lou was very pleased, though he wrote to his family that "anyone can get balloons who wishes to take the risk [and] is a good bullet dodger."[39]

Bennett's squadron mates noticed an undeterred resolve come over the aviator from West Virginia. Many sensed danger. Some said he was taken with "balloon fever." Pilot R. A. "Andy" Anderson wrote, "He immediately set out to down every captive balloon in the area and we were all talking about it in the squadron." Lieutenant Ian "Old Naps" Napier, who was temporary commanding officer of No. 40 Squadron at this time, said that Bennett "was 'full out' to do in as many Germans as possible from the very start." For members of No. 40 Squadron, attacking balloons was nothing new. During the previous spring and summer of 1917, the squadron organized attacks en masse against German balloons in support of the allied offensives. When Ludendorff launched the great German offensive the preceding March while Lou was graduating from the Central Flying School, No. 40 Squadron were actively ground strafing in an effort to "attack everything" and disrupt the German offensive. These veteran pilots were well aware of the dangers involved when attacking balloons at the front, especially by lone pilots. During "Bloody April" 1917, they supported an attack on Vimy Ridge and shot down seven balloons in flames using such tactics. Still, they dreaded attacking kite balloons because they were "about the worst thing to tackle."[40]

One may wonder why destroying observation balloons in the Great War captured headlines. Although newspapers sensationalized the exploits of fighter pilots for the propaganda value, little was actually known of the most successful contributions of aircraft in the war—namely, in observation and reconnaissance, infantry liaison, and artillery spotting. Artillery spotting became one of the most important missions that aircraft and balloons performed. Because artillery accounted for something like 75 percent of the casualties in the Great War, it played the pivotal role in battle. The accuracy of artillery fires improved dramatically with aerial observation. In 1918, both allied and German armies used this improvement in artillery fire control to develop new tactics that required close integration between artillery and advancing infantry. Aviation platforms that directed these fires often were the key component of successful maneuver.[41]

Both fixed-wing aircraft and balloons effectively controlled artillery fires. Observation aircraft could fly higher than balloons and could see activity deep in hostile territory. However, aircraft could only loiter over the desired area as long as they had the fuel to do so. Only a limited number of aircraft were available to cover a sector for a given period of time. The wireless, or radio, sets that crews used to relay information were not always reliable. Europe's poor weather hindered continuous observation from aircraft while balloons were a more consistent, accurate, and stable platform for artillery spotting.[42]

The balloon companies also lived and moved with the Army, and balloons could remain airborne (in theory) from dawn to dusk. They had direct phone lines from the observation baskets to headquarters. There were usually several balloons airborne over a given sector to provide continuous daylight observations for the Army. Their observation altitude was generally from 150 to 1,000 meters (500 to 3,300 feet), depending on weather or threat from enemy aircraft. A good observer with field glasses could see about 16 kilometers (10 miles) beyond the lines, depending on conditions and altitude. This was usually sufficient to cover the effective range of most artillery batteries. Balloons could still make observations in poor weather and had a crucial role of warning friendly forces of an impending assault.[43]

Because observation balloons were vital for consistently accurate fire control, efforts to attack and destroy them had great military value and were often a priority mission for pursuit squadrons. The consensus of many American combat airmen was that pursuit aviation had two most important roles:

1. Establish air superiority in order to protect allied observation platforms (balloons and observation aircraft).
2. Use allied air superiority to deny the enemy use of German observation platforms.

Therefore, air superiority was essential to success in the air, because it equated to protecting allied soldiers on the ground; since enemy observation platforms were negated, enemy commanders were blinded, and hostile artillery was then less accurate. It also frustrated enemy intelligence efforts. Air superiority implied that directed allied artillery fires were more accurate and deadly, countering enemy battery fires and negating German defenses. Additionally, allied commanders exercised better command and control when allied observation platforms reported on the position of friendly units. Corps observation aircraft were especially useful in this role when advancing ground units outdistanced their normal lines of communication. These "contact patrols" were often the fastest and most accurate means of information. For the commander of the 77th US Infantry Division, the 50th Aero Squadron was the sole source of position reports for a period of eighteen hours at one point.[44]

The importance of observation platforms was not lost on Army commanders, hence the air battles that evolved because of them. Great effort was put into protecting balloons in particular, since their construction and location on the battlefield made them vulnerable. Balloons were "gas bags" filled with flammable hydrogen gas, which incendiary ammunition readily ignited. It rarely took more than fifteen seconds from the spark of the first flames to the ultimate explosion and subsequent fall of the balloon. In order to be effective platforms for the artillery, it was imperative that balloons be as close to the front line as possible—two or three kilometers (about a mile) at best. Although enemy artillery was a hazard to balloons, their most dangerous adversary was the pursuit plane loaded with incendiary ammunition. Attacking pilots had to get close to the target, however, in order for this type of ammunition to be effective.[45]

The mere presence of attacking aircraft often forced entire balloon companies to winch down their balloons to the ground, where they were less vulnerable to attack, but useless in their primary mission since the entire sector was thus temporarily "blind." Therefore, "balloon busters" did not have to destroy a balloon to be effective. An attacker's effect on the battlefield was the same whether he successfully "killed" a balloon or not. Because the attacking pilot could easily switch targets, balloon units lowered all the balloons in proximity to the attack as a precaution. Armies designed elaborate defenses in depth to protect balloons. Attacking aircraft faced a formidable ring of opposition. Weather conditions permitting, patrols of pursuit aircraft orbited above the balloons, specifically detailed to protect them. On the ground, batteries of antiaircraft artillery, especially the dreaded "flaming onions"—a group of 37mm tracer rounds fired rapidly in a string—and machine-gun emplacements ringed the balloons. Of these, pilots considered the latter far more dangerous. Soldiers also launched balloon decoys in which the basket was loaded with high explosives that were detonated as the attacking pilot neared the balloon, engulfing the aircraft in the resulting fireball.[46] Pilots who successfully attacked balloons and lived needed great daring, great skill, and luck.

"Dud weather" on August 20 kept Lou grounded that day. He resumed flying offensive patrols the next day, flying an hour-and-a-half midday patrol and a two-hour evening patrol. To Lou's chagrin, he had no victories on either mission, though Lou recorded that his patrol "engaged [twelve] Fokker biplanes." His flight commander, Captain Dixon, destroyed a Fokker D VII southwest of Cambrai around 1740 hours. Another disappointment from this mission was Lou's "bus." It returned from a patrol with engine problems after a little over eighteen hours of flight time and was grounded afterward for repairs.[47]

During these intervals of inaction due to bad weather or mechanical trouble, Lou often went up to the airfield and visited with his rigger, William Reid. Reid, from Edinburgh, Scotland, found his young pilot to be one of the "nicest" men he'd ever met. He was "so quiet," and he "never seemed to mix with the other officers much." Instead, Lou's "heart was in his work." The young man was passionate to learn all he could about his aircraft, yet at times, he confided in the older Reid as he would a father figure. Lou told his rigger that he "wanted to be the first man to fly across the Atlantic Ocean." They talked "about various things," and as Lou's record improved, Reid concluded that his young lieutenant was both fearless and "one of the finest pilots in the world."[48]

Better weather and combat activity greeted Bennett on August 22. The RAF was supporting the allied push toward Cambrai and launched an aggressive campaign to seize command of the air by attacking German airfields along the front with large combat formations. In the north, the American 17th Pursuit Squadron joined Nos. 210, 211, 213, and 218 Squadrons, RAF, in attacking Varssenaere airfield, covered by No. 204 Squadron. A little farther south, Lou's No. 40 Squadron joined a strike force against Gondecourt airfield southwest of Lille. Both Nos. 40 and 208 Squadrons bombed the airfield while the Bristol F2B fighters of No. 22 Squadron acted as escorts. They hoped to build on the success of a previous mission on August 19 against Phalempin airfield, located a few miles southeast of Gondecourt. Bennett's squadron took off into a bright, sunny sky at 0500 hours to rendezvous with the other squadrons.[49] With his machine down for maintenance, Lou was flying S.E. 5a number C9258, the same "bus" Dixon had been flying the previous day when he shot down the Fokker. Allied airmen often flew a circuitous route to the target on these early morning raids, attacking from the east in order to strike "out of the sun" so as to achieve surprise and to prevent German gunners from shooting accurately. At about 0600 hours, the attack squadrons came in below 1,000 feet and dropped seventy-five 25-pound bombs on the airfield. They scored a direct hit on a hangar that burned and strafed numerous other targets with their machine guns, including more hangars, a locomotive and train at the railway station, and machine-gun emplacements. Coming off target, the airmen turned almost due west to fly home by the most direct route. Their flight paths carried them toward the town of La Bassée, slightly east of which, near the village of Don, they spotted several hostile kite balloons at 2,000 feet. Bennett, who had now established his reputation as a "balloon buster," dove to the attack. At 0610, he pressed in on the balloon "at close range," fired ¼ drum of incendiary ammunition, and watched as the "balloon caught fire and went down in flames, [while the] observer descended by parachute." Farther north, he saw more balloons.

Lou banked his machine into a hard right-hand turn, selected the highest *Drachen*, and fired about half a drum more of Buckingham ammunition into his target. It too went down in flames at about 0620 hours. Lou had again destroyed two balloons in one sortie and had used less ammunition to do it. He searched for another balloon but could not find any, apparently since they had been "hauled down" by their crews. His victories were confirmed by other pilots on the mission. "Dixie" Dixon also destroyed a balloon at nearby Hantay on that mission.[50]

Lou was back on the ground at 0640 hours. In one week, he had destroyed seven balloons, driven a Fokker scout down "out of control," and shared an LVG observation plane. He had done very well. That afternoon, Reid and Dredge finished maintenance on his own bus, which he took up for an hour-and-thirty-five-minute offensive patrol at 1700 hours. He returned with "engine trouble," so Lou continued to fly S.E. 5a C9258 on his first sortie the next day.[51]

Despite the allied successes, the hardened, disciplined German Air Service still struggled to provide their weary army with the intelligence it desperately needed to blunt the allied thrusts. Formations of two or three observation aircraft flew together in order to provide fire support, visual lookout for allied aircraft, and redundancy of observation in the event that one of the aircraft was downed. Losses to allied aircraft and strikes on German airfields had taken their toll. The Germans fought back aggressively, sending their best pursuit wings to oppose the air offensive. In turn, the RAF stepped up its offensive patrols, and Lou flew three of these on August 23. His first patrol led by Captain Dixon took off into the mist at 0620 hours. Around 0715, "C" flight observed three LVG observation aircraft below them at about 3,000 feet in the vicinity of Quiéry-la-Motte, a village west of Douai on the L'Autoroute du Nord. Spotting the British S.E. 5s, the Germans dove to the southeast to escape. "C" flight dove from 6,000 feet in pursuit. Lou pulled the nose of his machine farther east, well ahead of one of a German aircraft to cut off its escape. He attacked the German using textbook Mannock tactics; approaching head on with a slight offset from the nose of the observation ship; firing a short burst before aggressively maneuvering to reposition himself under the German's tail, where the observer could not take a clear shot at him. Lou followed the German's twists and turns as the aircraft dove from 3,000 to 800 feet, closing the distance as they dove. Lou wrote that he "literally filled him full of lead." He fired about three hundred rounds into the aircraft and noted that the cockpit was "full of smoke and [the] observer had disappeared." The enemy machine "continued straight down and crashed" just south of Quiéry-la-Motte.[52]

At this point, a patrol of three Fokker D VII scouts arrived and "prevented further action." The morning mist made it difficult to see if these were accompanied by other enemy fighters, so Lou returned to base. "Dixie" had seen this action and the destruction of the German observation ship. Lou was ecstatic; he had his first official fixed-wing "kill." He flew two more patrols that day but destroyed no aircraft or balloons. That evening, he sat down to write a quick note to tell his family the good news and enclosed another clipping of his previous four-balloon victory. Since another daylight raid was scheduled the following morning to keep pressure on the Germans, he kept his letter brief so he could get some sleep.[53]

The next morning's scheduled raid was canceled due to low clouds, but the weather improved throughout the morning. Lou volunteered for a midday offensive patrol between Lens and La Bassée. He accompanied another experienced American pilot, Lieutenant Reed Landis. Landis was an Air Service pilot, one of the "orphans" the USAAS had been unable to place in an American unit. He was "loaned" to the British in March 1918 and spent most of his career with No. 40 Squadron, where he destroyed one balloon and eleven enemy aircraft, including two on August 19. In September, he was chosen to command the 25th US Pursuit Squadron.[54] Dixon and Major Compston, the new squadron commander, noted Lou's penchant for fighting alone. By 1918, such tactics incurred considerable risk and were superseded by battle formations. Hence, Bennett flew with an experienced pilot since Dixon "wanted the greatest care taken of him until he mastered all the tricks of aerial fighting."[55]

Although it was still cloudy, the two Americans left the Bryas airfield at 1215 and headed east for a "voluntary 'strafe' . . . of German observation balloons" in the vicinity of Haisnes, a village just south of La Bassée, about twenty-nine kilometers (eighteen miles) northeast of their airfield. Their patrol area was small, only about six kilometers (four miles) separated La Bassée and Lens. Lou was again happy to be flying his own machine, which "sported" a bullet hole from a previous combat in the center of the British roundel on the left side of the fuselage. Approaching the front, the men spotted a line of balloons in their patrol area running north–south and spaced about three miles apart. The northernmost balloon was about six kilometers northeast of La Bassée near the village of Petite Hantay, while the southernmost was about six kilometers northeast of Lens near the village of Annay. Now it was Landis's turn to develop engine trouble, which forced him to return to base. Lou continued alone, deciding to swing his aircraft toward Lens and attack the southernmost balloon at Annay. By attacking from south to north with the midday sun at his back peeking through breaks in the clouds, he had the advantage of coming "out of the sun." At about 1240 hours, Bennett dove from around 10,000 feet on the hostile balloon near Annay. Antiaircraft guns opened up along the front as Lou's S.E. 5 closed on the balloon. He fired Buckingham ammunition, and the balloon fell in flames.[56]

Back at Bryas, Captain Dixon learned that Landis had aborted his flight while Bennett had pressed on the mission. Dixon stated, "I ordered my machine out in order to catch up with Bennett as he feared absolutely nothing." With all haste, Dixon took to the sky looking for his charge.[57]

Lou came off target, looked north, and saw that two balloons were still up. Destroying three balloons in a day was another achievement to write home about and "cheer up father."[58] Lou swung the nose of his ship north to set up an attack on the second balloon, which was slightly northeast of his position.

In the northernmost balloon, *Leutnant* Emil Merkelbach was scanning the front lines west of Petite Hantay at 1,000 meters (about 3,300 feet) for several hours on August 24, 1918. He was an observer and commander of Balloon Unit 9 of the 107th Infantry Division of the Imperial German Army. He was tired. Merkelbach had served for four long years of war and was awarded the Iron Cross for his valor. He was one of those soldiers transferred from Russia to the Western Front to support the Ludendorff offensives after Russia withdrew from the war. Sometime around 1300 hours, he was alerted to an attack in the south by the sound of antiaircraft guns when an allied machine attacked a neighboring balloon positioned at Annay, which burst into flames while he watched. Merkelbach telephoned his ground crew to winch down his *Drachen* while the allied scout attacked the adjacent balloon near the village of Provin in the Meurchin coal mining district.[59] This *Drachen* was the next kite balloon north from the burning Annay balloon.

Merkelbach was still 300 meters in the air (almost 1,000 feet) when the Provin balloon also erupted in flames. In horror, he saw the allied pilot turn and point the nose of his aircraft at Merkelbach's own balloon, approaching "at terrible speed." It was a race against time, and the experienced balloon observer knew it was too late. When the allied airman opened fire, Merkelbach's *Drachen* was still 50 meters (about 150 feet) above the ground—too low to parachute safely—though his ground crew frantically continued to winch down the balloon. Merkelbach and the allied pilot were now eye level with each other. As he looked at the allied pilot's face, he could only hope that the division's antiaircraft cannon and the battery of eight heavy machine guns of Machine Gun Detachments 920 and 921 that protected his *Drachen* might stop the enemy plane. Despite the raging antiaircraft fire from those guns, the enemy pilot pressed on, coolly ignoring the danger. Though terrified, Merkelbach marveled at his adversary's "heroic" courage, even as the antiaircraft batteries' barrage of incendiary bullets encircled the plane. There was nothing else the *Leutnant* could do but await the outcome. Merkelbach thought of his wife and children at home in their village of Grenzhausen while he stood alone in his basket waiting to "die miserably" by "being buried underneath [his balloon's] burning debris" as flaming rounds of Buckingham ammunition surrounded him.[60]

Louis Bennett Sr. with his two surviving children, Louis Jr. and Agra. (Louis Bennett Library, Weston, WV.)

Sallie Maxwell Bennett. (West Virginia and Regional History Center, WVU Libraries.)

Louis Bennett Jr. with his jalopy, circa 1906. (West Virginia and Regional History Center, WVU Libraries.)

Bennett's first aircraft, a Curtiss "tractor" biplane at Sheepshead Bay, New York. (West Virginia and Regional History Center, WVU Libraries.)

The main hangar at the airfield of the West Virginia Flying Corps (WVFC) in Beech Bottom, West Virginia. Mechanics prepare to start the JN-4D "Jenny" (left) and "penguin" ground taxi trainer (right) by pulling the propellers through, also known as "hand-propping." (West Virginia and Regional History Center, WVU Libraries.)

Close-up of the penguin, or "grass cutter," ground training aircraft in the foreground. A Curtiss Jenny is behind and to the right. (West Virginia and Regional History Center, WVU Libraries.)

West Virginia Aircraft Factory, Warwood, West Virginia. (West Virginia and Regional History Center, WVU Libraries.)

Interior of the West Virginia Aircraft Factory. (West Virginia and Regional History Center, WVU Libraries.)

RFC captain E. A. Kelly (left, with crutches) and Lou after Kelly was involved in a crash at Sheepshead Bay. (West Virginia and Regional History Center, WVU Libraries.)

Mechanics work on WVFC Aircraft Number One after a crash. Note broken propeller. (West Virginia and Regional History Center, WVU Libraries.)

Captain Louis Bennett Jr. (center), commander of the West Virginia Flying Corps. At right is instructor William Frey. The aviator at left is likely Lou's Yale classmate Tommy Kent. France considered Frey a deserter from the *Aéronautique Militaire*. (West Virginia and Regional History Center, WVU Libraries.)

The West Virginia Flying Corps, July 1917, in front of a Curtiss Jenny, Beech Bottom, West Virginia. Captain Louis Bennett Jr. is standing directly beneath the propeller hub. Instructor William Frey is to his left. At far right is Sergeant Snedecker, US Army, military instructor. (Louis Bennett Library, Weston, WV.)

Interior of the very basic rear cockpit of a Jenny. (USAF Image.)

WVFC Aircraft Number One. Records show that the tail number corresponds to the aircraft that had a mishap en route to West Virginia and later was involved in the crash of August 4, 1917, that killed Cadet C. B. Lambert of Welch, West Virginia. (West Virginia and Regional History Center, WVU Libraries.)

Lieutenant Louis Bennett Jr. and his niece in Wheeling, January 29, 1918, prior to his departure for Britain. (West Virginia and Regional History Center, WVU Libraries.)

Louis Bennett Jr. in Canada. (West Virginia and Regional History Center, WVU Libraries.)

British AVRO-504K scout similar to aircraft used for gunnery training at Hicks Field, Texas. (USAF Image.)

RFC aviation cadet Louis Bennett Jr. at Hicks Field, Texas. (West Virginia and Regional History Center, WVU Libraries.)

"Yale Men" (class year) undergoing flight training in Britain (left to right, both rows): 1. Irving Course (1919); 2. Henry Jackson Jr. (ex-1918); 3. David Beebe (1919); 4. Glen Wicks (ex-1918); 5. John Moffett (1915); 6. Jarvis Offutt (1917); 7. Louis Bennett Jr. (1917); 8. Samuel J. Walker (1917). (Division of Political and Military History, National Museum of American History, Smithsonian Institution, Bennett Collection.)

Lieutenant Bennett standing in front of his Sopwith Pup while saying goodbye to friends at their home in Drokes, Beaulieu, Hants, Britain before departing for France. Names listed on back are Verity, Mordaunt, Lettice Aceland, Ottilie, and Ethel Mills. (West Virginia and Regional History Center, WVU Libraries.)

British Sopwith Dolphin Scout. (Collections, Royal Air Force Museum.)

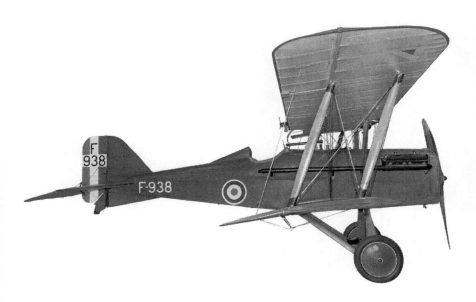

S.E. 5a (Scouting Experimental). (Collections, Royal Air Force Museum.)

Sitting on footlockers, Lou's friends Jarvis Offutt (left) and Orville A. "Tubby" Ralston (right) eat Whole Wheat cereal. This photo was found in Lou's RAF wallet. The back reads, "Lou—here you have the picture Bliss took. Wish you had been in it. Am ferrying now with H.B. at American Officers Inn, London.—Jarvis." Both men were from Nebraska. Offutt was killed in a crash. Offutt AFB is named for him. Ralston survived the war, became a USAAF officer in World War II, and died in a B-17 crash in the US. (West Virginia and Regional History Center, WVU Libraries.)

Employees of the West Virginia Aircraft Company pose for a group photo with their float in front of the Wheeling Suspension Bridge, July 4, 1918. (West Virginia and Regional History Center, WVU Libraries.)

A German ground crew works with their tethered or kite balloon, also known as a *Drachen*. (Division of Political and Military History, National Museum of American History, Smithsonian Institution, Bennett Collection.)

Defending the *Drachen*. A German antiaircraft machine gun and crew from Machine Gun Detachments 920 and 921 that protected Emil Merkelbach's *Drachen*. (Division of Political and Military History, National Museum of American History, Smithsonian Institution, Bennett Collection.)

Defending the *Drachen*. Another German antiaircraft machine gun and crew from Machine Gun Detachments 920 and 921 that protected Emil Merkelbach's *Drachen*. (Division of Political and Military History, National Museum of American History, Smithsonian Institution, Bennett Collection.)

Leutnant Emil Merkelbach in his balloon basket preparing to make an ascent in Russia, January 1918. (Division of Political and Military History, National Museum of American History, Smithsonian Institution, Bennett Collection.)

Leutnant Emil Merkelbach, observer and commander of Balloon Unit 9, 107th Infantry Division, German Imperial Army. (Dr. Ulrike Kunze and Herr Rüdiger Remy, Merkelbach's grandchildren.)

Press pass for Sallie Maxwell Bennett. (West Virginia and Regional History Center, WVU Libraries, Bennett Collection, Box 2, Folder 20.)

The retreating German Army dynamited the village of Wavrin, including its parish church. (West Virginia and Regional History Center, WVU Libraries.)

Occupation of Wavrin. A German Army band plays in the Church Square (place de l'êglise). (Jean Pierre Delecroix.)

Destruction of Wavrin along the train station street (Rue de la Gare). (Jean Pierre Delecroix.)

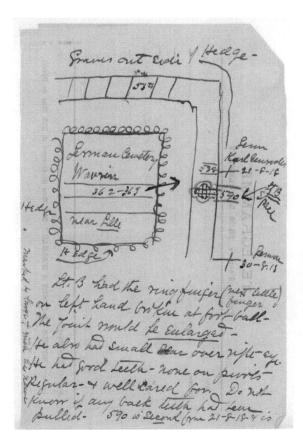

Sketch of the German military cemetery in Wavrin and the expected location of Lieutenant Bennett's grave. It includes a note with his physical description for purposes of identifying his remains. (West Virginia and Regional History Center, WVU Libraries, Bennett Collection, Box 2, Folder 20.)

Sallie Maxell Bennett in 1918, sent to her son in France. (Louis Bennett Library, Weston, WV.)

Curé Leon Delannoy, who assisted Sallie in recovering her son's remains. (West Virginia and Regional History Center, WVU Libraries.)

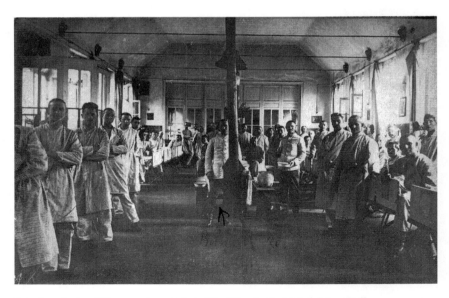

Interior photo of German hospital staff in Wavrin that Madeleine Dallenne gave to Sallie. "Richard" is at photo center marked by an arrow. (West Virginia and Regional History Center, WVU Libraries.)

M. Didier Delaval and descendants of Emil Merkelbach—Dr. Ulrike Kunze, Dr. Karl-Heinz Kunze, Herr Rűdiger Remy, and his wife, Ruth—at the site of the former German military hospital, Wavrin, France. (Author's photo.)

Scrapbook page that includes the memorial card for the chapel dedication on August 24, 1919. At upper right, a French priest prays at Lou Bennett's grave in Wavrin. At bottom, the memorial chapel Sallie commissioned there in 1919 with the small monument to Lieutenant Louis Bennett placed to the right of the entrance. A close-up view of the monument is on the lower right. According to the city of Wavrin website, this small monument was damaged in World War II. (Division of Political and Military History, National Museum of American History, Smithsonian Institution, Bennett Collection.)

In recent years, Sallie's chapel still stands and is used as a parish hall. (Author's photo.)

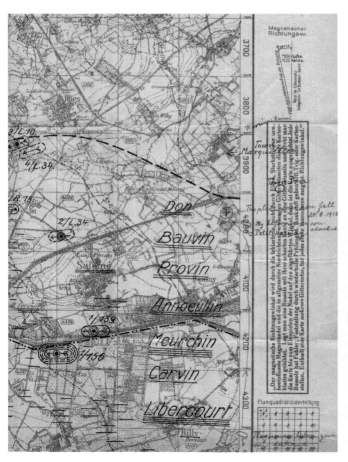

Emil Merkelbach's map indicating the position of two German balloons, Lou's route of flight and S.E. 5 crash site as well as German military unit boundary lines, names of nearby villages, and unit positions. (Division of Political and Military History, National Museum of American History, Smithsonian Institution, Bennett Collection.)

This field near Petite Hantay is where Lou's S.E. 5 crashed, near the buildings at upper left. *Leutnant* Merkelbach's balloon was tethered to a truck by this field surrounded by antiaircraft guns. (Author's photo.)

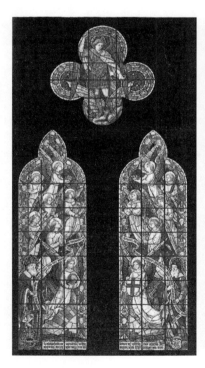

The original design of the RFC Window in Westminster Abbey as it appeared on the ceremony invitations. The angel holding the "shield of Faith" at lower right with the Cross of St. George had a generic face. (West Virginia and Regional History Center, WVU Libraries.)

The RFC Window as installed. The angel bearing the "shield of Faith" has the face of Louis Bennett Jr. (damaged in World War II). The West Virginia Flying Corps emblem is at lower right. (Ms. Christine Reynolds, Copyright: Dean and Chapter of Westminster, London.)

Sallie Maxwell Bennett in mourning attire. (Louis Bennett Library, Weston, WV.)

Photo of Augustus Lukeman's clay model rendering of *The Aviator* that Sallie sent to Major General Mason Patrick. This photo has never before been published. (USAF Image.)

The Aviator at Linsly School, Wheeling, West Virginia, 2022. (Author's photo.)

8

Mothers of Heroes

Waiting for News on the Home Front

A weary Sallie Maxwell Bennett spent Friday, August 2, 1918, sitting by her dying husband's bedside in Dr. Marvel's Sanitarium. She was reading a letter from her son, Lieutenant Louis Bennett Jr., announcing that he was going overseas "tomorrow." It was dated July 18. She had already received his July 20 cable from France telling her that his transfer succeeded. Now she completely understood that he was not coming home as she had hoped.

Sallie resigned herself and wrote to her son that "it *was* to be." She believed that had he received her July 10 cable, he would have asked for a furlough and come with all haste. She hoped that he would not blame her for keeping the gravity of his father's illness from him. The end of her husband's life had arrived. He was holding on but only because of stimulants. She added, "He is proud of your courage [and] this morning was glad to know you'd gotten your wish at last [to go to the front]."[1] She received Lady Frost's July 14 letter confirming Lou's transfer and that the Frosts admired him greatly. Alice Williams's letter arrived too. Through her friends, Sallie kept up with Lou's movements since his letters lagged from two weeks to a month or more. She was grateful Lou was "well and safe. It is these little things that help," she wrote to him. In thanks for Alice Williams's help, she sent a donation to one of her charities, the National Federation of Women's Institutes for its exhibition of women's art.[2]

Agra also wrote to her brother from her father's bedside in Atlantic City. She wasn't sure what to tell him but confided that their father was not improving like they had hoped, and that he was losing strength. Unlike her mother, Agra believed he would ultimately pull through and planned to stay there until he did. She missed Lou and wished he weren't so far away. Her husband, Johnson, kept their baby with him in Wheeling while she stayed with her father.[3]

The two women sat with the elder Bennett through most of the hot and humid day. Although he listened to Lou's letter with interest, Louis Bennett Sr. slept most of the time. Sallie felt overwhelmed and told her son that there was nothing he could do. Perhaps, she added, he would not have gotten leave anyway. She conceded that Lou was probably safer in Europe than in the United States since "so many instructors . . . have lost their lives here." Accidents claimed the lives of some of Lou's closest friends. Burt Tait, one of Lou's friends from training, was killed on July 16. He was a flight commander and instructor in Canada who died while testing an aircraft that had just come out of maintenance. The engine stopped on takeoff, and he and a colleague were burned to death in the crash. Even more devastating to Lou was the accidental death of his good friend Jarvis Offutt. Offutt finally made it to France and was posted to No. 56 Squadron, Royal Air Force (RAF), another S.E. 5 (Scouting Experimental) outfit. Like many newcomers, his first sortie was a practice strafing mission. While diving on his target, Jarve apparently fixated on it by peering through his Aldis telescopic sight while his aircraft continued to dive at the ground. Thus, he lost situational awareness of his height and when he did notice the ground "rushing up" at him, "it was too late and then [he] tried to pull out too fast." Jarve yanked the stick back as hard as he could, overstressing the wings of his machine in a desperate effort to keep from crashing. The wings collapsed, and his S.E. 5 dove into the ground, killing him instantly. Tubby Ralston lamented, "It seems that always the best go first." He, Bless, and Ralph Snoke from the 17th US Pursuit Squadron "flew up" to see Johnny Farwell from Yale to mourn Jarve's passing. They intended to fly over to Bryas to see Lou next, but bad weather prevented it.[4] Lou mourned the loss alone.

However, the intensity of combat at the front prevented a long mourning period. That night, German bombers attacked Lou's airfield, dropping star shells to illuminate the field before bombing it. Impressed, Lou drove to a salvage depot south of the field the next day in order to chip metal fragments from a "*five* engine Gotha—which was brought down in flames." Lou's friend Tubby Ralston also crashed. He "pancaked" into the ground and was almost killed. To him, the fighting was "hell on roller skates." Lou's squadron lost several American aviators: Grady Touchstone was shot down and made a prisoner of war (POW). He was joined in August by both Robert Anderson and A. J. Anderson. W. O. Archer became a POW in September. Lou's letters home reflected this growing fury of combat. The same day as the Gotha raid, his comrade from Baltimore Paul Burwell became separated from his flight and had "a lively scrap." Burwell was attacked by "[ten] Huns" on his tail. He did all sorts of dives and turns to escape being killed before a flight of Sopwith Camels came to his rescue. Burwell was fortunate to come out of the engagement unscathed. Many more skilled aviators were not so fortunate. During July and August 1918, the attrition of allied fliers, particularly to ground fire, seemed staggering. In one of his last letters to Lou, Jarvis Offutt portended that, "a man's superiority in flying seems to cut so little figure, in whether he gets archied [hit by ground fire] or not."[5]

This was indeed an astute observation. Lou's first flight commander, George McElroy, was killed by ground fire in July, as was the renowned British ace Mick Mannock, who died on July 26 when he was "archied." His friend James McCudden took off on a trench strafing mission two and a half weeks earlier, lost his motor on takeoff, and died in the crash. In the space of about two months, No. 40 Squadron lost two of its commanders, the second of whom, Major Arthur William Keen, crashed and burned on August 15, the day Lou forced down the Fokker D VII. Keen died from his injuries on September 12. Lou's new commander was Major Robert J. O. Compston. Lou's friend Bill Dillon was also killed in August. Twelve Yale aviators were killed in Europe in July and August 1918 alone. Half of the eight Yale men of Lou's training class in Britain were dead by the end of the war. The losses became both routine and feared. One American pilot wrote, "We've lost a lot of good men. It's only a question of time until we all get it."[6]

The war of attrition in the air mirrored the war on the ground, only at a numerically smaller scale. American "doughboys" sustained terrible casualties too. When Foch launched his counterattack on July 18 the US 1st and 2nd Divisions were in the vanguard. Casualties in some regiments were as high as 50 percent. Elements of the 28th "Keystone" Division captured the village of Fismette. After the German counterattack, only 30 of the 230 Pennsylvanians holding the village survived. At Belleau Wood, the US Marines lost about 4,600 men, almost half of their forces engaged. By the end of September, unofficial casualty estimates from the Meuse-Argonne battle reached 75,000.[7]

Although receiving such macabre news from loved ones in Europe was disconcerting to families at home, receiving no mail at all was more terrifying because of the implications a lack of mail suggested. Mary Hays wrote imploringly, "Dearest—Oh *where* are you? Not a line in more than a week. I am *so* worried ["so" is underscored five times]. I simply haunt the Post Office but so far haven't been rewarded." Mails were delayed by distance and sometimes interdicted by combat, such as by submarine attacks. Many combatants wrote in cheerful clichés so as to not give family members "the horrors." Censorship too imposed constraints against disclosing too much information to the home front. The British Army printed the Field Service Post Card, officially called the Form A 2042 but known popularly as the "Whizz Bang" or "Quick Firer," so soldiers could write home often. Many times battle survivors sent these immediately after combat with everything crossed out except "I am quite well," that way loved ones received welcome news from the front shortly after reading about the battle in the daily newspapers. The Form A 2042 represented the mass-produced archetype of the "form," a document unique to the modern world in which one communicated by crossing out things or checking them off. Ian LeRougetel sent a "Field Card" to notify his family that "I am quite well" and that he had "received your letters" after the heavy fighting on August 22 and 24.[8]

Lou did not use it, so Sallie had to be content with letters or an occasional cable from him. Sallie, like most mothers, thought of him "every moment" and wondered how and where he was. She worried about his zeal to make a name for himself, in her view worthy of "Stonewall" Jackson. She admonished Lou repeatedly to be patient and "take it easy—Don't get reckless [and] try to *Eat* Huns." She wanted him to write long letters about his squadron and his work but scolded, "[I] *want* you back when the war's over."[9]

She maintained her extended vigil with her husband, who thought of young Louis "until the end." She and Agra were together with him on Friday evening, August 2, when he "went away quietly in his own great way." Throughout his ordeal, he did not complain. The heat was oppressive with temperatures reaching 110 degrees "in the shade." Agra added in her letter that their father did not suffer. Weary and devastated, Sallie returned home to Weston with her daughter and the body of her husband. He was buried on the evening of August 6, "in the cool after a torrid day."[10]

Before leaving Atlantic City, a fatigued Sallie attended to the funeral arrangements, purchasing a bronze casket and copper outer box for her deceased husband. She bought tickets for the trip home. She sent telegrams to all the family relations and wrote some that she would mail at stops en route "for the funeral." The anxiety of the last three months took its toll, however. She was easily upset and overburdened by what she believed was the insensitivity of her relatives and the perceived indifference of her son-in-law, whom she felt interfered with her plans by rescheduling the funeral in the afternoon after she made all the arrangements. She was outraged that Johnson expected her to share the same roof with her husband's "housekeeper," which would invite "scandal for Mr. Bennett." Johnson's behavior offended her sense of Victorian decorum, and she accused him of ignoring the rights and propriety of the funeral by not being appropriately attired. She complained that he meddled in what she believed was her due as widow of the deceased. Most egregious, he had gone into the family home in Weston "giving orders as if *he* owned the house" and tried to sit in "Mr. B's chair." Her sister, Mary Maxwell, also did not escape Sallie's ire, since she too had "taken charge" of the Weston home before the mourners arrived from Atlantic City and did not let "the Weston family of Bennetts do things." Since it was "Primary Election Day," none of the men could attend before evening. Sallie was relieved when the "Knights Templar [and] Masons took charge of the funeral at sunset" and her husband "was laid to rest by their beautiful ceremony." She thought the sunset ceremony was more comforting, for to Sallie it "seems like saying good night in the evening" rather than "good bye."[11]

Questions surrounding her late husband's estate caused her more stress. She found she could not sleep. This was exacerbated by the fact that her husband named three men to be executors of the estate; son-in-law Johnson; nephew Hunter M. Bennett, a Weston attorney; and young Louis—at the front and not easily reached. The month or so lag in mails did not stop creditors from demanding payment from the estate, though she did convince some to wait. Sallie sent Lou a power of attorney to sign naming her to act in his absence, but August ended and she still had no word from him—not even something to acknowledge his father's death. Anticipating such a legal necessity earlier in the summer, Johnson insisted that Sallie send her son a power of attorney and have it "testified to before a U.S. Consul." The intensive combat operations precluded young Louis from doing that, so his commanding officer testified to it and sent it home on August 20.[12] Unfortunately for Sallie, it would not arrive until much later.

Although Johnson and Hunter embraced the problems arising from the estate and appear to have been trying to spare her further worry, Sallie was used to having her own way and was generally not happy with them. She thought they did not work together at all. Johnson had business affairs in the Northern Panhandle, while Hunter was the Lewis County prosecuting attorney. She felt they excluded her from important decisions and were insensitive to her desires. Worse, yet, in her "darkest hour" it appeared as if her daughter, Agra, was openly siding with Johnson against her. She neither approved nor understood their actions—especially Johnson's, who ordered auditors to examine her late husband's books. He and Sallie were at loggerheads. Even after she received Louis's power of attorney, which she immediately forwarded to the other executors, they ignored her as a colleague. She was not amused and fully expected to stand in her son's stead. Having managed her husband's business affairs for three months before his death, she was indignant at the slight. She was a Victorian Southern woman trapped in a modern man's world. Sallie grew increasingly frustrated at her helplessness with the situation.[13]

Not yet aware of Lou's combats on the Western Front, Sallie answered her son's early, frustrated letters by imparting her own miseries, telling him that in many ways they were sharing similar experiences. She felt she had gotten no recognition for the hard work she'd done for his father since May, just as Lou was working hard in No. 90 Squadron without apparent recognition. She added that they had to go on in the same way, doing their duty and working hard. She told him, "That's what the women are doing here—while someone else hands over the money." American women were doing important war work, but they were not being recognized for it. She was ready to "*Boss a job*" instead of being "bossed around," but experienced women "over 50 years [were] *not* accepted."[14] True, most of the roughly one million women who were doing war work were young single women who had previously been employed in less well-paid jobs. The war allowed them a degree of upward mobility. Some married women who were previously employed when they were single also temporarily reentered the workforce. Despite the belief by some feminists that they had shattered gender barriers in the workplace, this was only a temporary condition, and women were expected to return to their previous jobs or homes when the war emergency was over.[15] Although the war often symbolized the coming of the modern age, the reality for American women was that they were still excluded from first-class citizenship. Most women were precluded from business decisions or leadership. Although some served in traditional roles such as nurses, women were barred from military service. Most women were denied direct political participation, such as holding office or voting, though exceptions existed in some states in the Wild West. Woodrow Wilson provided a national catalyst for women's suffrage by linking that progressive issue to his war for democracy. Speaking to the Senate in 1918, he declared that women's suffrage was "vital to the winning of the war." However, in economic circles, there was no such impetus for change.[16]

Sallie wanted a change. Her Southern heritage stressed the "moral superiority" and "cultural authority" of women who were able to get things done.[17] She felt she needed to do something. Newspaper accounts of the recent tough fighting in Europe led her to believe why she had probably not received a letter from Louis in a month—nothing since mid-July. She wrote to him that she knew heavy fighting would please him and that she was "glad to have [him] there" but wanted him to come back safely. In fact, Sallie wrote, she too had a desire to serve overseas, but not as a nurse. She frankly thought she would be a poor nurse. Instead, she argued that the government could use "*old* folks—of experience." Sallie told Lou, "I *could* look after the boys I know [and] comfort their Mothers with letters—like your friends in England have me. I don't think I could have lived through the past three months with the care [and] anxiety for your father had I not been kept informed by them of your being well and safe. It is these little things that help." She wrote to a close friend of the Bennett family, John W. Davis, the solicitor general from the Justice Department, about getting a passport to go to wartime France. Davis was an attorney from Clarksburg and a future presidential candidate. He informed Sallie that "under existing regulations," she would be denied a passport with a son in the service. He further advised her that "this rule has been very rigidly adhered to." Undeterred, Sallie responded to Davis that since her son was fighting in British service, the law shouldn't apply to her. She insisted that Davis "find a loophole for me."[18]

Her desire to visit the combat zone and write letters for the troops was not an original idea. During what she called the "War of Secession," many women voluntarily wrote letters home for soldiers who were too wounded or sick to do so. In many cases, they wrote such letters after a soldier died so that families might have accurate and reliable news of a loved one's fate. These personal letters were a much more dependable means of learning about who did not survive a battle than were the casualty lists cobbled together by both armies, which mainly concerned themselves with military operations. Custom demanded that a soldier's comrades in the unit, his "band of brothers," write personal letters to his family advising them of his fate, but as historian Drew Gilpin Faust found, "months often passed before soldiers in the field found time, circumstance, or strength to write." On occasion, women stepped in and fulfilled that duty. As Union armies penetrated deeper into the heart of the Confederacy, it gradually disintegrated. Communications broke down as railroads deteriorated, waterways were cut off, and more Southern men were conscripted for combat. Southern women often found they were alone and left to deal with various matters, including the dead and wounded who remained after a battle—which could be staggering. Many women, Northern and Southern, volunteered to help in hospitals. Although charitable agencies such as the Christian Commission and the Sanitary Commission in the North played an important role in communicating with soldiers' families, especially those who were casualties, in the South such a role was usually filled by private individuals. Women increasingly found themselves "conscripted into the work of death by a war that invaded their homes and communities."[19] Sensing a similar need among the airmen at the Western Front, Sallie Maxwell Bennett saw her role shaping along these historic lines, and she aggressively pursued it.

She was also becoming more frustrated with estate matters. Johnson and Hunter hired a stenographer to copy her late husband's tax bills and receipts. Hunter thought Mr. Bennett's small memorandum books were too hard to read, so Sallie sat with the stenographer for two days reading off the items until they had covered every entry up to the day he died. She wrote to Lou that she "never was so tired in [her] life" from the additional strain.[20] Sallie spent her sleepless nights answering the piles of unanswered telegrams and sympathy letters on her desk. She was only able to get fresh air when she went to the cemetery in the evenings with her granddaughter.

Sallie was also worried the executors would blame her for the complete mess they made, when she "had nothing to say about matters." Until Louis came home and set things straight, she decided "that it would be safer for [her] to go away [and] leave them with full responsibility" until they fixed things, which she expected to take at least several months. Sallie made arrangements to take the train to New York. She still hadn't unpacked her trunk from Atlantic City even though it had been over three weeks, but at least she didn't have to worry about packing. Sallie at last had a letter from her son in France. His July 23 letter arrived on Sunday, August 18, but she was only able to answer it the following Thursday. She wrote to Lou that she was looking forward to a rest, as she had had none since early May, and she was sorry she could not get permission to send him candy but she would continue to pursue the issue. She wrote, "I'm *always* with you in spirit."[21]

On Tuesday, August 28, Sallie was awakened at 0530 hours by a knock at the door. It was the Western Union delivery boy with a cable for her. It read,

> Regret to inform you that Lt. L. Bennett, Royal Air Force, is reported missing on [August] twenty-fourth. Letter follows.
> Secretary Air Ministry[22]

The shocking cable came without forewarning twenty-six days after her husband's death. It offered no other information. Its ambiguity was traumatic. How was he missing? Was it because of combat or weather? Did "missing" mean that no body was recovered or was he just overdue at his airbase? The possibilities appeared limitless. One might certainly understand had Sallie succumbed to self-pity or despair at this point, coming as it did so soon after the death of her spouse of twenty-nine years while she was burdened with estate matters in which she felt herself becoming increasingly marginalized.[23] However, Sallie Maxwell Bennett immediately leaped into action, sending the delivery boy back to the Western Union office with two cablegrams. The first was to her influential friend Alice Williams, living at St. Mary's Mansions, London. She informed Alice that "Louis [is] reported missing" and asked her to offer the Air Ministry a reward for information. She concluded by adding, "Spare no expense to locate body if killed." She knew Williams had the connections to get answers.[24] Next, Sallie sent a cablegram to the commander of Lou's pursuit squadron at the front in France. She simply demanded that he "offer reward to Germans to locate Lieut Bennett reported missing."[25]

Having dispatched marching orders to those whom she believed could immediately obtain the results she needed, Sallie returned to New York and wrote to friends every day with news about her son's status. She sent letters to Etta LeRougetel and Lady Frost as well as to Augustus Post at the Aero Club of America and Postmaster General Albert Burleson. She also sent a letter to Cordelia Hays so she could break the news to her daughter, Mary.[26] Johnson rushed to Washington, DC, to inquire with numerous government agencies, such as the State Department, as well as the Red Cross whether they had any additional information. They had none. It would be two to three weeks, he estimated, before they had any definite news.[27] Before leaving, Johnson notified the Wheeling press that "West Virginia's foremost air flyer" had gone down somewhere along the Picardy front. The people of the Ohio Valley awoke to the headline, "Louis Bennett, Wheeling Air Fighter, Missing In Action." They hoped their favorite son was a prisoner of war and not "dashed to death."[28]

Sallie arrived in New York at the end of August and settled into her apartment on Fifth Avenue, better situated there than in Weston to respond to news of her son. Mail took an additional three days to travel from New York to Weston, and since New York is a port city, she could quickly sail to Europe if needed once she obtained the necessary permissions. When September arrived, Sallie received conflicting news about Louis. A hopeful cable arrived around September 12 from Lou's squadron commander, Major Compston, informing her:

> Cancel all letters. Louis prisoner. Leg broken, Slight Burns.
> Compston 40 Squadron RAF[29]

Later that month, she received a more troubling letter from Compston that was dated September 2. In that letter, Compston acknowledged receipt of her initial wire and advised her that "it is not a matter of expense to find out about your son." He told her that on Lou's last patrol, he had gone out with another pilot who had "come back to our side of the 'lines' owing to engine trouble." Additionally, during the time of Lou's patrol, "a machine was reported as brought down in flames." Compston feared Lou had "met his death." Sallie did not give up hope, however, and concluded that the earlier letter was superseded by more recent news. Compston also promised in his letter to keep a map for her that marked the position where Lou's machine fell, which he did.[30]

Sallie's friends in London informed her that if Louis were a prisoner she would know in "[two] weeks if unwounded, [three] if wounded." More news trickled. A letter arrived addressed to her late husband from Lou's ground crew, expressing "deepest sympathy in the hour of your great loss." Thinking it their "duty to write [Mr. Bennett] a line or two," William Reid and Charles Dredge gave Sallie a glimpse of her son's last combat sortie. They had "every reason to believe he was struck by an Archie after bringing down two balloons in flames." Reid added, "It is a very great loss to me to think that I have lost such a noble young man. I hope to God [that] he is still alive. His last words to me before he left were—'I will get them all right.' He left the ground with a smile on his face—which he always did."[31]

Another letter arrived from Lou's flight leader that day, Reed G. Landis. From Landis, an experienced combat pilot who already had twelve victories, Sallie for the first time got a sense of the importance of her son's "work" in France. Whereas the ground crew wrote of having "great affection" for him and described him as "a thorough gentleman and a splendid pilot," Landis wrote:

> My dear Mrs. Bennett,
>
> It is with very deep regret that I write to you about your son's loss. He was a member of my flight, and we have worked and played together a great deal since he came out to the Squadron.
>
> As to his work, I can truthfully say that it has been most remarkable. He has shown ability, keenness of thot [sic] and bravery never excelled, and equaled by only a very few. If he had been allowed to carry on I am sure he would have made a most astounding record—as it was he shot down nine balloons in flames and two enemy aircraft. That alone is quite sufficient to make his name among the effective pilots over the lines.
>
> Some slight comfort may come to you in the fact that he went "missing" after having exacted heavy toll from the enemy—and to the very last moment he was doing his work—our work—over the lines.
>
> Personally, your son was gifted with a most lovable disposition and manner. We all loved him here at 40. And he is such a son as any Mother should be inordinately proud of. He is one more of the wonderful pals—and sons—who have given their best—their all for the cause we fight for.
>
> > Very Truly,
> > Reed G. Landis
> > 1st Lt. Sig. R.A.C.A.
> > 40 Squad. R.A.F., B.E.F.[32]

The arrival of the Landis letter must have been bittersweet for Sallie. On one hand, she could be proud Lou's colleagues held him in such esteem. Her son's accomplishments through his talent and skill as an aviator were also something of which she could be proud. On the other hand, there is a finality to its tone that must have troubled her.

Shortly thereafter, a letter arrived from the British Air Ministry that was sent three days after the Landis letter. It merely confirmed the earlier Air Ministry telegram that reported Lou as missing. It also only pointed out "that this does not necessarily mean that he is killed or wounded and to say that you shall be immediately informed as any definite news is received." Sallie stayed in New York waiting for news. Still unaware of the elder Bennett's death, Airman Reid sent a follow-on letter to him on September 5 in which Reid joyously announced that he believed Louis was alive. The squadron had interviewed several German prisoners who reported that Lieutenant Bennett had been brought down, receiving burns and a broken leg in the crash. It now seemed as though Lou was a prisoner of the Germans—but where? Sallie immediately cabled the Air Ministry, Mrs. LeRougetel, Major Compston, the Aero Club of Paris, and her friends General Mason Patrick with the American Expeditionary Force and Solicitor John Davis.[33]

Mary Hays took the news of her love's "being missing" very hard. Her mother told Sallie that Mary's heart was breaking. "Mary has been quite miserable for several days. The Doctor says [it's] shock [and] if she could relax [it] would be better. Mary had a letter [from Louis] this morning dated Aug. 8—of course too long ago to tell anything but [it] did say he had been doing very little Patrol Duty." Mary also received letters from him dated July 31 and August 2, 3, 7, and 8, none of which could confirm that he was alive. When Cordelia learned that Lou was unofficially a POW, she decided to keep that from Mary in her present state. Cordelia and Sallie were coming to an understanding as mothers, and Cordelia wrote to Sallie that she appreciated her correspondence, considering their letters "strictly *entre nous* [between us]." On her own initiative, Cordelia sent a cable to the International Red Cross in Switzerland to learn if Lou were a POW.[34]

Other letters from Sallie's friends in Britain expressed sympathy for the loss of her husband and hope for her son. From Dora Frost, she received "unofficial" word that Lou was a prisoner. She received a letter from Lieutenant W. Laurie Field in No. 40 Squadron. He confirmed Lou had been "brought down by anti-aircraft guns after attacking a balloon." He was injured, with slight burns and a broken leg. Field added that Lou was "a great favourite with us all" and hoped that they would receive official news of Lou's capture soon. There was no supporting information from outside of No. 40 Squadron. Sallie's British friends corresponded with each other in their efforts to gather information about Lou. From Etta LeRougetel, Sallie learned about the intense fighting along the front the week Lou went missing. Her son Ian had been up in the line and his "company was up to its eyes in it [and] had a very hard time on Thursday [August] 22nd [and] Saturday [August] 24th." Etta had gone to both the War Office and the Air Board in hopes of learning something about Lou's fate, but both offices had no "fresh information" and believed it was still "*very early*" to expect any information from Germany on the events of August 24.[35]

The plummeting morale in the Imperial German Army finally dissolved. In Germany, military leaders met with the kaiser to discuss the deteriorating situation at the front. The Allies were advancing rapidly. German leadership concluded that the war could no longer be won militarily and that "we have reached the limits of our endurance." Soldiers and airmen at the front were certainly not aware of the kaiser's meeting and continued fighting. No. 40 Squadron maintained its support of the infantry, and infantrymen like Ian LeRougetel were "with the pursuing army now which is moving rapidly after the Hun."[36] It seemed the end was at last in sight.

Meanwhile, Sallie's problems with the estate continued to hound her. Cordelia Hays wrote to Sallie about the car Lou had given to Mary "for the war." She thought it was inappropriate for her daughter to keep it and wanted her to return it, but she thought Sallie should ultimately decide. Lou had written to Mary that if the car were giving her trouble, she should sell it and put the money toward a new Packard, which was the car he thought he'd like when he returned. Agra confirmed everything. This new "problem" added another "burden" to Sallie's weary shoulders. She understood Cordelia's wishes and agreed to take the car back. She wrote that she'd "probably store the car" until Louis returned and then she would let him decide what to do. Sallie was especially upset that Cordelia had paid for the repairs, and it seemed to her the "Philistines" at the dealership had robbed them—literally. Lou's auto tool kit was missing and the mechanics were not forthcoming on what work was done.[37]

Mary misunderstood the arrangement. Brokenhearted, agonizing with worry for her love, she thought Sallie wanted everything back from her son, including his coat that he had given Mary at Christmas. She treasured it because it was Lou's coat, and she had worn it when they were together during his furlough. She agreed to return the car but pleaded to keep the coat so she could have "something that belongs to him." Mary promised to "take the very best care of it" and hoped they'd have good news soon. She ended with, "I don't think I could stand it otherwise." Despite her own misery, Sallie sensed Mary's agony and sent a compassionate response in which she apologized for "butting in" on Mary's personal affairs. Sallie told the girl that she was overwrought with all that had happened, and as a result she had not explained herself well to Mary as it was "so hard to keep [things] straight." Sallie begged Mary to keep the coat and that if Lou did not come back, Sallie wanted Mary to have the car too, "for keeps." She added that she knew that Mary would be hurt and disappointed if Lou did not return, "but he got his wish at *last* [and] went down *fighting*."[38]

About the same time, son-in-law Johnson McKinley wrote to Sallie about further trouble with the elder Bennett's estate since Lou was still not available as executor. Johnson asked Sallie to consider making her late husband's estate a corporation in order to expedite resolution of outstanding debts and other issues that remained, aggravating her immensely.[39]

At this point, the first wave of another global disaster intruded into the story. The influenza pandemic, erroneously called "Spanish flu" by contemporaries, struck New York City. This particularly lethal form of influenza killed more people than did the war. It is estimated that somewhere between forty million and one hundred million people died worldwide by the time it disappeared in 1919. No one at the time knew its origins or why it vanished. It was especially lethal to young adults, and its suddenness was worse than the epidemics of cholera, smallpox, or typhus in the nineteenth century. The first wave struck in mid- to late 1918; the second, in the spring of 1919. It hit the rich as well as the poor. It struck its victims with a high fever, and they were usually dead within days. The influenza epidemic of 1918–19 was the worst pandemic since the Black Death of the fourteenth century, and Sallie Maxwell Bennett contracted it.[40]

"Burning with fever" and fearing that she was near death, Sallie sat down and bared her soul on a common pad of paper in her apartment. For several weeks, she was "far from well" with "the Spanish Influenza" but kept on her feet, driven to make "continuous inquiries for [her] son—Louis—reported Missing in France." She felt terribly alone, seemingly abandoned by her sister and her daughter, Agra. She feared her son-in-law, Johnson, was seeking to take over her late husband's estate for himself and was not consulting with the second executor, Hunter Bennett. Instead, Johnson was "hiding behind his wife's skirts." Despite receiving a clipping from the *Charleston (West Virginia) Gazette* announcing Lou had been killed around August 28, Sallie was certain he would be home soon and set things straight. She was outraged that Johnson sought to make the estate a corporation without waiting for Louis. After three months in Atlantic City watching her husband die, having her son reported missing, and finally contracting the Spanish flu, she wrote it was an "awful burden to bear alone now—seems more than my share."[41]

Illness and stress took its toll on the fifty-year-old widow, and she fired off a sharp letter to Johnson and Agra questioning their hurry to act without her son. Sallie protested that she did not understand them, and she cited how her own father's estate as well as those of other prominent West Virginians had been settled, declaring that no one made those estates corporations. Why, therefore, did Johnson propose such a preposterous, irrevocable change to her husband's estate?[42]

When Johnson proposed converting her husband's estate into a corporation held jointly by herself, Agra, and Lou, Johnson merely offered this option as an expeditious solution to their problems. Sallie would gain control and, as a corporate head, would no longer need executors or reports to the court. She could dispose of the property as she and her children saw fit. Johnson thought it was a desirable option. He urged her to consult an attorney and "think it over." One suspects Johnson also wanted to extricate himself from his role as executor, having to respond to Sallie's steady complaints.[43] Johnson had his own businesses to run.

Unconvinced, Sallie wrote to Johnson to "take no steps of any importance until Louis comes back." She intended to remain in New York "until I can find Louis and get him safe back home." She boasted that she could manage herself and never had need for a doctor or lawyer of her own. She also admonished her daughter and son-in-law to "butt out" of her quest to find Louis.[44] Although it seemed she had turned a corner, Sallie would not fully recover for some time.

Her nephew Hunter Bennett, the Lewis County prosecuting attorney and second executor to the elder Bennett's estate, sent Sallie an encouraging letter that matters of the estate were at last "progressing." He told his aunt that, nonetheless, he was more interested in the return of his cousin Louis than in estate matters. Hunter warned her about the mounting crisis in Germany, which was seeing famine and riots. He was especially concerned that if the war did not end in the fall of 1918, conditions would become very difficult on prisoners of war. Hunter cautioned, "I would not leave anything undone to get [Louis] out of there" and urged her to write to John W. Davis about arranging a prisoner exchange. Davis was now a member of the US Special Diplomatic Mission in Berne, Switzerland, seeking to promote official terms covering the exchange of prisoners with the Imperial German government.[45]

Sallie took Hunter's advice. In early October, she received a letter from Davis, who informed her that he had "put the Red Cross Headquarters" in Berne to work on securing any information that "could be had concerning [Louis]." However, since Lou was a member of the British Forces, prisoner exchanges had to be conducted based on agreements "between the British and German Governments on that subject."[46] Although still tired and weak from the flu, Sallie felt better and finally had some hope.

However, in mid-October, she received a disturbing letter from Cordelia Hays that included a cable from the Red Cross in Geneva, Switzerland, that simply stated, "Regret inform Lt. Louis Bennett RAF reported dead—writing." Cordelia added that she was still optimistic about Lou, that it said "nothing *really* definite." She reminded Sallie that mistakes had been made before. She and Mary were on their way to visit family in Toronto, Canada, and she would ask "Sir Thomas [and] Lady Tait" how they could trace her son. Cordelia added that she wanted to "ease your heartache."[47]

However, Sallie's world at last came crashing down. At midnight on October 30, Sallie once again picked up the notepad on which she had bared her soul while she battled with influenza. It was, she bitterly declared, "the end of a 'perfect day.'" Postmaster General Burleson sent her a message that he received a cable from the American Military Attaché in London that read, "'Lieutenant Louis Bennett, R.A.F. reported dead—in telegram from Copenhagen dated September 29th, 1918'—No further details are given but should something be received you will be notified." In desperation she wrote, "Can this be the end of my brave boy!" Still clinging to hope, Sallie avowed, "until the Air Ministry confirms it, I will *not* believe it."[48] In gratitude, Sallie sent the postmaster general a blank check to cover his expenses, which he naturally returned.

The next day, Sallie wrote a quick letter to Hunter that she was "nearly crazy with the estate discussion . . . and looking up Louis." She implored him to protect her "best interest" with the estate and to help her "*all* you can." Hunter answered a few days later with a hopeful suggestion that Sallie should write to Pope Benedict XV in Rome and ask him for help in locating Louis, since "they have the greatest [organization] in the world." In fact, Benedict had founded a bureau that not only searched for the missing but also worked to exchange wounded prisoners. Hunter went to school at Notre Dame, and he offered to write to its president and ask for his help with the formalities. Hunter added that the Pope "had located a great many lost soldiers when other means failed."[49]

Shortly thereafter, two letters arrived from the Red Cross that crushed Sallie's remaining hopes. The first letter came from Mr. R. E. Bailey, the director of the Bureau of Prisoners of War of the American Red Cross in Berne, Switzerland. He informed her:

> The Frankfurt German Red Cross has requested us to inform you that Aviator Lieut. Louis Bennett, 40th Squadron Brit. A.F. dropped to his death August 24th, 1918.
>
> His grave is located at the Zivilfriedhof Wavrin Grab 590. They are unable to give any further details.
>
> In complying with the request of the German Red Cross we express to you our deep regret and sympathy.
> R.E. Bailey
> Director Bureau of Prisoners
> Information and Communication[50]

The second letter was from the International Committee of the Red Cross, International Agency for Prisoners of War in Geneva. Expressing their sympathies, they informed Sallie that they learned from a German Red Cross telegram that Lou was reported killed on August 24 and that the International Red Cross was investigating "for the source of their information."[51]

Other correspondence arrived supporting the Red Cross confirmation. Etta LeRougetel forwarded two letters from Major Compston concerning Louis. In the first, he notified Mrs. LeRougetel that he had received an unofficial report, although "fairly reliable," that Louis was dead. Compston surmised that his former pilot had died of his injuries and he advised Etta that he (Compston) had not informed Mrs. Bennett. In his second letter, the major wrote that he had received a cablegram from Mary Hays inquiring about Lieutenant Bennett's status. He asked LeRougetel to "break the sad news to . . . Louis' people." He added, "May God help his Mother to bear their second terrible loss."[52]

Lou's faithful rigger, William Reid, sent Sallie a heartfelt letter from the front on November 16. Besides expressing his sympathies, Reid described the efforts of No. 40 Squadron to obtain information about Lieutenant Bennett from the Germans. Pilots flew over the lines risking hostile fire and dropped inquiries about Louis. These proved fruitless. He told Sallie what they knew and what the pilots in the squadron thought had happened. Reid expressed his hope that at least he would be able to visit his former pilot's grave. Since the fighting had ceased, the government allowed him to carry a camera, and he promised to take a photo of the grave for her if he could find it.[53]

Despite the devastating news, Sallie did not abandon her quest to obtain a passport and go to France herself. Throughout the months of October and November 1918, she maintained correspondence with Franklin Polk, counselor at the US State Department. Through Polk, she tried to obtain a passport and gain confirmation of her son's status. It was Polk who informed Sallie that the Red Cross was the official international agency for determining the status of prisoners of war and thus the agency that she should contact regarding Lou's status. Polk returned a blank check Sallie had sent State Department officials to cover their expenses. On November 18, 1918, the assistant secretary of state officially denied her request for a passport.[54]

Undaunted, Sallie Maxwell Bennett next sought political help in her quest to get to Europe. Unbowed by the death of her husband, the influenza pandemic, the loss of control over his estate that had made her "nearly crazy," and the emotional roller coaster over the disappearance and death of her only son, this remarkable West Virginia mother was not about to be defeated by mere bureaucrats. She turned to Senator Howard Sutherland for his assistance in bypassing the system in order to have her way. Sutherland responded enthusiastically, not only providing information and contacts but also making a "personal appeal to the Passport Division" on her behalf.[55]

However, it appears Sallie was not content to try only one avenue to obtain a passport. Mr. William Brice, a newspaperman from the *Wheeling News Register*, offered her a promising option: Would she agree to "represent the *Wheeling Register*" and "act as correspondent for the *Wheeling Register* in Foreign Service, either England or France?" It is unclear if this request came from inquiries made by Senator Sutherland or by Sallie herself, for Brice follows up his correspondence on December 7 informing her that he did not exactly understand what she wanted and hoped the "new arrangements" would be satisfactory.[56] Nonetheless, on December 27, 1918, Mr. H. Howell from the State Department, acting in Polk's absence, wrote to Sallie informing her that her passport had been issued and sent to New York. The next day, her press credentials approved, Sallie Maxwell Bennett sailed for Great Britain aboard the *Walmer Castle* with nine pieces of luggage.[57] At long last, she was on her way to find her son.

Before she left, she sent Governor Cornwell a set of buttons she had originally given Louis. Cornwell, who had lost a son earlier and regarded young Bennett as such, wrote, "This has touched me more than I can tell you." He promised to return the buttons should Sallie find Louis alive or to wear them in his memory if not. Also before her departure, a letter arrived from Lou's flight commander, Captain George Dixon, who was recovering in hospital. Dixon related his version of Bennett's last combat to Sallie, how her son continued alone to attack German balloons when Landis's machine developed engine problems; how Dixon had hurried to "catch up" to Lou in order to take care of him until he had gained more experience. When Dixon reached the area of her son's last combat, he found no trace of either Bennett or the balloons he had destroyed. Reluctantly, Dixon pointed the nose of his bus westward and returned to base. He thus could only offer her the "bare facts of the heroic death of one of the bravest boys that I ever met" and his sympathy. Perhaps she could find small comfort knowing Lou had been "awarded the Distinguished Flying Cross" for his actions.[58]

Upon arriving in Europe, Sallie began inquiries at once into the location of her son's grave. She gave her address as "American Express, 6 Haymarket, London." During this time, Sallie addressed issues concerning her late son's estate with British authorities. It is unknown if she also learned that the recommendation for his Distinguished Flying Cross (DFC) was not approved. She did inquire after it. As to why it was not approved, the official British story was that Britain did not award the DFC posthumously. That story, of course, is completely false. In September 1918, a DFC was awarded posthumously to a member of Lou's own flight and squadron, Indra Lal "Laddie" Roy, from Calcutta, India. Roy originally joined the Royal Flying Corps in July 1917 as a member of No. 56 Squadron. He was only there a week, apparently without any significant combat experience, when he crashed his S.E. 5a and was injured. He was ordered back to Britain for more training but was pronounced medically unfit to fly. Eventually, he was able to have the decision reversed and was posted to McElroy's "C" flight in No. 40 Squadron on June 19, 1918. He destroyed five German aircraft and drove another five down out of control from July 6 to July 19 before he was shot down in flames over Carvin in a battle with Fokker D VIIs on July 22. He was at the front with No. 40 Squadron for just thirty-three days.[59]

There is some evidence that suggests that when Sallie was first advised of "official" British policy, that it did not award posthumous DFCs, she immediately applied for a Memorial Cross for her son. According to the Harry Creagan Papers at the Canadian National Aviation Museum, however, this request was also denied. Before issuing an award, the RAF made inquiries with the Canadian government regarding Bennett's service record serving with Canadian Forces since Lou first enlisted in Canada. The Canadian Department of Militia responded that Louis Bennett was a deserter from the Canadian Expeditionary Force's 213th Battalion in December 1916. It reported he had enlisted at Camp Borden in September 1916 and deserted when the unit moved to St. Catharines, Ontario in December. The RAF could not issue a decoration to a deserter.[60]

It is unlikely that the British told this to a grieving widow who had also lost a son in combat for the British Empire. One also cannot imagine that Sallie Maxwell Bennett would let such an accusation go unchallenged—especially since it was untrue. Lou was busy at Yale in the fall of 1916 and had not yet decided to join British forces. However, Canadian records show that on September 25, 1916, Louis Bennett from Brooklyn, New York, did indeed enlist in the 213th Battalion and was assigned a regimental service number of 764553. He was born in Philadelphia in 1890 and claimed to have served eight years with the US Army's field artillery. Two bullet wound marks on his left hip were identified in the physical exam as inflicted during that service. Evidence shows that after this Louis Bennett from Brooklyn deserted, he became a fireman in Detroit, Michigan. He registered for the US draft in Detroit on June 5, 1917, the same day Lou registered for the draft in Wheeling. It is clear from the signatures that these were two different men and that the signature on the draft registration card in Detroit matches the Canadian attestation records of the 213th Battalion. Besides having almost identical names, both men also had almost identical service numbers. The Louis Bennett who deserted was born on June 26, 1890, and he was issued the service number 764553. The service number for Louis Bennett Jr. was 264553, only one digit removed from the other, and Lou's service number is erroneously handwritten on top of the attestation paper for the Brooklyn Bennett. It appears Canadian officials based their reply on a case of mistaken identity and that the DFC should have been awarded to Lieutenant Louis Bennett Jr., RAF.[61]

In any event, Sallie received a letter from Major General Sir Harold Ruggles-Brise from the British War Office regarding a decoration for Lieutenant Bennett. Ruggles-Brise was the military secretary of Field Marshal Sir Douglas Haig. Using passive bureaucratic language, the secretary informed her that the War Office had made "full inquiries" into the case of her son. Although his actions at the front "displayed gallantry, his services did not attain to the standard required for the award of a decoration. In these circumstances it is regretted that no further action can be taken in the matter." Ruggles-Brise added that the field marshal extended his sympathies and intended to mention her son in dispatches in future. This, he ultimately did. The bureaucracy thus quietly put to rest the embarrassing situation of having to decorate a hero of the British Empire whom its colonial bureaucracy had (erroneously) labeled a deserter. Lou's mother was politely kept ignorant of the situation.[62]

It is also unclear at this time what information Sallie received regarding her son's death. From Dixon, Compston, and a few others, she learned that on August 24, 1918, after Landis returned to base, Lou pressed on to the vicinity of Provin, a village five miles east of his original patrol area at Haisnes. At about 1300 hours, he attacked a German balloon near Annay. Flying through heavy antiaircraft fire, Bennett destroyed that balloon and attacked and destroyed a second nearer Provin. A British antiaircraft artillery battery reported the two balloons destroyed and that German defenses had brought Lou's plane down in flames. Lou apparently leapt from the burning plane and broke his leg.[63] Beyond that, British officials could not help her.

In December 1918, Sallie introduced the first memorial to her son in the form of a $500 prize through the Aero Club of America to develop a practical airplane parachute. Speaking for the organization, Henry Woodhouse accepted the offer and announced that members of the club would plan the parachute competition. The club's selection committee included Major Thomas S. Baldwin, an Army balloonist who made his first parachute jump in 1895; Congressman Fiorello LaGuardia, the Air Service pilot who led the US Army Air Service (USAAS) detachment in Italy to which Fred Weyerhaeuser was assigned; Brigadier General Frank Lahm, who organized the American First Balloon Group in Europe and served as chief of Air Service, Second US Army; William Thaw, a Pittsburgh native, Yale graduate, ace, and member of the famed Escadrille Lafayette who was probably the first American airman in aerial combat against the Germans; and naval commander John H. Towers, who set an early aviation endurance record in 1911 and helped Trubee Davison establish the Millionaires' Unit as a naval aviation reserve unit. Although balloon observers used parachutes on a regular basis during the war to escape attacks from pursuit aircraft, Woodhouse conceded that parachute use from aircraft "has not become general and the relative merits of different types have not been established." German pilots were issued parachutes late in the war, and many allied airmen wanted the device. Eager inventors such as Joseph T. Gribbin and businessmen such as George McCadden took up the contest's challenge.[64]

Nonetheless, Sallie was not distracted in her quest to recover her son. She remained in London through February 1919, speaking with officials and British pilots who knew Lou. She was awaiting permission to go to France, which she apparently secured by the end of the month. Son-in-law Johnson kept her up-to-date with news of the estate as well as with the business dealings of the West Virginia Aircraft Company. In February, Johnson congratulated her on getting her way with British officials—something he attributed to her management talents, of which he spoke admiringly. Encouraging her, Johnson also asked her to get any advice from British airmen that might help the company. It had started making furniture since the war ended in order to remain solvent, but Johnson saw the potential of aviation and wanted to continue making aircraft and running flying schools. Competition was stiff, since government contracts were canceled and surplus Army aircraft were "dumped" on the market for sale at low prices. Johnson clearly indicated the vital role Louis played in the success and direction of the company, and he clearly missed Lou's counsel. Lady Frost wrote congratulations, citing that "as usual" Sallie had gotten her way and added that she would keep Sallie's plans quiet.[65] What was she up to?

By March 1919, Sallie established herself at the Hôtel de l'Europe in Lille, France, forwarding her mail by American Express in Paris. She received conflicting information as to the location of her son's grave and searched for it at both locations. The Red Cross letter she received from R. E. Bailey placed the grave in the French village of Wavrin, while another Red Cross source put it in Wavre, Belgium. She investigated each location, eventually rejecting Wavre because "no British Air Force had been there." During her search, she once again found herself at war with bureaucrats. The French government opposed removing the remains of the war dead, which infuriated many families and increased their bereavement. It was not until 1920 that the French government finally gave permission to repatriate fallen soldiers, and it was not until the summer of 1922 that the repatriation movement officially began.[66] Their timing was, of course, much too sluggish for Sallie Maxwell Bennett.

She turned to her own countrymen for assistance, and the nearest Americans in France in the spring of 1919 were in the US Army. Sallie enlisted their help to find Louis. Since her press credentials restricted her travel to Britain and France, she had no access to German grave records. However, the US and allied armies had already begun the occupation of Germany. US soldiers traveling into Germany relayed her inquiries to other allied personnel who were in positions to help.[67] Sallie also searched for any Germans who might have witnessed her son's death. She was especially keen to locate the doctor who treated Louis in his last moments and removed his identification bracelet.

Sallie found even greater assistance from a friend closer to home. Major General Mason Patrick of Lewisburg, West Virginia, commanded all remaining USAAS units in Europe during the occupation. Patrick enthusiastically gave Sallie his assistance, designating subordinates to assist her and writing letters on her behalf. Because of his position and access to the Army command structure, Patrick was able to get faster results for her. Several officers were dispatched to look for Lou's grave since there were discrepancies regarding its precise location. Captain Frederick W. Zinn commanded the Graves Commission after the Armistice. The commission's task was to "seek out and identify graves of American flyers fallen in combat." Zinn himself was an aviator. He enlisted in the Foreign Legion and transferred to the Lafayette Flying Corps where he flew Sopwiths. When the United States entered the war, Zinn joined the USAAS and was assigned to headquarters. He oversaw the transfer of American pilots from French squadrons to American units. After the Armistice, Zinn traveled to Berlin and across Germany searching for records. He recovered some $65.89 taken from Lou and held by the Germans. In late March or early April, after a diligent search, Zinn determined that Lou's actual grave number in the German cemetery in Wavrin was 590, which matched the information obtained earlier by the International Red Cross. Zinn also expected to obtain a complete plan of the cemetery and list of graves to help Sallie locate the grave accurately.[68] Such help proved invaluable to her.

Sallie did not completely neglect her duties to the *Wheeling Register* while she searched for Louis. She reported the arrival of Mr. Benedict Crowell, assistant secretary of war, and members of the American aviation mission, which arrived in late May aboard the transport *Mount Vernon*. They arrived for the discussions at Versailles.[69] Sallie also did not neglect her friends and acquaintances. Aware that she was the only mother of a fallen aviator in Europe, Sallie wrote to several other mothers who lost sons and offered to visit their sons' graves. Each of these women wrote heartfelt letters of thanks, that Sallie was taking time out from her quest to honor their sons. Sallie's simple gesture further bonded them together in grief and compassion. Etta Hoskins was one of these mothers who expressed her thanks. Etta was moved by the devastation that Sallie described in her search, especially the difficulties in traveling through the war-torn French countryside. She was genuinely touched by Sallie's effort for each of them despite these difficulties. Etta told Sallie how important it was to her and her husband that Sallie saw their son's grave for them and sent them "a description of the place." She was especially moved that Sallie remembered to put flowers on her son Paul's grave. Hoskins remarked that an Army officer told her to "not even think of" having her own son's body returned to America. She wanted to know Sallie's opinion. In her letters to these mothers, Sallie fervidly urged them to demand that the government keep its promise and bring their fallen sons home. Sallie corresponded with many others. Mrs. Meigs "Lutie" Bland of Kansas City wrote to Sallie about her offer to visit her son's grave and asked her to describe the grave site for the Bland family. Although she felt bitter sorrow over her own loss, she felt Sallie had it much harder with multiple sorrows.[70]

For Walter Kerr and his family, Sallie's investigation into their son's whereabouts brought official confirmation that their son was dead. Not only did Sallie find the grave, but she also sent the official certificate confirming his death. The family never received one from the US government. In gratitude, Kerr sent Sallie a "bill of exchange for 750 francs" for her to erect a fitting memorial. Asking her to command him if she should need anything, Kerr added, "My best wishes and great respect for your bravery in doing all in the memory of your beloved son that you have is most keen."[71]

In early March, Sallie arrived in the village of Wavrin. It was a small village of around three thousand souls, only twelve kilometers (about eight miles) southwest of Lille on the main railway to Bethune. The Germans occupied this little village for three years, and it was close to the front lines at the end of the Great War. On September 29, 1918, the Germans ordered the village inhabitants to leave. On October 3, the German Army began its retreat, but as it retreated, soldiers dynamited the village in a desperate attempt to slow the advance of the allied armies. It proved to be a futile "scorched earth" policy that left the villagers destitute through the winter of 1918–19. The Germans did not even spare the village church. It was to the German field hospital in Wavrin that stretcher-bearers took the wounded Lieutenant Bennett, and it was in Wavrin that he died and was buried.[72]

When Sallie arrived, only a few months had passed since the German Army destroyed the village. The destruction was unlike anything she had ever seen before. The villagers themselves had only recently returned to find their homes in ruins, yet they warmly received her and shared their accounts of her son's combats. They told her that "almost every day a pilot in a single seated machine came from the British lines alone. He would dart down out of the clouds [and] destroy a German balloon." They attributed these attacks to Lieutenant Bennett. Sallie was moved very deeply, and she wrote to Johnson to see if there were estate moneys available to build a memorial chapel there. On March 24, 1919, Johnson wrote back that although it was a bit unusual to dispense moneys before all debts were paid on the estate, funds were indeed available and "can be provided whenever you wish them." He added that Agra thought it was a splendid idea and supported it. Sallie had another good reason to build the chapel for the village. Local townspeople assisted her in finding Louis's grave, which was unmarked without cross or headstone—a reasonable expectation given the circumstances that late in the war. The Germans had not updated their plans of the Wavrin military cemetery since June 1918, and as a consequence, Sallie was unsure exactly which grave belonged to her son. All she had when she arrived was a rough sketch of the cemetery. Marie-Louise Plancque, whose family lived in nearby Don located just north of Provin, wrote to Sallie in January that she visited the young man's grave and placed flowers there.[73]

Despite the sketch and eyewitness information, Sallie wanted to be certain of the grave location and, most importantly, that it contained her son's body. The local parish priest, *Curé* Leon Delannoy, offered to help her. He met with Monsieur Gantois, the village gravedigger, to verify the information. Gantois remembered burying the body of an American aviator on August 24, 1918. He placed the body in grave number 590. He dug only four more graves there before the war ended, so he did not forget. Additionally, a twenty-year-old Frenchwoman substantiated his statement. The Germans employed Madeleine Dallenne as an assistant nursing orderly. She was present as a German doctor treated Bennett's injuries. He was severely injured with a head wound, burns, and broken legs. Bennett was stripped of his uniform and bandaged from his thighs to his head. The doctor ordered Dallenne to remove Lou's boots. Before she could, she told Sallie, Bennett regained consciousness, called out for his parents, and died.[74]

Madeleine Dallenne gave a detailed description of the bandaged body to *Curé* Delannoy and M. Gantois. Sallie therefore asked them to open the grave. She wanted the identity confirmed and the body removed so that she could take it with her back to Weston. All of this, of course, was a violation of French law. Nonetheless, the townspeople of Wavrin helped her circumvent French government officials to remove the body and smuggle Louis Bennett Jr. home. It was important, however, for them to be as vague as possible, especially when writing anything down. Sallie needed an abettor who was both competent and knowledgeable—and one who could keep quiet. Her main accomplice in Wavrin was no less a figure than *Curé* Delannoy. He made the arrangements for the exhumation and to ship the body to another cemetery and grave until Sallie could return home. It was much easier to smuggle the remains out of the country from a grave in a private cemetery than from a military cemetery, where officials and prying eyes might see something.[75] It appears Sallie intended to have Lou buried in Paris, initially at the Cimetière de Malakoff, and later at Cimetière de Montrouge. Sallie first had to be sure of the remains and asked to view the body. On the back of a hotel telegram form, she left specific instructions for Gantois and described features of her living son. Lou had broken his ring finger on the left hand playing football, so the joint was enlarged. He also "had a small scar over [the] right eye. He had good teeth." Of course, after six months in the ground, decomposition was advanced. Facial features would be indistinguishable and probably distorted by then. She also wanted Gantois to cut off several locks of hair "if possible" for her and then restore the grave to look undisturbed.[76]

On Sunday, March 9, 1919, Gantois opened the grave, viewed the body, and cut off the locks of hair. The description of the remains matched Dallenne's account. Lou's "heavy gold ring" was missing, and Madeleine informed *Curé* Delannoy that a German officer had taken the ring, Lou's pocketbooks, and his boots after he had died.[77] Gantois could not remove the body at that time and left the grave site. French authorities were cracking down on gravediggers and undertakers who were removing deceased soldiers all across France. Authorities arrested a transport contractor at Lyons and charged him with "unlawfully removing bodies from graves on the battlefield." As a result, families were finding it almost impossible to contract with gravediggers or undertakers to recover their loved ones. Gantois believed he was possibly being watched. *Curé* Delannoy certainly believed he was.[78]

While Sallie worked clandestinely with *Curé* Delannoy and selected villagers in Wavrin to quietly exhume and remove her son's body, she also corresponded with her network of friends in officialdom to see if she could obtain legitimate approval to do it. Sallie wrote to an old acquaintance from Washington, DC, for help, Elise Jusserand, wife of the French ambassador to the United States. Sallie advised Elise that she wanted "to work quietly, so that if my request should be granted, it may not embarrass the French Government by publicity." Jusserand wrote letters on Sallie's behalf but cautioned her that she feared "nothing can be done." Since that area of France was still under the jurisdiction of the Army, Jusserand asked one of her friends to speak with the military commander of artillery for the Lille sector. Elise also wrote a letter of introduction to André Tardieu, a deputy of President Clemençeau and high commissioner of the Franco-American War Cooperation Commission, whom she told Sallie to contact for advice.[79]

General Patrick also spoke with French authorities on her behalf. He was advised that Sallie should delay removing Lou's remains for the time being. Mme. Jusserand's friend received a similar answer from French military authorities in Lille. The French general graciously offered to provide a car for Sallie so she "had every facility for visiting [her son's] grave," but he emphasized that "she could *not* remove her son's body." Sallie politely thanked her official friends for their help, telling Elise that "words cannot express my gratitude to M. l'Ambassador [and] yourself." Claiming that she was still uncertain of the grave's location, Sallie promised to "let them know what happens."[80]

Having exhausted "official" permissions to exhume the body of her son for burial in Weston, Sallie continued with her clandestine arrangements. Through *Curé* Delannoy, Sallie hired some men to disinter Lou's body in the night. She gave them written instructions that directed them to meet with "*Monsieur le Curé* Leon Delannoy" who would take them to the grave. Everything proceeded successfully. Father Delannoy wrote:

> Dear and Venerable Madam Bennett,
> All right! I have seen your men Tuesday and I have conducted them at the cemetery for showing the grave. We have fixed rendezvous at ten o'clock in night; I was exact, but the men arrived too late and was afraid for attracting attention, because some men had seen me going through, so that I was not able to say a prayer when the body was removed, but I prayed before. I had met the men about twenty past ten o'clock. The grave is very well in order. M. *P'abbé* and Elise and none in people know nothing. I am very happy that everything was done with satisfaction.
> Please you say me if return was good, and if you are satisfied about everything. Receive, if you please, my deep respects.
> L. Delannoy[81]

Although Sallie was successful in removing her son's remains from the military cemetery, she could not find anyone who would risk shipping them out of the country, and she could not do that herself. While she waited, Sallie characteristically took action. Despite ill health, she went back to Britain and sought British governmental assistance in removing Lou's body from France and returning home with it. He had fought with them, after all, she reasoned. However, British officials refused to contradict French policy and did not approve her request. Back in France, Sallie pursued her quest to remove Lou's body, making time for a pleasant visit with General Patrick to express her gratitude. She monitored the construction of the memorial chapel that was being erected in her son's honor in Wavrin. Its dedication ceremony was set for August 24, 1919—the first anniversary of Lou's death.[82]

However, what most consumed her time in France during the summer of 1919 was her tireless zeal in finding, identifying, and visiting the graves of other fallen Americans for their grieving families at home. Sallie saw firsthand the immensity of death and devastation in Europe, and she also experienced the overwhelming grief of mothers across France. Their sorrow was so like her own. At the same time, she received letters from friends back home who had lost their sons, letters from mothers who, like her, voiced their anguish, mothers who, unlike Sallie, were an ocean away and unable to search for their child's grave. She was moved profoundly, and being Sallie Maxwell Bennett, she translated that collective grief into action, taking upon herself the responsibility to find, visit, and photograph each grave and, when possible, to send a precise map of its location to the families.[83]

9

A Job So Sacred

Women, Governments, and Care for the Fallen

Word of Sallie's private quest spread throughout the countryside while she traveled around war-torn France searching for American graves. Eventually, eyewitnesses to Lou's final combat wrote or came forward with their versions of what transpired on that August afternoon in 1918. One of these was Marie-Louise Plancque from Don. Plancque and her family remained during the German occupation, and she voluntarily wrote to Sallie with her account of the battle, how Lou fell "gloriously in the La Bassée sector after having destroyed two German balloons." Plancque described how on Saturday, August 24, 1918, his aircraft came directly from the English lines just after 1300 hours and aggressively attacked the German observation balloon above the village of Provin. The balloon caught fire and its balloonists parachuted to earth while antiaircraft cannon and machine guns opened up. Nonetheless, the pilot continued "his heroic aerial raid with great coolness and courage against a second German balloon a few kilometers from the first near the village of Hantay." The Germans desperately hauled it down, while the allied aircraft followed its descent and attacked it. The balloon suffered numerous hits and deflated as it fell but didn't catch fire.[1]

Plancque continued, "Although not more than a hundred meters above the ground, the intrepid pilot doggedly pursued it despite the easy target he presented to the balloon's machine gun ground defenses. It was probably a machine gun bullet that punctured his fuel tank since the airplane was low to the ground. We saw everything—the aircraft jolt from taking fire and coming down near the balloon over which it had just triumphed." Plancque told

Sallie that the villagers in Hantay knew the exact place where Lou's plane fell, near the Marquillies railroad station, and that a young boy from Hantay saw the crash and the injured brave pilot. She added that the boy knew the pilot was American because his identity papers were not burned. She concluded, "We can also attest, Madame, to the heroic courage of the injured pilot, who earned the admiration of his adversaries and was treated with humanity by the German soldiers, who burned their hands in their rush to pull him out of the burning machine."[2]

When Plancque visited Hantay, she did not meet this boy since he worked elsewhere, but she spoke with his mother who told her that she thought the pilot had burns and a broken leg. Her son knew that the injured pilot was transported to the medical aid station at Marquillies, but he probably only received first aid there because Marquillies was very close to the front and the Germans did not keep the injured there long. His mother believed the pilot was evacuated to a rear area hospital, the closest being in nearby Wavrin. Plancque was uncertain of this because the German Army had forced the citizens of Marquillies to leave.[3]

Sallie knew that Lou was admitted to the Wavrin military hospital through the testimony of Madeleine Dallenne and continued trying to locate the doctor who treated Lou and took his identification disk after he died. She wanted to recover all of his possessions—notebooks, pocketbooks, ring, watch, identity disk, a locket from Agra, and boots. Sallie pressured Madeleine for the information, but Dallenne seemed guarded in what she revealed, claiming that she did not know the Germans who were there or took the items. She found a photo of the hospital staff for Sallie, and Dallenne finally identified a nurse—one she claimed she did not know personally—who took the items.[4] Madeleine told Sallie that the commander of the German hospital was "*Oberatz* Hans Herchenroder [sic]," believed to be a native of Hamburg. She was uncertain if he was present when Lou died. Sallie asked *Curé* Delannoy to speak with Madeleine further and gave him a list of questions that Sallie wanted him to ask her. He agreed to do so but was not happy about it because Dallenne had "not been modest during the war."[5] Through *Curé* Delannoy, Sallie learned that the name of the nurse Dallenne identified in the photo was "Richard" and that he and the other nurses in the photo were sent elsewhere three or four months after Lou's death. The girl knew four of the doctors in the photo but claimed that they weren't the ones that treated Bennett. Sallie made inquiries into Germany through the allied armies, and she eventually received Lou's pocketbooks, identity disk, locket, and broken watch.[6]

Sallie also wanted information on Lou's aircraft and hoped to recover pieces of it. She contacted the Royal Air Force (RAF), but they had no additional information about it since Lou went missing.[7] Plancque, however, thought the Hantay boy might be able to help Sallie in that regard.

Henri Mortelecque was close by when Lou's S.E. 5a (Scouting Experimental) was struck by machine-gun fire and burst into flames. Henri thought the machine was "only fifty meters above the ground" when it was hit. As it fell, he saw the aviator climb out of his burning ship at about 25 meters in altitude and jump clear. The aircraft was engulfed in flames and crashed near the Marquillies rail station and burned almost completely. The Germans could not approach the wreck because ammunition was exploding in the fire. Mortelecque approached to within only a few feet of the aviator "three or four minutes after the terrible fall." A junior German officer and "one or two soldiers" tended the pilot. Henri saw another German—perhaps a medical orderly though not a soldier—set the injured pilot's head on a handkerchief on his knee. The officer stayed until the ambulance and orderly came. The orderly briefly chatted with the pilot in English. Mortelecque could see three breaks in the leg. He also saw a bleeding wound above the left eye. When the medic opened Lou's tunic to allow him to breathe more easily, the boy mistook Lou's brown hair as black, not knowing that it had been singed by the flames. He watched the Germans make a careful inventory of the prisoner's possessions before he was carried away. Resourceful as are most children, Mortelecque managed to come away with "some pieces of wood, iron, and aluminum tubes which were part of the fuselage" of the downed aircraft. Henri took Sallie to the place where Lou's machine fell, and more importantly, where he found her son. He also gave her some of his treasured pieces of Lou's S.E. 5.[8]

Sallie received more answers to her inquiries about the locations of other American grave sites. The British Air Ministry sent her the name of the cemetery near St. Omer where William Dillon was buried, but that was all they knew. The information she received from the Graves Registration Service (GRS) of the US Army's Quartermaster Corps, however, was thorough in its precision. From their correspondence, Sallie received not only the cemetery where the deceased were buried but also the grave number, section number, and plot. They notified her when remains were in transit from temporary battlefield graves to a permanent military cemetery. If unable to give her "definite information as to their location," the GRS at least gave her what little information they had and a point of contact at the permanent cemetery where she ultimately obtained specific information. At times, these even included directions and rail lines to the cemeteries.[9]

Graves of Americans who were buried by allied or hostile armies were noteworthy for incomplete documentation. Painstaking work by Fred Zinn and other soldiers of the GRS often led to the recovery and reburial of these American dead as well. As in the American Civil War, African American troops did much of the work clearing the battlefield of corpses and reinterring the deceased in military cemeteries.[10] As more of the war dead were recovered and entered into the bureaucratic files of the GRS, the ability to locate the "final" resting place of individuals became more accurate. Thus, Sallie could write to her family and friends that she either knew the locations of the graves or had visited them and placed flowers on the "last" resting places of Jarvis Offutt, William Dillon, Tingle W. Culbertson, Stephen Paul Hoskins, William J. Bland, and James E. Miller. She sent their families documents, maps, and photographs.[11]

It may seem ironic that an army that was so woefully unprepared to mobilize, train, produce matériel, and fight the Great War was also the most efficient at finding, documenting, and relocating its war dead. Unlike European armies, for which the Great War was their first total war of the Industrial Revolution, the United States Army had already been baptized in the blood of industrialized warfare during the American Civil War, albeit on a lesser scale than the Great War. Nonetheless, at the time the resulting slaughter from the military technologies and tactics employed during the Civil War stunned soldiers and civilians alike. It proved bloodier than any war in US history with over 700,000 soldier dead and an estimated 50,000 civilian dead. For the American South, it produced an overall mortality rate that exceeded "any country in World War I and that of all but the region between the Rhine and the Volga in World War II." It exceeded the entire 1860 populations of Arkansas or Connecticut. Neither side had anticipated such a death toll. Staggered by the casualty lists of Shiloh, Antietam, Gettysburg, and Cold Harbor, Americans on both sides were aghast by the scale of carnage. After the three days of Gettysburg, for instance, "7,000 slain men and 3,000 dead horses" were scattered around the various sections of the battlefield decaying in the hot summer sun. The resulting stench shrouded the area from early July until the first frost came in October. Collecting and burying the dead after Civil War battles was done with whatever resources were available, what historian Drew Gilpin Faust called "an act of improvisation."[12]

However, the Union Army did not wait for a Shiloh or Gettysburg before it began to identify and bury its war dead. As early as the First Battle of Bull Run (Manassas) in July 1861, the unexpected numbers of casualties forced the Army to take action. In September, the US Army issued General Order 75, which made commanders responsible for interring the dead within their jurisdiction. They also were required to record the deaths on a form and submit it to the office of the adjutant general. Additionally, the orders required them to place headboards on each grave. By 1862, the Army issued further instructions to allocate individual burial plots and headboards, including name and grave numbers, "when practicable." It authorized commanders to select a suitable spot near every battlefield as a cemetery. Also in 1862, Congress passed legislation authorizing the president to permit the War Department to purchase sites for cemeteries, "for the soldiers who shall die in the service of the country."[13]

Since the Revolutionary War, the US Army obviously had experience burying those who died on active duty, even on the frontier where interment duties were left to garrison commanders. However, previous casualty numbers seemed minuscule in comparison with those of the Civil War. In July 1864, Congress enacted a measure that established a new organization to process casualties, designated as a "special graves registration unit." By the time the United States entered the Great War, that unit had become the GRS of the Quartermaster Corps. Since American combat soldiers of World War I carried an identification tag on their persons and Army bureaucracy had a mature processing system, the GRS did efficient, though not perfect, work. European armies were often rediscovering a process that bitter experience had taught Americans a half century before. Nonetheless, the work for all belligerents was still painstakingly difficult given the nature of twentieth-century weapons and the tactics used during the Great War. The GRS had an estimated twenty-four hundred burial sites where US servicemen were reportedly interred. Tens of thousands of graves had been destroyed by fighting before war's end or by farmers after the Armistice who were eager to prepare their fields for the spring planting season. The GRS faced a monumental task.[14]

When war was declared against Germany, the Wilson administration followed the precedent established after the Spanish-American War and the Philippine Insurrection, promising families that it would repatriate the bodies of American soldier dead in the World War as well. However, when reports from the Western Front revealed the grim realities of industrialized warfare in the Great War, many realized that some of the dead could be neither recovered nor identified. Nonetheless, as casualties mounted, administration officials and legislators came under enormous pressure from the families of the fallen to honor the government's commitment and return the soldier dead. Their voices were joined by the lobbying of the Purple Cross, a recently organized association of American funeral directors who, like their Civil War predecessors, sensed a lucrative business opportunity. Secretary Newton Baker rejected the self-interests of the Purple Cross. Although Baker said he had no authority to interfere with "any propaganda" that undertakers used in their lobbying campaign for a congressional bill to force the Army to return the war dead, he emphasized that the War Department would only respond to the wishes of the next of kin. Members of Congress were even more critical of the undertakers' pressure.[15]

The transport and burial of all American soldier dead remained under the professional care of the GRS. When General Pershing voiced concerns that making such efforts while hostilities were still in progress might waste resources and possibly more lives, it was decided to delay the recovery of the war dead until after the fighting stopped. Besides, battlefield conditions were not conducive to collecting or transporting the dead and barely allowed the GRS to identify or decently bury the fallen in temporary graves. Therefore, the decision was not necessarily unacceptable under the circumstances of war.[16]

Sallie was certainly grateful for the information the GRS provided her. Likewise, the families—and especially the mothers—of these slain Americans were thankful for Sallie's exertions on their behalf and wrote her to tell her. "Lutie" Bland wrote, "What a friend you have been . . . there is no use in my saying thank you. Thanks mean nothing. I can only say I am with you in love [and] sympathy [and] sorrow." Lutie was overwhelmed at the "ordeal you have been going through for yourself [and] then for us, the mothers and fathers you have been helping [and] comforting by making them feel there is some one over there who cares." Bland went on to say that her son's widow, Mary Bland, was "nearly heart-broken over the knowledge that she cannot have even that comfort of having William back here."[17] Sallie Maxwell Bennett hoped to change all that.

Unable to find the words to fully express her gratitude, Mrs. J. D. Culbertson expressed her deep appreciation to Sallie, writing, "Oh! Thank you, thank you so much" for the "trouble, painstaking and discomfort of it all and for me!" She and her husband feared that their son's remains were lost, or worse, "possibly some other man was placed in [his] grave." But after receiving the papers Sallie sent them, their fears were put to rest. Culbertson was moved by the "crown of violets and roses fastened to the cross" that Sallie placed at the grave. She also took a photo for the Culbertson family and sent it along with the information.[18]

Sallie's kindnesses were not without precedent. In the midst of civil war, while Union and Confederate armies struggled to locate and identify the dead, grieving families on both sides immediately ventured out to the recent battlefields in order to find and recover their loved ones. Civilians were touched directly by the war, through newspapers, photographs, and lithographs. The telegraph brought news of recent battles quickly and made distant war and death more accessible. For tightly knit nineteenth-century Victorian families, the death of a loved one away from home disrupted their understandings of a "Good Death." It struck at the core of home and family. Because neither army had an adequate system for notifying families of casualties, the bereaved sought to recover the bodies themselves so that they knew their loved ones were "truly dead and had not just been misidentified." Even families of "moderate means" descended on the battlefields to reclaim their loved ones, to encase them in good coffins, and to escort them home. If families could not make the trip, a trusted friend or neighbor went in their stead. Eventually, voluntary organizations funded either by states or by philanthropists stepped in to help fulfill this role. In the North, the Sanitary Commission and the Christian Commission were among those that helped survivors recover their loved ones. In the South, the Central Association of South Carolina and the Louisiana Soldiers' Relief Association played similar roles. The South, however, had not experienced the same abundance of voluntary associations as did the North, and families there relied on individual efforts, not all of which were "philanthropically inclined." Undertakers on both sides made a considerable profit in removing, transporting, and reinterring the dead. It was not uncommon for these families to request that an undertaker "secure a lock of his hair as a memento" before encasing and shipping the remains.[19]

As Kurt Piehler discussed, the American Civil War denoted a change in the way soldier dead were treated. Previously, individual graves were usually reserved for the nobility or officers with the masses of the ranks relegated to a common grave or a common funeral pyre. During the American Civil War, the belief arose that each common soldier must be honored in death. The greatest honor survivors could bestow was to find the dead, identify them if able, and bury them in a designated cemetery with an appropriate monument or headstone. Drew Gilpin Faust agrees. Despite the impersonal, industrialized massed killing the war produced, nineteenth-century Americans addressed the issue within the context of a duty to humanity. It was the mark of civilization to respect human remains. There was also religious justification. Americans emerged from the Second Great Awakening with a renewed vigor for the tenets of Protestant doctrine, which included the belief that the human body faced divine resurrection on the Last Day. This belief placed the human body apart from other matter, demanding "sacred reverence and care." It belonged to the dead individual and was a promise of a "surviving identity" of "immortal selfhood."[20] Therefore, it demanded appropriate rituals and burial.

As the war dragged on, another transformation occurred in attitudes toward the fallen. Soldier dead gradually came to be regarded as martyrs for their side's cause. This was especially true in the South. Each dead soldier became a symbol of the national sacrifice, in effect a Christlike figure, each of whom—like their Redeemer—had been willing to, in the words of one soldier, "sacrifice my life upon the alter [sic] of my country." Etta Hoskins invoked this imagery after the Great War when she sent her thanks to Sallie for enduring hardship to find, decorate and photograph her son Paul's grave. She wrote, "Christ died for others; so did our boys. They gave their all." In this way, these men who could no longer fight the battles gave meaning to the war and its many dead. They were not just dead individuals but part of the collective identity of the nation. It was only fitting and proper to recover these heroes, embalm their bodies, place them in a coffin for shipment home, and bury them in "a marked and honored grave" near their loved ones to give dignity and meaning to their deaths. Nineteenth-century Americans were eager to do this after such a bloody civil war. In the North, clergyman Horace Bushnell tried to explain the massive death and suffering endured by the United States, preaching that the war had changed the understanding of nationhood. From war, he remarked, a new divinely incarnated nation had come at the price of "our acres of dead." Its new role was as a "redeemer nation" with a broader purpose, a "Manifest Destiny" ordained to save the world at large.[21] Just such a nation could make the world "safe for democracy."

Theodore Roosevelt, Woodrow Wilson, and many Yale "heelers" echoed these sentiments to justify America's entry into the war. One American aviator with the British in France noted this characteristic in a newly arrived American division, writing, "These boys certainly have got funny ideas. They think they are crusaders and talk like headlines. They are full of catch-phrases and ideals." Newspapers certainly did their part to indoctrinate the young men. Headlines trumpeted the "romance and adventure of the Civil War" during the fiftieth anniversary celebrations, and George Creel's propaganda fed the flames with embellished, pithy slogans to proselytize the troops.[22]

Not all Americans shared Bushnell's religious convictions at the end of the War of 1861–1865. Indeed, the slaughter of so many by the machinery of the Industrial Revolution had the opposite effect and left them doubting their faith or all religion. Such "modernist" disillusionment foreshadowed the 1914–1918 War. For Union veteran Ambrose Bierce, the "afterlife" that many of his contemporaries sought was simply the grave. After touring the Virginia battlefields, Herman Melville considered the only byproduct of modern warfare as death. There was no glory or inspiration in battle. Men were simply tools of industrialized war—a cog in the machine, to use a modern expression. Walt Whitman, likewise, was in no way a believer like Bushnell. Whitman witnessed the suffering and death of war firsthand. He wrote letters from hospitals to the loved ones of dead and dying soldiers so families would know of their fate. For Whitman, the dead embodied "the majesty and reality of the American common people." They were, therefore, the true justification for the war. He did come to believe, like Bushnell, that the nation owed a debt to its fallen soldiers.[23]

However, the official policy of the federal government toward its soldier dead evolved slowly and only after a period of time. Reports from US Army agents tasked with finding the graves of the fallen throughout the devastated South, of increasing Southern defiance and angry desecration of Union graves shaped this policy. Only gradually did the government realize it had an obligation to the fallen. When the war ended in 1865, only 101,736 of the 359,520 total Union dead were in "permanent recorded graves" as directed by Army regulations and congressional legislation. The Union dead were interred in just twenty-seven new national cemeteries, just over half of the total needed for the scale of dead. In response to public opinion, in July 1865 Quartermaster General Montgomery Meigs ordered all commanders to compile an inventory "of all internments registered during the war" to account for the over 250,000 remaining unburied or hastily buried Union dead. Lack of resources, records, and cooperation from the local white populace left US Army commanders frustrated, and they had to improvise in their efforts. Delay made the bodies vulnerable to further deterioration and made identification less likely. Many soldier dead still lay where they fell on the battlefields of 1864–1865. Factors such as the wooded terrain in areas like the Wilderness or the speed at which commanders transitioned from one battlefield to the next pursuing Grant's "Hard War" strategy, meant that many thousands who were killed in the fighting remained unburied. This was especially true of Confederate dead, who were deliberately left to decay in many cases as a matter of official Union policy. Similarly, the scale of slaughter overwhelmed the infant graves registration units, and procedures for recording graves were often ignored.[24]

More reports from the field arrived that local Southern whites expressed their outrage by mistreating Union graves. Sometimes, farmers plowed the graves under. Near Memphis, Tennessee, a road was built over a Union cemetery. When these conditions became known in the North, the public demanded that the federal government act on its obligation toward its fallen citizen-soldiers who sacrificed their lives in the holy cause of the Republic. In February 1867, Congress passed legislation "to establish and protect national cemeteries." For the first time, the national government assumed responsibility for its soldier dead. Eventually, this became the National Cemetery System. As government intentions became better known, agents searching for the dead received letters and records from the comrades of the fallen who had made lists and drew maps of grave sites during the war. Agents discovered that the combat soldiers were also an "army of record keepers" who only needed to be asked in order to provide them with carefully preserved details of graves and the identities of the occupants. Defying the massive, impersonal industrial carnage that could obliterate a man's identity, veterans kept details of graves in order to preserve the identities and humanity of their fallen brothers in arms. Additionally, Southern freedmen responded to inquiries about the location of Union graves, often at great risk to themselves. Some of these African Americans maintained graves or cemeteries, while others kept the locations hidden from vengeful white Southerners. In this way, War Department agents gathered the remains and identities of the Union dead for the national cemeteries. By 1870, almost 300,000 Union soldiers were recovered and reinterred in some seventy-three national cemeteries.[25]

Ultimately, the National Cemetery System served a twofold purpose. First, these cemeteries fulfilled their traditional role of honoring fallen soldiers—Black and white—of the United States Army. Second, they allowed the federal government to establish a very visible presence across the conquered South. They served "an ideological agenda as a permanent, systematic embodiment of Federal authority within the former Confederacy." Both Northerners and Southerners understood this point. It inspired similar commemoration efforts by Southerners, especially Southern women.[26]

The gradual establishment of the National Cemetery System contrasts markedly with Southern practices for recovering and honoring fallen Confederate soldiers. Southerners, too, worried about the condition of graves and corpses. The official US Army policy of neglecting Confederate dead, as well as desecration of graves by Northerners whose farmers also often disregarded enemy dead and plowed over graves, rankled many Southerners and spurred them to action. As soon as the fighting ended, local communities—generally led by Southern women—established associations to find, identify, rebury, and honor Confederate dead in dignified cemeteries of their own. These local associations shared Southern attitudes and justification for fighting the war, which helped gain support for their cause. Thus, they obtained faster results than the cumbersome bureaucracy of government. The scale of difficulty that they faced was made greater by the fact that they lacked the organization and resources of the US government. Invoking the martyrdom of each soldier for the Confederate cause, Southern women appealed for help. Mrs. William McFarland of the Hollywood Memorial Association of the Ladies of Richmond declared that these soldier dead belonged to the entire South. When they died, she declared, they "left us the guardianship of their graves." It was every Southerner's duty to care for them out of gratitude as much as sorrow. Through skillful organization, these voluntary associations of white Southern women demonstrated a very impressive ability to raise money for their projects through private donations, fundraisers, and state legislatures from the former Confederacy to establish cemeteries for Confederate soldiers throughout the South.[27]

One might thus assume that more effort and care were put into Southern efforts to gather their dead in an honored resting place than were put into Northern ones, which were administered by War Department bureaucracy but this was not the case. Americans from both sides of the conflict approached this duty as sacred work. Brevet Major General J. L. Donaldson, the chief quartermaster for the Military Division of the Tennessee, recognized this important precedent established by the federal government. He circulated a unique set of general orders noted for their uncharacteristically informal, personal tone. Donaldson directed that since "the Government in assuming to perform a work, which belongs as a special right only to kindred and friends of the deceased," War Department's agents must "discharge the duty, with the delicacy and tenderness of near and dear friends." He also distributed an announcement addressed to the "Friends of Deceased Union Soldiers" that invited them to be present during the exhumations of the soldier dead. That way, those still searching for unidentified or missing family members might find them at last. Whenever possible, Americans tried to bring the remains of their loved ones home for burial, and Southerners especially wanted their dead returned from "foreign" soil.[28]

On the surface, it may seem that the actions of Sallie Maxwell Bennett to find and return her son, to exhume the body late at night, and to keep her plans secretive were uniquely American in their precedent. The fact is that during and after the Great War, many people—particularly the French—took similar actions to bring their departed loved ones home. It was one of the tragic features of bereavement from the Great War that linked it to the American Civil War and separated these wars from previous wars. In the 1914–1918 War, the unprecedented scale of modern industrial war and extreme violence on an unprecedented scale—violence of a magnitude that had never been seen before on earth—inflicted horrendous casualties and lasting physical damage as well as terrible psychological damage that is inevitable whenever one is immersed in extreme violence for a protracted period. Amplified since the belligerent powers' global empires drew in soldiers from around the world to fight in their armies, the resulting carnage from the war's violence had a global impact. The casualties, scars, and bereavement emulated the American experience of its Civil War but multiplied it on a global scale. Just as Americans learned in what Sallie called the "War of Secession," families in World War I found that both personal and collective bereavement intensified with the absence of the traditional stages that helped prepare individuals and communities for mourning. Great War soldiers frequently died without the support of close family members. The grieving process in the 1914–1918 War, though, was exacerbated by the reversal of the normal succession from one generation to the next on a huge scale, for it was an entire generation of young men who died in numbers that were unparalleled before 1914–1918.

That which was the most cruel for those "bereaved by the Great War was that they lacked the *bodies* of those who died." One can gain a sense of the acute psychological suffering this caused by the enormous amount of energy that was spent to disinter bodies when "the law did not yet allow one to do so."[29]

The ferocity of total warfare challenged attempts to maintain the identities of the fallen, compounding the psychological fear and pain felt by families. Americans in the Civil War tenaciously searched for loved ones who sometimes seemed to have simply disappeared. Even the relatively less destructive weapons of that war could obliterate entire bodies. After receiving no word from her brother for three months after the Battle of Antietam, one Southern woman corresponded with both Confederate and Union generals hoping that they knew his whereabouts. After three years, she still doggedly pursued the search. Even if families recovered the remains, they needed to be certain that it was indeed that of a loved one. To have the wrong corpse suggested the unspeakable horror that their loved one languished alone in some unknown grave. A half century later, Mrs. J. D. Culbertson shared similar fears with Sallie. Dora Frost found it "distressing to have to give up hope" of finding Louis alive, yet she thought Sallie was still "very fortunate to have had so much information" and *know* that she had found "her brave hero." One of Frost's nephews went missing in October 1914, and it was only as 1919 began that his mother began to give up hope after suffering "untold suspense."[30]

Over the course of the Civil War, soldiers became increasingly careful to carry some identification with them into battle, such as a small inscribed Christian Bible, a metal badge, or letters, so that their remains were easily identified. This tradition carried into the Great War. Lou also wore a small pewter identification disk. In both wars, to have one's identity obliterated struck terror into the hearts of soldiers and civilians alike. Yet the weapons and firepower of the modern age sometimes annihilated the bodies of the dead. This was a concept many civilians unfamiliar with the scale of industrial total warfare could not grasp. After Gettysburg, a Union chaplain walked the battlefield and found "little fragments so as hardly to be recognizable as any part of a man." The theological implications of vaporized bodies were troubling to nineteenth-century Americans. Hence, families searched for their loved ones with tenacity.[31] The destructiveness of modern weapons increased even more substantially during the Great War, which American soldiers quickly learned.

As American fatalities mounted and the logistical problem of recovering and transporting huge numbers of decaying remains became apparent, some in the War Department questioned the administration's repatriation policy. Since each soldier had been required to complete a form with an emergency notification address for next of kin, the War Department was able to send each person named on that form a survey, asking them whether the deceased soldier's remains should be repatriated or buried overseas. After the Armistice, both those who were for and those who were against repatriating the American soldier dead made fervent arguments for their respective positions. Those who argued that the dead should remain overseas believed that they would forever represent the American sacrifice made in the name of democracy. Former president Theodore Roosevelt wrote that he and his wife, Edith, wanted the remains of their son, Quentin, to remain in Europe, because "we have always believed that where the tree falls, let it lay." Others believed that leaving the bodies of American soldiers in Europe represented the nation's emergence as a great world power, a kind of status symbol. Behind closed doors, some officials also expressed concerns about both the expense and practicality of returning thousands of deteriorating bodies from Europe.[32]

They were in the minority, however. More families agreed with Sallie, and it became increasingly clear that the vast majority wanted the government to return their loved ones' remains. Some feared that foreign governments would hold the dead as "hostages" in some future European conflict, forcing the United States to intervene. Others believed Europeans would seek to profit from visits by bereaved families who made "pilgrimages" to the graves of their loved ones in Europe. Most, like Sallie Maxwell Bennett, held that the final decision as to where the deceased were buried belonged to the families, and like their Civil War–era ancestors, the majority of relatives believed that the greatest honor survivors could bestow on their dead was to identify them and bury them in a cemetery at home with an appropriate monument or headstone.[33]

After Armistice Day 1918, most of the bodies rested on the former battlefields or in military cemeteries established nearby. It was only the Americans and the French who "by national law or decree had the right to request that bodies be sent home for private burial," but that did not occur until after the summer of 1922. Significantly, once official bureaucracy approved the measure, nearly 240,000 coffins—slightly over one-third—of the 700,000 identified bodies were repatriated. Nor was Sallie Maxwell Bennett's desire to go to France and find her son's body before the cessation of hostilities extraordinary. Jane Catulle-Mendès, the widow of the poet Catulle Mendès, "used her social connections and contacts to get behind the front lines at the *Chemin des Dames*" in 1917 to retrieve her youngest son's body. She, like Sallie, had the boy disinterred at night. French fathers clandestinely exhumed their sons from the temporary military cemeteries by night, both during and after the war, in defiance of official regulations. Inspired by Sallie's quest, Mary Bland set off for Europe resolved not to come home until she had secured William's remains and brought them with her to the United States.[34]

They followed in the tradition of American women, and particularly Southern women, during what they called the "War of Southern Independence." As historian John R. Neff found, these Southern women likened their efforts to those of the Mother of God. Like Mary, they were "the first at the graves of their beloved dead," even if that meant traveling to distant battlefields where their loved ones were buried "in a far-off, stranger's land."[35]

The process of repatriation was consequently an emotionally wrenching experience for the families. It often was worse after official sanction was authorized. In order to retrieve their sons, husbands, or brothers, many parents, wives, and sisters went through a horrifying experience of disinterring their loved ones' skeletons so that they could be identified. They leveled intense anger at government bureaucrats in the Great War for refusing the reclamation of war dead. One Frenchman spoke for many when he declared, "I can bring back my son on my own, without asking anything of the government." Perhaps government officials thought that the honored dead should remain together as a symbol of their collective struggle, but families "felt that the sacrifice of their children was enough, and now it was time for them to be returned." Lutie Bland, too, felt "bitterly towards our government [and] everyone who has had anything to do with this." She shared her anger with Sallie. Bertha Offutt penned her frustration that the government had not officially notified her that Jarvis's remains had been moved to a "permanent" location "*for France*." She, too, was distraught with the policy toward American soldier dead. Like Sallie, she wanted to bring her son's body back home and wondered "if even that small privilege and consolation will be denied the mothers?"[36]

Sallie encouraged this activism while she waited for the official policy to change. She scrutinized the progress of the Wavrin church and sent out memorial cards with the invitations. Only a month before the dedication ceremony, it hit a snag. She had donated 20,000 francs to construct the building and a small memorial with it, of which materials cost 9,500 francs.

Curé Delannoy wrote to her that the builders were running out of money, and had asked him if she could give more. Sallie was furious. On August 9, she responded that she had sent "*all* the 20,000 francs" that he and "*l'abbé* Dewailly [from the Lille diocese] had assured [her] *that* was the full amount." Sallie opined the local people should give something too, and if they did not have the money, then the workmen should freely work overtime beyond an eight-hour day. She was doing without things herself and thought it unfair that they expected "a stranger to pay *extra* [and] they do nothing."[37]

The problems were worked through eventually, though it appears she donated another 10,000 francs to complete the chapel on time. Exactly a year to the day after Louis was killed in action, the memorial church was dedicated. It was the first one to be erected in that devastated region of France. Sallie invited numerous dignitaries to the dedication ceremony as well as her son's ground crew. The bishop of Arras attended and addressed the gathering. Also in attendance were the lord mayor of Chester and his wife, Dora Frost. They stopped near Ypres on their way to the ceremony, because the mayor's youngest son was buried there. *Curé* Delannoy was happy to receive the guests. The memorial Mass was scheduled for ten o'clock, dinner at noon, and Vespers at three in the afternoon.[38]

While she waited in France, Sallie received more responses from Germany to her inquiries. At last, she received the German death certificate confirming her son had been shot down and died on August 24, 1918. According to the *Kommandeur der Flieger*, he crashed in the Sixth Army zone near Hantay, was taken by German Field Ambulance 25 to Wavrin, and subsequently died from burns. The certificate was sent by the British occupation forces in Cologne and accompanied by a letter from the German Red Cross in Frankfurt.[39]

She also received word from Cologne regarding the doctors who had treated her son in the Wavrin field hospital. Dr. Hans Herchenröder responded that he was indeed at Wavrin during that time period, but he did not recall treating any casualties with severe burns. Such an injury "seldom occurred in our surgical hospital" and as such it "would have been remarkable." He thought perhaps that Sallie should contact the other surgeons, Doctors Renner, Meyer, and Baumgarth, or Surgical Assistant Cauer. He assured her that any "valuable articles" were "handed by our staff to our inspectors" with a report sent to the "Sanitary Department of [the] War Office" in Berlin. Herchenröder categorically denied any allegations that he had taken Lou's ring.

"As [a] royal Prussian Medical Officer I reject such a suspicion very firmly," he protested. He denied Dallenne's claim that he bandaged the wounded aviator "with a girl—apparently the daughter of my French host and hostess, shall be in question."[40] Sallie's quest was still unfulfilled.

Sallie's inquiries into Germany produced a surprise, however. A German lieutenant, who not only had been present when Lou's aircraft was shot down but also had a unique view of the battle and watched Bennett jump from his burning machine, wrote to her. This junior officer "went to him [and] took care of him till the ambulance came." From the village of Grenzhausen near Coblenz, Sallie received an eyewitness account from Emil Merkelbach about her son's last combat. Assuming that the Bennett family would be interested in hearing his description, Merkelbach took this unusual and courageous step to share this very vivid, personal experience with her. In fact, for years after the war, Merkelbach could never shake the memories of that "fatal hour" when he expected to die "from being buried underneath [his balloon's] burning debris."[41]

In Merkelbach's letters, one senses his fear as he watched Bennett's aircraft destroy a neighboring balloon (Bennett's second of the day), turn off target, and point directly at Merkelbach's own balloon. He shared his own desperation as he watched his adversary coming at "terrible speed" to close the distance on his *Drachen*, while his ground crew frantically winched his balloon down in a race against time. Emil told Sallie he marveled at his adversary's "heroic" courage, despite the antiaircraft fire, even as the hostile incendiary bullets surrounded him. Still 50 meters above the ground and too low to parachute to safety, Merkelbach stoically awaited the outcome. Suddenly, he watched the British aircraft erupt in flames—incendiary rounds from his heavy machine-gun defenses had struck the fuel tank. The wounded aircraft banked to the left toward the allied lines as it fell. The allied aviator tried to save himself by jumping from the flaming machine only a few moments before it hit the ground. He landed just some ten meters from the burning wreckage, which came to rest near the railroad station at Marquillies. "Miraculously," Emil Merkelbach was unhurt. He was relieved that "fate" had saved him. Soon after, the German balloonist was on the ground and ran over to the injured pilot. Besides burns and two broken legs, the enemy aviator also had a bullet wound to the left side of the head. Merkelbach had no way of knowing if that wound was caused by his own balloon's defenses or if the allied pilot was struck while attacking the second *Drachen* at Provin before he hurled himself in a final gesture of defiance against his third target, the northernmost balloon at Petite Hantay. However, the German lieutenant found the man unconscious and badly injured, and gave him immediate assistance. He called for a medical orderly and ambulance from his unit to provide proper care. The pilot wore a pewter identification disk, "Louis Bennett, Jr., Weston, W.VA., U.S.A."[42]

Once the injured flier received treatment and was evacuated to the hospital at Wavrin, Merkelbach walked over near the smoldering wreckage and picked up a link of seven machine-gun cartridges that were thrown from the crash of the S.E. 5. He took them "to show [his] wife and children the weapons of war, which nearly dealt out Death to their father." Merkelbach later heard that Bennett died that evening without regaining consciousness. The Germans buried him the next day with full military honors, "in a row with many German and enemy warriors, who shed their lives' blood in France for their Fatherland." As commander of a balloon company, he felt that this was a worthy tribute for such a "heroic enemy." Later, he sent Sallie a map of his sector that showed the position of the two northernmost *Drachen* as well as Lou's flight path and crash site.[43]

No doubt, it was a bittersweet moment for Sallie. At last, she had the "full details" of her son's "last moments." She was moved that German soldiers had buried Louis with full military honors. However, her patience with government bureaucracies was growing thin. During her wait, the French government notified her that she could not remove her son's body until three years had passed. Its aggressive campaign against those who tried to illegally remove the soldier dead had frightened off the undertakers she needed. Others who were without work notified the authorities of those who were transporting the bodies, frustrating Sallie's plans. Without the assistance of an undertaker or shipping agent, there was little else she could do. She wrote to Elise Jusserand to see if there was not some way to circumvent the red tape. Jusserand thought there might be, but it would take a little time. Cordelia Hays offered to write to her brother, who commanded a US Navy cruiser, USS *Charleston*, engaged in ferrying American "doughboys" home from Europe, and she thought perhaps he might be able to likewise transport Lou's body home. Unfortunately, by the time her letters reached her brother, the *Charleston* had finished with the ferry mission and could not help.[44]

As August came to a close, Sallie could be satisfied that she had seen the construction and dedication of the memorial church in Wavrin to completion. She believed that if she only stayed a few more months and applied persistent pressure, she would achieve her goal of returning home with Louis's body—just as she had succeeded in "locating him [and] getting his kit." Unfortunately, letters from home urged her to return so as to address important estate matters. She was not amused, but recognizing the exigency of the situation, Sallie reluctantly prepared to leave France. She presented gifts to *Curé* Delannoy, Marie-Louise Plancque, Madeleine Dallenne, and other townspeople to thank them for their help. These included cassocks to *Curé* Delannoy and *M. l'abbé* Dewailly from the diocese, a necklace from Liberty's in London for Madeleine Dallenne, and a brooch with an American aviator's emblem to Marie-Louise Plancque.[45]

Sallie left for New York aboard the SS *Rotterdam* on August 28 from Boulogne-sur-Mer, still determined to bring Louis home for burial in Weston. She was biding her time, and advised M. Jeanmonod, a Parisian undertaker, to make arrangements to ship the body once the political climate allowed him to do so. He protested that he could not get the authorization papers to remove bodies from "the front" and, therefore, she could not do what she wanted. Sallie was already in a combative mood while she prepared for departure because of the contentious estate matters awaiting her. She rebuked him, "Don't ask permission—I shall get papers in due time." The newspapers told Sallie that public opinion had turned against the government's position on repatriating the bodies.[46]

The contentious estate matters included growing friction between Hunter and Johnson, which developed into a rift.[47] Although she kept pace with financial statements and business matters of the estate from afar, Sallie felt she needed trustworthy counsel.[48] Sallie therefore wrote to her friend Governor Cornwell and asked him to intervene personally in the estate affairs, because she was "having an annoying time" with it. In the meantime, she hoped for a peaceful return voyage.[49] It was not.

A fellow passenger aboard the *Rotterdam* was associate justice of the US Supreme Court Louis D. Brandeis, who was returning to the United States after an unofficial visit to the Holy Land. They arrived in New York late at night on Sunday, September 7, but had to wait to clear customs and immigration the next day before they could dock and disembark. Normally, the process should have been completed by eight o'clock the following morning. However, there were not enough health inspectors aboard for the 1,030 passengers, and two of the inspectors "forgot about the passengers and played a game of chess in a corner of the social hall until they were reminded of the passengers waiting on deck" in the broiling sun. This delayed the process for three hours, resulting in a near riot by the passengers. The angry mob "descended to the dining saloon as a body," confronted the government officials, "and demanded to have their landing cards stamped." One could picture an irate and impatient Sallie Maxwell Bennett inciting the disgruntled crowd to action, though the journalist mentions no names. Eventually, the ship left quarantine and docked in Hoboken, New Jersey, about noon.[50]

Sallie at last returned to the United States after nearly nine months overseas with much on her mind. Besides the unfinished business abroad of returning her son's remains and recovering his ring and boots, she faced lingering estate problems. Sometime after returning home, she was injured in an accident and broke her collar bone, a painful injury that confined her to her apartment. On top of this, Sallie was going deaf. It seemed to her that there was no end to the sorrows and aggravations that continued to build since the spring of 1918, leaving her impatient and irritable. There were bright spots, though. Letters of condolence, thanks, admiration, and respect arrived in the mail praising her achievements—going to France, finding the fallen, sharing her efforts with families and friends, advocating for families, locating her son's grave and building a memorial church in his honor. Emily Campbell lauded her for giving "the greatest gift a woman is capable of—her only son!" Campbell's son returned home from the war in June but was "a perfect wreck and has been ill for weeks." Despite the war's trauma on the living, Campbell saw women like Sallie as role models for society.[51]

Mrs. R. W. Jones from the New York Division of the United Daughters of the Confederacy welcomed Sallie back from her "sad mission abroad." Tributes came from Lou's fellow pilots, like Edward Payne Larrabee, Major Robert Compston, RAF, Colonel T. DeWitt Milling, USAS, and Tubby Ralston.[52]

More good news arrived regarding the estate when Governor Cornwell agreed to intervene on Sallie's behalf after reviewing some of the papers she had sent him. He already decided not to seek a second term in office, and he advised her to avoid "any kind of friction" with the executors until the governor had a chance to talk with her personally. Cornwell was very much concerned that Sallie would "worry 'til [her] health is impaired." It certainly eased her mind to know that her friend, an experienced attorney for the Baltimore and Ohio Railroad, was now acting as her legal counsel. Although estate matters occupied her time for several more months, they became more manageable and less aggravating with Cornwell's help.[53]

Other good news followed. The Aero Club of America had named the winners of the Lieutenant Louis Bennett Jr. memorial parachute competition. President Hawley of the Aero Club considered the contest "very successful" and expressed his gratitude to her for aiding "aeronautics in a very material way."[54] She was pleased to see people respond so warmly to her gifts—both the parachute competition and the small church and memorial in Wavrin.

She still thought the British should do the right thing and award Lou the Distinguished Flying Cross he earned at the cost of his life, a cause that she pursued for the rest of her life. Tubby Ralston agreed with her, adding "he more than deserved the medals he was recommended for." She may have received some consolation or inspiration when she received a letter from Buckingham Palace. The letter from the Privy Purse Office of the British Royal Family informed her that the British sovereign, King George V and his wife, Queen Mary, heard of her loss and expressed their "deep regret" for the death of her son who died "in the service of his Country," expressing "their Majesties [sic] sympathy with you in your sorrow." The letter assured her that their "thoughts have been constantly with you [and] those who have been called upon to endure this exceptional burden and anxiety."[55]

Throughout the autumn and winter, Sallie answered the many letters and cards she received while she waited for an opportunity to bring Lou's body home. She shared details of her son's death to friends and family, and gave Yale her son's biography for the war record it compiled for the Class of 1917. In gratitude for his help in France, she offered to further Mason Patrick's career, proposing to write influential politicians on his behalf. No longer a general officer, he had left the Air Service and returned to the Corps of Engineers. Air Service headlines belonged to the controversial and outspoken William "Billy" Mitchell, who expected to lead that branch after the war and was frustrated when the Army selected an infantryman for the post. Mitchell was caustically critical of the Army and its leadership, including Patrick. Sallie was concerned for Patrick's future, but he graciously declined her offer, joking that he had "never asked for anything yet" and that he was "too old to alter my ways." As for Mitchell, Patrick remarked that he had been his subordinate in France, and although "in some ways he did quite well" and was enthusiastic, Mitchell ultimately was "erratic and not well balanced." Sallie still sent Grace and Mason Patrick a membership to the prestigious Chevy

Chase Club in Maryland as a token of thanks, which was cordially received. Eventually, Patrick was recalled to command the USAS and promoted to major general. He reorganized the Air Service in the 1920s, established a flight test center, promoted international goodwill flights, and was the key figure in the creation of the Air Corps.[56]

Shortly after Sallie blazed the trail, other Americans followed by visiting the European battlefields and cemeteries to find their soldier dead. The Young Men's Christian Association (YMCA) assisted them. The YMCA came overseas with the American Expeditionary Force and remained with the Army of Occupation. The War Department permitted relatives of the fallen to stay in rest huts erected by the YMCA, stating this was "only a continuation of the co-operation and service the YMCA has given the army and civilians in arranging accommodations for their convenience, comfort, and well-being while abroad." The American Legion also supported families by rendering military honors at the funeral services of the returning war dead.[57]

However, in February Sallie received a fright. Mrs. Anna Devera from Chicago arrived in New York aboard the *Britannia* with the body of her son, a US Navy seaman who was mortally wounded aboard ship during the war and buried near Marseilles. Like Sallie, she was unable to obtain official permission to return the body and had great difficulty securing an undertaker. Therefore, Devera applied the "liberal use of her money" in order to bring his remains home, costing her some $2,000. By enlisting the help of the Knights of Columbus (KofC), a Catholic men's fraternal benefits organization, she was able to obtain the necessary transportation permits to return her son to Chicago. The members of the local KofC chapter agreed to help her because, as combat veterans, they believed "that the only person who has a right to say whether a soldier's body should be returned from France is that man's mother."[58]

Sallie was alarmed, in part because Devera "had been *the first* to arrive with her son," but mainly because she went public with it. Sallie read about it in the newspaper, and when she went to the railroad station to speak with Devera, Sallie was stunned to learn that Devera intended "to publish 'her experiences.'" Sallie begged her not to do so and asked her escort, a KofC officer, "to impress upon her the necessity of 'keeping quiet.'" Sallie told her that she would "upset all future plans of other mothers because it would *make* both [the] French [and] U.S. Governments *take notice* [and] forbid this sort of thing." With Lou's body still in France, this was a very serious threat to her plans. Johnson and Agra offered to step in, but Sallie told them not to discuss it and not be like "some people, *á la* Wilson [who] can't keep their mouths shut or a finger out of every pie." She admonished them, "No matter what laws are passed, you must *leave this matter to me until* I 'call for help.'"[59]

Nonetheless, Sallie learned from Devera that at last the French government had relented and allowed Americans to repatriate their dead buried behind the battle zones. Sallie sent Lutie Bland the news, and Lutie forwarded this information to her daughter-in-law in France. Mary Bland in turn confirmed it and made arrangements to return her own husband's body. This was exactly the loophole Sallie wanted. Since she had removed her son's body from the military cemetery in Wavrin, it would be much simpler for her undertaker, M. Jeanmonod, to obtain the necessary papers. He only needed to document that Lou had died and been buried somewhere behind the lines of "natural causes," and then the powers that be would permit the remains to be repatriated. She immediately sent Jeanmonod his orders, and he replied from Paris on March 24 that he had recovered her son's remains and shipped them to New York via Le Havre aboard the SS *France*. Jeanmonod assured her that "everything is done in a very quiet way." On Saturday, April 10, 1920, the remains of Louis Bennett Jr. returned home to the United States at last after seven days at sea. An undertaker, Nathaniel H. Stafford, received them, obtained the transit and burial permit from the State of New York for one Louis Bennett who died in Paris, France, on August 24, 1918, of "natural causes." Stafford shipped the body to Weston where Louis was buried next to his father in Machpelah Cemetery in Lot 82, Space Four, on April 14, 1920.[60]

Secretary of War Newton Baker also did not allow the repatriation debate to become protracted. In 1919, he decided that the War Department must honor its pledge to the American people at the beginning of the war, allowing each family to choose. Baker wrote, "That no body will remain abroad which is desired in this country and that . . . no effort will be spared to accord fitting and tender care to those which, by request of the families concerned, will remain overseas in the Field of Honor." Either way, the dead would be returned or reburied at government expense. Additionally, Baker announced that the War Department was "prepared to furnish transportation from Hoboken to their homes to one relative or friend to accompany the body of each soldier who died abroad and whose body is being returned to this country for interment." Ordinarily, an Army officer accompanied the remains from the port to the hometown, but US Army regulations, shaped by the experience of the Civil War, made provision for a friend or relative of the deceased to accomplish that sacred duty.[61]

Seven out of ten American families chose to repatriate the remains of their loved ones. This required a major effort for the GRS and took several years. By contrast, about thirty-one thousand American families agreed with Theodore Roosevelt that their loved ones should be interred alongside their comrades on the battlefields where they fell. By March 1921, some 14,849 remains were returned home; approximately 500 were at the port of Hoboken, New Jersey, "ready for shipment;" another 3,293 were waiting for shipment in French ports, while 3,577 remained at "concentration points" near the Great War battlefields awaiting transportation to the ports.[62]

This decision to repatriate the remains of the war dead may also reflect Americans' growing isolationist attitude. In contrast to the euphoric, cooperative spirit of victory across the nation in early spring of 1919 in which many Americans favored endorsing the Treaty of Versailles and American membership in the League of Nations, by March 1920 the Senate had rejected the treaty and membership in the League by a vote of 49–35. At home, Americans faced skyrocketing inflation, terrorist bombings, strikes and labor unrest, and, in some cities, violent race riots. Returning American soldiers who went to war embracing Wilson's idealistic rhetoric returned disillusioned by the war and disgusted by the vindictive European powers at Versailles. These veterans helped nurture a growing national conviction that the United States should never again become involved in a European war. Writers of the Lost Generation gave them a voice. Americans in ever increasing numbers turned their backs on Europe and wanted their dead brought home.[63]

After the trauma of the Great War, the influenza pandemic, and the repatriation of thousands of war dead, it is small wonder that families and survivors went to great lengths to permanently remember the fallen. Sallie herself embarked on a campaign to dedicate some twelve memorials recalling her son's sacrifice, generally located in those cities she frequented the most, such as London, New York, Wheeling, and her home in Weston, though the majority of them were in West Virginia.

In Weston, Sallie offered the Bennett family home to the city as a memorial library for her son. In Europe, she visited villages smaller than Weston that had public libraries with reading rooms and frequently a museum. Sallie presented the library to the citizens of Weston in a Christmas letter in December 1921. The people of Weston were very eager to establish a county library, and Sallie challenged their public spirit. Following Andrew Carnegie's model, Sallie based her donation on the stipulation that Weston would raise enough money to endow the library and property, to generate sufficient annual income "for salaries, books and papers, and upkeep." However, due to the region's postwar recession, the endowment was not met. Both the coal and glass industries—the area's two main economic pillars—were hit hard after the war when demand for their products declined. As a result, this region of Appalachia entered an economic downturn that did not abate until World War II.[64]

Sallie convinced the state legislature to pass a measure that authorized county courts to acquire "a suitable site and to erect, equip, and maintain thereon" a war memorial for the World War, and with the backing of the local American Legion post, the county commission, and a charitable organization called the "Friends of the Louis Bennett Public Library," the Bennett home became the Louis Bennett Jr. War Memorial and Public Library.[65] Sallie donated books that Louis had kept as a child for a children's section. Her own library was given as a nucleus for a lending library.[66]

Sallie donated a plaque and silver wreath in St. Paul's Episcopal Church in Weston, where the family attended services. She established the Louis Bennett League to preserve her son's memory, and donated Lewis County airport—known as Louis Bennett Field—as a practical memorial to her son. In New York, Sallie donated a tapestry to St. Thomas Episcopal Church near the choir loft where Louis sang as a child. She gave a statue of George Washington to a Paris museum in Louis's memory and prize money for a poetry contest sponsored by the Poetry Society of Great Britain in honor of Louis.[67]

Sallie celebrated the new year of 1921 with a world tour, visiting Corsica, South Africa, Victoria Falls, New Zealand, and Australia before traveling to Great Britain. After all she endured, Sallie was exhausted and hoped to regain her strength with a relaxing sea voyage. Consequently, Sallie packed up her Manhattan apartment, put her goods in storage, and sailed with an appreciation of a job well done, for while pursuing her own holy quest, she reverently performed similar duties for friends and neighbors who waited an excruciatingly long time for the US government to make good on its prewar pledge to repatriate the war dead. Her persistence on their behalf helped speed the wheels of an obdurate American bureaucracy.[68]

When Sallie erected one of the first war memorials in Europe after the Armistice, she joined a global movement of commemoration and public mourning characteristic of the Great War. By commissioning the other abovementioned memorials, she established herself as one of the more prolific sponsors of memorials. Next, Sallie wanted to give Britain a permanent Louis Bennett Jr. memorial. Once Sallie stepped off the railroad platform in London in 1921 after her world tour, she was about to raise the bar.[69]

10

The Gratitude of All Those Present

Commemoration on the World Stage

Late in the day on Saturday, October 15, 1921, Sallie Maxwell Bennett arrived back in Britain after a long sea voyage from Australia. She braced herself to again do battle with British bureaucrats in order to claim any decorations her son had earned. Despite Britain's reluctance to award Lou's Distinguished Flying Cross, Sallie resolved "to make a memorial in England" for her son "as he had served with the British."[1] When she registered at the Carlton Hotel in London, she had in mind placing a bronze wreath at the Cenotaph in Whitehall, one of Britain's more important war memorials and one of many such monuments erected across Europe.[2] An avid newspaper reader, Sallie undoubtedly combed the British press after attending Sunday Anglican services, where she learned that General of the Armies of the United States John J. Pershing, who commanded the American Expeditionary Force in the war, had also arrived in London to honor Britain's Unknown Warrior with the highest decoration of the United States in a ceremony scheduled for Monday, October 17.

Realizing the importance of the event and that it was "too late to ask for a card" for reserved seating, Sallie decided to attend as part of the crowd. She considered herself "fortunate enough to get in with the general public" while Pershing, on behalf of the United States, presented the Congressional Medal of Honor to Britain's Unknown Warrior at his tomb in Westminster Abbey.[3] As Sallie filed past the tomb in the queue in the West Nave, she noticed that harsh sunlight was falling on it "thro' an *unpainted* window above." Sallie was suddenly inspired to commission a stained glass window so as to soften the glare of the morning sun on the tomb while at the same time commemorating her son. The idea to endow a memorial window came to her "most unexpectedly," almost as if her "dear son's spirit were guiding [her]." She later wrote, "Wouldn't a stained glass window *there*, to guard this tomb be a fitting memorial" for Louis. It would be "a memorial for him among his British friends and include all flying men." On one level, Sallie admitted she was "trying to keep [Louis] from being forgotten." On another level, she wanted to honor "*all* 'the fallen air heroes of the world,' the gift of *one* mother for *all* mothers; a window to typify *Love* of country, *Faith* in the Resur[r]ection, *Hope* of meeting our lost ones again."[4]

Sallie was not the only one present who observed that "it seemed more than mere accident . . . that, just at the beginning of the ceremony, the sun should stream down in its natural gold through a window not yet painted, upon the Union Jack that was spread at the foot of the Unknown Warrior's grave." Pershing, too, remarked that he was overcome by an "overpowering emotion" upon entering the abbey, knowing its ancient walls enshrined the remains of many distinguished figures, most notably the Unknown Warrior who had "unselfishly given their services and their lives."[5]

The years after the Great War certainly witnessed a prodigious commemoration effort. Sallie was by no means alone in her zeal. Some thirty-six thousand monuments were erected in France. They are ubiquitous throughout western Europe. After the Great War began in August 1914, commemoration became an act of citizenship: "To remember was to affirm community, to assert its moral character, and to exclude from it those values, groups, or individuals that placed it under threat." Community gatherings could be secular, religious, or both, but the presiding institutions normally structured the commemoration ceremonies in such a way as to avoid any responsibility for the "enormous collective loss" and cast themselves as "the guardians and protectors of the dead as individuals." Institutions of church and state were represented by an official of the ecclesiastical or state hierarchies appropriate to the occasion. For instance, a village presiding official might be the mayor or parish priest; a government minister or bishop at the departmental or state level; a head of state, archbishop or cardinal bishop at the national level. The themes of commemoration might follow a set pattern: ennobling the dead and the warriors by appealing to "ancient tradition;" highlighting their sacrifice and the community's debt to that sacrifice; or preserving their memory through the community's "unending duty of dedication to some noble communal task." These themes were especially prominent during the war. After 1918, however, British and French ceremonies became more somber affairs. Local mourners, local dignitaries, veterans, and schoolchildren walked in procession to the local war memorial. In Europe—and in America of the 1920s—Great War commemoration followed these classical rubrics: the community gathered together; they assembled at an appropriate place, which was oftentimes the local war memorial (or in France, a monument to the dead); they also congregated at an appropriate time, which was customarily on Armistice Day.[6]

A similar impulse gripped Americans after their Civil War. In both the North and the South, survivors set aside a day of commemoration and mourning to decorate graves and honor the men who died as well as the cause for which they fought. Over time, Confederate Decoration Day and the Union's Memorial Day merged into one US national holiday, which became the proper time to gather at an appropriate place and remember. Historian John Neff explains that the "desire throughout the United States to claim Memorial Day's origin bears eloquent testimony to the importance of the dead in the structure of sectional interpretations of the war and its meanings." It certainly underlined the deep sectional divisions that remained present after the war. Neff disagrees with historians Drew Gilpin Faust and David Blight, who argue that commemoration speeded the reconciliation process of the nation. Rather, Neff argues it perpetuated division because it cemented the relationship between the soldier dead and the survivors. Importantly, it promoted "the cause they championed." The fact remained that they were dead because of enemy action and nothing could ever change that.[7] Citizens of the former Triple Entente held a similar view toward Germany.

Sallie consciously followed the rubrics set by her Southern ancestors after what they called the "War Between the States." Yet she came to personify many of the changes taking place for both the women and the nation in the aftermath of World War I. She considered herself a traditional person from a traditional, affluent Southern family, and after the turmoil of the Great War disrupted her life, she became actively involved in the efforts to memorialize World War I, very much as her Southern ancestors had the Civil War. She gradually emerged as a force that helped shape the identity of the Great War through commemoration.

Sallie followed through with her plan to place a bronze wreath at the World War Cenotaph at Whitehall, London, in November 1921. It was dedicated to Lou's memory as well as to No. 40 Squadron. From Air Marshal Hugh Trenchard, Royal Air Force (RAF) commander, she obtained the names of officers or surviving families of officers who served with her son and wrote to them about the bronze wreath.[8]

Having secured at least one memorial to her son in Britain, Sallie now executed her more ambitious plan for Westminster Abbey so that the British could *never* forget the sacrifice her son had made—and the sacrifices that she and other mothers had likewise made for the empire. Sallie was strategic in selecting this window for her memorial. Light from the morning sun passes through the Royal Flying Corps (RFC) Memorial Window's stained glass onto Britain's Tomb of the Unknown Warrior, where at the burial of an unknown soldier on Armistice Day 1920, Britain's King George V led the mourners. The intent behind the Tomb of the Unknown Warrior was to inter an unidentified soldier's body in a sacred, national space that would serve as *the* site for imperial mourning and remembrance. The Unknown Warrior was chosen from the dead of the original British Expeditionary Force of 1914 so that his remains would be as greatly decayed and as unidentifiable as possible. Four bodies were considered, but one was finally chosen (by lot) and shipped across the English Channel via Royal Navy destroyer before being taken to Westminster Abbey for the ceremony.[9]

What Britain created was "perhaps the first national holy site." It was an immediate success, since more than one-and-a-quarter million mourners slowly filed past the open tomb in the days following the ceremony. What gave the commemoration at the tomb its greatest significance, as the *Spectator* observed, was "that the great symbolic act of allowing an unidentified body to represent all the mighty inarticulate sacrifice of the nation is justified, because all people heartily understand it and approve of it." Yet the glue that bound the people to the act, the paper continued, was that "every bereaved man or woman can say, 'that body may belong to me.'" The soldier in the tomb was therefore less a "personality" and more of "an idealization." This unknown soldier thus appealed to everyone. As an ordinary soldier, veterans groups often claimed him, but so could mothers whose soldier-sons were obliterated from the earth.[10] The concept of a tomb of an unknown soldier was international.

In the United States, the Unknown Soldier buried at Arlington National Cemetery—formerly Robert E. Lee's home seized by the Union Army during the Civil War—was equally embraced by veterans groups and by African

Americans, who identified with him as a symbol of Black service and sacrifice in the war. In many ways, the Tomb of the Unknown Soldier at Arlington was the Great War memorial of the United States for many years, since his war was "the War to End All Wars."[11]

This mass identification with the Unknown Warrior or Unknown Soldier was significant for two reasons: First, the impact of the Industrial Revolution on the Great War was more profound than just its technology, scope, or scale. Soldiers in the trenches were subjected to intense artillery barrages. During World War I, artillery accounted for over 70 percent of all combat casualties. Soldiers were buried alive or completely blown to pieces in these barrages. Thus, for the first time in the history of warfare, "both the number of missing and the number of unidentifiable bodies for all the belligerent parties" reached unprecedented proportions. In France, for instance, *half* of all corpses were in this category. When the British finally finished reburial of their unknown dead in 1938, they had reinterred some 517,000 soldiers that could not be identified.[12]

Nor were aviators spared this fate. Pilots "went missing" over the lines and were often not found for months—if at all. Several months after the Armistice an RAF officer, Lieutenant F. Thomson, wrote to Sallie and mentioned that they only recently found the wreckage of a British plane in a lake that contained the body of "Lt. Malcom of Buenos Aires." Two days after Lou was killed, American pilot George Siebold of the 148th US Pursuit Squadron was shot down in his Sopwith Camel over no-man's-land. He went down in a slow spin, attacked all the way down by *Leutnant* Hermann Frommherz, who continued to pour fire into the Camel until it crashed. German ground troops also fired on Siebold's aircraft. His demise was witnessed by members of the 17th US Pursuit Squadron as well as by a wingman, Jesse Orin Creech, who marked the crash site on his map. It was very unusual for the death of an airman to have so many witnesses who marked the crash site with such precision. Despite this care, pilots from the 148th Squadron flying over the area the next day hoping to find that Siebold had miraculously survived or at least to definitively mark the location of the wreck so the Graves Registration Service could recover the remains, instead found nothing. Most likely, the aircraft was obliterated by artillery fire, though it possibly—but unlikely—was moved. Either way, no trace of Siebold's body or his aircraft was ever found.[13]

Because the scale of unidentified corpses was so vast, it was not uncommon for family, survivors, or communities to have no grave or tomb where they could grieve. The rupture to life produced when the soldier was killed became more intense because the families did not know either the details of his death or his final resting place. This condition "tormented the survivors and made their bereavement almost impossibly difficult." One could visit cemeteries, but a sea of markers identified only as "unknown" greeted the bereaved. Which one, they might well ask, is where my loved one was buried?[14]

Second, what made this inherent need for a communal monument more profound in Britain, specifically, was the War Office decision in 1915 that banned repatriation of the war dead. This decision affected families and communities worldwide. With no dead upon which to focus grief, families had to rely on war memorials in general and the Tomb of the Unknown Warrior specifically as surrogate graves for each bereaved individual to express that grief. Because of the sanctity of the place of honor and the absence of a loved one's grave, commemoration ceremonies acted as substitute funeral services. Hence, loss became something collectively experienced in Britain, intertwining many thousands of private memories in a communal ceremony at the war memorial. The significance of the Unknown Warrior as the only British soldier repatriated from the Continent was that he represented the national community.[15]

Sallie keenly shared the acute pain other mothers were feeling for these missing sons, having also suffered in her agonizing search for Louis. Sallie's letters unmistakably indicate that maternal grief was one of her motives for commissioning the RFC Memorial Window, but she also remembered others whose sense of loss was no less painful. Cordelia Hays wrote to Sallie about Mary's grief. She was in constant mourning since receiving news of Louis. She spoke often of writing a sympathy letter to Sallie but would stop, distracted, and say, "Oh! Mother, I shall wait a little longer." It took her almost a year before she could do so. Cordelia described her daughter as being "very brave," but Mary had changed dramatically.[16] Like millions of other wives and sweethearts around the world, Mary Hays was devastated by the loss of her love in the war and struggled to grapple with the reality of that loss.

Sallie's friend "Bunnie" Burdett likewise tried to live with her grief. In her 1920 Christmas letter, she reflected on how she and Sallie were spending the holidays with their "dear dead." The holidays brought her only depression and sadness. Despite many invitations from family and friends over the Christmas holidays, Burdett planned to dine alone, "as I do on all holidays."[17]

Her sentiments were multiplied across continents. Mass bereavement was central to the proliferation of monuments and commemorative efforts after tragic wars like the Civil War and the Great War.

By participating in the memorialization process, Sallie joined the rest of the populations from the belligerent nations. At the same time, by placing memorials to Louis in Wavrin, Paris, London, New York, and West Virginia, she linked these places of collective bereavement with her own private bereavement, easing her sorrow. Other examples exist that reflect how commemoration at a given place alleviated individual sorrow. At a Verdun museum, a father who lost his son in the battle (and whose body was most likely never found) made a large model of the Arc de Triomphe in Paris. A large portrait of his son filled the space of the arch, the bas-relief showing a helmeted child, gazing intently, leaning on the guard of a sword set in a bouquet of victory laurels. In the background were a Christian cross and sunrays. Thus, the monument or memorial became a unifying focal point for grief.[18]

Unsurprisingly, there were political motives for not repatriating the soldier dead and for the construction of monuments and cemeteries on the fields of battle. G. Kurt Piehler emphasizes this nationalist/political aspect of commemoration. Piehler examines how governments and institutions used memorials, tombs of the unknown, and war cemeteries "to nationalize the war dead and [create] an official memory of this conflict." By making its war dead the central symbol of American power and national identity, US government leaders after the Great War hoped to minimize "divisive ties of class, ethnicity, religion, and region." Simultaneously, they sought to establish a series of American cemeteries and monuments across the former battlefields of Europe that would reflect the "power and prestige" of the United States as a Great Power.[19]

As mentioned previously, the United States did this after the American Civil War, when the federal government established a very visible presence across the conquered South through the establishment of the National Cemetery System. These cemeteries not only fulfilled their traditional role of honoring fallen soldiers of the United States Army but also served "an ideological agenda as a permanent, systematic embodiment of Federal authority within the former Confederacy." This point was understood by both Northerners and Southerners and helped inspire corresponding commemoration efforts by Southerners, especially Southern women. Such symbolism reinforced Northern myths and interpretations of the war's meaning, what historian

John R. Neff calls the "Cause Victorious," the Northern counterpart to the South's "Lost Cause." Neff argues that for the North the Union victory signified the new, happily reunified United States forged in the fires of war and finally void of all sectionalism. Its language and symbolism implied a reconciliation that was in reality decades in coming.[20] Nonetheless, these works were powerful symbols of national identity, and as a Southern woman, Sallie Maxwell Bennett knew this.

Similarly, after World War I, the United States sought to demonstrate its new prestige and identity in world affairs. Piehler argues that this was in part because the United States entered the war late and thus was spared the enormous casualties of the European powers. Europe was also bankrupt and owed billions of dollars to the US government and banking industry.[21] Perhaps more importantly, American leaders still bristled from European attitudes toward American arms. Americans saw attempts to amalgamate US soldiers into European armies as condescending and stung American pride. After the war, Europeans still regarded the United States as having played a subordinate role in the war, thus minimizing American sacrifices. Building an impressive American Cemetery System fulfilled a similar role in Europe as it had in the postbellum American South—a permanent, dignified embodiment of American power in Europe. Eventually, the United States constructed eight such cemeteries in Europe, completed without any scheme of segregation by rank or military division. Only the unknown soldier dead were buried in a separate section to facilitate future identification efforts. Each grave received an individual stone marker, and like the National Cemeteries of the Civil War, appropriate symbolic monuments were added to the landscape. When the Europeans saw the systematic, orderly, and dignified US military cemeteries, they tried to imitate them, and the Europeans also were not above efforts to nationalize the memorialization of the war.[22]

Nationalist identity was intense at times. For instance, at the commemoration of the Tomb of the Unknown Warrior and the unveiling of the Cenotaph in Whitehall, Britain "self-consciously excluded foreign dignitaries, including those of its former allies." Such rabid nationalism almost prevented Pershing's visit and presentation of the Congressional Medal of Honor to Britain's Unknown Warrior. Despite the US ambassador's explanation that the decoration was to "add whatever we can to the imperishable glory won by the deeds of our allies" and "further cement the friendly relations which have so long existed" between Britain and the United States, the

British government refused to acknowledge the offer or schedule a date for the ceremony until it was almost too late and Pershing was to return to the United States. He received approval only four days before he could last possibly present the medal. It seems that Britain's King George V was the problem, since such a gesture by the Americans required a similar gesture by Britain to award its highest decoration, the Victoria Cross, to the Unknown Soldier in Arlington Cemetery. His parochial view was stated diplomatically: "His Majesty considers that to compare the Victoria Cross, the highest military decoration in the world, as an equivalent to the Congress Medal, which has only now been struck and with no history behind it, is to lose sight of all proportion." Not only were the king's remarks boorish, but they were inaccurate, since the Congressional Medal of Honor was created in 1861, merely five years after the creation of the Victoria Cross. Additionally, the Medal of Honor had been baptized in the blood of America's deadliest war.[23] As Sallie Maxwell Bennett discovered, such profound nationalism had not diminished three years after the war, when in October 1921 she proposed the idea of a memorial window to the Air Ministry.

Sallie originally intended for the window to commemorate her son, Louis. However, from her conversations and correspondence with the dean of Westminster Abbey, she came to realize that she could not commemorate him personally. This exclusion may have been due to the false allegations that Lou was a deserter, something of which Sallie was never aware. If she could not so honor her son, she then envisioned an "international window," so that all of Britain's Allies could "feel that [Britain] remembered their services." Both the Air Ministry and the dean objected "on religious grounds to making the memorial of an international character." They urged her to commemorate British airmen, but they did concede she could make it "Anglo-American" if she could secure the permission of the US government.[24]

When Sallie received this official approval in April 1922, she had already waited in Europe for almost six months, delaying her departure for home until the window was completed and dedicated. She expected this process to only take a few months. After the Pershing ceremony in October, she made inquiries at several artistic glass firms and received a promising design by Burlison and Grylls in early November. Despite bureaucratic hurdles and frequent revisions of the design that delayed her objective, Sallie doggedly pursued the issue, in the meantime urging work to go ahead on the window. She rejected waiting for US government approval. Besides her resentment at the government's equivocation on its promise to return American soldier dead, Sallie expressed bitterness about its refusal to accept the West Virginia Flying Corps into the US Air Service (USAS).[25]

Also, Sallie had cleverly found a means by which she could commemorate Louis and his personal identity within the nationalistic memory and identity of the British Empire, with whom he had fought and died. This blending of collective memory and identity with personal memory and identity in war memorials was not unknown, but in the case of the RFC Memorial Window, it is certainly done in a unique way. In order to honor the memory of her son, Sallie had the artist use Louis's image as the model for one of the angels. The face of the angel holding the shield of Faith is the portrait of Louis Bennett Jr. The shield he holds is emblazoned with the Cross of St. George, the national emblem of England, and the central cross on the imperial flag, the Union Jack. This was not the design submitted to British authorities, nor was it printed on the official invitations distributed before the ceremony. In the design submitted, the angel bore a generic face and held the shield of Faith. It was only during the ceremony, when the window was unveiled, that Sallie surprised those present with the existing design.[26]

Louis's identity is artistically anchored in a touching and singular manner. At the lower right-hand corner of the window is the emblem of the West Virginia Flying Corps situated to symmetrically balance the window's design with the RAF/RFC badge and motto on the left. The flying corps design incorporates the State Seal of West Virginia with its motto in Latin, "Montani Semper Liberi" ("Mountaineers are always free"), fixed between a set of wings. Over the seal is a scroll bearing, "W. Va. F. C." Sallie admitted it was Louis Bennett's "own special design" which was embroidered on the tunics of the flying corps personnel. From Sallie's point of view, the seal of a "sovereign" state of the United States in the design satisfied the "Anglo-American" character approved by the Air Ministry. As her son's own design that incorporated the seal of his home state, it identified the window specifically with his memory and allowed Sallie to commemorate her son yet again. Placed in the nave of the Abbey, where its light shone upon the Tomb of the Unknown Warrior, the window also linked the memory of Louis Bennett with *the* site for national mourning and remembrance of the British Empire.[27]

Nationalistic governments weren't the only ones who could create "powerful symbols of identity." Sallie Maxwell Bennett came from a tradition where private individuals did that too. Although the Royal Air Force failed to award Lieutenant Bennett the decoration he had earned, his mother saw to it they could never forget him. She intended to forever link the British war memorial to her son and the state he called home.

Of all the mourners who came there, however, Sallie specifically had in mind all mothers who lost sons in the war. It was "the gift of *one* mother for *all* mothers." Sallie elevated an issue that the war had thrust to the fore—the role of women in commemoration and in society. When the letter came that notified Sallie Maxwell Bennett that Louis had died, she unwillingly joined a sorority of maternal grief on a scale that had never been previously experienced. The war was conceived in a world where men had an official political voice and women did not. A woman's wartime role was—as it had been in the nineteenth century—that "of chief mourners and mediums," to remember the men and make the required sacrifices. These women who did so much for the world's first global total war did not expect to receive monuments. In Europe especially, the Great War reinforced traditional gender stereotypes. These stereotypes, of course, overlooked the mass deportations of women from German-held France, or the violent demonstrations by German women against shortages inflicted by the allied blockade.[28]

Historian Jay Winter describes how in postwar commemoration, unlike prewar Europe, men no longer held a privileged place over women. European women took a more prominent role at the unveiling of war memorials, with a war widow or a mother who lost a son often performing the actual unveiling. This was also done in the aftermath of the American Civil War, as both a further effort to link personal grief with public remembrance and an attempt to reinforce traditional archetype gender roles of sacrifice and mourning. A woman who lost several sons and perhaps her husband unveiled the monument; her loss served to "reiterate ideals," and other mothers (or widows) could associate with someone who had suffered the most. If a mother who had lost so much "could still believe in truth and justice," the reasoning went, so should they all.[29]

The symbolism of having a mother or war widow unveil this commemorative window was part of Sallie's strategy. She suggested it would be fitting to ask Queen Mary to unveil the window "as a *Mother*." Many women who lost sons and husbands also noted the prominence that women were gaining in commemoration ceremonies and agreed with Sallie that they too "gave all" and were justified in their demands that their sons "are not forgotten." Sallie's friend Bunnie Burdett concluded that "women are better than men, and value so highly the communions and the constant prayer" for the souls of their loved ones as well as the commemoration ceremonies. She saw to it that at least five services were celebrated for her son in Jerusalem at the Basilica of the Holy Sepulchre.[30]

Despite the efforts to perpetuate gender stereotypes, industrial scale total wars like the Civil War and the First World War eroded the fiction that war was solely a masculine undertaking. Total war required full mobilization of a nation's resources, and during the Great War women's labor gained importance as women replaced men in many factories and offices. Women joined the military as nurses, operated military telephone switchboards, served as Young Men's Christian Association girls and performed other support functions. Even in the domestic sphere, the wartime role of women changed as they were called upon "to conserve food, clothing, and fuel as well as to serve as volunteers" in various organizations. This was especially true in the United States. Although the federal government expected women to mourn their dead, it also did not want that bereavement to disrupt the war effort. The Great War in America saw the blending of the women's suffrage movement with the war effort. These forces merged to force American society—and especially American women—to "define an identity for women as citizens." Because of their war experiences, many American women, including mothers, defined new civic roles for themselves. They demanded and expected to play a greater public part in society. Out of the sheer necessity of total war, they embraced tasks that were historically held by men. World War I thus expanded both roles and opportunities for women, although this was often temporary. It also further divided American women between those who favored this path and those who followed the more traditional ways. Historian David Blight found seeds of this division in the years after the Civil War too, when Southern women who were actively engaged in memorial work began using those energies in the struggle against some of the obstacles to women's rights. One woman in particular, Janet Randolph, declared that "I am not a suffragist" but that injustices toward women would "cause the women of Virginia to become suffragists."[31] This division became conspicuous at the turn of the century, when women's public roles were being redefined because women had assumed leadership roles in various causes—from commemoration to education reform and to suffrage.[32]

The influence of the American Civil War cannot be ignored when one studies its impact on the roles of women after World War I. Since the dawn of the Republic, American women followed the traditional gender divisions of duties—men were expected to fight and women were expected to mourn the dead and preserve their memories, just as women elsewhere were expected to do. After the trauma of the American Civil War, however, women began to assume a leadership role promoting commemoration. Although women's groups were active in both the North and the South, they became "more central to the commemoration of the Confederacy." During the war, commemoration in the South was identified with patriotism. White Southern women embraced it as their duty, and that role endured long after the war.[33] When the war ended, women expanded on this duty. As historian Lee Ann Whites found, the horrific mortality rate the war caused in the South eroded the traditional base of gender hierarchy in Southern families. With more and more Southern men serving in the military or becoming casualties, Southern women were forced to take a more active role in the community or the workplace. By war's end, Southern men also found themselves unable to actively engage in "treasonous" activities, such as honoring the defunct Confederacy and its soldiers, since they were "under parole and were pledged not to aid or encourage any movement of that kind." Therefore, Southern women who were not under any kind of parole aggressively accepted the mantle of honoring both the Confederacy and their soldier dead "with a vengeance." Known as "ladies' memorial associations," they organized parties, plays, and fetes to raise monies for their cause. Eventually, these became organized women's associations.[34]

Ladies' memorial associations that formed throughout the South after the Civil War assumed a crucial responsibility for trying to ease the Southern sense of loss and helped Southerners regain hope in the future. Accordingly, they perpetuated the explanation that the South only lost the war because the North possessed overwhelming numbers and industrial supremacy. Therefore, Southern men suffered no shame in defeat. This idea was known as the Lost Cause, and ladies' memorial associations shaped its communal memory and provided cultural expression and meaning of the war. Responding to the federal government's National Cemetery System, Southern women ensured that Confederate dead also received a proper burial and were honored with the appropriate symbols of the Lost Cause. Other women's groups, such as the United Daughters of the Confederacy (UDC), a group that Sallie Maxwell Bennett joined, actively preserved Lost Cause memory by lobbying for monuments, organizing fundraisers for them, controlling their construction, and participating in the unveiling ceremonies. Sometimes, the galleries of state legislatures were packed with UDC members as a show of "force" that reacted vocally to any opposition to their ends.[35]

As we have seen, commemoration is not a phenomenon unique to the United States or the American South. However, commemoration did acquire some unique qualities there. In contrast to most memorials, in the United States commemoration was the primary concern of voluntary associations and not governmental authorities. Private individuals or groups commissioned most monuments; thus, it was a decentralized process. President Ulysses S. Grant observed that in the South, "memorials are the chief business of the United Daughters of the Confederacy."[36]

Such activity was not lost on Sallie Maxwell Bennett, who already identified with her Confederate heritage and applied to have Lou registered on the Daughters' role of honor. In the face of obstructive government bureaucracies, she identified even more strongly with it. In her correspondence to the dean at Westminster Abbey, she clearly links her son with his Confederate ancestry, particularly his relationship to its revered general, Thomas "Stonewall" Jackson, citing that the UDC awarded Lou their Cross of Service for those "men of lineal Confederate descent who served honorably in the World War."[37] She continued to do so with each of her son's memorials. Civil War commemoration peaked in the United States between 1903 and 1914, with a number of monuments unveiled during the First World War. The UDC may have had as many as 100,000 members at this time. For many Americans of the period, Civil War commemoration was still a fresh experience when the guns ceased on November 11, 1918. This was the commemorative tradition Sallie knew.[38]

Southern women of property who promoted the "history" of the "Lost Cause" through monuments and commemoration were not the only group of women seeking to define American nationalism or identity between the Civil War and the Great War. Historian Francesca Morgan studied the nationalist vision of divergent women's voluntary organizations including the UDC as well as the Woman's Relief Corps (WRC), the Daughters of the American Revolution (DAR), and the National Association of Colored Women (NACW). Despite the fact that these women's groups acted separately with often disparate ideas, they should be studied together, Morgan argues, because each of these dissimilar organizations shared the desire to inspire a conviction in their countrymen that they were part of an American nation called the United States, to which "they imparted a national past and a national destiny." Nonetheless, their respective visions of this American national identity were as distinct as their backgrounds. At one extreme, women expressed a nationalism that extended beyond their households to the greater community, conveying a vision that encouraged political activism and the woman's role in nation building. Like Sallie's friend Bunnie Burdett, these women nationalists regarded women as morally superior to men and therefore uniquely qualified by their "cultural authority" to direct the commemoration of the war dead.[39]

African American clubwomen argued that their nation and their country were identical, a position that eventually became fundamental in the Civil Rights Movement. On one hand, these clubwoman took a contrary stand to the position of white America and of white ladies' memorial clubs that identified nation with race. On the other hand, African American women seemed to reject the concept of the "twoness" experience in their own community, as W. E. B. Du Bois articulated as being both "Negro" and "American." Rather, groups like the NACW returned to the Reconstruction-era idea of nation based on the XIV Amendment, where birth on American soil established one's national citizenship. As an auxiliary to the organized Union Civil War veterans, the WRC focused on national patriotism. It promoted Memorial Day ceremonies, performed charity work in the veterans' community, put the national flag in school classrooms, commemorated the Union dead, and cemented its vision of patriotism and nationalism through allegiance to the flag. At another extreme were women who expressed nationalism more conventionally, honoring their historical fertility role as mothers (actual or potential). As mothers, they had an obligation to society to raise their children as solid citizens of the national community and sacrifice their sons to that national community if necessary. Rather than demean the role of women, these more traditional groups still sought to uplift women themselves and others through character and patriotism. Their sons' sacrifices in battle on the altar of the nation were for them the "highest form of patriotism" and tacitly reinforced the official exclusion of women from voting and military service and therefore full citizenship.[40]

Sallie enthusiastically embraced the traditional role to commemorate the fallen, drawing from a heritage where private individuals bore the greatest burden of memorialization. However, a study of any memorial is often less about those remembered than the individual or individuals who commissioned it. Historian Thomas Brown observed, "The power to install and dedicate a monument implied authority to shape the public realm and define the conduct that deserved admiration."[41] The significance of the memorial or monument, therefore, depended on the sponsors. Nation-states did not hesitate to employ memorialization to exert their national or imperial power and prestige.

Neither did Sallie Maxwell Bennett. By commissioning the RFC Memorial Window, she similarly intended to both "shape the public realm and define the conduct that deserved admiration" toward her son and his brother airmen. She succeeded: first, dedicating a memorial to them and second, utilizing the symbol of the West Virginia Flying Corps at the "first national holy site" of the British Empire to secure Louis Bennett Jr. and his home state to its collective memory. Finally, she was able to overcome the intense nationalistic bias of the imperial bureaucracy to do it. Her actions were not just those of a bereaved mother desperately seeking to remember her son and finding meaning for his death, although her grief was truly genuine. She clearly intended to influence the imperial bureaucracy to achieve her goals.

Sallie Maxwell Bennett is also representative of the erosion of gender stereotypes accelerated by the First World War and the changing identity for women as citizens. She took a leading role in establishing those dozen memorials to Louis in France, Britain, and the United States. She sought to increase the prestige of other mothers who lost sons. Beginning with the window in Westminster Abbey, her public monuments were subsequently designated as a "gift of *one* mother for *all* mothers." After each commemoration ceremony, Sallie gained prominence in the community including at the national level. In 1924, she was selected as an alternate delegate to the Democratic National Convention. After being notified by Cordell Hull, chairman of the Democratic National Committee of her nomination, she wrote presidential candidate John W. Davis in disbelief and asked him if she (a woman) really was an alternate. Indeed she was, and although some of her duties included sponsoring teas and luncheons for other delegates with Mrs. Davis, party officials asked for her help identifying important local party members or influential citizens that might support their candidate.[42] Through these commemorative monuments, gifts to all mothers, she helped define the conduct that deserved admiration. As she wrote the Air Ministry, "these boys *gave all* and we, who lost them—*gave all* and I want the world to feel that they did not die in vain."[43]

At noon on Friday, May 26, 1922, Herbert E. Ryle, the dean of Westminster Abbey, accepted a memorial window dedicated to the "memory of officers and men of the British flying services who fell in the Great War, 1914–1918." Presented by the Secretary of State for Air the Honorable Captain Frederick Edward Guest, the memorial window overlooked Britain's Tomb of the Unknown Warrior in the Nave of Westminster Abbey. Unlike other public monuments in Britain, which historian Thomas Laqueur described as "little more than venues for names" no matter how imposing they appeared, the RFC Memorial Window was unique in that it embodied both public and private commemorative characteristics.[44]

As one might expect, the dedication ceremony of the Bennett window at Westminster Abbey in May 1922 followed the conventional precepts of public commemoration, serving as a fair example of a combined religious and civil patriotic commemorative ceremony. Dignitaries in attendance included Dean Ryle of Westminster Abbey; Frederick Guest, the secretary of state for air; Lord Gorell, the undersecretary for air; Ambassador and Mrs. Harvey, representing the United States; Air Chief Marshal Sir Hugh Trenchard, commander of the RAF; General J. E. B. Seeley, a member of Parliament; and representatives of the US, French, and wartime allied air services. The congregation included Sallie Maxwell Bennett and other "American and British mothers, dressed in black to show their grief." While the community gathered, the Central Band of the Royal Air Force played a selection of music that included works from Mendelssohn, Bach, Grieg, and Handel. At noon, the ceremony proper began, and they played the hymn "The Supreme Sacrifice" by John S. Arkwright, which was followed by an opening prayer led by the abbey's precentor. After the assembly recited several prayers, including the Lord's Prayer and an anthem, Frederick Guest asked the dean to accept the RFC Memorial Window with some brief remarks of tribute to the donor.[45]

The dean gratefully accepted the gift of the window for the abbey, saying that it "would remain among the Abbey's most cherished possessions." He also found it "peculiarly fitting we think, that this window which is to commemorate these men who fell, and that it should look down on the grave of the Unknown Warrior in memory of common sacrifice." The dean closed his remarks adding, "So far as possible we mean to keep the window in good condition and repairs. We are not going to be unmindful of the great generosity of the donor, whose name does not appear but who has the gratitude of all those present."[46]

Dean Ryle then recited a sixteenth-century prayer that was described as the "keynote of the service." The assemblage then sang the hymn "O God, Our Help in Ages Past." After the blessing, the Order of Service concluded with a bugler playing "The Last Post." The ceremony concluded with the RAF band playing the British national anthem, "God Save the King," and the congregation left the church to Sir Edward Elgar's "Imperial March."[47]

Although brief, the dean's remarks echoed the standard formula: commemoration of the dead, their sacrifice and the promise of preserving their memory for the future. The *Paris Herald* observed, "The service was simple but moving," and paid tribute to the memorial's future role, as "for years to come, the inscription on the grave of the Unknown Warrior in Westminster Abbey will be read by the light that streams through the window bearing the arms of the American [sic] and British air forces."[48] Frederick Guest described it as an "impressive dedication service" for "a memorial to the deep spirit of patriotism and self-sacrifice exhibited by British airmen in the war." The *Washington Post* likewise wrote that the "permanent memorial" given by "Mrs. Louis Bennett of Wheeling, W. Va." to those "who died in the air service of the great war" were honored "with impressive services" of commemoration. The ceremony received the attention of "every American news agency and photographic agency . . . together with about 200 British and Dominion papers."[49] Sallie also received correspondence from the French ambassador to the United States regarding the event.

The design of the RFC Memorial Window in Westminster Abbey reflects the desire to ennoble and glorify the fallen airmen, while its location in the abbey's nave above the Tomb of the Unknown Warrior situates it in a fitting place for mourning. Designed by T. Harry Grylls of Burlison and Grylls, the window is in three sections. The theme is appropriately "flying men and wings," with Saint Michael the Archangel—patron saint of airmen—in the top section trampling a devil angel. In the lower sections, four large angels "hold the breastplate of Righteousness, the sword of the Spirit, the helmet of Salvation and the shield of Faith." The prophets Isaiah and Ezekiel flank the design, while quotes from each prophet fill the scrolls that traverse the window ("They that wait upon the Lord shall renew their strength, they shall mount up with wings as eagles" and "I heard also the noise of the wings of the living creatures as they touched one another"). At the base, an inscription reads: "To the Glory of God and in proud and thankful memory of those members of the British Flying Corps who fell in the Great War 1914–1918."[50]

She had done it. Sallie Maxwell Bennett had at last triumphed over the imperial bureaucracy that refused to honor her son with the decoration he had earned at the cost of his life. What she had in mind next was something more along the lines of her UDC heritage that would be perpetual and inspirational—a statue in the United States. But equally important, she had to erect the monument in the right place. It is through her efforts to build this last monument to her son, *The Aviator* statue, that Sallie tried to cement the legacy of Louis Bennett Jr. and thus ensure he did not "die in vain." She did this by seeking to find a place in the United States where his memory would be preserved and perpetuated as she had done in Europe, again linking the importance of a war memorial and place so as to convey the meaning of his life and death in the war for future ages. Not long after returning from the dedication of the RFC Memorial Window in Westminster Abbey, Sallie contemplated putting this memorial for Lou at his alma mater, Yale. She had in mind a statue that would catch the "spirit" of sacrifice of the war class of Yale, the Class of 1917. Therefore, in August 1922, Sallie traveled to New Haven to offer the university a war memorial to its treasurer, George Parmly Day. She proposed to erect the monument in the "circle at Vanderbilt Hall . . . because the Class of 1917 lived there," and from Vanderbilt the class "left for service." This location followed her desires to link her son's sacrifice overseas with those places unique to him. Day, however, was out of town and unable to answer her until late September.[51]

In the meantime, Sallie searched for an acceptable sculptor who could create a statue that would both be "a work of art" and still "perpetuate the spirit of service" that Louis had displayed. As a member of the National Association of Women Painters and Sculptors, Sallie did not just appreciate art but was keenly aware of the latest trends and artists. She frequented the National Arts Club at 15 Gramercy Park in Manhattan. She had seen some of the statues that other individuals had erected to honor American servicemen from the Great War, and she was disturbed by the inaccuracy of their uniforms. Sallie viewed this as a serious departure from tradition, asserting that monuments to Civil War soldiers "of both armies" correctly portrayed their full uniforms. She wanted to "perpetuate the World War uniform" and depict Lou's figure wearing "the full aviator equipment." Her idea for the monument was a statue with "the figure surmounting a granite pedestal with [an] inscription" to remind Yale heelers trying to prove their sand "of the heroism of 'The Class of 1917.'" It would also serve as a "place where the mothers, wives [and] families of fallen aviators" would see it, mourn, and perform the appropriate rituals of commemoration.[52]

She found a promising artist in Henry Augustus Lukeman. Lukeman was born in Richmond, Virginia, in 1871. He studied at the National Academy of Design in New York and continued at L'École des Beaux-Art in Paris. Lukeman later created the bronze statue of Jefferson Davis in the National Statuary Hall Collection in the US Capitol, given in 1931 by the State of Mississippi. He was commissioned to carve the Confederate Memorial at Stone Mountain, Georgia, replacing Gutzon Borglum because, in Sallie's view, as a Southerner Lukeman "put patriotism before artistic ego." Borglum argued with the UDC memorial's association, which led to him being fired. He is most known for his sculpture on Mount Rushmore. Lukeman had a studio in New York City, where Sallie no doubt paid him a call. One of Lukeman's works that caught Sallie's eye was the North Carolina monument to Confederate women in Raleigh, a work of art that captured both the accuracy of clothing and the "spirit" Sallie was seeking. It was commissioned by a Confederate veteran, Colonel Ashley Horne, and dedicated on June 10, 1914. Horne wanted to build the monument because, as a "soldier of Lee's Army for four years and seeing the work that the women of my State did in carrying food and clothing," he believed that Confederate women also should be remembered.[53]

The statue itself depicts a careworn Southern grandmother attired in an antebellum dress of her youth, reading from a book to her grandson of "the heroic story of that tragic four years" of the "War for Southern Independence." The boy, dressed in postbellum clothing, holds his deceased father's sword, gazing ahead into the distance. Although it stimulates many questions, the statue communicates Horne's explanation of the cultural role of Confederate women by passing on the "true history" of the Confederacy. Two bas-reliefs on the monument's base commemorate the traditional and "sacred" roles of women as mothers. In the first, a Southern woman raises an arm and sends soldiers off to war. In the second, a Southern woman tenderly kisses a returning survivor, while another Southern matron receives the corpse of a son sacrificed in battle.[54]

When Lukeman showed Sallie *The Aviator* design, she knew that she had found her artist. Sallie, characteristically, immediately put her plans in motion. Yale officials were less enthusiastic. At first, Sallie was told that the campus was too small for the monument. She persisted. Claiming they needed Vanderbilt circle for recreation space, the Yale monuments committee next asked Sallie to "give a memorial gate opposite Harkness Hall." She declined since Lou's class "knew *that* building not at all." Appealing to her artistic nature, the committee offered that the site was more aesthetically pleasing, but since it was not "properly placed" and had no linkage to the Class of 1917 or her son, Sallie rejected it.[55]

Lukeman suggested the nation's capital as a possible location for his work. He of course wanted his art prominently displayed where it could be seen by large numbers of people, such as in front of the State, War and Navy Building—an appropriate place. Like the RFC Memorial Window in Britain, Lukeman's statue would be Sallie's gift to the United States representing fallen aviators from all branches of the Armed Forces. Sallie agreed to consider it and wrote to Major General Patrick about placing the memorial there. Patrick thought the idea a good one and offered to help.[56]

About this time, Edward Stifel from Wheeling came to visit Sallie in New York. He learned about Sallie's idea and wanted to convince her to erect the monument in Wheeling.[57] Stifel was a prominent businessman who was assisting a local private school, Linsly Institute, in its Second Century Fund Drive Campaign. The school, which is the oldest college preparatory school west of the Alleghenies, was founded by Noah Linsly and had been part of the Wheeling community since 1814. The Linsly Board of Trustees wanted the school to expand in its second century of existence in order to be relevant in the modern age. They launched the Linsly Campaign in 1924 to raise $400,000 in order to move the school from downtown Wheeling to a new campus location at Thedah Place. The new campus was more centrally located in the expanding greater Wheeling area, situated along Wheeling Creek and the National Road. It was only fifteen minutes by streetcar or ten minutes by automobile from downtown, conveniently located for many of the growing affluent neighborhoods that surrounded Thedah Place. The board wanted the school to grow with the city—and the nation. The Linsly Campaign sought to add an engineering junior college, the Linsly Technical Institute, to the existing school in order to prepare Linsly graduates for the escalating new technologies of the modern era with "the latest scientific equipment in the laboratories."[58]

Stifel believed that the statue was symbolic of the new age of technology and the spirit of service the age required. He was convinced it was the perfect centerpiece to the new campus because, Stifel told Sallie, "your son Louis was well known and highly regarded by Wheeling people, not only on account of his family connections, his spirit and his brave deeds, but also on account of the part he took in establishing an aviation field, an airplane plant, and an aviation corps in Wheeling for the United States when it was so badly needed." Although Stifel was persuasive, she had already agreed to try the Washington, DC, location but refrained from dismissing Stifel's offer outright. Stifel returned home and immediately contacted two other prominent Wheeling men, Lee C. Paull and Carl O. Schmidt, to marshal support to place the monument that was now being called *The Aviator* on the grounds of the new Linsly campus.[59]

Through Mason Patrick's auspices, Sallie's proposal was proceeding to place *The Aviator* on the "pavement in the sunken garden on the north side of the State, War, and Navy Building, or on the terrace on the south side of the same building." Patrick recommended that Sallie write to Lieutenant Colonel C. O. Sherrill of the Army Corps of Engineers, who was responsible for public buildings and grounds in the nation's capital. Sherrill thought it "an excellent site" and advanced the proposal to the Commission of Fine Arts. The commission, however, "unanimously disapproved placing the Aviator Memorial in that location" claiming the scale was not aesthetically desirable. Instead, they suggested a more appropriate site was Bolling Field, the USAS airfield south of Washington along the Potomac.[60]

General Patrick told Sallie that Bolling was isolated and "difficult to access." Only USAS personnel would normally view the statue. Patrick wrote, "Under no circumstances would I recommend this field as a site." Sherrill, who also sympathized with Sallie, recommended that she seek congressional help. They could pass a bill that would identify a location "entirely satisfactory to you and to which no objection from an artistic standpoint can be furnished." Sallie naturally enlisted Patrick's help. He was only too happy to assist her and wrote to his superiors in the War Department suggesting that they join with the Navy Department to request "the desired legislation to enable the Memorial to be erected." However, the next day, a dejected Patrick wrote to her to say that the assistant secretary of war had ordered that neither Patrick nor the War Department were to seek this legislation, although the assistant secretary "approves the idea in general." Patrick wrote to apologize, "in which I have failed you" despite doing "all that I could under the circumstances."[61]

Undoubtedly, the assistant secretary's decision was a result of an interservice political brouhaha over just who should control military aviation in the United States. In an effort to modernize American military air power, in late 1923 Patrick attempted to secure government support for a new aviation policy whereby the Army and Navy would coordinate their aviation requirements, including a single congressional appropriation for all military aviation. The Army, naturally, would get the larger share of it. A report was approved by the Army's Lassiter Board and forwarded to the Joint Board. Patrick hoped this change might improve, modernize, and synchronize military aviation development in the United States. He had wisely sent his most outspoken and volatile subordinate, William "Billy" Mitchell, on an inspection tour of American security interests in the Far East so as not to exacerbate a delicate political process. Despite this precaution, the Navy saw the proposal as a threat to its own aviation branch and declined taking part in it. A second attempt to gain Navy acceptance occurred in September 1924, and when it too failed, Mitchell was back in the United States and launched a sensationalist publicity campaign that ultimately ended his military career.[62]

Unfortunately for Sallie Maxwell Bennett, the political climate was not favorable for a jointly sponsored monument to fallen Army, Navy, and Marine airmen of the Great War. Once again, it seemed to her, an ungrateful government had rejected an offer by the Bennett family "to do something for the United States," and she was going through "the same experience" as her son when he offered the services of the West Virginia Flying Corps to the government. Unsure of the outcome for the memorial in Washington, DC, Sallie promised her friend Edward Stifel that should the negotiations to place *The Aviator* there collapse, she would offer it to Linsly.[63]

Meanwhile, enthusiasm grew in Wheeling about the proposition to bring *The Aviator* to that city. Sallie's friends, Nancie and J. J. Holloway, asked her to consider donating the monument to the new Chapline Street Extension that connected the downtown with the National Road on Wheeling Hill.[64] In Washington, Lukeman met with Lieutenant Colonel Sherrill to see if he could yet somehow secure the State, War, and Navy Building site. Sherrill was confident that a joint bill would pass Congress during the legislative session. Despite his confidence, the bill only passed the Senate, not the House.[65] Sallie would have to wait until the next session before her plans might move forward to have the memorial in Washington, DC.

Faced again with government indifference, Sallie had enough, complaining to Sherrill that the Commission of Fine Arts "showed *how little* they appreciated the *Spirit* of this Memorial" by suggesting she place it at distant Bolling Field. Her sympathetic friends in Washington were unable to budge the bureaucracy to accept her gift. If her "dear son's spirit" were indeed guiding her, then clearly the memorial statue belonged in Wheeling. Since her meeting with Edward Stifel, she received constant entreaties from him and Robert Hazlett from the Linsly Board of Trustees, as well as J. J. Holloway. Both groups lobbied vigorously to convince her to donate *The Aviator* to them. Stifel persuaded Sallie to travel to Wheeling in December and visit the campus construction site at Thedah Place along the bank of Wheeling Creek. Sallie wrote to thank Sherrill for his efforts on her behalf and to inform him of her decision to put the monument in Wheeling. There, her son "was known, admired, and loved. There, like his ancestor, Stonewall Jackson, he will be remembered [and] this memorial to him [and] all soldiers of West [Virginia] who gave their lives in [the] World War [will] be appreciated [and] pointed out to future generations, whereas in Washington it would only be 'one of many.'"[66]

Although she had agreed to give the statue to Linsly, construction delays slowed the new campus project. In the meantime, the statue was nearing completion and she had to pay Lukeman, yet the memorial could not "be fully completed until [the] location is *definitely* decided on." Meanwhile, J. J. Holloway doubled his efforts to secure *The Aviator* for the Chapline Street Extension. Sallie was not sure how to proceed. She had promised the statue to Stifel personally and intended to keep her word, but she didn't want to burden the school with the statue if it would no longer fit their plans. In addition, both Stifel and Holloway were close friends, and she wanted to please both. She wrote to Holloway, asking him to meet with Stifel and together come to an amicable arrangement.[67]

Since the Chapline Street site was still some time away from completion and since Linsly construction was proceeding more rapidly, the speedier choice was the Thedah Place location. In addition, both Hazlett and Stifel wrote to Sallie to assure her that Linsly was the ideal place to capture the spirit of *The Aviator* memorial. Besides being the oldest college preparatory school west of the Appalachian Mountains, Linsly served as the first capitol building of the state of West Virginia during the American Civil War. Its new campus location at Thedah Place overlooked the National Road, which first linked the US capital with the West. The grounds at Linsly were spacious enough to hold commemorative services of any kind, and the cadet battalion would assemble twice daily on the field in front of the statue. It would overlook most major campus functions, football games, and final drills as a constant reminder and pedagogue to Linsly cadets for generations to come. Furthermore, the Linsly trustees vowed that the statue was to "be under the constant supervision and protection of . . . Linsly." Finally, by dedicating the sculpture at a military school, Louis would leave—as the inscription on the pedestal reads—"his spirit as an example of able courage, not only unto young men but unto all the nation." Robert Hazlett added that the trustees suggested the dedication ceremony for Sallie's finest memorial to her son be held at "eleven o'clock on the eleventh day of November," Armistice Day. He concluded, "The significance of which hour and date you well know."[68]

It was a convincing argument. Linsly's earnestness touched her deeply. Knowing that Linsly would honor the statue and prominently position it along the National Road, where it could be continually seen by the American public, Sallie gave orders for Lukeman to ship the newly completed sculpture there. Sallie made arrangements to attend the dedication. Despite suffering from a skin ailment and weary from her exertions, Sallie looked forward to the ceremony. Once she finished this work, she would "feel free 'to let myself go.'"[69]

Conclusion

Ready to Serve: The Monument as Exemplar

Fair weather with rising temperatures greeted Sallie Maxwell Bennett as she arrived at Thedah Place. *The Aviator* dedication ceremony was scheduled for two o'clock in the afternoon on Wednesday, November 11, 1925. American aviation was headline news that Armistice Day. The *Wheeling Intelligencer* announced that Mrs. Margaret Lansdowne, widow of the commander of the doomed US Navy airship *Shenandoah* was called to testify in court. A naval officer had previously tried to coerce her into giving false testimony at a court of inquiry into the fatal crash of her husband's airship in bad weather. The officer wanted her to retract public statements she made that her husband "had been ordered to take the *Shenandoah* on her fatal flight over his protests" about the deteriorating weather. The outspoken US Air Service (USAS) advocate William "Billy" Mitchell used the *Shenandoah* catastrophe as an example of "incompetent, negligent and almost treasonable" policies by both the War and Navy Departments toward aviation. Mitchell charged that both departments gave Congress "misleading information about aeronautics," and that the lives of airmen in each service were "used as pawns." Mitchell was on trial by court-martial—also a front-page headline across America—in part for his criticism.[1]

Sallie's thoughts were elsewhere: Armistice Day 1925. She was determined that the ceremony for this most important memorial follow the rubrics that the decorum of the age demanded. As we have seen, she was not alone in her efforts since "the huge amount of commemorative activity that took place in the 1920s and 1930s can be seen as a way for contemporaries to alleviate their grief by experiencing bereavement collectively." We saw how commemoration began as early as the summer of 1914 with the shocking numbers of casualties inflicted by industrialized warfare. After the Armistice, commemoration continued with greater care. Each individual who died in the war, like Louis Bennett Jr., "was *remembered* in his family, his village, his parish, his workplace," just as Sallie, Linsly, and the city of Wheeling were preparing to do at the unveiling of *The Aviator*. Nor were the collective grief and these memorial ceremonies exclusive to the victorious Allies. Emil Merkelbach and many German mothers attended similar kinds of ceremonies at like memorials that Sallie, Bunnie Burdett, and Lady Frost had attended. In each belligerent nation (except Russia) and the territories of its empire, each of the war dead was remembered by the state—whether at the local or national levels or both—following various rubrics of commemoration: readings of the names of the war dead, "words spoken at ceremonies, the images offered in inscriptions and commemorative monuments, the stained-glass windows, the cemeteries and ossuaries." Most of these memorials have endured and remind those of us in the twenty-first century of the endless commemorations where "political liturgy and private bereavement were complementary." The collective loss created so strong an emotion that it became important to commemorate each individual, and the masses of unidentified dead were honored with a ceremonial tomb to the Unknown Soldier or the Unknown Warrior.[2]

These tombs and memorials became "works of art at the service of memory" that usually depicted three scenes: courageous warrior, martyr, or death. Although these memorials "glorified the courage of the survivors and united them in their ordeal, they were above all, places of mourning where bereavement and religious and patriotic fervor were complementary." Perched high atop impressive pedestals, these statues cut heroic postures: "Their war is sanitized. No mud, no lice, no blood." In this way, both the process of mourning and the remembrance of sacrifice were "inextricably connected." The memorial was a place where survivors could "identify with the heroes and justify their sacrifice."[3] The sanitized sculpture and the ceremony had a kind of cleansing effect upon the observers, distilling both grief and memory.

Although Sallie's efforts were largely lauded by the community, she certainly had her critics—including her own sister. In October 1918, while Sallie was in the throes of the influenza pandemic, grieving for her late husband, and apprehensive for her missing son, her sister Mary Maxwell sent her a scolding letter, chastising Sallie for writing "personal and unofficial letters" on Lou's behalf because she felt Sallie was "doing more harm than good." She added, "You forget that you cannot (as you always wish to) dictate, or, advise people without their resenting it." As for Sallie's impatience, Mary declared that officials had "thousands of appeals from Mothers and Fathers about their sons and all must be treated alike." Mary asked, "What have you or Louis ever done since the beginning of this dreadful war to help either with *your money* or *time* that would entitle you to extra consideration now?"[4] Was this behind Sallie's motivation to memorialize Louis throughout West Virginia? Were these monuments—these gifts—her way of atoning with the people of the Mountain State? Were Sallie's numerous inquiries and letters extraordinary? Was she indeed seeking "extra consideration"?

As we have seen, one of the characteristics about the scope of trauma inflicted on family members by the Civil War and—to a larger extent—the Great War was the "lack of details about the fate of loved ones." Many families besieged their loved ones' comrades and commanders with insistent questions in their letters. "What were the loved one's last moments like? What were the exact circumstances of their death? Where was he wounded? How much did he suffer?" This rupture created by the absence of the loved one during death, and intensified by the families not knowing the details, "tormented the survivors and made their bereavement almost impossibly difficult."[5] Mary Maxwell could throw worded spears, but Sallie Maxwell Bennett had been pierced by far worse. It was not Mary's son, after all, who had "gone missing" over the lines.

Although Mary had a point that thousands of mothers and fathers wanted information regarding their sons, one must remember that "mourning was first and foremost an individual ordeal experienced in dreadful solitude." One war widow described the "pity that I see in their eyes" and others' selfish gratitude that "she's the widow, not me." The looks were often too much to bear, and therefore the "bereaved often wanted to be alone," much like Sallie's friend Bunnie Burdett. For them, the war was permanent in their lives, since a loved one was torn from them because of it. After the cards, letters of condolences, and visits were finished, "the bereaved are *alone*." After the war, Agra complained to Sallie that she didn't like to go out much because people did not want to see women wearing black in public and be reminded of the war.[6]

Survivors of the Great War believed it was crucial to erect monuments "on the sites where the men had fought and died as well as on their home territory." This effectively linked the European battlefields to the home front and brought the Great War "to nations that had been spared the war itself, like the United States." Sallie understood this, and when she built the chapel at Wavrin and dedicated it to her son, she hoped to forever join the village of Wavrin, France with Weston, West Virginia. Besides being a symbol of her gratitude for Wavrin's help in finding and returning her son, the Wavrin Chapel would also be a reminder there of Weston's sacrifice—Sallie's own personal sacrifice—for the people of France. Although the bronze plaque on the chapel wall simply reads, "to the memory of Lieutenant Bennett, U.S.A. aviator," it remains a permanent fixture on the church's stone walls.[7]

What about the other part of Mary's criticism—did Sallie respond to it by dedicating the greatest number of memorials to Louis in West Virginia as a means of "doing something" for the state? She certainly had already shown her gratitude in the past. Sallie donated money to an organization with which Alice Williams was affiliated, possibly in gratitude for inquiring about Louis at the Air Ministry.[8] She also sent the State Department a blank check to cover expenses for inquiring after Louis. These were done before the letter from Mary. True, Sallie showed her gratitude to the villagers in Wavrin by erecting a chapel there, but one must remember that in the context of Great War memorialization, it was essential for survivors to make those links between the battlefront and the home front. Although one cannot rule out Mary's letter as a factor in Sallie's decision to favor her home state with the preponderance of memorials to her son, one must also keep her actions within the greater context of what was happening in the rest of the world. Sallie Maxwell Bennett was not the only one seeking to memorialize the fallen in the vicinity of home.

When Sallie arrived at Thedah Place that Armistice Day 1925, it was the seventh anniversary of the day the fighting stopped in the eleventh hour of the eleventh day of the eleventh month of the fifth year of the war, when the guns fell silent. For most of those who had survived the Great War or lost loved ones in the war, Armistice Day ceremonies at the local war memorial took on a hallowed, cathartic purpose, whereby "an entity was created that perfectly obeyed the classical precepts of tragedy: unity of time, 11 November; unity of place, the war memorial; unity of action, the commemorative ceremony." Whether the day became a national holiday or not depended on the country, but "the day itself, or the previous Sunday, is everywhere a day of reflection and remembrance."

In many countries, veterans and families gathered around the war memorial at eleven o'clock for a commemorative ceremony. This combination of location, time, and place became central to commemoration and bereavement in the years after World War I. This was true in London, Paris, Berlin, and Wheeling, West Virginia, on Armistice Day 1925. Articles and advertisements in the *Wheeling Intelligencer* were full of references to the memory of the Great War. The Rose Company on Main Street featured an advertisement that stated, "The Paths of Glory Lead to Immortality," backed by a drawing of marching allied soldiers over a crowded cemetery of crosses and wreaths. The George Stifel Company described the Armistice Day ceremony as "a simple rite . . . dedicated to those who carried on to the end and 'went-west.'" The advertisement urged everyone to "face east in respect to the dead; give thought to the living victims; and be thankful for the many heroes of the war." Stone and Thomas entered a modest advertisement that simply stated, "Armistice Day: Seven years ago today . . . the world celebrated the signing of the Armistice . . . which meant the cessation of the World War, with its terrible toll of suffering and death." Although KDKA radio in nearby Pittsburgh listed no Armistice Day programming, WJZ in New York City planned an Armistice Day program for the evening. Also that evening, a military ball was scheduled for the Market Auditorium in Wheeling. Members of the Four Minute Club met to enjoy a dinner with General J. Sumner Jones as the guest of honor.[9]

At eleven o'clock in the morning, Wheeling observed two minutes of silence throughout the city. Traffic stopped and bells tolled. Police enforced the observance. At the end of the two minutes, the city returned to life. Traffic and trade carried on as usual. Although schools and banks were closed, for many the day passed as any other day and some criticized what they called "Wheeling's apathy" since Armistice Day was not an official civic holiday.[10]

According to the *Intelligencer*, Linsly Institute was "the only institution or organization to recognize the importance of the event. An immense celebration was held in connection with the unveiling of the statue of Lieut. Louis Bennett, Jr." More significant than just observing the appropriate ceremonial rites, however, the newspaper praised Linsly for erecting a memorial statue to "serve as [a] source of inspiration to the youth" of the Ohio Valley. By dedicating the sculpture at a school, Louis would leave, as the inscription read, "his spirit as an example of able courage, not only unto young men but unto all the Nation." The *Intelligencer* reminded its readers that *The*

Aviator depicted a likeness of Louis Bennett Jr., who founded the West Virginia Flying Corps and the West Virginia Aircraft Company in the Upper Ohio Valley. He had kept an office in the Schmulbach Building on Market Street. Wheeling and the counties in the Northern Panhandle had enthusiastically embraced the unit, the air base, and the factory Lou established there. The community gratefully remembered too that he and his pilots invited the citizens of the Upper Ohio Valley to the airfield for flights around the area before the unit disbanded. When Lou was reported missing, the local newspapers identified him as a Wheeling aviator. He and the unit were accepted and included into the community. Now, the community honored him and identified itself with the heroic sacrifice of this courageous warrior.[11]

As a war memorial, *The Aviator* certainly fit the theme of the courageous warrior. The base was cut from Greens-Landing granite from Maine, and polished marble. The statue was seven and a half feet in height and cast from bronze. It depicted Louis in his "aviator uniform" atop the six-and-a-half-foot pedestal. The belted coat is depicted as "furling in the breeze while he looks boldly off to the horizon." The figure was fitted with "enormous bird-like wings, one of which is high, the other dipped—or broken—and touching the ground." The broken wing hinted at Lou's martyrdom in combat, reminding the observer that he had been sacrificed upon the altar of his country.[12]

Such a magnificent monument required an equally impressive ceremony to make the memorialization rite complete. Once again, Major General Mason Patrick of the Air Service came through to help. The USAS dispatched five aircraft from Langin Field, the Army Air Base located south of Wheeling in Moundsville, West Virginia. As they appeared like specks over the hills to the south, "a great shout rose from hundreds of humans" who thrilled at the aerial display. The flight of aircraft, led by the commander of Langin Field, A. E. Simonin, opened the ceremony with a fly-past in the "missing man" formation, followed by a forty-five-minute demonstration "of thrilling aerial stunts." As it approached the gathered throng, Simonin's ship "swooped by with a hideous roar of its motor not two hundred feet above the crowded bleachers, much to the excitement of all witnesses." Having delighted the crowd with an "elaborate display of air tactics," the Army fliers rejoined their formation, turned toward Langin Field, and disappeared over the southern hills near the Linsly campus.[13]

The Linsly cadet major called the battalion to attention, and Linsly president Dr. George Mecklinburg opened the ceremonies by asking "Dr. Jacob

Brittingham, the rector emeritus of St. Luke's [Protestant Episcopal] church in Wheeling, to ask an invocation." Fittingly, Brittingham "called upon the Heavenly Father to bless the school, the teachers and students thereof; the city and Nation; the brave mothers who sent their beloved sons to battle." So that peace might become eternal on earth, Brittingham also prayed that the example set by the "honored dead" would inspire "all young manhood in America." He closed by asking the crowd to join him in reciting the Lord's Prayer.[14]

Next, the statue was presented by former West Virginia Senator Howard Sutherland, who noted that *The Aviator* was a mother's gift to Linsly, the city of Wheeling, the state of West Virginia, and the nation. But, he continued, *The Aviator* was more than a gift, more than "a beautiful tribute of a Gold Star Mother [sic] of West Virginia" dedicated "to the glorious memory of all Americans who sacrificed their lives in the World War, 1914–1918." It was much more. On another level, as Senator Sutherland remarked, it "not only commemorates the memory of her own son, but her gift speaks for all the mothers who yielded up their sons to their country's call." He concluded by adding that "the great dominating and compelling thought that has inspired this gift and which this gift should inspire in others is service, service to God, service to the Nation, service to state and to the community." Those so inspired "to lives of service" by Lou's example personified in *The Aviator* would bring the "loving thought of Mrs. Bennett" to fulfillment.[15]

As Senator Sutherland concluded his remarks, Jack Adams and Dan Burns, original members of the West Virginia Flying Corps, and Edwin Bailey and Mentir Ralston Jr. of Weston, who were members of the Louis Bennett League, pulled a cord that released a large American flag that covered the statue. The flag flew back and rested above the main entranceway into the new school building, serving as a patriotic backdrop for the memorial statue.[16]

Otto Schenk, president of the Linsly Board of Trustees, accepted the monument on behalf of the school. Wheeling Mayor William J. Steen accepted the statue on behalf of the city. Speakers from the National Aeronautic Association and the Wheeling American Legion Post Number One added the appropriate tributes, reflected on the sacrifices made during the Great War, and looked toward the future. Doctor Clarence True Wilson of the National Council of the Methodist Church in Washington, DC, a close personal friend of President Calvin Coolidge, next gave a discourse on the influence of biblical teachings on American democracy. In particular, Wilson stressed the sanctity of self-sacrifice both in peace and war.[17]

Mr. Henry Woodhouse, president of the Aerial League of America, stood next to a small bronze figure while he paid tribute to "Lt. Bennett," whom he had known before the war. Woodhouse concluded by presenting the figure, inscribed with the words "Winged America" and the names of American aviators who were killed in the Great War, to Sallie Maxwell Bennett. He declared that he and the Aerial League of America "wished to bestow some honor on the mother" who had given so much. These speakers all added to the dignity and official solemnity that the occasion required. The Fort Henry Club band and the cadets from Linsly rounded out the occasion with the appropriate martial display that befitted the ceremony. Those in attendance sang "America" and listened to patriotic band music while many inspected the statue. Finally, "Retreat" was sounded and the flag was lowered. The cadet major dismissed the Linsly battalion, and the commemorative Armistice Day ceremony was concluded.[18]

By celebrating the commemoration on Armistice Day, the "classical precepts of tragedy" and closure were completed. Sallie Maxwell Bennett had not only given an appropriate gift to the nation, the state of West Virginia, the city of Wheeling, and Linsly, but she also united with them in the commemoration of all the war dead from 1914–1918. As a prominent mother who had "yielded up" her son, she could represent all mothers who had sacrificed their sons in the war so that the monument was not only her own gift but also a gift on their behalf. It thus joined the nation with their own personal bereavements. Finally, the monument was a legacy to future generations in order to inspire them through Louis's "example of able courage." Thus, *The Aviator* was a more lasting monument, a more permanent institutional memory in that it sought to connect Bennett's spirit of sacrifice in the Great War with the youth of the future. It was here that America's first mega-celebrity, Charles A. Lindbergh, came to pay his respects.[19] In this, too, Sallie Maxwell Bennett got her way, for succeeding generations of Linsly cadets graduated with the image of *The Aviator* and Lou's words "Ready to Serve" as the engraved motto on their class rings—a testament to this inspiration. *The Aviator* remains central to the school's identity today. Louis Bennett Jr. and Sallie Maxwell Bennett are still remembered to some degree in Wheeling to this day.

Unlike Europe, in the United States the memories and wounds of the American Civil War, World War II, Vietnam, and more recent wars overshadow those of the Great War. In the marketplace, memorabilia from the Second World War and the American Civil War command high prices, while similar items from the Great War are cheap by comparison. Of the many American military cemeteries in France, the largest is from the Great War, the Meuse-Argonne American Cemetery and Memorial near Romagne. It is largely deserted and seldom visited by American tourists, while daily bus tours from Paris venture out to the World War II cemetery near Omaha Beach, Normandy. By contrast, among Europeans the Great War continues to be remembered on television and in print media. Each Armistice Day, Great Britain observes a two-minute silence across the country. British officials and business people buy and wear a poppy from the Royal British Legion to commemorate the fallen in Flanders Fields. Europeans still strive to remember their first total war of the Industrial Revolution, just as their American cousins energetically strive to remember theirs—the American Civil War. It is estimated that over fifty thousand books on that war were published before the beginning of the twenty-first century alone.[20]

When American doughboys returned home from the Great War, they were welcomed and honored by the surviving veterans of the Civil War. In Wheeling, for instance, both Union and Confederate veterans marched in a parade of honor with the returning members of the American Expeditionary Force. Those too old or feeble to march rode alongside in automobiles provided by local owners. Having these ancient veterans participate was "one of the features of the parade." The symbolism of these two generations of veterans marching through the hometown streets was important, as it confirmed that the veterans of the Great War had achieved a milestone, a rite of passage, and were also worthy of acclamation.[21]

Equally significant and indicative of the changes in American society, women of the Ohio Valley were asked to both welcome the soldiers and join in the parade. Appealing to "Mothers, Wives, and Sweethearts" to march in the parade, the *Wheeling Register* added, "Women have never failed to show their patriotism and will proudly come forth at this, the last call for patriotic service and demonstration." It was a historic event, because "women have never before been asked to come forth in a body to prove they can be mobilized as citizens and when women are asking for the privileges they are doing, it is to be hoped that this first attempt for county mobilization will find no slackers." Attitudes toward women in American society had slowly changed as women campaigned for suffrage, achieved in 1920 with the XIX

Amendment. Much was due to the "total war" nature of World War I, because women too were "ready to serve." They went into the factories and served in roles overseas. But one can trace these changes further back to the American Civil War, when the traditional gender hierarchy eroded as the war became more "total" in nature. Northern women's clubs pressed for abolition well before the guns fired on Fort Sumter, and later Northern women entered military hospitals as nurses. Meanwhile, Southern women broke gender barriers too, some becoming nurses while others—forced by the realities of total war—embraced roles previously dominated by their men folk.[22]

While the federal government erected official cemeteries and monuments, ladies' memorial associations picked up the mantle of their traditional duty of commemorating the dead and led the way in private commemoration. True, wealthy individuals, like Sallie Maxwell Bennett, had the means to commission monuments and did so without censure, leading to a surfeit of Confederate statues across the United States. However, even women of modest means found a way to express their desires through these ladies' memorial associations. While women—and especially Southern women—became more actively engaged in this memorial work, they also became more politically active and used some of those energies in the struggle against obstacles to women's rights. By the end of the nineteenth century, women had assumed leadership roles in various causes—from commemoration to education to industrial reform and suffrage.[23]

Sallie Maxwell Bennett is representative of this changing identity for women as citizens. She took a leading role after the Great War, establishing memorials to Lou in France, Britain, and the United States. She sought to increase the prestige of mothers who had lost sons and advocated for family rights for the return of American soldier dead. Beginning with the window in Westminster Abbey, her public monuments were subsequently designated as a "gift of *one* mother for *all* mothers."[24] After each commemoration ceremony, Sallie gained prominence in the community and in 1924 was chosen as an alternate delegate to the Democratic National Convention. Through these commemorative monuments, gifts to all mothers, she helped define the conduct that deserved admiration.

It should not be any surprise, then, that the American experience in the Great War was directly inspired by the country's Civil War heritage, both in how the country prepared for war and in how it commemorated the war. Lou's efforts to create a state aerial militia is representative of that volunteer heritage. Americans who celebrated the Civil War fiftieth anniversary commemorations when war erupted in Europe naturally compared the European conflict to their own measuring stick. These Civil War celebrations, reunions, preparedness camps, and ceremonies often converged around a monument or cemetery erected by the Civil War survivors. The Civil War monuments, as works of art, were more than just a memorial or a place to grieve. They also had a pedagogical purpose for future generations of Americans. These seemingly ordinary monuments celebrated a shared national, tragic experience while they imparted a message about that experience, which their creators sought to convey. The rituals of commemoration conducted by the Civil War generation and their progeny appeared to confirm the mutual respect they held for both "the blue and the gray," while at the same time these memorials and rituals indicated the "tremendous meaning" the war experience gave to villages and towns across the United States. Additionally, these monuments and ceremonies were instrumental in reinforcing an American national identity and sculpting a shared memory of the war and its meaning. Though Americans often dispute which concept of national identity the war represented, it nonetheless became a cornerstone of American national identity. It has therefore been burned into the core of American identity for succeeding generations.[25] According to historian James McPherson, the Civil War was "the central event in the American historical consciousness."[26] Sallie Maxwell Bennett knew this and incorporated this knowledge into her efforts.

Her son Louis Bennett Jr. was clearly influenced by Civil War heritage. Like Sallie, he ardently read newspapers and periodicals, and these touted the "forgotten romance and adventure of the Civil War." The US Army used its fiftieth anniversary celebrations to "implant sound fundamental ideas" of military policy among students from colleges "and other institutions of learning." Under the direction of General Leonard Wood, camps at Plattsburgh, New York; Tobyhanna, Pennsylvania (where Lou trained); and elsewhere fueled the Preparedness Movement.[27] The national consciousness of the American Civil War was so prevalent on the Great War generation that it gave credibility to an Army myth. Supposedly, before Pershing sailed for France, Army Chief of Staff Hugh Scott told him, "Now Jack, this is not the Army of the Potomac." Thus inspired with patriotic fervor, Americans such as Theodore Roosevelt, Trubee Davison, and Louis Bennett Jr. sought to form elite volunteer units in the Great War, which Americans had done since the Mexican War and which, during the Civil War, bore the brunt of the fighting.[28] Unlike his contemporaries who embraced the war declaration as a means to "do something for Yale" and create elite units associated with their caste and alma mater, Louis Bennett Jr. returned to his roots to raise a volunteer aerial militia under the auspices of the state of West Virginia.

Louis Bennett, Jr. also exemplified the many changes that faced his generation. He was reared with a Confederate family history and an identity rooted strongly in tradition. Unlike Sallie, he rarely mentions his heritage or relationship to "Stonewall" Jackson. Rather, his letters emphasize his desire—his commitment—to make his own mark in the world. Like many of his generation he embraced and mastered the new aviation technology that symbolized the modern potential of the early twentieth century and sought to create a national aviation reserve that was "ready to serve" the nation in time of war. As a modern man, he recognized that this reserve needed a collaborative public and private financial and industrial base to sustain it in a global industrial war. While Army bureaucracy lurched toward organization before turning to Canada for assistance, he had a clearer vision of the way forward and tried to put it into practice.

Still, in applying that vision, he drew on the traditions of his ancestors, which was stronger than the indoctrination of Yale or the sporting club tradition of his class. For Lou, the identity with home and state led to the formation of the West Virginia Flying Corps. Because of his bitterness over the government's rejection of his unit and problems within the Army Air Service, he chose to fight with Britain's air arm. It was Reed Landis though, his flight leader that accompanied Lou on Bennett's last sortie, who suggested Lou's inner struggle between the modern world and his heritage. Landis believed that Lou relied too much on traditional values of personal courage and individual skill instead of the massed battle formations and coordinated tactics of the Industrial Age. Consequently, Lou tended to fly alone into battle to prove his sand.[29] This unresolved tension between the old and the new ultimately led to his untimely death.

Sadly, Louis Bennett Jr. died before his true potential could be fully realized. In some ways, he was years ahead of his contemporaries. His effort to establish a national aerial militia was extraordinarily ambitious. It ultimately took the vast resources of the federal government, the help of the Allies' air services, and a great deal of trial and error by the Army and Navy to eventually bring such an idea to fruition. Still, had he received the support of the War Department, who knows if he might have achieved at least part of his goal? Lou's ideas did not die with him, however. In the 1920s, the vocal and volatile Billy Mitchell captured headlines while advocating the national aviation system Lou tried to put in place in 1917. Several Yale "heelers" from Lou's aviation circles, including F. Trubee Davison and Robert A. Lovett from the Class of 1918, were postured after the Great War to advance Lou's ideas about the roles of government and industry toward developing aviation and had a profound impact on American military aviation. Davison was the first assistant secretary of war for air and shaped the Army Air Corps. Lovett served as assistant secretary of war for air during World War II and later became the secretary of defense.[30]

But over time, Lou's ideas became associated with those who survived the 1914–1918 War and moved them forward. Once the Great War generation faded away, fewer remained to remember Louis Bennett Jr., his ideas, his accomplishments, his courage. The aviation community expanded with World War II, further distancing Lou from the tribe he had helped advance. In the twenty-first century, he was largely forgotten. In 2022, while serving as the director of history for Space Launch Delta 45 at Patrick Space Force Base, the former air base named for Major General Mason Patrick, the author came across photos from General Patrick's secretary, including Trubee Davison and several generals from both world wars. Also in the collection was a photo of the clay model of Augustus Lukeman's *The Aviator* statue which Sallie had sent to Patrick in her quest to place it in Washington, DC. On the reverse, someone printed in pencil, "Statue of Charles Lindbergh, first to fly the Atlantic."[31]

For Sallie Maxwell Bennett, there was still much ahead of her. She moved to Wheeling to live with her daughter, Agra, after Johnson died unexpectedly. It fell to Sallie to run the affairs of the corporation and help her daughter and grandchildren weather the storm of the Great Depression. Sallie lived to see another generation of young American men go off to war and watched them take to the skies in war machines like her son had done in the Great War. In 1944 when victory was at last in sight, Sallie Maxwell Bennett died. She was buried next to her husband and son in Weston.

Sallie's commemorative efforts were not completely in vain, even though Lou was largely forgotten, or at best a footnote on tours in Westminster Abbey. Perhaps, having grown up watching the Civil War generation, Sallie saw how the world moved on and was thus spurred to her prolific commemoration efforts. At least in Wavrin, Weston, and Wheeling, the memory of Sallie and Louis Bennett Jr. live on to a degree.

The Aviator statue remained central to Armistice Day and Memorial Day ceremonies at Linsly for many decades thereafter. When the school outgrew its campus at Thedah Place and moved to a site near Knox Lane, the monument moved with the school. On a crisp, sunny autumn afternoon dotted with scattered clouds, *The Aviator* was rededicated on November 11, 1975, its fiftieth anniversary. One of the honored guests was an original member of the West Virginia Flying Corps, Jack Adams, who participated in the 1925 dedication of the statue. Once again, the cadet battalion was drawn up in formation around *The Aviator* to provide the appropriate military honors, while Lou's nephew, Johnson Bennett McKinley, presented the statue. Accepting the statue for Linsly was Robert C. Hazlett, president of the board of trustees. Once again, a flight of military aircraft made a fly-past of the site, as A-7 Corsair jets of the Ohio Air National Guard streaked overhead in the missing man formation, thrilling the cadets assembled there. The ceremony again concluded with "Retreat."[32]

By dying in British service, Lou did not receive the wider recognition of his countrymen. Through a clerical error, the British denied him the honors he had earned with them. Despite the family's best efforts to achieve justice for him, the world did move on. Like the American experience of the Great War, the heroism and foresight of Lou Bennett have been relegated to near obscurity. As World War I in the United States remains eclipsed by the American Civil War, Louis Bennett Jr., too, still seems to remain veiled in Stonewall's shadow.

Acknowledgments

Many people helped make this book possible. First, thanks to the outstanding staff at the West Virginia Regional History Center, West Virginia University Libraries, Lori Hostuttler, Lemley Mullett, Michael Ridderbusch, Christy Venham, and Viktoria Ironpride. Thanks to archivist Debra Basham and historian Mary Johnson at the West Virginia Archives and History Library in Charleston, West Virginia. Thanks also to renowned military historians Michael Neiberg and the late Walter J. Boyne for their insights. Thanks to Kay Peterson and Jennifer Locke Jones at the National Museum of American History, Smithsonian Institution, for permission to use their photos, and thanks also to Michael Frost and William Wallace at the Yale University Library for their research support.

Other assistance came from overseas. Troy Kitch from the Joint Prisoner of War/Missing in Action Accounting Command at Hickam Air Force Base, Hawai'i, supplied important documentation on the recovery of American war dead. In France, thanks to Raymond Loyer, Michel Beirnaert, Frederick Vienne, and *Pere* Francis Maillard for directing me to sources in Wavrin. Special thanks to Jean Pierre Delecroix for his photos of war-ravaged Wavrin and Didier Delaval, who gave me and the grandchildren of Emil Merkelbach a tour of the village and cemeteries. Thanks also to the Merkelbach family—Dr. Ulrike Kunze, the late Dr. Karl-Heinz Kunze, Herr Rűdiger Remy, and his wife, Ruth—for the photos of their grandfather and accompanying me on our visit to the battlefield.

I'm very grateful to Westminster Abbey, especially Christine Reynolds, assistant keeper of the muniments, as well as the staff at the Royal Air Force Museum, London, for kind permission to use their images. Many thanks to Patrick Osborne and Mary Munk at Library and Archives, Canada. She confirmed my research that the Canadian military confused Weston's Louis

Bennett Jr. with a deserter with a similar name and service number. Bill Rawling from the Canadian National Defense Headquarters' Directorate of History and Heritage also corroborated the validity of this error. Thank you for the outstanding research support.

Grateful thanks are due to the late Guy Croston and Bob Gall in Morgantown, West Virginia. Thanks also to Max Houck, director of the Forensic Science Education Program at West Virginia University, for his insights on identifying human remains. In Weston, West Virginia, I'm grateful to Katrina Johnson and Karen Enderle at the Louis Bennett Library for kind permission to use their photos. Thanks to local historian Otis Reed and the Reverend John Valentine, rector of St. Paul's Episcopal Church. In Wheeling, West Virginia, grateful thanks to Thomas O. James, historian and author Margaret Brennan of Warwood, and the late Very Reverend Eugene Ostrowski, pastor of Corpus Christi Church. I'm also grateful to Justin Zimmerman, headmaster of Linsly School, and Terry Miner, Ron Miller, and the late Dr. Robert Schramm at the Linsly museum. Thanks also to Dr. Sean Duffy at the superb Ohio County Public Library for permission to use the Lindbergh video. I'm very grateful to former congressman David B. McKinley, great-nephew of Louis Bennett Jr., who shared photos and notes that greatly focused this work. He showed me one of Lou's notebooks from RAF flight training, which is not unlike my notebook from USAF flight training. I'm especially grateful for his assistance.

Thanks also to Gayathri Umashankaran and her editing staff for catching and correcting my errors. Sincere thanks are due to Tara Dugan, project editor, for her patience and extra effort in bringing this work to print.

Special thanks to Dr. Karen Petrone, professor of history, University of Kentucky, and Dr. Ronald L. Lewis, professor emeritus at West Virginia University, for the tedious task of reviewing the manuscript and offering substantial improvements that were invaluable. Thank you. Finally, thanks to my colleague Dr. Brian Laslie, command historian at the US Air Force Academy, and Natalie O'Neal, acquisitions editor at the University Press of Kentucky. You all made this book possible. Thank you.

Notes

ABBREVIATION GUIDE TO NOTES

Because the Great War was a global catastrophe that pulled in soldiers and resources from around the world, I used the date format established by the International Standards Office (ISO) in the notes of this book: year-month-day. For example, August 5, 1927, is annotated as 1927-8-5 in the notes. Other abbreviations are listed here:

Abbreviation	Meaning
BC	Mrs. Louis Bennett Collection, West Virginia and Regional History Center, West Virginia University Libraries, A&M 1590
BCR	Bennett Combat Report
CP	Governor John J. Cornwell Papers, West Virginia State Archives, Charleston, WV, AR 1734
Dad	Louis Bennett Sr.
EM	Emil Merkelbach
JCM	Johnson Camden McKinley
JJC-WVRHC	John J. Cornwell Papers, West Virginia and Regional History Collection, West Virginia University Libraries, Morgantown, WV
LB	Louis Bennett Jr.
NMAH	Division of Political and Military History, National Museum of American History, Smithsonian Institution, Bennett Collection
SMB	Sallie Maxwell Bennett
WVCD	West Virginia State Council of Defense Papers 1917, State Archives, AR 1721
WVRHC	West Virginia and Regional History Center, West Virginia University Libraries, Morgantown, WV

INTRODUCTION

1. Conversation with Frank A. "Bud" Dusch, 2008-11-2. Hereafter, Bud Dusch, 2008-11-2; "Col. Lindbergh Greeted by 100,000," *Wheeling Intelligencer*, 1927-8-5. Hereafter *Intelligencer*, "Col. Lindbergh." See also Thomas O. James, "Lindbergh Lands in Moundsville," Charles Lindbergh: An American Aviator, https://www.charleslindbergh.com/history/moundsville.asp.

2. *Intelligencer*, "Col. Lindbergh."
3. Ibid. See also James, "Lindbergh Lands in Moundsville."
4. Ibid.
5. Sallie Maxwell Bennett to Dean Ryle, Westminster Abbey, 1921-11-26, Westminster Abbey Muniments, 66991 (hereafter SMB to Ryle, 1921-11-26, Muniments-66991); Robert W. Schramm, *The Linsly School* (Charleston, SC: Arcadia Publishing Company, 2003), 29.
6. Bud Dusch, 2008-11-2; James, "Lindbergh Lands in Moundsville"; *Intelligencer*, "Col. Lindbergh."
7. Charles A. Lindbergh, *We* (New York: G. P. Putnam's Sons, 1927), 294; "Lindbergh Takes Dayton by Surprise," *New York Times*, 1927-8-6.
8. Hiram Bingham, *An Explorer in the Air Service* (New Haven, CT: Yale University Press, 1920), 175; Hudson, *In Clouds of Glory* (Fayetteville: University of Arkansas Press, 1990), 188.
9. "Louis Bennett and His Birdmen Will Uphold Honor of W.VA. in the Clouds," *Wheeling Sunday Register*, 1917-7, West Virginia and Regional History Collection, West Virginia University Libraries, Mrs. Louis Bennett Collection, Box 3, Folder 9 (hereafter "Louis Bennett and His Birdmen," *Sunday Register*, 1917-7, WVRHC, BC3/9); Family History of Louis Bennett Jr., 1919-11-4, Louis Bennett Jr., Yale Alumni Files, RU 830, Box 315, 2 folders, Yale University Libraries, New Haven, Connecticut (hereafter Yale Alumni folder).
10. Cynthia Mills, introduction to *Monuments to the Lost Cause: Women, Art, and the Landscapes of Southern Memory*, ed. Cynthia Mills and Pamela H. Simpson (Knoxville: University of Tennessee Press, 2003), xix.
11. "Forgotten Romance and Adventure of the Civil War," *New York Times*, 1913-7-13; "Four Thousand Wheeling Citizens Rally to Support of President," *Intelligencer*, 1917-4-3; Edward G. Lengel, *To Conquer Hell: The Meuse-Argonne, 1918* (New York: Henry Holt, 2008), 32.
12. James M. McPherson, *Ordeal by Fire: The Civil War and Reconstruction* (Boston: McGraw-Hill, 2001), 180; "Wheeling Ideal Location for Airport, Says Airman: Henry Woodhouse, President of Aerial League, Speaks Here," *Intelligencer*, 1925-11-12; Louis Bennett Jr. to Louis Bennett Sr. (hereafter LB to Dad), 1916-5-2, 1916-5-26, 1916-5-31; LB to Albree, 1916-7-6, BC1/4; F. S. Blackall Jr., "An Aerial Coastal Patrol of Yale Men," *Yale Courant (Illustrated)* 53, no. 1 (October 1916): 38.
13. LB notes on envelope, postmarked 1917-3-30, BC1/9.
14. George H. Williams, "Louis Bennett, Jr., No. 40 Squadron, RFC/RAF," *Cross and Cockade Journal* 21, no. 4 (Winter 1980): 333; Giulio Douhet, *The Command of the Air* (1942; repr., Washington, DC: US Government Printing Office, 1983); William Mitchell, *Winged Defense: the Development and Possibilities of Modern Air Power Economic and Military* (1925; repr., New York: Dover Publications, 1988).
15. Harold Hartney, *Up and At 'Em* (Garden City, NY: Doubleday, 1940), 309; James J. Hudson, *Hostile Skies: A Combat History of the American Air Service in World War I* (Syracuse, NY: Syracuse University Press, 1968), 3, 26; Rebecca Hancock Cameron, *Training to Fly: Military Flight Training 1907–1945* (Washington, DC: US Government Printing Office, 1999), 93.
16. Bingham, *Explorer*, 25.

17. LB to DuPont Aeronautical Interests, 1917-8-17, Bennett Collection, 1/11; LB to Dad, 1917-4-3, BC1/10; David M. Kennedy, *Over Here: The First World War and American Society* (New York: Oxford University Press, 1980), 148–49; Marc Wortman, *The Millionaires' Unit: The Aristocratic Flyboys Who Fought in the Great War and Invented American Airpower* (New York: Perseus Books Group, 2006), 77–78, 80–82.

18. Hudson, *In Clouds of Glory*, 188.

19. Hudson, *Hostile Skies*, 30–31; Hudson, *In Clouds of Glory*, 188.

20. Bingham, *Explorer*, 14–22, 51.

21. John L. Frisbee, *Makers of the United States Air Force* (Washington, DC: US Government Printing Office, 1996), 24, 25.

22. L. Wayne Sheets, "'Able Courage': The Monumental Sallie Maxwell Bennett," *Goldenseal*, Spring 2000, 30.

23. Ibid., 30–33.

1. IN STONEWALL'S SHADOW

1. Sheets, "'Able Courage,'" 28.

2. Family History, Bennett Alumni folder, 1919-11-4 (hereafter, Alumni Folder); David B. McKinley, "Ready to Serve: The Life of Lt. Louis Bennett, Jr.," 2, BC4/6 (hereafter, McKinley, "Ready to Serve").

3. Dennis Norman, *Under the Shade of the Trees: Thomas (Stonewall) Jackson's Life at Jackson's Mill* (Charleston, WV: Mountain State Press, 2000), 70–84.

4. Ibid., 85–86; Yale Alumni folder; "Louis Bennett and His Birdmen," *Sunday Register*, 1917-7, BC3/9.

5. "Louis Bennett and His Birdmen," *Sunday Register*, 1917-7, BC3/9; Charles Woolley with Bill Crawford, *Echoes of Eagles: A Son's Search for His Father and the Legacy of America's First Fighter Pilots* (New York: Dutton, Penguin Group, 2003), 55; Wortman, *Millionaires' Unit*, 31; Edward V. Rickenbacker, *Fighting the Flying Circus* (1919; repr., Garden City, NY: Doubleday, 1965), viii.

6. McKinley, "Ready to Serve," 3; Merritt to SMB, 1912-6, BC1/2; handwritten testament, Friday, 1912-10-8, signed Louis Bennett Jr. and twenty-one others, BC1/3, Yale 1917 Statistical Questionnaire, XIV, Alumni Folder.

7. Wortman, *Millionaires' Unit*, 5; Railroad Freight bill, 1913-9-17, BC1/3; Dad to LB, 1913-9-21, BC1/3; Note, Elmer to LB, 1913-8-28, BC1/3; *Yale Yearbook*, Class of 1917, 1–2, 89 (hereafter *Yearbook* 1917); *Yale Directory* 1916.

8. Wortman, *Millionaires' Unit*, 4–5, 15–17, 99.

9. Ibid.

10. *Yearbook* 1917, 1; Owen Johnson, *Stover at Yale* (New York: Grosset & Dunlap, 1912), 54–56.

11. *Yearbook* 1917, 1–2; Johnson, *Stover at Yale*, 55–59.

12. McKinley, "Ready to Serve," 3; Williams, "Louis Bennett, Jr.," 332–33; LB to Dad, 1916-3-15, BC1/3; Berbudran to SMB, 1919-6-24, BC3/1.

13. Wortman, *Millionaires' Unit*, 15.

14. *Yearbook* 1917, 1–2; McKinley, "Ready to Serve," 3; Williams, "Louis Bennett, Jr.," 332–33; Johnson, *Stover at Yale*, 13–14.

2. THE WAR TO END ALL WARS THROUGH THE LENS OF COLLEGE BOYS

1. Farr to SMB, 1913-8-21, BC1/3; Yale Academic Recitation Card, Spring 1915, BC1/3.
2. Letter of Introduction, Thomas to All Cadillac Distributors, 1914-6-10, BC1/3.
3. SMB to Dad, 1914-9-29, Bennett Collection, 1/3.
4. Ibid.; *Yearbook* 1917, 89; *Yale Directory* 1916.
5. Jay Winter and Blaine Baggett, *The Great War and the Shaping of the 20th Century* (New York: Penguin Books, 1996), 10, 15; Wortman, *Millionaires' Unit*, xiii.
6. Holger Herwig, *The Marne, 1914: The Opening of World War I and the Battle That Changed the World* (New York: Random House, 2009), 36–61, 73; Winter and Baggett, *Great War*, 79; Jim Powell, *Wilson's War: How Woodrow Wilson's Great Blunder Led to Hitler, Lenin, Stalin & World War II* (New York: Crown Forum, 2005), 54.
7. Herwig, *Marne, 1914*, 36–51, 64; Winter and Baggett, *Great War*, 59–60.
8. Herwig, *Marne, 1914*, 64–67; Wortman, *Millionaires' Unit*, 24–25; Michael S. Neiberg, *Fighting the Great War: A Global History* (Cambridge, MA: Harvard University Press, 2005), 11–15.
9. "Elis Beat Navy Grapplers. Middies then Turn Tables and Win in Gymnastics and Fencing," *New York Times*, 1917-2-24.
10. Winter and Baggett, *Great War*, 68–70, 83; Neiberg, *Fighting the Great War*, 29; Herwig, *Marne, 1914*, 262; Hew Strachan, *The First World War* (New York: Penguin Books, 2004), 55–56.
11. Neiberg, *Fighting the Great War*, 32–37.
12. John H. Morrow Jr., *The Great War in the Air: Military Aviation from 1909 to 1921* (Washington, DC: Smithsonian Institution Press, 1993), 63.
13. Henry Serrano Villard, *Blue Ribbon of the Air: The Gordon Bennett Races* (Washington, DC: Smithsonian Institution Press, 1987), 203–5; Claude Grahame-White and Harry Harper, *The Aeroplane in War* (London: T. Werner Laurie, 1912).
14. Morrow, *Great War in the Air*, 63–69.
15. Villard, *Blue Ribbon of the Air*, 203, 207; Morrow, *Great War in the Air*, 63–69.
16. "Yale Is to Open Course in Aviation: Prof. L. P. Breckenridge Here, Talks with Many Aero Club Members," *New York Times*, 1914-4-2.
17. Ibid.
18. "Wheeling Ideal Location for Airport, Says Airman: Henry Woodhouse, President of Aerial League, Speaks Here," *Intelligencer*, 1925-11-12; McKinley, "Ready to Serve," 3.
19. Wortman, *Millionaires' Unit*, 25; LB-Dad, [circa June 1916], BC6/9.
20. "Easy for Harvard Vets. Yale's Green Lacrosse Team an Easy Prey—Attendance Small," *New York Times*, 1915-5-22.
21. Raymond H. Fredette, *The Sky on Fire: The First Battle of Britain, 1917–1918* (Washington, DC: Smithsonian Institution Press, 1966), 63, 87, 91–92, 160–61, 262; James M. Morris, ed., *Readings in American Military History* (Upper Saddle River, NJ: Prentice Hall, 2004), 55–58; Morrow, *Great War in the Air*, 109–10.
22. Wortman, *Millionaires' Unit*, 25–26.
23. Winter and Baggett, *Great War*, 134; Foster Rhea Dulles, *America's Rise to World Power, 1898–1954* (New York: Harper & Row, 1954), 97–98; Arthur S. Link, *Woodrow Wilson and the Progressive Era, 1910–1917* (New York: Harper & Row, 1954), 164–67.

24. Wortman, *Millionaires' Unit*, 25–26.
25. "Inviting War, Says Hadley," *New York Times*, 1915-5-23; Wortman, *Millionaires' Unit*, 26.
26. Wortman, *Millionaires' Unit*, 26–27.
27. John Garry Clifford, *The Citizen Soldiers: The Plattsburg Training Camp Movement, 1913–1920* (Lexington: University Press of Kentucky. 1972), 57–58, 60.
28. Ibid.
29. Link, *Woodrow Wilson*, 132–33.
30. Clifford, *Citizen Soldiers*, 57–58, 70; Link, *Woodrow Wilson*, 133–35, 168–69.
31. Clifford, *Citizen Soldiers*, 57–58, 70; Link, *Woodrow Wilson*, 133–35, 168–69, 200.

3. AERIAL MILITIA

1. Yale *Directory* 1916; LB to Dad, 1916-3-2, BC1/4.
2. Yale *Directory* 1916; Wortman, *Millionaires' Unit*, 29–39.
3. *Yearbook* 1917, 48; LB to Dad, 1916-1-9, 1916-1-17, 1916-1-21, 1916-2-1, 1916-2-12, 1916-3-15, 1916-3-27, BC1/4.
4. LB to Dad, 1916-1-18, BC1/4.
5. LB to Dad, 1916-1-9, 1916-1-21, 1916-2-1, 1916-2-12, 1916-3-2, BC1/4.
6. Daniel R. Beaver, *Modernizing the American War Department: Change and Continuity in a Turbulent Era, 1885–1920* (Kent, OH: Kent State University Press, 2006), 68–69; "Wheeling Ideal Location for Airport, Says Airman: Henry Woodhouse, President of Aerial League, Speaks Here," *Intelligencer*, 1925-11-12.
7. Ibid., 226–27n33, 70.
8. Link, *Woodrow Wilson*, 183–84; Beaver, *Modernizing the American War Department*, 69–70.
9. Link, *Woodrow Wilson*, 184; Beaver, *Modernizing the American War Department*, 70–71.
10. Beaver, *Modernizing the American War Department*, 70–72; Link, *Woodrow Wilson*, 183–88, 184nn.
11. Beaver, *Modernizing the American War Department*, 68–76; Link, *Woodrow Wilson*, 186–88.
12. "Yale Wins on the Mat," *New York Times*, 1916-2-13; "College Men Grapple," *New York Times*, 1916-2-20; "Elis Beat Navy Grapplers," *New York Times*, 1916-2-25; LB to Dad, 1916-1-9, 1916-3-15, BC1/4; *Yearbook* 1917, 89; "Yale Wrestlers Best," *New York Times*, 1916-3-5.
13. LB to Dad, 1916-3-15, 1916-4-18, 1916-5-2, BC1/4; *Yearbook* 1917, 89.
14. Link, *Woodrow Wilson*, 136–38.
15. Ibid.; Roger G. Miller, *A Preliminary to War: The 1st Aero Squadron and the Mexican Punitive Squadron of 1916* (Washington, DC: Air Force History and Museums Program, 2003), 1–2.
16. Link, *Woodrow Wilson*, 136–38.
17. "'Tap Day' at Yale," *New York Times*, 1916-5-19; *Yearbook* 1917, 89; LB to Dad, 1916-5-2, 1916-5-26, 1916-5-31; LB to Albree, 1916-7-6, BC1/4.
18. Link, *Woodrow Wilson*, 140, plate 24; John Patrick Finnegan, *Against the Specter of a Dragon: The Campaign for American Military Preparedness, 1914–1917* (Westport, CT: Greenwood Press, 1974), 165; "Facts of the Raid as Learned by Funston and Made Public

by the War Department," *New York Times*, 1916-5-8; "Yale Favors Roosevelt: 934 of 1,923," *New York Times*, 1916-6-3; Clifford, *Citizen Soldiers*, 54–69.

19. LB to Dad, [no date; content is summer 1916], BC6/9; SMB to LB, [no date], BC 1/9.

20. "Expedition to Chase Bandits," *New York Times*, 1916-6-16; Link, *Woodrow Wilson*, 140–41; Wortman, *Millionaires' Unit*, 24, 27–28; "Sailors in Fight with Mexicans," *New York Times*, 1916-6-20; Finnegan, *Specter of a Dragon*, 166.

21. Wortman, *Millionaires' Unit*, 7, 19, 23–33; F. S. Blackall Jr., "An Aerial Coastal Patrol of Yale Men," *Yale Courant (Illustrated)* 53, no. 1 (October 1916): 38.

22. Telegram, Alden to LB, 1916-6-28, BC1/4; LB to Dad, 1916-8-16, 1916-8-27, BC1/5; "Yale Battery Needs Men," *New York Times*, 1916-6-27; "Yale Battery Open: Still Needs 106 Men," *New York Times*, 1916-7-8; telegram, Stinson Flying School-LB, 1916-7-2, BC1/4.

23. "Sailors in Fight with Mexicans," *New York Times*, 1916-6-20; "More Refugees Reach Coast: Vera Cruz Crowded with Americans Who Can Find No Quarters," *New York Times*, 1916-6-24; "Three Other States Go: Connecticut to Follow New Jersey and Massachusetts Thursday, Border Camps Await Them," *New York Times*, 1916-6-25; Link, *Woodrow Wilson*, 142–43; "Lull in Movement of Troops to West," *New York Times*, 1916-6-30; "Gen Wood to Send 130,000 Soldiers to Mexican Line," *New York Times*, 1916-7-3; LB to Dad, 1916-8-16, BC1/5; Blackall, "Aerial Coastal Patrol," 38; Alumni folder.

24. Blackall, "Aerial Coastal Patrol," 38–39.

25. Ibid.; Wortman, *Millionaires' Unit*, 43–44; LB to Dad, 1916-8-10; Albree to LB, 1916-7-6, BC1/5.

26. LB to Dad, [no date; content is June–July 1916], BC6/9.

27. "Gen. Wood Reviews Plattsburg Men," *New York Times*, 1916-7-30; "Mexicans Protest Over Border Shots: Gen. Gonzales Charges Militiamen Crossed and Attacked the Homes of Natives—Villistas Blamed by Bell," *New York Times*, 1916-7-25; "Americans Slain in Mexican Raid," *New York Times*, 1916-8-1; "Mexico Is Ready to Help Us Again: Obregon Lauds Co-operation in Fort Hancock Fight, Saying It Proves Good Faith," *New York Times*, 1916-8-2; "War Game at End of Plattsburg Camp," *New York Times*, 1916-7-15; "Yale Guns Drive Foes to Flight: Battery B Scatters Invading Force Which Threatens Stores at Tobyhanna," *New York Times*, 1916-9-1.

28. LB to Dad, 1916-8-10, 1916-8-27, 1916-9-4, 1916-9-6, BC1/5.

29. LB to Dad, 1916-9-6, 1916-9-12, BC1/5; "Recalled Troops to Be Demobilized," *New York Times*, 1916-9-8.

30. "Yale Battery Members Join Football Squad," *New York Times*, 1916-9-26; *Yearbook* 1917, 89.

31. *Yearbook* 1917, 1; Johnson, *Stover at Yale*, 54–56.

32. LB to Dad, 1916-10-19, 1916-10-30; Receipt, Oliver Magnetic Car Company, 1916-11-1, BC1/6.

33. LB to Dad, 1916-11-11; Meeting Notice, 1916-11; SMB to LB, 1916-11-16; Langrock-Garner Receipts, 1916-12-1; Chase Company to LB, 1916-12-1; Yale College Semi Annual Exam, 1916-12-4, BC1/6.

34. LB to Dad, 1916-12-8; Baker Company Receipt, 1916-12-23, BC1/6.

35. Link, *Woodrow Wilson*, 252–55, 255n10; "Lloyd George Calls All Peace Talk Unfriendly," *New York Times*, 1916-9-29.

Notes to Pages 46–56   237

36. Link, *Woodrow Wilson*, 255–62.
37. LB to Dad, 1917-1-11; Gladys to LB, 1917-1-18; Dance card, de Ropp to LB, 1917-2-3, BC1/8.
38. LB to Dad, 1917-2-18; LB to SMB, 1917-1-24, BC1/8.
39. LB to SMB, [no date]; Patterson to LB, 1917-2-22; telegram, Cooke to LB, 1917-2-23; Williams to LB, 1917-2-28, BC1/8; Finnegan, *Specter of a Dragon*, 169.
40. Amy Bennett to LB, [no date], 1917; Vernon Hall invitation to tea, 1917-3-11; SMB to LB, Wednesday, [no date], 1917, BC1/9.
41. Wortman, *Millionaires' Unit*, 73.
42. Link, *Woodrow Wilson*, 265.
43. Ibid., 144; LB to Dad, 1917-1-27, BC1/8.
44. Lengel, *To Conquer Hell*, 15.
45. Link, *Woodrow Wilson*, 263–64, 265–67; Finnegan, *Specter of a Dragon*, 184.
46. "Mr. Taft Advocates a Conscription Law," *New York Times*, 1917-2-5; also cited in Finnegan, *Specter of a Dragon*, 185.
47. Link, *Woodrow Wilson*, 268–69; Finnegan, *Specter of a Dragon*, 185.
48. Link, *Woodrow Wilson*, 267–68.
49. Ibid., 267–70; Powell, *Wilson's War*, 88; "St. Louis and St. Paul Will Be Held Here," *New York Times*, 1917-2-11; "For American Convoys," *New York Times*, 1917-2-8.
50. Link, *Woodrow Wilson*, 271, 144; Lengel, *To Conquer Hell*, 15.
51. "America Has Practically Declared War on Teuton, Says Zimmermann," *Intelligencer*, 1917-3-31; Link, *Woodrow Wilson*, 271–74.
52. Telegrams, Cooke to LB, 1917-3-8, 1917-3-11; Thompson to LB, 1917-3-8; Dad to LB, 1917-3-11, BC1/9.
53. Aunt Marie to LB, 1917-3-3; SMB to LB, 1917-3-12; Assistant Secretary of State to SMB, 1917-3-29, BC1/9; "Yale Men Organize Second Air Corps," *New York Times*, 1917-3-12.
54. LB notes, 1917-3-30, BC1/9.
55. Telegram, Johnson Camden McKinley (hereafter, JCM) to LB, 1917-3-26, BC1/9.
56. LB to Dad, 1917-3-27; telegrams, Thompson to LB, 1917-3-28, 1917-3-29, BC1/9.
57. Telegram, Dad to LB, 1917-3-27; LB to Dad, 1917-3-29, BC1/9.
58. LB to DuPont Aeronautical Interests, 1917-8-17, BC1/11.
59. Link, *Woodrow Wilson*, 276.

4. "A MORE DISTINGUISHED WAY OF DOING GREATER GOOD"

LB to Cornwell, 1917-5-10, Governor John J. Cornwell Papers, West Virginia State Archives, Charleston, WV, AR 1734 (hereafter, CP).
1. Powell, *Wilson's War*, 96–97; Link, *Woodrow Wilson*, 25–32, 186–87, 276.
2. Link, *Woodrow Wilson*, 276; Powell, *Wilson's War*, 96–97; "Cabinet Has Decided on a State of War," *Intelligencer*, 1917-3-31.
3. LB to Dad, 1917-4-1, 1917-4-2, 1917-4-3, BC1/10.
4. LB to Dad, 1917-4-2, BC1/10; "Gerard Exposes Great Folly of Not Preparing," *Intelligencer*, 1917-3-31; Finnegan, *Against the Specter of a Dragon*, 102–3; Ronald L. Boucher, "The Colonial Militia as a Social Institution: Salem, Massachusetts, 1764–1775," ed. James M. Morris, *Readings in American Military History* (Upper Saddle River, NJ: Prentice Hall, 2004), 14–15.

5. Cameron, *Training to Fly*, 92; Charles J. Gross, *Prelude to the Total Force: The Air National Guard, 1943–1969* (Washington, DC: US Government Printing Office, 1985), 1.

6. Finnegan, *Specter of a Dragon*, 102–3; Clifford, *Citizen Soldiers*, 184–85; Gross, *Prelude to the Total Force*, 1; Cameron, *Training to Fly*, 92–97.

7. George Ficke, "Augustus Post: 1874–1952," Early Birds of Aviation, accessed July 15, 2008, http://www.earlyaviators.com/epostaug.htm; LB to Dad, 1917-4-2, BC1/10.

8. Hartney, *Up and At 'Em*, 309; Hudson, *Hostile Skies*, 3, 26; Cameron, *Training to Fly*, 93; LB to DuPont Aeronautical Interests, 1917-8-17, BC1/11; LB to Dad, 1917-4-3, BC1/10; Mitchell, *Winged Defense*, 21–22; Beaver, *Modernizing the American War Department*, 83.

9. Hartney, *Up and At 'Em*, 309; Hudson, *Hostile Skies*, 3, 26; Cameron, *Training to Fly*, 93; LB to DuPont Aeronautical Interests, 1917-8-17, BC1/11; LB to Dad, 1917-4-3, BC1/10; Mitchell, *Winged Defense*, 21–22; Beaver, *Modernizing the American War Department*, 83; LB to Dad, 1917-4-17, Brook Watson Private Collection, Wheeling, West Virginia (hereafter Watson Collection).

10. LB to Baker, 1917-5-5, CP; Williams, "Louis Bennett, Jr.," 333; telegram, Burdett to LB, 1917-4-3, BC1/9; Clifford, *Citizen Soldiers*, 26–27; Hartney, *Up and At 'Em*, 94; "Aviator Posing as Royal Flier Now in Trouble," *Clarksburg Exponent*, 1917-12-7.

11. Cameron, *Training to Fly*, 124; LB to Dad, 1917-4-9, Watson Collection.

12. Cameron, *Training to Fly*, 124; aircraft linen samples, 6 artifact envelopes, 1917-4-3; letter, 1917-6-18 with 3 business cards and aircraft linen samples from Courtrai Manufacturing Company; telegram, SMB to JCM [1917]; note, SMB to JCM [no date] referring to Curtiss Aeroplane Company linen, BC1/10.

13. Link, *Woodrow Wilson*, 281–82; Powell, *Wilson's War*, 97–98; "Champ Clark Is Re-elected House Speaker," *Intelligencer*, 1917-4-3; "Mr. Wilson's Address to the Legislatures," *Intelligencer*, 1917-4-3; "War Clouds Hover," *Weston Democrat*, 1917-4-4.

14. "Comment of Today's Newspapers on the President's Address," *New York Times*, 1917-4-3; "Patriotic Weston," *Weston Democrat*, 1917-4-6; "Four Thousand Wheeling Citizens Rally to Support of President," *Intelligencer*, 1917-4-3.

15. William A. Carney Jr. and Brent E. Carney, *Wheeling in Vintage Postcards* (Charleston, SC: Arcadia Publishing, 2003), 104–5; "Four Thousand Wheeling Citizens Rally to Support of President," *Intelligencer*, 1917-4-3; "Seven Thousand Charleston Men in Big Demonstration," *Intelligencer*, 1917-4-3; "Wellsburg in Outburst of Patriotism," *Intelligencer*, 1917-4-3.

16. Carney and Carney, *Wheeling in Vintage Postcards*, 91; "Lafollette Blocks War Resolution," *Wheeling Daily News*, 1917-4-3; "Pacifists Hiss President and Defend Neutrality," *Wheeling Daily News*, 1917-4-3; "America's Probable Declaration of War," *Wheeling Daily News*, 1917-4-3.

17. "Baltimore Patriots and Pacifists Clash; Lights Go Out on Dr. Jordan," *Intelligencer*, 1917-4-2.

18. Link, *Woodrow Wilson*, 282; Draft, SMB to Sherrill, [1925]-10-14, BC5/8; Williams, "Louis Bennett, Jr.," 333. Yale later awarded the Class of 1917 their degrees.

19. LB to Dad, 1917-4-17, Watson Collection.

20. Frederick Palmer, *Newton D. Baker: America at War*, vol. 1 (New York: Dodd, Mead, 1931), 285, 287; Hudson, *Hostile Skies*, 3; Villard, *Blue Ribbon of the Air*, 203, 211.

21. Mitchell, *Winged Defense*, 22–25; Douhet, *Command of the Air*, 79, 83.

Notes to Pages 64–70   239

22. Ronald L. Lewis, *Transforming the Appalachian Countryside: Railroads, Deforestation, and Social Change in West Virginia, 1880–1920* (Chapel Hill: University of North Carolina Press, 1998), 7; *Wheeling News Register*, 1917-7-6, travel advertisements; Conversation with Guy Croston, 1981-5-17; Bud Dusch, 2008-11-2.

23. Ken Fones-Wolf, *Glass Towns: Industry, Labor, and Political Economy in Appalachia, 1890–1930s* (Urbana: University of Illinois Press, 2007), 62, 75, 85; *Fourteenth Biennial Report of the Bureau of Labor of West Virginia, 1917–1918* (Charleston, WV: Tribune Publishing Company, 1918); "Beech Bottom's Immense Power Plant Ready for Partial Operation July 1," *Intelligencer*, 1917-3-15.

24. Secretary of State Papers, AR 1065, Corporation Book 99, West Virginia State Archives, Charleston, WV, 128–29, 304–5; JCM to Louis Bennett Sr., 1917-8-24, BC1/11.

25. Christine Reynolds, *Stained Glass of Westminster Abbey* (London: Jarrold Publishing, 2002), 20–21; cash ledger, WVFC, 1917-4-21 to 1917-7-5, BC1/10; LB to Dad, 1917-4-29, Watson Collection.

26. Williams, "Louis Bennett, Jr.," 333, also in CP; LB to Baker, 1917-5-5, CP.

27. Cornwell to Chief, Militia Bureau, 1917-9-1, CP; John J. Cornwell Papers, West Virginia and Regional History Collection, West Virginia University Libraries, Morgantown, WV, Boxes 51, 52, 53 (hereafter JJC-WVRHC); "Beech Bottom's Immense Power Plant Ready for Partial Operation July 1," *Intelligencer*, 1917-3-15; "Charleston Hopes to Land U.S. Plant," *Intelligencer*, 1917-4-3.

28. Hudson, *Hostile Skies*, 12n, 13; Cameron, *Training to Fly*, 12–13.

29. LB to Baker, 1917-5-5, CP 302; "1st Regiment to Mobilize," *Intelligencer*, 1917-4-2; "Second Regiment Will Be Mobilized at Charleston," *Intelligencer*, 1917-4-3; Cornwell to Jackson, 1917-7-7, JJC-WVRHC, Box 54, July; Beaver, *Modernizing the American War Department*, 84.

30. Kennedy, *Over Here*, 148, 150; Beaver, *Modernizing the American War Department*, 83.

31. "Roosevelt's Big Army," *Weston Democrat* from *New York World*, 1917-5-11.

32. Ibid.; Kennedy, *Over Here*, 148–49.

33. Kennedy, *Over Here*, 149; Wortman, *Millionaires' Unit*, 41, 77–78.

34. Kennedy, *Over Here*, 149; Wortman, *Millionaires' Unit*, 77–78, 80–82.

35. Beaver, *Modernizing the American War Department*, 83.

36. Dad to SMB, [1917]-5-8, BC1/10.

37. LB to Baker, 1917-5-5; Cornwell to Baker, 1917-5-10, CP.

38. LB to Cornwell, 1917-5-10, CP; *Weston Democrat*, 1917-5-18, "Opportunity Given to Become Aviator."

39. Telegram, LB to Dad, 1917-4-21; Telegram LB to Dad, 1917-4-28; LB to Dad, 1917-4-29; LB to Dad, [no date]; SMB to Dad, 1917-5-27, Watson Collection; LB to Dad, 1917-6-29, Watson Collection.

40. *New York Times* clipping, "New School for Aviators," with letter from SMB to Cornwell, 1917-5-15, CP.

41. Hudson, *Hostile Skies*, 6–8, 27–30; Cameron, *Training to Fly*, 112–13; Hiram Bingham, *An Explorer in the Air Service* (New Haven, CT: Yale University Press, 1920), 10–13.

42. Williams, "Louis Bennett, Jr.," 333; James J. Sloan, *Wings of Honor: American Airmen in World War I* (Atglen, PA: Schiffer Military/Aviation History, 1994), 401; Certificate

of Inspection Enlistment, WVFC, CP; "West Virginia Flying Corps Has Started Real Training," *Wheeling Sunday News*, 1917-7-29.

43. Williams, "Louis Bennett, Jr.," 333.

44. LB to Cornwell, 1917-6-22, CP; "Louis Bennett and His Birdmen," *Sunday Register*, 1917-7, BC3/9; Cameron, *Training to Fly*, 89–90; LB to Dad, 1918-2-25, BC1/14.

45. LB to Cornwell, 1917-6-22, CP; Grahame-White and Harper, *Aeroplane in War*, 151–52; Cameron, *Training to Fly*, 119; Hudson, *Hostile Skies*, 28; "West Virginia Flying Corps Has Started Real Training," *Wheeling Sunday News*, 1917-7-29.

46. Telegram, LB to Cornwell, 1917-6-10; Cornwell to Bell, 1917-6-11; LB to Cornwell, 1917-6-22, CP; LB to Dad, 1917-7-4, BC1/10; Cameron, *Training to Fly*, 93–94; Fred Weyerhaeuser diary excerpt, in letter: Mrs. Marian E. Aamodt to Mrs. Johnson B. McKinley, 1975-11-11, Watson Collection.

47. LB to Dad, 1917-7-3; Dad to SMB, 1917-6-12, BC1/10; LB to Dad, [no date], BC1/17; Carney and Carney, *Wheeling in Vintage Postcards*, 104–5.

48. Beaver, *Modernizing the American War Department*, 83; Louis Bennett Draft Card, Ancestry.com, World War I Draft Registration Cards, 1917–1918, Lewis County West Virginia, accessed August 29, 2008, http://content.ancestrylibrary.com/iexec/default.aspx?htx=View&r=5542&dbid=6482&iid=WV-1992561-2959&fn=Louis&ln=Bennett+Jr.&st=r&ssrc=&pid=22501003.

49. Dad to SMB, 1917-6-12, BC1/10; LB to Cornwell, 1917-7-6; telegram, LB to Stewart, 1917-7-11, CP; governor's secretary to Frank Rowan, 1917-8-14, JJC-WVRHC, Box 54, August; Cornwell to W.W. Jackson, 1917-7-7, JJC-WVRHC, Box 54, July.

50. LB to Dad, 1917-7-6, Watson Collection.

51. "Lafayette Escadrille Transferred to U.S. Army Air Service," *Intelligencer*, 1917-7-5.

52. Proclamation, 1917-7-16 (signed 1917-8-24); LB to Cornwell, 1917-7-28, CP.

53. "Louis Bennett and His Birdmen," *Sunday Register*, 1917-7, BC3/9; "West Virginia Flying Corps Has Started Real Training," *Wheeling Sunday News*, 1917-7-29.

54. "Louis Bennett and His Birdmen," *Sunday Register*, 1917-7, BC3/9.

55. "Louis Bennett and His Birdmen," *Sunday Register*, 1917-7, BC3/9; "West Virginia Flying Corps Has Started Real Training," *Wheeling Sunday News*, 1917-7-29.

56. "Louis Bennett and His Birdmen," *Sunday Register*, 1917-7, BC3/9; "West Virginia Flying Corps Has Started Real Training," *Wheeling Sunday News*, 1917-7-29; Cameron, *Training to Fly*, 114–15.

57. Cordelia Hays to SMB, 1918-9-21, BC2/14; LB to Cornwell, 1917-7-25, 1917-7-28, CP; "West Virginia Flying Corps Has Started Real Training," *Wheeling Sunday News*, 1917-7-29.

58. LB to Cornwell, 1917-7-28, CP.

59. Cordelia Hays to SMB, 1918-9-6, BC2/13; Agra to SMB, 1918-10-1, BC2/15.

60. "Through Car Schedule," *Intelligencer*, 1917-4-3; Bud Dusch, 2008-11-2; William A. Carney Jr. and Brent E. Carney, *Wheeling*, Images of America (Charleston, SC: Arcadia Publishing, 2003), 29.

61. Carney and Carney, *Wheeling in Vintage Postcards*, 64, 121; Mabel Hinrichs Bissett and Bertha Cupp Jones, *Warwood: A History, 1669–1975* (Wheeling, WV: Ernest St. C. Bentfield, 1993), 27; Carney and Carney, *Wheeling*, 25.

62. Bissett and Jones, *Warwood: A History*, 49; Carney and Carney, *Wheeling*, 30.
63. Bissett and Jones, *Warwood: A History*, 39, 48, 53, 54, 63, 65, 80.
64. Carney and Carney, *Wheeling in Vintage Postcards*, cover, 87; Rev. Msgr. Eugene Ostrowski, 2008-4-26; Bissett and Jones, *Warwood: A History*, 59, 83.
65. "Student Aviator Dashed to Death," *Intelligencer*, 1917-8-4; "Beech Bottom's Immense Power Plant Ready for Partial Operation July 1," *Intelligencer*, 1917-3-15.

5. UNUSUAL COURAGE

1. Dad to SMB, 1917-6-12, BC1/10; "Student Aviator Dashed to Death," *Intelligencer*, 1917-8-4; LB to Dad, [no date], BC1/17.
2. "Student Aviator Dashed to Death," *Intelligencer*, 1917-8-4; Air Force Handbook 11-203, vol. 1, *Weather for Aircrews* (HQ USAF/XOO, March 1, 1997), 34–38; Frank Tallman, *Flying the Old Planes* (Garden City, NY: Doubleday, 1973), 130.
3. Ezra Bowen, *The Epic of Flight: Knights of the Air* (Alexandria, VA: Time-Life Books, 1980), 24, 46.
4. Tallman, *Flying the Old Planes*, 130; "Student Aviator Dashed to Death," *Intelligencer*, 1917-8-4.
5. "Student Aviator Dashed to Death," *Intelligencer*, 1917-8-4; Tallman, *Flying the Old Planes*, 130; "West Virginia Student Aviator Killed in Fall of Airplane at the Beech Bottom Camp," *Wheeling Register*, 1917-8-4.
6. "West Virginia Student Aviator Killed in Fall of Airplane at the Beech Bottom Camp," *Wheeling Register*, 1917-8-4; "Student Aviator Dashed to Death," *Intelligencer*, 1917-8-4.
7. "Student Aviator Dashed to Death," *Intelligencer*, 1917-8-4.
8. Telegram, LB to Cornwell, 1917-8-3, CP; "West Virginia Student Aviator Killed in Fall of Airplane at the Beech Bottom Camp," *Wheeling Register*, 1917-8-4; "Student Aviator Dashed to Death," *Intelligencer*, 1917-8-4.
9. "Student Aviator Dashed to Death," *Intelligencer*, 1917-8-4; "Dead Aviator, Capt. Taylor, Was Former Wash-Jeff Student," *Intelligencer*, 1917-8-4; Woolley with Crawford, *Echoes of Eagles*, 45; Elliott White Springs, *War Birds: Diary of an Unknown Aviator* (New York: Grosset and Dunlap, 1926), 62–87; Dad to SMB, 1917-6-12, BC1/10.
10. "Student Aviator Dashed to Death," *Intelligencer*, 1917-8-4; Cornwell to Army Adjutant General, 1917-8-24, CP; SMB to Hadley, 1922-6-6, Yale Alumni folder.
11. Dad to SMB, 1917-7-20, BC1/10; Dad to SMB, 1917-8-18, BC1/11; LB to Cornwell, 1917-9-9, CP.
12. Cornwell to Chief, Militia Bureau, 1917-9-1; LB to Cornwell, 1917-8-29, CP.
13. JCM to Louis Bennett Sr., 1917-8-24; LB to DuPont Aeronautical Interests, 1917-8-17, BC1/11; LB to Cornwell, 1917-8-29, CP; Cameron, *Training to Fly*, 112–15; Hartney, *Up and At 'Em*, 322; Sloan, *Wings of Honor*, 38.
14. LB to DuPont Aeronautical Interests, 1917-8-17; JCM to Louis Bennett Sr., 1917-8-24, BC1/11.
15. LB to DuPont Aeronautical Interests, 1917-8-17; JCM to Louis Bennett Sr., 1917-8-24, BC1/11; LB to Dad, "Tue," BC1/10.
16. JCM to Louis Bennett Sr., 1917-9-10; Dad to SMB, 1917-9-5; telegram Dad to SMB, 1917-9-17, BC1/11.

17. LB to Cornwell, 1917-9-9, CP; Bissett and Jones, *Warwood: A History*, 36; Williams, "Louis Bennett Jr.," 334; Harold Hartney, *Up and At 'Em*, 342; SMB to LB, Christmas season 1917, BC1/13; Cameron, *Training to Fly*, 108, 122; Wortman, *Millionaires' Unit*, 85–103.

18. LB to SMB, 1917-9-6; Weyerhaeuser to LB, 1917-9-20, BC1/11; Sloan, *Wings of Honor*, 296–308.

19. Dad to SMB, 1917-9-5; Howell to SMB, 1917-9-6, BC1/11; Dad to SMB, 1917-9-3, BC1/12.

20. Cornwell to LB, 1917-9-7; McCain to Cornwell, 1917-9-27, CP; "Yale Battery Held Up," *New York Times*, 1917-5-4; Dad to SMB, 1917-8-18, BC1/11.

21. LB to Cornwell, 1917-9-9; Cornwell to LB, 1917-9-11; McCain to Cornwell, 1917-9-27, CP.

22. Bussler to Cornwell, 1917-10-17, CP; LB to Sullivan, 1917-9-28, State Council of Defense Papers 1917, state archives, AR 1721, Box 1, Folder 1 (hereafter, WVCD).

23. LB to Sullivan, 1917-9-26; Cornwell to LB, 1917-9-27; LB to Cornwell, 1917-9-29, WVCD.

24. Agra to SMB, 1917-10-3, BC1/12.

25. LB to Cornwell, 1917-9-29, WVCD; Mitchell, *Winged Defense*, 87–89.

26. Agra to SMB, 1917-10-3, BC1/12; Williams, "Louis Bennett, Jr.," 334; LB to Dad, 1918-1-14, BC1/14; Hartney, *Up and At 'Em*, 318–23; Wooley and Crawford, *Echoes of Eagles*, 41.

27. Cameron, *Training to Fly*, 120, 107–8, 149, 160; Springs, *War Birds*, 25, 32–35, 107–9; Hudson, *Hostile Skies*, 30–31; Wortman, *Millionaires' Unit*, 117–21.

28. Springs, *War Birds*, 101; Cameron, *Training to Fly*, 108.

29. Williams, "Louis Bennett, Jr.," 334; Hudson, *In Clouds of Glory*, 188; Dad to SMB, 1917-10-5; Agra to SMB, 1917-10-10; Dad to SMB, 1917-10-6, BC1/12.

30. Williams, "Louis Bennett, Jr.," 334; Hudson, *In Clouds of Glory*, 188; Agra to SMB, 1917-10-3, 1917-10-10; LB to Dad, 1917-10-13; Prentice to LB, 1917-10-4; Prentice to Kemp, 1917-10-4; Phillips to Musson, 1917-10-27, BC1/12; LB to Dad, 1917-11-18; LB to Dad, 1917-11-23, BC1/13; LB to Dad, "27th" [1917-10-27], BC1/17.

31. Cameron, *Training to Fly*, 124; LB to Dad, "27th" [1917-10-27], BC1/17.

32. Larrabee to SMB, [1919]-1-7, BC2/20; LB to Dad, "27th" [1917-10-27], BC1/17; Agra to SMB, 1917-10-3, BC1/12.

33. Cameron, *Training to Fly*, 114–15.

34. Springs, *War Birds*, 35–36.

35. Cameron, *Training to Fly*, 115–16.

36. LB to Dad, "27th" [1917-10-27], BC1/17; Gerald F. Linderman, *Embattled Courage: The Experience of Combat in the American Civil War* (New York: The Free Press, 1987), 17; Springs, *War Birds*, 134; Sloan, *Wings of Honor*, 194–95.

37. Cameron, *Training to Fly*, 124–25, 145; LB to Dad, 1918-1-1, BC1/14; Williams, "Louis Bennett, Jr.," 334.

38. Cameron, *Training to Fly*, 108, 128, 197.

39. Special Order No. 1918-1-16, Jerry C. Vasconcells Collection, Clark Special Collections Branch, USAF Academy McDermott Library, Colorado, MS15, Box 1, Volume 1 (hereafter, Vasconcells Collection); RFC Canada Transfer Card, R.F.C.

Can. 380, Vasconcells, J., 175, Vasconcells Collection (hereafter, RFC Canada Transfer Card).

40. Cameron, *Training to Fly*, 128, 130; RFC Canada Transfer Card, Vasconcells Collection; Special Order No. 16, Vasconcells Collection.

41. Numerous cards and telegrams, Christmas 1917; Mary Hays to LB, "Christmas 1917"; telegram, SMB to LB, 1917-12-24, BC1/13; SMB to LB, 1918-7-28, BC1/8.

42. Telegram, Mary Hays to LB, 1917-12-24; SMB to LB, Christmas season 1917, BC1/13.

43. LB to Dad, 1918-1-1, BC1/14; Cameron, *Training to Fly*, 128, 130.

44. LB to Dad, 1918-1-1, BC1/14; Cameron, *Training to Fly*, 128, 130.

45. LB to Dad, 1918-1-14, BC1/14; Cameron, *Training to Fly*, 124; Williams, "Louis Bennett, Jr.," 334 and photo, 335; George H. Williams, "To Whom It May Concern," 1918-1-21, BC2/6; SMB to LB, "Tuesday 2 p.m.," BC1/13; Dad to SMB, 1918-1-22, BC2/10. Sallie attended in his place.

46. SMB to LB, "Tuesday 2 p.m.," BC1/13; SMB to LB, 1918-3-20, BC1/19.

47. Springs, *War Birds*, 9; William R. Griffiths, *The Great War*, West Point Military History Series, ed. Thomas E. Griess (Wayne, NJ: Avery Publishing Group, 1986), 145–46.

48. LB to Dad, 1918-2-15, BC1/14; Springs, *War Birds*, 10–21; William Sowden Sims, *The Victory at Sea* (Annapolis, MD: Naval Institute Press, 1984; originally published by Doubleday, Page, 1920).

49. Frederick Libby, *Horses Don't Fly: The Memoirs of the Cowboy Who Became a World War I Ace* (New York: Arcade Publishing, 2000, 2012), 157–58.

50. LB to Dad, 1918-2-25, BC1/14.

51. Graduation Certificate, RAF No. 12306, March 6, 1918, BC2/6; Hudson, *In Clouds of Glory*, 188; Hudson, *Hostile Skies*, 33; Cameron, *Training to Fly*, 127, 159, 168–69.

52. Cameron, *Training to Fly*, 159–60.

53. Record of Service of the Late Lieutenant Louis Bennett, Royal Air Force, BC4/6 (hereafter, Bennett Record of Service); LB to Dad, 1918-3-10, BC1/14; LB to SMB, 1918-4-21, BC1/15; Mary Hays to LB, 1918-8-16, BC2/3.

54. Savoy Hotel receipt for room 463, 1918-3-13–1918-3-15; Room 33, 1918-7-17–1918-7-19; LB to Dad, 1918-4-4, BC1/15; SMB to LB, 1918-4-2, BC1/19.

55. LB to SMB, 1918-4-21, BC1/15; Williams to SMB, 1918-4-25; Perkins to Williams, 1918-4-23, BC2/10; LB to Dad, "Easter Sunday" [1918-3-31], BC1/15.

56. LB to Dad, "Easter Sunday" [1918-3-31], BC1/15; LB to Dad, 1918-4-11, BC1/15; Cameron, *Training to Fly*, 172; Ralston to SMB, 1919-7-21, BC3/3.

57. Springs, *War Birds*, 67.

58. MacDonald to LB, 1918-3-20, BC1/19; Springs, *War Birds*, 75, 79; LB to Dad, 1918-4-11, BC1/15.

59. MacDonald to LB, 1918-3-20, BC1/19; Bowen, *Knights of the Air*, 24–25; Springs, *War Birds*, 86–87, 104; Duff to LB, [no date], Brockworth Aerodrome, BC1/13; LB to Dad, 1918-4-11, BC1/15.

60. LB to Dad, 1918-4-14; LB to SMB, 1918-4-21; LB to SMB, 1918-4-22; LB to Dad, 1918-5-23, BC1/15.

61. LB to SMB, 1918-4-21, BC1/15.

62. Perkins to Williams, 1918-4-23, BC2/10; LB to SMB, 1917-4-29, BC1/15.

63. LB to Dad, 1918-4-4, BC1/15; Williams to SMB, 1918-4-25, BC2/10; Springs, *War Birds*, 84; Bennett Record of Service, BC4/6; LB to SMB, 1917-4-29, BC1/15; LB to Dad, 1918-4-11, BC1/15.

64. Griffiths, *Great War*, 131; Martin Marix Evans, *1918: The Year of Victories* (Edison, NJ: Chartwell Books, 2002), 44–47; Lengel, *To Conquer Hell*, 40–41; Evans, *1918*, 17.

65. Griffiths, *Great War*, 131–32, 139; Evans, *1918*, 12–14.

66. Griffiths, *Great War*, 139–40; Evans, *1918*, 44–51; Robert A. Doughty, et al., eds., *Warfare in the Western World: Military Operations Since 1871*, vol. 2 (Lexington, MA: D. C. Heath and Company, 1996), 614–17; William Mitchell, *Memoirs of World War I* (New York: Random House, 1928), 187–88, 189; Lengel, *To Conquer Hell*, 40.

6. MOST REMARKABLE WORK

LeRougetel to SMB, 1918-7-21, BC2/11.

1. Peter Kilduff, *Richthofen: Beyond the Legend of the Red Baron* (New York: John Wiley and Sons, 1993), 193, 199–202; LB to SMB, 1918-4-21, BC1/15.

2. Kilduff, *Richthofen*, 202–3; Bowen, *Knights of the Air*, 139.

3. Kilduff, *Richthofen*, 193.

4. Lengel, *To Conquer Hell*, 41–43.

5. LeRougetel to SMB, 1918-4-26, BC2/10.

6. LB to Dad, 1918-5-23, BC1/15.

7. Gene Gurney, *Flying Aces of World War I* (New York: Random House, 1965), 107.

8. Springs, *War Birds*, 104–5, 138; Hudson, *In Clouds of Glory*, 48; LB to Dad, 1918-5-23, BC1/15.

9. Walter J. Boyne, email to the author, 2002-10-28.

10. Cecil Lewis, *Sagittarius Rising* (1946; repr., London: Greenhill Books, 2006), 163.

11. Ibid.; Springs, *War Birds*, 140.

12. Hudson, *In Clouds of Glory*, 48; Libby, *Horses Don't Fly*, 136.

13. Springs, *War Birds*, 119, 138, 139; Lewis, *Sagittarius Rising*, 146; Hudson, *In Clouds of Glory*, 79, 154.

14. LB to Dad, 1918-5-23, BC1/15.

15. Norman Franks, *Dog-Fight: Aerial Tactics of the Aces of World War I* (London: Greenhill Books, 2003), 119, 173; Springs, *War Birds*, 119; LB to Dad, 1918-5-23, BC1/15.

16. LB to SMB, 1918-4-29, BC1/15; Mary Hays to LB, 1918-8-5, BC2/2.

17. Maxwell to LB, 1918-7-9, BC1/20; Vira? to LB, 1918-3-17, BC1/19; Stewart to LB, [no date], BC1/8; Mary Hays to LB, 1918-8-5, BC2/2; Mary Hays to LB, 1918-3-25, BC1/19; Agra to LB, 1918-7-4, BC1/20; SMB to LB, 1918-7-4, BC1/20.

18. LB to Dad, 1918-5-23, BC1/15; SMB to Marvel, 1918-6-22, BC2/10; Howell to SMB, 1918-6-26, BC2/10.

19. SMB to LB, [1918]-7-28, BC1/8; SMB to LB, 1918-5-8, 1918-5-20, BC1/19.

20. Hudson, *In Clouds of Glory*, 188; LB to Dad, 1918-6-2; LB to SMB, 1918-6-8, BC1/16; LB to Aunt Mary, 1918-6-2, BC1/20.

21. LB to SMB, 1918-6-8; LB to Parents, 1918-7-23; LB to Parents, 1918-6-18, BC1/16; Mary Hays to LB, 1918-8-16, BC2/3.

22. LB to SMB, [no date], "[received] June 23d My *Birthday*," BC1/16; Weyerhaeuser to LB, 1918-7-11, BC1/20.
23. Ralston to LB, 1918-7-13, BC1/20; Gurney, *Flying Aces*, 107; Sloan, *Wings of Honor*, 195; LB to Parents, 1918-7-23, BC1/16.
24. Sloan, *Wings of Honor*, 198; Ralston to LB, 1918-7-13, BC1/20.
25. Neiberg, *Fighting the Great War*, 323, 321, 326–27, 329–30.
26. SMB to LB, 1918-7-4, BC1/20.
27. Agra to LB, 1918-7-4; Williams to LB, 1918-6-7, BC1/20; Frost to SMB, 1918-7-14, BC2/11.
28. LB to Parents, 1918-7-18; LB to SMB, 1918-7-16, BC1/16; Williams to SMB, 1918-7-20, BC2/11.
29. Williams to SMB, 1918-7-20; LeRougetel to SMB, 1918-7-21, BC2/11.
30. SMB to LB, 1918-7-18, BC1/20; Agra to LB, 1918-7-18, BC2/1.
31. SMB to LB, Army Form C 2123, Messages and Signals, [no date], SMB BC1/19.
32. SMB to LB, 1918-7-18, BC1/20.
33. SMB to LB, 1918-7-18; SMB to LB, 1918-7-7, BC1/20; "Major General Patrick Dies," *Charleston Gazette*, 1942-1-30; Hudson, *Hostile Skies*, 56.
34. SMB to LB, 1918-7-18, BC1/20.
35. Williams to SMB, 1918-7-20, BC2/11.
36. Telegram, LB to SMB, 1918-7-21; telegram, SMB to Williams, [no date], BC1/16; postcard, Williams to LB, 1918-7-31; SMB to LB, 1918-7-26, BC2/1.
37. Agra to LB, 1918-7-27, BC2/1.
38. Agra to LB, 1918-7-26, BC2/1.

7. TO DIE A FIERY "MISERABLE DEATH"

Emil Merkelbach to SMB, [1922]-2-26, BC2/10; Emil Merkelbach to Bennett Family, 1922-11-22; Emil Merkelbach to SMB, 1923-1-6, BC4/14 (hereafter, EM to SMB).
1. JCM to LB, 1918-8-1, BC2/2; LB to Parents, 1918-7-23, BC1/16; LeRougetel to SMB, 1918-7-29, BC2/11; "List of Officers Killed Whilst Serving with 40 Squadron from June to October 1918," attached to Air Ministry letter, Mullan to SMB, 1921-11-8, BC4/6.
2. LB to Parents, 1918-7-23, BC1/16; Hudson, *In Clouds of Glory*, 188–89.
3. LeRougetel to SMB, 1918-7-29, BC2/11; Hudson, *In Clouds of Glory*, 188.
4. Hudson, *In Clouds of Glory*, 188; Williams, "Louis Bennett, Jr.," 336–37.
5. LB to Parents, 1918-7-23, BC1/16. McElroy had forty-seven confirmed victories. Hudson, *In Clouds of Glory*, 78.
6. Mary Hays to LB, 1918-8-16, BC2/3.
7. Hudson, *Hostile Skies*, 200, 30–43; Sloan, *Wings of Honor*, 211–12, 216–17, 219–21, 228–29, 231; Mary Hayes to LB, 1918-8-23, BC2/3; Offutt to LB, 1918-7-29, BC2/1.
8. Griffiths, *Great War*, 143; Hudson, *Hostile Skies*, 90–92, 99–106; Lengel, *To Conquer Hell*, 47–48; Sloan, *Wings of Honor*, 198; Springs, *War Birds*, 202–3, 167; Napier to SMB, 1922-1-8, BC4/7.
9. Ralston to LB, 1918-7-13, BC1/20; Hudson, *Hostile Skies*, 97–98. None of Roosevelt's squadron mates saw his final combat, see Samuel Hynes, *The Unsubstantial Air:*

Notes to Pages 117–122

American Fliers in the First World War (New York: Farrar, Straus and Giroux, 2014), 208–9; Woolley with Crawford, *Echoes of Eagles*, 146.

10. Hudson, *Hostile Skies*, 102–4; Hynes, *Unsubstantial Air*, 198–99.

11. Sloan, *Wings of Honor*, 198; Bennett Record of Service, BC4/6; Lieutenant Bennett's Flying Time Summary, BC2/4 (hereafter Bennett Flying Time); Springs, *War Birds*, 158; Hudson, *In Clouds of Glory*, 79; Ralston to LB, 1918-7-28, BC2/1; Ralston to LB, 1918-8-18, BC2/3.

12. Hudson, *In Clouds of Glory*, 189; Williams, "Louis Bennett, Jr.," 334, 336–37; Bennett Record of Service, BC4/6; Bennett Flying Time, BC2/4; Libby, *Horses Don't Fly*, 142; Springs, *War Birds*, 160.

13. Franks, *Dog-Fight*, 213; Christopher Shores, Norman Franks, and Russell Guest, *Above the Trenches: A Complete Record of the Fighter Aces and Units of the British Empire Air Forces 1915–1920* (London: Grub Street, 1990), 271–72; Hudson, *In Clouds of Glory*, 189; Williams, "Louis Bennett, Jr.," 334, 336–37; Mary Hays to LB, 1918-8-24, BC2/3.

14. Stéphane Audoin-Rouzeau and Annette Becker, *14-18: Understanding the Great War* (New York: Hill and Wang, 2000), 42, 150; Drew Gilpin Faust, *This Republic of Suffering: Death and the American Civil War* (New York: Alfred A. Knopf, 2008), 32–34.

15. Neil Hanson, *Unknown Soldiers: The Story of the Missing of the First World War* (New York: Alfred A. Knopf, 2006), 187. Of the 115 casualties, those suffering psychological damage numbered around 17 percent.

16. Audoin-Rouzeau and Becker, *14-18*, 42.

17. Mary Hays to LB, 1918-8-25, BC2/3. Lou never received her encouraging words.

18. Hudson, *Hostile Skies*, 113–14; Neiberg, *Fighting the Great War*, 338–44; Ralston to LB, 1918-8-18, BC2/3.

19. Springs, *War Birds*, 159–60; Weyerhaeuser to LB, 1918-10-7, BC2/15; Bennett Record of Service, BC4/6; Bennett Flying Time, BC2/4; weather conditions from Hudson, *In Clouds of Glory*, 88.

20. Williams, "Louis Bennett, Jr.," 337; Yale 1917 Statistical Questionnaire, Alumni Folder; Hudson, *In Clouds of Glory*, 189.

21. USAF, *Multi-command Manual 3-3* (Doctrine) 17, June 1, 1994, 3-14 to 3-19; also author's experience as USAF F-4 and F-15 fighter aviator and instructor, circa 1986–2000.

22. Lewis, *Sagittarius Rising*, 157.

23. Williams, "Louis Bennett, Jr.," 338; Bennett Record of Service, BC4/6.

24. Blessley to LB, 1918-8-27, BC1/13. American S.E. 5 pilot William Lambert also saw no enemy aircraft in the midst of battle on a bright, sunny day. See Hudson, *In Clouds of Glory*, 79.

25. Neiberg, *Fighting the Great War*, 338–44.

26. Hudson, *In Clouds of Glory*, 88–89; Bennett Record of Service, BC4/6.

27. Hudson, *In Clouds of Glory*, 89.

28. LB to Parents, [1918]-8-14, BC1/18.

29. Ibid.; Shores, Franks, and Guest, *Above the Trenches*, 272; Bennett Record of Service, BC4/6; Bennett Flying Time, BC2/4.

30. Bennett Record of Service, BC4/6.

31. Ibid. This lists engine serial numbers as M.N. 17930, W.D. 59362. Lewis Gun No. 15142 and Vickers Gun D. 8627; Springs, *War Birds*, 164; Williams, "Louis Bennett, Jr.," 339, 347; Libby, *Horses Don't Fly*, 234.

32. Springs, *War Birds*, 139–40; Beaumont to Officer Commanding (O.C.) 288 POW Camp, 1919-3-11, attached with letter, Beaumont to SMB, 1919-3-17, BC3/4; Hudson *In Clouds of Glory*, 189.

33. Bennett Record of Service, BC4/6; LB to Mother, Father, and Sis, 1918-8-15, BC1/18; Franks, *Dog-Fight*, 127–28, 234; Springs, *War Birds*, 220–22, 227, 233; Hudson, *In Clouds of Glory*, 189–90. Hudson describes the weather conditions as "the bright sunny day," whereas Lou writes of mist and cloud.

34. LB to Mother, Father, and Sis, 1918-8-15, BC1/18; Bingham, *An Explorer in the Air*, 144; Woolley with Crawford, *Echoes of Eagles*, 288.

35. Bennett Record of Service, BC4/6; Hudson, *In Clouds of Glory*, 190; Bennett Flying Time, BC2/4; LB to Dad, 1918-8-17, BC1/18; Bennett Combat Report, 1918-8-17, "7-40 a.m.," Army Form W. 3348, 40 Sq. RAF (hereafter, "BCR").

36. Knobel Combat Report, 1918-8-17, "7-40 a.m."

37. LB to Dad, 1918-8-17, BC1/18; BCR, 1918-8-17, "About 8 a.m." Bennett's Flying Time log records only one sortie on August 17, from 0630 to 0825 hours.

38. Bennett Record of Service, BC4/6; Bennett Flying Time, BC2/4; Hudson, *In Clouds of Glory*, 191; BCR, 1918-8-19, "10 am . . . 10-10 am"; LB to Family, 1918-8-20, BC1/18.

39. Stephen Longstreet, *The Canvas Falcons: The Men and Planes of WWI* (New York: Barnes and Noble Books, 1970), 187–89; LB to Family, 1918-8-20, LB to Family, 1918-8-22, BC1/18; *London* and *Manchester Daily News*, 1918-8-21, "15 ½ Tons of Bombs in a Day. Big Raid on Aerodrome Near Lille. Unnamed Pilot Brings Down 4 Balloons," clippings in BC1/18.

40. Williams, "Louis Bennett, Jr.," 339; Napier to SMB, 1922-1-8, BC4/7; Hudson, *In Clouds of Glory*, 188–89; Landis to Otis L. Reed, response to 1969-2-16 inquiry, courtesy of Otis Reed; BCR, 1918-8-19, "1-40 pm."

41. Daniel P. Morse, *The History of the 50th Aero Squadron* (Nashville: Battery Press, 1920), 11–15; Hudson, *Hostile Skies*, 86; Albert Manucy, *Artillery Through the Ages: A Short Illustrated History of Cannon, Emphasizing Types Used in America* (Washington, DC: US Government Printing Office, 1949), 20; John Buckley, *Air Power in the Age of Total War* (Bloomington: Indiana University Press, 1999), 47–48; Neiberg, *Fighting the Great War*, 276, 344; Doughty et al., *Warfare in the Western World*, 2:578–81, 597.

42. Lewis, *Sagittarius Rising*, 86–88.

43. Hudson, *Hostile Skies*, 87–88, 290; Sloan, *Wings of Honor*, 124, 331; Lewis, *Sagittarius Rising*, 72–74.

44. Mauer Mauer, ed., *The U.S. Air Service in World War I*, vol. 4, Postwar Review and Lessons Learned (Washington, DC: Office of Air Force History, 1978–79), 71, Lessons Learned, 27th US Aero Squadron; Morse, *50th Aero Squadron*, 11–14.

45. Hudson, *Hostile Skies*, 87; Sloan, *Wings of Honor*, 96, 332.

46. Hudson, *Hostile Skies*, 87; Hudson, *In Clouds of Glory*, 84; Springs, *War Birds*, 167, 199, 203; Mauer, *USAS in World War I*, 72.

47. LB to Family, 1918-8-20, SMB BC1/18; Bennett Flying Time; Bennett Flight Log, BC2/4; Hudson, *In Clouds of Glory*, 192; Bennett Record of Service, BC4/6, Shores, Franks, and Guest, *Above the Trenches*, 141.

48. William Reid to SMB, 1925-12-20, BC6/1.

49. Hudson, *In Clouds of Glory*, 131, 192; Hudson, *Hostile Skies*, 213; Springs, *War Birds*, 261; Sloan, *Wings of Honor*, 191–94; *Paris Herald*, 1918-8-21, clipping with letter, LeRougetel to SMB, 1919-8-22, BC3/5; Bennett Flight Log, BC2/4.

248   Notes to Pages 131–138

50. Shores, Franks, and Guest, *Above the Trenches*, 141; Williams, "Louis Bennett, Jr.," 341; Hudson, *In Clouds of Glory*, 192; BCR, 1918-8-22, "6-10am" and "6-20am."

51. Bennett Record of Service, BC4/6; Bennett Flight Log, BC2/4; BCR, 1918-8-23, "7-15 A.M."

52. Hudson, *Hostile Skies*, 213, 215; LB to Family, 1918-8-23, BC1/18; BCR, 1918-8-23, "7-15 A.M."

53. LB to Family, 1918-8-23, BC1/18; Bennett Flight Log, BC2/4.

54. Norman Franks, *SE 5/5a Aces of World War I* (Oxford: Osprey Publishing Limited, 2007), 28; Hudson, *Hostile Skies*, 255; Sloan, *Wings of Honor*, 379; Hartney, *Up and At 'Em*, 354.

55. Franks, *Dog-Fight*, 117; Williams, "Louis Bennett, Jr.," 345; Dixon to SMB, 1918-11-30, BC2/19.

56. Dixon to SMB, 1918-11-30, BC2/13; Compston to SMB, 1918-9-2, BC2/13; Hudson, *In Clouds of Glory*, 193; Beaumont to Officer Commanding (O.C.) 288 POW Camp, 1919-3-11, attached with letter, Beaumont to SMB, 1919-3-17, BC3/4; EM to SMB, 1923-1-6, BC4/14.

57. Dixon to SMB, 1918-11-30, BC2/19; Williams, "Louis Bennett, Jr.," 345.

58. LB to Parents, 1918-8-14, BC1/18.

59. EM to SMB, 1918[sic]-2-26, BC2/10. The date on the letter is incorrect. *Drachen* (dragon) was a nickname the Germans gave observation balloons and the one Merkelbach used in his letters.

60. EM to Bennett Family, 1922-11-22, EM to SMB, 1923-1-6, BC4/14; EM to SMB, [1922]-2-26, BC2/10; Williams, "Louis Bennett, Jr.," 343.

8. MOTHERS OF HEROES

Etta LeRougetel to SMB, 1918-4-26, BC2/10.

1. SMB to LB, 1918-8-2, BC2/2.

2. SMB to LB, 1918-8-16, BC2/3; Letter/receipt, Williams to SMB, 1918-8-15, BC2/12.

3. Agra to LB, [no date], BC1/19; JCM to LB, 1918-8-1, BC2/2.

4. Agra to LB, 1918-8-8; SMB to LB, 1918-8-2; Tait to "Benny," 1918-8-13; Blessley to LB, 1918-8-13, BC2/2; Ralston to LB, 1918-8-18, BC2/3.

5. LB to Parents, 1918-8-14, BC1/18; Springs, *War Birds*, 234–35, 274; Sloan, *Wings of Honor*, 211, 219–20; Offutt to LB, 1918-8-11, BC2/2.

6. Longstreet, *Canvas Falcons*, 190–91; Williams, "Louis Bennett, Jr.," 339; Compston to SMB, 1918-9-2; Etta LeRougetel to SMB, 1918-9-6, BC2/13; Sloan, *Wings of Honor*, 212; Booklet, "Commemorative Exercises in Honor of the Yale Men Who Gave Their Lives in the War," 1919-6-15, BC8/3; Springs, *War Birds*, 236, 267.

7. Lengel, *To Conquer Hell*, 47–49, 191; Neiberg, *Fighting the Great War*, 328.

8. Mary Hays to LB, 1918-8-14, BC2/2; Paul Fussell, *The Great War and Modern Memory* (Oxford: Oxford University Press, 1975), 181–85; LeRougetel to SMB, 1918-9-6, BC2/13.

9. SMB to LB, 1918-8-16, BC2/3; SMB to LB, 1918-8-22, BC2/12.

10. "To Whom It May Concern," SMB, 1918-10-8, BC2/15; Agra to LB, 1918-8-8, BC2/2.

Notes to Pages 139–147   249

11. "To Whom It May Concern," SMB, 1918-10-8, BC2/15.
12. LB to Family, 1918-8-20, BC1/18.
13. "To Whom It May Concern," SMB 1918-10-8, BC2/15.
14. Ibid.
15. Kennedy, *Over Here*, 284–85.
16. Francesca Morgan, *Women and Patriotism in Jim Crow America* (Chapel Hill: University of North Carolina Press, 2005), 3–4; Kennedy, *Over Here*, 284–85.
17. Morgan, *Women and Patriotism*, 2–3; W. Fitzhugh Brundage, "Woman's Hand and Heart and Deathless Love," in *Monuments to the Lost Cause: Women, Art, and the Landscapes of Southern Memory*, eds. Cynthia Mills and Pamela H. Simpson (Knoxville: University of Tennessee Press, 2003), 730.
18. SMB to LB, 1918-8-16, BC2/3; Davis to SMB, 1918-8-20; SMB to Davis, 1918-8-21, BC2/12.
19. Faust, *This Republic of Suffering*, 85, 106–7; McPherson, *Ordeal by Fire*, 408–9.
20. SMB to LB, 1918-8-16, BC2/3.
21. "To Whom It May Concern," SMB, 1918-10-8, BC2/15; SMB to LB, 1918-8-16, BC2/3; SMB to LB, 1918-8-22, BC2/12.
22. "To Whom It May Concern," SMB, 1918-10-8, BC2/15; Western Union Cablegram, British Air Ministry to "Bennett Weston WV," 1918-8-28, BC2/7.
23. "To Whom It May Concern," SMB, 1918-10-8, BC2/15.
24. Western Union Cablegram, SMB to "Miss Williams, seventy-eight St. Mary's Mansions, London" [sent 1918-8-28; Williams to SMB, 1918-9-1, BC2/18, originally attached to 1918-10-26 letter], BC2/7.
25. Western Union Cablegram, SMB to "Commander Fortieth Squadron—Air Force British Expedition—France" [sent 1918-8-28], BC2/7.
26. LeRougetel to SMB, 1918-9-6; Frost to Williams, 1918-9-12; SMB to Agra, [no date]; Cordelia Hays to SMB, 1918-9-4, BC2/13.
27. "To Whom It May Concern," SMB, 1918-10-8, BC2/15; JCM to SMB, 1918-9-4, BC2/13.
28. "Louis Bennett, Wheeling Air Fighter, Missing In Action," *Intelligencer*, 1918-8-29.
29. SMB to LB, 1918-8-22, BC2/12; Western Union Cablegram, Compston to SMB, 1918-9-12, BC2/13.
30. Compston to SMB, 1918-9-2, BC2/13.
31. Williams to SMB, 1918-10-9, BC2/16; LeRougetel to SMB, 1918-9-6, BC2/13; Reid and Dredge to Louis Bennett, Sr., 1918-8-26, BC1/8 (typed copies and extracts), BC2/7 (original).
32. Sloan, *Wings of Honor*, 206, 220–21, 377, 379, 388; Williams, "Louis Bennett, Jr.," 342–43; McKinley, "Ready to Serve," 15–16; Compston to SMB, 1918-9-2, BC2/13; copy of letter, Landis to SMB, 1918-8-25, BC1/18.
33. McNally to SMB, 1918-8-28, BC1/18; Reid to Louis Bennett Sr., 1918-9-5, BC2/13 "To Whom It May Concern," SMB, 1918-10-8, BC2/15.
34. Cordelia Hays to SMB, 1918-9-4, BC2/13; Cordelia Hays to SMB, 1918-10-5, 1918-10-10, BC2/15.
35. Field to Frost, 1918-10-1, enclosed with letter, Frost to SMB, 1918-10-6, BC2/15; LeRougetel to SMB, 1918-9-6, BC2/13.

36. Neiberg, *Fighting the Great War*, 331; Doughty et al., *Warfare in the Western World*, 2:624; Powell, *Wilson's War*, 134–35; LeRougetel to SMB, 1918-9-6, BC2/13.

37. Cordelia Hays to SMB, 1918-9-21, SMB to Cordelia Hays, 1918-9-29, BC2/14; Agra to SMB, 1918-10-1, BC2/15; "To Whom It May Concern," SMB, 1918-10-8, BC2/15.

38. Mary Hays to SMB, 1918-10-10, SMB to Mary Hays, 1918-10-18, BC2/16.

39. JCM to SMB, 1918-9-24, BC2/14.

40. Winter and Baggett, *Great War*, 314–17.

41. "To Whom It May Concern," SMB, 1918-10-8, BC2/15.

42. SMB to Agra and JCM, 1918-9-26, BC2/14. Curiously, Sallie changed her birth year to make herself appear older. Her tombstone is engraved "1857," but she isn't on the 1860 federal census with her family in Wheeling. She appears with the Maxwell family on the 1870 federal census, as age six. Her 1903 and 1911 passport applications list it as 1864, matching the 1870 census. In 1915, she changed it to 1860. In 1922, it's 1862. On her 1921 passport application it's 1859.

43. JCM to SMB, 1918-9-24, BC2/14; SMB to Hunter Bennett, 1918-10-11, BC2/16.

44. SMB to Agra and JCM, 1918-9-26; telegram, SMB to Agra, 1918-9-27, BC2/14.

45. Hunter Bennett to SMB, 1918-9-28, BC2/14; Polk to SMB, 1918-10-16, BC2/16.

46. John W. Davis to SMB, 1918-10-7, BC2/15.

47. Cordelia Hays to SMB, 1918-10-18; cablegram, Red Cross to [Cordelia] McClurg Hays, 1918-10-13, BC2/16.

48. SMB note, 1918-10-30, attached with "To Whom It May Concern," SMB, 1918-10-8, BC2/15.

49. SMB to Hunter Bennett, 1918-10-31, BC2/18; Hunter Bennett to SMB, 1918-11-7, BC2/19.

50. Bailey to SMB, 1918-10-30, BC2/18.

51. *Comité International de la Croix-Rouge* to SMB, 1918-10-31, BC2/18.

52. Compston to LeRougetel, 1918-10-10, 1918-10-16, BC2/16.

53. Reid to SMB, 1918-11-16, BC2/19.

54. Polk correspondence to/from SMB, 1918-10-10, 1918-10-16, 1918-11-18, BC2/16, BC2/19.

55. Sutherland to SMB, 1918-11-23, 1918-11-26, BC2/19.

56. Brice to SMB, 1918-11-29; four telegrams (undated) asking her to act as correspondent and copy to Herman Mayer in New York; Brice to SMB, 1918-12-7, BC2/19.

57. Howell to SMB, 1918-12-27; Baggage Declaration, 1918-12-28, BC2/19; Press passes/credentials BC2/20.

58. Cornwell to SMB, 1918-12-29, BC2/20; Dixon to SMB, 1918-11-20, BC2/19.

59. 11254 Supplement to the *London Gazette*, 1916-9-21; Shores, Franks, and Guest, *Above the Trenches*, 327; "Indra Lal Roy's Achievements as Pilot," Lives of the First World War, accessed June 28, 2024, livesofthefirstworldwar.iwm.org.uk.

60. Ruggles-Brise to SMB, 1919-5-8, BC3/1; https://www.bac-lac.gc.ca/eng/discover/military-heritage/first-world-war/personnel-records/Pages/item.aspx?IdNumber=38339.

61. Harry Creagan Papers, Canadian National Aviation Museum, see http://data2.archives.ca/cef/well2/238878a.gif, accessed December 15, 2006; https://www.bac-lac.gc.ca/eng/discover/military-heritage/first-world-war/personnel-records/Pages/item.aspx?IdNumber=38339.

62. Ruggles-Brise to SMB, 1919-5-8, BC3/1.
63. Compston to SMB, 1918-9-2, BC2/13; Dixon to SMB, 1918-11-20, BC2/19.
64. "$500 as Airplane Parachute Prize: Mother of Lieut. Bennett, Killed Aviator, Offers It to Develop Invention," *New York Times*, 1918-12-30; Gribbin to SMB, 1919-1-24; McCadden to SMB, 1919-3-19, BC2/20.
65. JCM to SMB, 1919-2-4, BC2/20; "Aeronautics in America," *New York Times*, 1919-8-14; "The Neglect of Aviation," *New York Times*, 1919-8-21; Frost to SMB, 1919-2-9, BC2/20.
66. SMB to Osborn, 1920-3-20, Yale Alumni folder; Audoin-Rouzeau and Becker, *14-18*, 215-16.
67. Kittredge to SMB, 1919-3-21, BC2/20.
68. Patrick to SMB, [no date]; Patrick to US Army Effects Depot, 1919-6-20; Taylor to SMB, 1919-4-4; Patrick to SMB, 1919-6-27, BC2/21; Sloan, *Wings of Honor*, 54.
69. Typewritten/unsigned document of Crowell mission, BC2/20; "American Mission of Aviation Experts Sails to Study Flying Progress Abroad," *New York Times*, 1919-5-23.
70. Hoskins to SMB, 1919-5-19; Bland to SMB, 1919-4-6, BC2/21.
71. Kerr to SMB, 1919-4-18, BC2/21.
72. SMB to Yale, [no date], Yale Alumni folder; Williams, "Louis Bennett, Jr.," 344.
73. SMB to Yale, [no date], Yale Alumni folder; JCM to SMB, 1919-3-24, BC2/21; Williams, "Louis Bennett, Jr.," 343-44. Williams misspells her name as "Planey." Wavrin military cemetery sketch and expected location of Lieutenant Bennett's grave, BC2/20.
74. *Curé* Leon Delannoy to SMB, [1919]-5-29, BC3/1; Williams, "Louis Bennett, Jr.," 344. Williams misspells her name as "Dallene."
75. *Curé* Delannoy to SMB, [no date]; Plancque to SMB, [1920]-1-2, BC2/20; Undertaker Jeanmonod to SMB, 1919-6-30, BC3/1.
76. Instructions and map, [no date], BC2/20; Author's phone conversation with Max M. Houck, director, Forensic Science Initiative, chairman, Forensic Science Educational Program Accreditation Commission, WVU, 2008-7-7; William D. Haglund and Marcella H. Sorg, eds., *Forensic Taphonomy: The Postmortem Fate of Human Remains* (Boca Raton, FL: CRC Press, 1997). This work is graphic.
77. *Curé* Leon Delannoy to SMB, [1919]-5-29, BC3/1; Berbudran to SMB, [1919]-6-24, BC3/1; Berbudran sent Sallie a "souvenir," a pinned, rolled ribbon. The author opened this artifact and a lock of Lou's hair fell into the author's hand. It was quite thick and light brown.
78. Unidentified/undated newspaper clipping, "War Graves Swindle: France's Action against Battlefield Ghouls," with Berbudran to SMB, [1919]-6-24, BC3/1; *Curé* Delannoy to SMB, [no date], BC2/20.
79. SMB to Jusserand, 1919-5-22; Jusserand to SMB, 1919-5-20; Craven to Jusserand, 1919-5-20; Jusserand to SMB, 1919-5-21; Jusserand to Tardieu, 1919-5-21 (author's translation), BC3/1.
80. SMB to Jusserand, 1919-5-22; Craven to Jusserand, 1919-5-20, BC3/1.
81. Instructions and map, [no date]; *Curé* Delannoy to SMB, [no date], BC2/20.
82. Jeanmonod to SMB, 1919-7-23 with unidentified newspaper clipping, 1919-8-9, "Remarques: Le Scandale des Tombes," BC3/3; Compston to SMB, 1919-10-22, BC3/10;

Curé Delannoy to SMB, [no date], with receipt, Tabourdeaud et Fils to SMB, 1919-7-19, BC3/2; Burder to SMB, 1919-8-13, BC3/4; Patrick to SMB, 1919-7-5, BC3/2.

83. Bissell to SMB, 1919-7-2, BC3/2; Bland to SMB, 1919-8-1; Culbertson to SMB, 1919-8-1, BC3/4.

9. A JOB SO SACRED

Bland to SMB, 1918-8-1, BC3/4.

1. Plancque to SMB, 1919-4-25, BC2/21. Author's translation.

2. Ibid.; Williams, "Louis Bennett, Jr.," 343–44. Williams offers a slightly different version of this account and mistakenly spells Plancque's name as "Planey."

3. Marie Louise Plancque to SMB, 1919-4-25, BC2/21.

4. Meigs Bland (Lutie's husband) to SMB, 1919-4-6, BC2/21; McCulloch to SMB, 1919-9-8, BC3/6; Dallenne to SMB, 1919-7-14, BC3/2.

5. Beaumont to Officer Commanding (O.C.) 288 POW Camp, 1919-3-14, attached with Beaumont to SMB, 1919-3-17, BC3/4; *Curé* Delannoy to SMB [attached to receipt, *Tabourdeaud et Fils*] to SMB, 1919-7-19, BC3/2.

6. *Curé* Delannoy to SMB, 1919-7-21, BC3/3; 1919-5-29; McCulloch to SMB, 1919-6-18, BC3/1.

7. Thomasson to SMB, 1919-4-25, BC2/21.

8. Plancque to SMB, 1919-7-22, BC3/3; McCulloch to SMB, 1919-9-8, BC3/6; McCulloch to SMB, 1919-6-18, BC3/1.

9. Glen to SMB, 1919-6-3; GRS Paris to SMB, 1919-6-14; Zinn: Memorandum for Major Crampton, 1919-5-20 (Patrick forwarded to SMB); Pierce to SMB, 1919-6-18, BC3/1; Bissell to SMB, 1919-7-2, BC3/2.

10. Hanson, *Unknown Soldiers*, 253–54; Faust, *This Republic of Suffering*, 227.

11. Offutt to SMB, 1919-9-10, BC3/6; Hoskins to SMB, 1919-5-19; Kerr to SMB, 1919-4-18, BC2/21; Bland to SMB, 1919-8-1; Culbertson to SMB, 1919-8-1, BC3/4.

12. Hanson, *Unknown Soldiers*, 253–54; Faust, *This Republic of Suffering*, xi–xii, 266, 55, 81, 69, 65.

13. Faust, *Republic of Suffering*, 64–65, 99; Catherine W. Zipf, "Marking Union Victory in the South: The Construction of the National Cemetery System," in *Monuments to the Lost Cause: Women, Art, and the Landscapes of Southern Memory*, ed. Cynthia Mills and Pamela H. Simpson (Knoxville: University of Tennessee Press, 2003), 27–28.

14. Zipf, "Marking Union Victory in the South," 35–36; Faust, *This Republic of Suffering*, 103, 135; Michael Sledge, *Soldier Dead: How We Recover, Identify, Bury, & Honor Our Military Fallen* (New York: Columbia University Press, 2005), 111; Hanson, *Unknown Soldiers*, 254; Paul Fussell, *The Great War and Modern Memory* (1975; repr., New York: Oxford University Press, 2000), 70.

15. Hanson, *Unknown Soldiers*, 241–42; "Baker Cannot Combat Undertakers' Efforts," *New York Times*, 1920-1-15.

16. Hanson, *Unknown Soldiers*, 241–242; Sledge, *Soldier Dead*, 135–36.

17. Hoskins to SMB, 1919-5-19; Kerr to SMB, 1919-4-18, BC2/21; Bland to SMB, 1919-8-1; Culbertson to SMB, 1919-8-1, BC3/4.

18. Culbertson to SMB, 1919-8-1, BC3/4.

19. Faust, *This Republic of Suffering*, 84–85, 87–88, 110–11, 117; John R. Neff, *Honoring the Civil War Dead: Commemoration and the Problem of Reconciliation* (Lawrence: University Press of Kansas, 2005), 39.

20. G. Kurt Piehler, *Remembering War the American Way* (Washington, DC: Smithsonian Institution Press, 1995), 6; cited in Sledge, *Soldier Dead*, 202; G. Kurt Piehler, "The War Dead and the Gold Star: American Commemoration of the First World War," in *Commemorations: The Politics of National Identity*, ed. John R. Gillis (Princeton: Princeton University Press, 1994), 175.

21. Faust, *This Republic of Suffering*, 61–62, 80, 83, 190–91; James M. McPherson, *For Cause & Comrades: Why Men Fought in the Civil War* (Oxford: Oxford University Press, 1997), 95; Neff, *Honoring the Civil War Dead*, 2; Hoskins to SMB, 1919-9-16, BC3/7.

22. "War Call Sounded by Col. Roosevelt," *New York Times*, 1917-3-20; Link, *Woodrow Wilson*, 281–82; Wortman, *Millionaires' Unit*, 27–28; Springs, *War Birds*, 204 (quote); Hynes, *Unsubstantial Air*, 213; "Forgotten Romance and Adventure of the Civil War," *New York Times*, 1913-7-13; Lengel, *To Conquer Hell*, 32.

23. Faust, *This Republic of Suffering*, 200, 202, 208, 123.

24. Sledge, *Soldier Dead*, 200–202; Faust, *This Republic of Suffering*, 213 (quote), 217–26, 237; Zipf, "Marking Union Victory in the South," 29.

25. Faust, *This Republic of Suffering*, 219–27, 234; Sledge, *Soldier Dead*, 201.

26. Zipf, "Marking Union Victory in the South," 27, 40.

27. Ibid.; Faust, *This Republic of Suffering*, 238–40, 246. Neff, *Honoring the Civil War Dead*, 29; Brundage, "Woman's Hand and Heart and Deathless Love," 73.

28. Faust, *This Republic of Suffering*, 238–40, 233–34, 84–85, 246.

29. Audoin-Rouzeau and Becker, *14-18*, 42, 214–15.

30. Faust, *This Republic of Suffering*, 127–28, 105–6; Frost to SMB, 1919-1-28 1919, BC2/20.

31. Faust, *This Republic of Suffering*, 119–21, 127–28 (Chaplain's quote on 128); Williams, "Louis Bennett, Jr.," 344 photo.

32. Sledge, *Soldier Dead*, 135–36; Hanson, *Unknown Soldiers*, 242.

33. Sledge, *Soldier Dead*, 136; Hanson, *Unknown Soldiers*, 242; Piehler, *Remembering War the American Way*, 6; cited in Sledge, *Soldier Dead*, 202.

34. Audoin-Rouzeau and Becker, *14-18*, 193, 215; Bland to SMB, 1919-9-22, BC3/7.

35. Neff, *Honoring the Civil War Dead*, 143, 147–48.

36. Audoin-Rouzeau and Becker, *14-18*, 193, 216; Bland to SMB, 1919-8-1, BC3/4; Offutt to SMB, 1919-9-10, BC3/6.

37. *L'abbé* Dewailly to SMB, 1919-6-5, BC3/4; JCM to SMB, 1919-4-7, BC2/21; Curé Delannoy to SMB, 1919-7-24; Summary, SMB to Curé Delannoy, 1919-8-9, BC3/3.

38. M. *l'abbé* Dewailly to SMB, 1919-8-3, BC3/4; George M. Murray, ed., *1917 in the War: History of the Class of 1917, Yale College*, vol. 2 (New Haven, CT: Yale University Press, 1919), 15; Reid to SMB, 1919-10-8, BC3/9; Curé Delannoy to SMB, 1919-7-21, BC3/3; Frost to SMB, 1919-6-29; Curé Delannoy to SMB [attached to receipt, Tabourdeaud et Fils to SMB, 1919-7-19], BC3/2.

39. British Administrator, Cologne to SMB, 1919-7-28; duplicate Death Certificate from the Acting Inspector of the Air Corps, 1918-8-27; Frankfurt Red Cross to "Commandant, Cologne," 1919-7-25, BC3/3.

40. Cologne Red Cross, Enquiry Office of Wounded and Missing to British Commander, Cologne, 1919-5-30, attached with translation/cover letter, from "Blaise" *An den Herren britischen Kommandanten Koeln*, 1919-6-7, BC3/1. Translation reads, "Dr. Herchenröder bandaged him, but he died on the operating table, after having spoken only once some words in the English language. The doctor took off his identity disk and said to the young lady who assisted, 'This was an American who served with the British.' Then he also took off a weighty golden ring" (SMB to German Red Cross, no date, BC3/1).

41. McCulloch to SMB, 1919-9-8, BC3/6; EM to SMB, "1918" [*sic*—probably 1923]-2-26, BC2/10; EM to SMB, 1923-1-6 January, BC4/14.

42. Emil Merkelbach to Bennett Family, 1922-11-22; EM to SMB, "1918" [*sic*—probably 1923]-2-26, BC2/10; EM to SMB, 1923-1-6, BC4/14; Merkelbach's map, NMAH, Bennett Collection Acc. No. 88843; Williams, "Louis Bennett, Jr.," 344 photo.

43. EM to SMB, 1923-1-6, BC4/14; Merkelbach's map, NMAH, Bennett Collection Acc. No. 88843.

44. Reid to SMB, 1919-10-8, BC3/9; L'Intendant Général Chef de l'Office des Sépultures to SMB, 1919-6-5; Cordelia Hays to SMB, 1919-6-5, BC3/1; letter copy/draft, SMB to JCM, 1920-2-23, BC4/1; Cordelia Hays to SMB, 1919-7-2, BC3/2.

45. Letter draft/copy, SMB to JCM, 1920-2-23, BC4/1; Memorandum of Inquiries to make of Johnson Camden McKinley and Edward Waddell, [no date], BC3/2; JCM to SMB, 1919-4-4, 1919-4-7, BC2/21; *Curé* Delannoy to SMB, 1919-7-21, BC3/3; Madeleine [Dallenne] to SMB, 1919-7-14, BC3/2; Plancque to SMB, 1919-9-11, BC3/7.

46. Holland-America Line to SMB, 1919-7-28, BC3/3; Jeanmonod to SMB, 1919-8-24, BC3/4; Jeanmonod to SMB, 1919-6-30, BC3/1.

47. Hunter Bennett to SMB, 1919-9-29, BC3/7 (missing the beginning); Agra to SMB, "Sunday Night," [no date]; attached clipping from *Wheeling Majority*, 1919-11-13, BC3/11; Cornwell to SMB, 1919-9-29, BC3/8; Carroll to JCM, 1922-7-30; JCM to SMB, 1922-8-2, BC4/12.

48. JCM to SMB, 1919-2-4; Atkins to SMB, 1919-3-12, BC2/20; JCM to SMB, 1919-3-24, 1919-4-7, BC2/21; Memorandum of Inquiries to make of Johnson Camden McKinley and Edward Waddell, [no date], BC3/2; Waddell to JCM, 1919-9-26, BC3/9.

49. Cornwell to SMB, 1919-10-25, BC3/10; Memorandum of Inquiries to make of Johnson Camden McKinley and Edward Waddell, [no date], BC3/2; JCM to SMB, 1919-3-24, 1919-4-7, BC2/21.

50. "Brandeis Sails for Home," *New York Times*, 1919-8-29; "Justice Brandeis Back from Syria," *New York Times*, 1919-9-9.

51. SMB to Osborn, 1920-3-20, Yale Alumni folder; Bland to SMB, [1920]-3-13, BC4/2; McCulloch to SMB, 1919-9-8, BC3/6; Campbell to SMB, 1919-9-29, BC3/8; numerous letters in BC, Box 3, folders 4, 6, 7, 8, 9, 10, 11.

52. Jones to SMB, 1919-10-2, BC3/9; Larrabee to SMB, [1920]-1-7, BC2/20; Compston to SMB, 1919-8-21, BC3/4; Compston to SMB, 1919-10-22, BC3/10; Milling to SMB, 1919-10-20, BC3/10; Ralston to SMB, 1919-7-21, BC3/3. By 1919, Air Service officers used USAS (US Air Service) instead of USAAS (US Army Air Service).

53. Cornwell to SMB, 1919-7-2, BC3/2; Cornwell to SMB, 1919-9-29, BC3/8; Cornwell to SMB, 1919-10-25, BC3/10.

54. Hawley to Atkins, 1919-6-16, BC3/1; "$500 As Airplane Parachute Prize," *New York Times*, 1918-12-30.

55. Sheets, "Able Courage," 30; Ralston to SMB, 1919-7-21, BC3/3; copy letter, Privy Purse Office to SMB, 1919-7-30, Yale Alumni folder.

56. Yale Assistant Secretary to SMB, 1919-9-27, BC3/8; Mason Patrick to SMB, 1919-11-10, BC3/11; Patrick to SMB, 1920-1-4; Grace Patrick to SMB, 1920-2-11, BC4/1. Patrick Space Force Base in Florida was named for him circa 1950.

57. "Y.M.C.A. Aids Visitors to Graves in France," *New York Times*, 1920-6-13.

58. "Costs Mother $2,000 and Great Worry to Bring Soldier Son's Body from French Cemetery," *New York Times*, 1920-2-22.

59. Letter copy/draft, SMB to JCM, 1919-2-23, BC4/1.

60. Bland to SMB, 1920-3-13; Jeanmonod to SMB, 1920-3-24; Stafford to SMB, 1920-3-19 (plus attachments), BC4/2; "Shipping and Mails," *New York Times*, 1920-4-11.

61. Sledge, *Soldier Dead*, 136; "To Accompany War Dead: War Department to Pay Way of One Relative or Friend," *New York Times*, 1920-6-9.

62. Hanson, *Unknown Soldiers*, 242–43.

63. Dulles, *America's Rise to World Power*, 115–18.

64. Sheets, "Able Courage," 32; South American cruise documents, BC3/12; world tour and offer to donate home as library: Oldham to SMB, 1921-1-18, BC4/5; Miller to SMB, 1921-7-19; SMB to people of Weston, 1921-12-9, Bennett files, Lewis County Public Library; JCM to SMB, 1919-4-7, BC2/21; Ken Fones-Wolf, *Glass Towns: Industry, Labor, and Political Economy in Appalachia, 1890–1930s* (Urbana: University of Illinois Press, 2007), 109; Brevick to SMB, 1921-12-31, BC4/7.

65. Imlay and Pritchard, Subcommittee on Ways and Means to SMB, 1922-2-1, BC4/7.

66. Sheets, "Able Courage," 33.

67. McKinley, "Ready to Serve," 20; Thomas B. Haines, ed., *Aircraft Owner's and Pilot's Association Airport Directory*, 2003–2004 ed. (Frederick, MD: AOPA Membership Publications, Inc., 2003), 3 and 577. The airfield's International Civil Aeronautics Organization (ICAO) designator is 49I—author.

68. Miller to SMB, 1921-7-19; JCM to SMB, 1921-8-6 August 1921, Air Ministry to SMB, 1921-10-28, BC4/5; Paly (?) to SMB; receipt, Manhattan Storage and Warehouse Company for SMB, 1922-6-15, BC4/11; SMB to Stokes, 1921-6-9, Yale Alumni folder.

69. SMB to. Paly (?), 1922-6-30, BC4/11.

10. THE GRATITUDE OF ALL THOSE PRESENT

Remarks of Herbert E. Ryle, Dean of Westminster Abbey, 1922-5-26, attached Weller to SMB, 1922-5-29; "American Memorial Unveiled in Abbey," *Paris Herald*, 1922-5-27, attached to Ludlow-Hewett to SMB, 1922-6-1, BC4/10.

1. SMB to Nettleton, 1922-5-18, Yale Alumni folder; Mullan to SMB, 1921-10-28, BC4/5; Boddington to SMB, 1922-5-18, BC4/9. "Ribands" in BC-WVRHC.

2. "Memorial to Heroic West Virginian Placed on England's War Monument," *Wheeling Register*, 1921-12-4, Yale Alumni folder.

3. SMB to Nettleton, 1922-5-18, Yale Alumni folder (quote); Christine Reynolds, *Stained Glass of Westminster Abbey* (London: Jarrold Publishing, 2002), 20–21.

4. SMB to Nettleton, 1922-5-18, Yale Alumni folder; Sheets, "Able Courage," 29; SMB-Ryle, 1921-11-26, Muniments66991.

5. *London Times*, 1921-10-18, cited in Hanson, *Unknown Soldiers*, 313–16. Quotes are from Hanson.

6. Daniel J. Sherman, "Art, Commerce, and the Production of Memory in France after World War I," in *Commemorations: The Politics of National Identity*, ed. John R. Gillis (Princeton, NJ: Princeton University Press, 1994), 187, 460; Audoin-Rouzeau and Becker, *14-18*, 186.

7. Neff, *Honoring the Civil War Dead*, 154, 6–7.

8. Williams, "Louis Bennett, Jr.," 347 (the wreath was removed to the Central Flying School in Upavon); Warson to SMB, 1921-11-5; Mullan to SMB, 1921-11-5; Warson to SMB, 1921-11-7, attached list of officers; Boddington, 1921-11-8; confidential letter/attached listing name of officers "serving with 40 Squadron from June to October 1918," Mullan to SMB, 1921-11-8, BC4/6; Napier to SMB, 1922-1-8, 1922-3-4, BC4/7; Roy to SMB, 1922-4-29, BC4/8.

9. Thomas W. Laqueur, "Memory and Naming in the Great War," in Gillis, *Commemorations*, 156–64.

10. Ibid. (quote on 157); Daniel J. Sherman, "Bodies and Names: The Emergence of Commemoration in Interwar France," *American Historical Review* 103 (April 1998): 465.

11. Piehler, "War Dead and the Gold Star," 175.

12. Audoin-Rouzeau and Becker, *14-18*, 217–18; Laqueur, "Memory and Naming in the Great War," 156–64.

13. Thomasson to SMB, 1918-4-25, BC2/21; Hanson, *Unknown Soldiers*, 218–19, 236.

14. Audoin-Rouzeau and Becker, *14-18*, 217–18.

15. Catherine Moriarty, "Private Grief and Public Remembrance: British First World War Memorials," in *War and Memory in the Twentieth Century*, ed. by Martin Evans and Ken Lunn (Oxford: Berg, 1997), 126; Laqueur, "Memory and Naming in the Great War," 170; Piehler, "American Commemoration of the First World War," 168, 171–73; Sherman, "Bodies and Names," 451.

16. Cordelia Hays to SMB, 1919-7-2, BC3/2; Cordelia Hays to SMB, 1919-10-26, BC3/10.

17. Burdett to SMB, 1920-12-23, BC4/4.

18. Audoin-Rouzeau and Becker, *14-18*, 219, 184–85.

19. Piehler, "American Commemoration of the First World War," 169.

20. Zipf, "Marking Union Victory in the South," 27; Neff, *Honoring the Civil War Dead*, 8–9.

21. Piehler, "American Commemoration of the First World War," 168–69. Some 30,587 US servicemen were buried in Europe (Sledge, *Soldier Dead*, 204).

22. Lengel, *To Conquer Hell*, 50–51, 419; Piehler, "American Commemoration of the First World War," 168–69; Sledge, *Soldier Dead*, 203–4.

23. Laqueur, "Memory and Naming in the Great War," 157; Hanson, *Unknown Soldiers*, 315–16.

24. SMB to Air Ministry, 1922-3-9, Westminster Abbey Muniments67006 (hereafter, Muniments); Air Ministry to SMB, 1922-4-7, Muniments67006. The "religious grounds" were not specified.

25. Grylls to SMB, 1921-11-5, Muniments66985; SMB to Air Ministry, 1922-3-9, Muniments67006.

26. Reynolds, *Stained Glass of Westminster Abbey*, 20-21; RFC Window Dedication ceremony program, BC4/10.

27. SMB to Air Ministry, 1922-3-9, Muniments67006; Reynolds, *Stained Glass of Westminster Abbey*, 20-21.

28. SMB to Ryle, 1921-11-26, Muniments66991; Gillis, *Commemorations*, 12; Audoin-Rouzeau and Becker, *14-18*, 62-24.

29. Jay Winter, *Sites of Memory, Sites of Mourning: The Great War in European Cultural History*, (Cambridge: Cambridge University Press, 1995), 53; Moriarty, "British First World War Memorials," 135-36.

30. SMB to Knapp-Fisher, 1922-5-12, Muniments67009; SMB to Air Ministry, 1922-3-9, Muniments67006; Burdett to SMB, 1919-9-24, BC3/8.

31. Piehler, "American Commemoration of the First World War," 168-71; David W. Blight, *Race and Reunion: The Civil War in American Memory* (Cambridge, MA: Belknap Press, 2001), 279.

32. Catherine W. Bishir, "A Strong Force of Ladies: Women, Politics, and Confederate Memorial Associations in Nineteenth-Century Raleigh," in *Monuments to the Lost Cause: Women, Art, and the Landscapes of Southern Memory*, ed. Cynthia Mills and Pamela H. Simpson (Knoxville: University of Tennessee Press, 2003), 23.

33. Piehler, "American Commemoration of the First World War," 170-71; Thomas J. Brown, *The Public Art of Civil War Commemoration: A Brief History with Documents* (Boston: Bedford/St. Martin's, 2004), 22-23, 63-64.

34. LeeAnn Whites, *The Civil War as a Crisis of Gender: Augusta, Georgia 1860-1890* (Athens: University of Georgia Press, 1995), 5, 18, 47-48; Neff, *Honoring the Civil War Dead*, 146.

35. Bishir, "A Strong Force of Ladies," 4-23.

36. Brundage, "'Woman's Hand and Heart and Deathless Love,'" 66; Brown, *The Public Art of Civil War Commemoration*, 22.

37. NMAH, Bennett Collection-General Information file; Application in the WVRHC, BC2/20, "World War Record of Lineal Descendants of Confederate Veterans"; SMB to Ryle, 1921-11-26, Muniments66981.

38. Cynthia Mills, introduction to Mills and Simpson, *Monuments to the Lost Cause*, xix; Blight, *Race and Reunion*, 273.

39. Morgan, *Women and Patriotism*, 1, 2-5, 8-9, 12-13.

40. Ibid.

41. J. Bartlett and K. M. Ellis, "Remembering the Dead in Northrop: First World War Memorials in a Welsh Parish," *Journal of Contemporary History* 34, no. 2 (1999): 231; Brown, *Public Art of Civil War Commemoration*, 22.

42. 1924 Democrat National Convention miscellany, BC9/1; Hull to SMB, 1924-6-17; SMB to Davis, 1924-6-20; telegram, Davis to SMB, 1924-6-16; tea invitation, 1924-6-22, BC5/7.

43. SMB to Air Ministry, 1922-3-9, Muniments67006.

44. RFC Window Dedication Program and entry passes, BC4/10; Laqueur, "Memory and Naming in the Great War," 163.

45. "American Memorial Unveiled in Abbey," *Paris Herald*, 1922-5-27, plus various unidentified newspaper clippings with Ludlow-Hewett to SMB, 1922-6-1, BC4/10; RFC Window Dedication Program, BC4/10.

46. Weller to SMB, 1922-5-29, plus attachments; "American Memorial Unveiled in Abbey," *Paris Herald*, 1922-5-27, with Ludlow-Hewett to SMB, 1922-6-1, BC4/10.

47. "American Memorial Unveiled in Abbey," *Paris Herald*, 1922-5-27, plus various unidentified newspaper clippings with Ludlow-Hewett to SMB, 1922-6-1, BC4/10; RFC Window Dedication Program, BC4/10.

48. "American Memorial Unveiled in Abbey," *Paris Herald*, 1922-5-27, clipping with Ludlow-Hewett to SMB, 1922-6-1, BC4/10.

49. Guest to SMB, 1922-5-29; "Aviators' Window Dedicated: Memorial Gift of West Virginia Woman Honors British Heroes," *Washington Post*, 1922-5-27, with Ludlow-Hewett to SMB, 1922-6-1, BC4/10.

50. Reynolds, *Stained Glass of Westminster Abbey*, 20–21; various unidentified newspaper clippings with Ludlow-Hewett to SMB, 1922-6-1, BC4/10.

51. Draft letter, SMB to Nettleton, 1925-11-3, Yale Alumni folder; Day to SMB, 1922-9-27, BC4/12; SMB to Phelps, 1922-11-1, BC4/13.

52. SMB to Phelps, 1922-11-1, BC4/13; membership receipt SMB, 1919-11-10, BC3/11; draft letter, SMB to Sherrill, [1925]-1-5; draft letter, SMB to Sherrill, [1925]-10-14, BC5/8.

53. Robert W. Schramm, *The Aviator* (Wheeling, WV: JR Enterprises, 2005); Grace Elizabeth Hale, "Granite Stopped Time: Stone Mountain Memorial and the Representation of White Southern Identity," 226, and Cynthia Mills, "Gratitude and Gender Wars," both in Mills and Simpson, *Monuments to the Lost Cause*, 193–94.

54. Schramm, *The Aviator*; Grace Elizabeth Hale, "Granite Stopped Time: Stone Mountain Memorial and the Representation of White Southern Identity," 226, and Cynthia Mills, "Gratitude and Gender Wars," both in Mills and Simpson, *Monuments to the Lost Cause*, 193–94.

55. SMB to Phelps, 1922-11-1, BC4/13; SMB to Nettleton, 1925-11-3, Yale Alumni folder, 1919-11-4.

56. Yale Alumni folder, 1919-11-4; Patrick to SMB, 1924-2-15, 1924-6-23; SMB to Sherrill, [1925]-10-14, BC5/8.

57. Stifel to SMB, 1924-11-26, BC5/8.

58. Stifel to SMB, 1924-11-26; numerous letters/telegrams, Stifel to SMB, 1924-10-28, 1924-11-3, 1924-11-10, 1924-11-18, 1924-11-26, 1925-4-8, 1925-4-9, BC5/8; Robert W. Schramm, *The Linsly School* (Charleston, SC: Arcadia Publishing Company, 2003), 25–33, quote on 31; "Bud" Dusch, 2008-8-4.

59. Stifel to SMB, 1924-11-26, 1924-10-28, BC5/8.

60. Sherrill to SMB, 1924-9-25, 1924-10-11, BC5/8.

61. Patrick to SMB, 1924-10-20, BC3/7; Sherrill to SMB, 1924-10-11, BC5/8; Patrick to SMB, 1924-5-10, BC5/7.

62. Alfred F. Hurley, *Billy Mitchell: Crusader for Air Power* (New York: Franklin Watts, 1964), 84–93.

63. Patrick to SMB, 1924-10-20, BC3/7; SMB to J. J. Holloway, 1925-4-2, BC5/10.

64. Nancie Holloway to SMB, 1924-11-22, BC5/9; Nancie Holloway to SMB, 1925-1-13; J. J. Holloway to SMB, 1925-2-6; "Urge Statue Be Placed on New Extension," *Wheeling Telegraph*, 1925-7-9, BC5/10.

65. Lukeman to SMB, 1925-12-18, BC5/12; Sherrill to SMB, 1925-7-1, BC5/8.

66. SMB to Sherrill, Sherrill, [1925]-10-14, 1924-10-11, BC5/8; numerous letters, Stifel to SMB, Hazlett to SMB, J. J. Holloway to SMB, BC5/10, BC5/11; SMB to Hazlett and Linsly Institute Board of Trustees, 1925-6-8, BC5/10.

67. SMB to Holloway, 1925-4-2; SMB to Hazlett and Linsly Institute Board of Trustees, 1925-6-8, BC5/10.

68. Hazlett to SMB, 1925-6-25, BC5/11; Letter/sketch of Linsly grounds, Stifel to SMB, 1925-6-29; telegram Stifel to SMB, 1925-7-3; Stifel to SMB, 1925-7-25, BC5/12; Sheets, "Able Courage," 31-32.

69. "Marie" to SMB, 1925-11-15, BC6/1; SMB to J. J. Holloway, 1925-4-2; SMB to Hazlett and Linsly Institute Board of Trustees, 1925-6-8, BC5/10.

CONCLUSION

1. "Naval Court of Inquiry Reopens Session Monday," *Intelligencer*, 1925-11-11; "Charges of Col. Mitchell Are Upheld by Army Air Officer"; "'The Aviator' Will Be Unveiled Here Today"; "505 Airmen Killed in Obsolete Craft, Says Aviation Major."

2. Audoin-Rouzeau and Becker, *14-18*, 219, 184–85; Winter, *Sites of Memory, Sites of Mourning*, 91, 108–13.

3. Audoin-Rouzeau and Becker, *14-18*, 188, 190.

4. Maxwell to SMB, 1918-10-22, BC2/16.

5. Audoin-Rouzeau and Becker, *14-18*, 217–20.

6. Ibid., Agra to SMB, 1919-6-7, BC3/1.

7. Audoin-Rouzeau and Becker, *14-18*, 219, 184–85; Williams, "Louis Bennett, Jr.," 348; Wavrin town website, accessed August 11, 2007, http://translate.google.com/translate?hl=en&sl=fr&u=http://tortue.brodeuse.free.fr/wavrin.htm&prev=/search%3Fq%3Dwavrin,%2Bfrance.

8. Receipt, undated, "Donation to Mrs. Alice Williams, £2," BC2/12.

9. Audoin-Rouzeau and Becker, *14-18*, 186, 188, 190 (quote); "Radio Today," *Intelligencer*, 1925-11-11; "Wheeling Quietly Pays Tribute to Her War Dead," *Intelligencer*, 1925-11-12; "4-Minute Men Enjoy Dinner," *Intelligencer*, 1925-11-12.

10. Editorial, "Seven Years Later," *Intelligencer*, 1925-11-12.

11. "Wheeling Quietly Pays Tribute to Her War Dead," *Intelligencer*, 1925-11-12; "Statue to Serve as Source of Inspiration to Youth," *Intelligencer*, 1925-11-12; Sheets, "Able Courage," 31–32.

12. Sheets, "Able Courage," 31.

13. "Statue to Serve as Source of Inspiration to Youth," *Intelligencer*, 1925-11-12; Sheets, "Able Courage," 31.

14. "Statue to Serve as Source of Inspiration to Youth," *Intelligencer*, 1925-11-12; Sheets, "Able Courage," 31.

15. "Memorial to Heroes of World War," *Intelligencer*, 1925-11-12.

16. "Memorial to Heroes of World War," *Intelligencer*, 1925-11-12; "Moral Equivalent of War Is Needed by All Nations," *Intelligencer*, 1925-11-12; Schramm, *Linsly School*, 28, photo caption.

17. "Memorial to Heroes of World War," *Intelligencer*, 1925-11-12; "Moral Equivalent of War Is Needed by All Nations," *Intelligencer*, 1925-11-12; Schramm, Linsly School, 28, photo caption.

18. "Memorial to Heroes of World War," *Intelligencer*, 1925-11-12.

19. Schramm, *Linsly School*, 29.

20. Sledge, *Soldier Dead*, 293; Lengel, *To Conquer Hell*, 2–4; John M. Taylor, *While Cannons Roared: The Civil War behind the Lines* (Washington, DC: Brassey's, 1997), ix.

21. "Civil War Men to Honor Boys: G.A.R. and Confederate Veterans Will March in 80th Division Parade with Young Soldiers," *Wheeling Register*, 1919-6-7.

22. "Women of 3 Counties Are Asked to Parade and Welcome Soldiers," *Wheeling Register*, 1919-6-4; Whites, *Civil War as a Crisis in Gender*, 5.

23. Bishir, "Strong Force of Ladies," 23.

24. SMB to Ryle, 1921-11-26, Muniments66991.

25. Mills, introduction, xix; Blight, *Race and Reunion*, 4.

26. William R. Ferris, "'The War That Never Goes Away': A Conversation with Civil War Historian James M. McPherson," *Humanities* 21, no. 2 (March/April 2000), 4–9 (quote 2).

27. "Forgotten Romance and Adventure of the Civil War," *New York Times*, 1913-7-13; "Mobilize Students to Study Warfare: Six Weeks' Camp of Military Instruction to Open at Gettysburg Next Monday," *New York Times*, 1913-7-5.

28. Beaver, *Modernizing the American War Department*, 83; McPherson, *Ordeal by Fire*, 180.

29. Landis to Otis Reed, [undated], attached to Otis Reed to Landis, 1969-2-16, courtesy Otis Reed.

30. John L. Frisbee, *Makers of the United States Air Force* (Washington, DC: US Government Printing Office, 1996), 24, 25, 60, 115, 122, 181, 274.

31. Space Launch Delta 45 History Office Archives (no accession number) marked "Patrick photos."

32. Schramm, *Linsly School*, 76; Schramm, *Aviator*; author's recollections of the event.

Index

Aero Club of America, 6, 25, 44, 54, 56–59, 63, 93, 143, 146, 155, 184; Thomas S. Baldwin, 155; Alan R. Hawley, 25, 57, 93, 184; Albert B. Lambert, 25, 57; parachute contest, 10, 155, 184; Robert E. Peary, 25, 57; Augustus Post, 57, 143; Alberto Santos-Dumont, 25, 57; John H. Towers, 156; Henry Woodhouse, 25–26, 57, 155–56, 222

Aéronautique Militaire, 70

African Americans, 67, 173

aircraft, 1–2, 6–7, 22–25, 37–39, 41, 46, 53, 57–59, 62–65, 68–71, 73–75, 77–81, 83–84, 86–87, 89–90, 92, 95–98, 100–104, 109, 112, 114, 116–34, 136, 145, 153, 156, 164, 166, 180, 194, 220, 228; A-7 Corsair, 228; Aviatik, 24; Avro 504, 90, 92, 96; Caproni bomber, 84, 106; Curtiss "Jenny" (JN-3, JN-4), 33, 37, 41, 51, 57, 71, 75, 78–83, 90–92, 109; Curtiss model F flying boats, 41; Deperdussin (Dep) flight control system, 41; Fokker D VII, 120–21, 123, 126, 129–32, 137, 154; Fokker Triplane, 100, 126; Gotha bomber, 136–37; Hispano-Suiza liquid-cooled engine (Brasier Hispano engine), 101, 122; LVG, 124–26, 131; Nieuport 17, 38; Nieuport 28 (USAS), 115–16; S.E. 5, 101–4, 109, 113–14, 120–23, 125–26, 130–31, 133, 136, 153, 166, 181; Sopwith Camel, 96–97, 103–4, 114, 124, 137, 194; Sopwith Dolphin, 96–97, 101, 105; Sopwith Pup, 96–97; Taube, 24; Voisin, 24

airship, 26, 215

Alden (captain of Yale Battery), 40

American Civil War, 4–6, 9–13, 19–20, 22, 24, 40, 49, 52, 56, 58, 60–61, 66–68, 76, 89–90, 106, 112, 118, 167–72, 175–77, 187, 192–93, 196–97, 200–204, 208, 213, 217, 222–25, 227–28; memorabilia, 223; Memorial Day, 192, 204, 228; War of 1861–1865, 172; "War of Secession," 6, 12, 141, 175; "War of Southern Independence," 178, 209

American Expeditionary Force (AEF), 99–101, 111, 146, 185, 190, 223; 1st Infantry Division, 101, 137; 2nd Infantry Division, 101, 137; 3rd Infantry Division, 108; 26th Infantry Division, 101; 28th "Keystone" Division, 137; 32nd Infantry Division, 101; 42nd Infantry Division, 101; 77th Infantry Division, 128

American League Against Militarism, 62

American Legion, 185, 188, 221; Post Number One, 221

Anderson, A. J., 115, 137

Anderson, R. A. "Andy," 126

Anderson, Robert, 115, 136

Annapolis, USS, 39

Arabia, SS, 45

Arabic, SS, 30

Archer, W .O., 115, 137

Arlington National Cemetery, 3, 193–94, 198; Tomb of the Unknown Soldier, 3, 194, 216
Armistice Day, 177, 192–93, 214–15, 218–19, 222–23, 228
artillery, 21, 23, 28, 32, 91, 99, 121, 124, 127–29, 154, 161, 194; antiaircraft ("Archie"), 116, 125–26, 129, 133–34, 137, 144, 146, 155, 164, 180; "flaming onions," 129
Atlantic City, NJ, 87, 105, 108, 110, 135, 138–39, 142, 149
Aviator, The (statue), 3, 24, 209, 211, 213, 215, 221, 227; Jacob Brittingham, 221; Henry Augustus Lukeman, 209–10, 212–14, 227; Lee C. Paull, 211; Edward Stifel, 210–13; Thedah Place, 3, 213, 215; Clarence True Wilson, 221–22

Bailey, Edwin, 221
Bailey, R. E., 151, 156
balloon, observation, 25, 57, 73, 114, 119–21, 123–34, 144–46, 153, 155–56, 159, 164, 180–81
Baltimore and Ohio Railroad, 63, 183
Beech Bottom, WV, 64, 71–72, 74–78, 80–84, 87, 90, 92, 94; Windsor Power Plant, 64, 77, 80
Belleau Wood, Battle of, 108, 137
Benedict XV (pope), 45, 150–51
Bennett, Agra (sister of LB), 12, 33, 78, 87–88, 92, 105, 110, 112, 135, 138, 140, 147–49, 159, 165, 186, 217, 227
Bennett, Amy (cousin of LB), 46
Bennett, Hunter (cousin of LB), 139–40, 142, 148–51, 182
Bennett, Jonathan M., 12–13
Bennett, Louis, Jr. (LB), 2, 4–5, 7, 9, 216–22, 224–28; accounts of his combats, 159, 164–66, 179–81, 226; Aero Club of America, 6, 24–25, 44, 54, 56–59, 63; childhood and youth, 12–14; commemorations, 3, 10, 155–56, 178–79, 181, 184, 187–222,

224–25, 227; creating the WVFC, 6–8, 25–26, 32, 51–77, 59, 60, 62–65, 68–86; missing in action, 137–60; in Preparedness Movement, 29, 32–54; in RFC/RAF, 87–112; trip out West, 1914, 18; on Western Front, 113–34, 136; at Yale, 14–34, 36–53, 56–62
Bennett, Louis, Sr. (father of LB), 4, 6, 12, 19, 33, 38, 42–44, 46, 48, 51, 53–54, 56, 58, 61–62, 68–69, 70, 72–73, 81, 83, 87–88, 90, 94–95, 98, 101, 103–5, 121, 140; business activities, 6, 18, 33, 39, 44, 56, 65; family history, 12–14; financial lessons, 19, 33–34, 37, 44, 59, 70, 82; funeral, 138–39; illness, 53, 84, 87, 93, 105–6, 108, 110–12, 121, 135–36, 138–39; politics, 12, 56, 65, 68; United Confederate Veterans, 4–5, 52, 60, 93
Bennett, Sallie Maxwell (mother of LB), 2, 9–10, 12–13, 18–19, 39, 44, 52, 69, 87–88, 92–93, 95–96, 98, 101, 106, 108–9, 114, 140–41, 184, 225–27; as alternate delegate to DNC, 205, 224; estate concerns, 139–40, 142, 147, 149–50, 182–84; husband's illness, 105, 110–12, 121, 135–36, 138–39; influenza, 148, 150; journalist credentials, 152–53; memorials, 155–56, 178–79, 181, 184, 187–222, 224–25, 227; recovery of son's remains, 161–63, 175, 178, 182, 185–86, 194; search for the fallen, 153–61, 164–67, 169–71, 175, 179–81, 182–83, 190; son reported missing/killed, 143–48, 150–52
Bernstorff, Johann Heinrich Graf von, 48
Bethmann Hollweg, Theobold, 45
Bingham, Hiram, 70, 75
Birth of a Nation, The (Griffith), 5; Ku Klux Klan, 5
Bishop, William A. "Billy," 107, 114, 121
Bland, "Lutie," 158, 169, 178, 186
Bland, Mary, 158, 169, 178, 186

Index

Bland, William J., 158, 167
Blessley, Rowland "Bless," 106, 120–21, 136
Bliss, Tasker, 66
Bolling, Raynal, 57; Bolling Field, Washington, DC, 211, 213
Borglum, Gutzon, 209
Brandeis, Louis D., 182
Breckenridge, Lester Page, 25
Britannia, RMS, 185
British Expeditionary Force (BEF), 21, 111, 115, 119, 193; Field Service Post Card (Form A 2042), 138
Bryan, William Jennings, 27–28, 49, 55
Bryas, France, 114, 119, 122–23, 125, 132–33, 136
Buckingham ammunition, 123, 125, 131, 133–34
Burdett, "Bunnie," 195, 200, 204, 216–17
Burgess Aeroplane Company, 40
Burleson, Albert, 143, 150
Burwell, Paul, 115, 137
Bush, Prescott, 17, 32

Cadillac, 18, 33, 43–44
Campbell, Emily, 183
Canada, 8, 70, 87–88, 90–91, 136, 150, 226, 229; 213th Battalion, Canadian Expeditionary Force, 154; Louis Bennett as deserter from Brooklyn, NY, 154, 229–30; Camp Borden, Long Branch, Ontario, 88; Canadian Department of Militia, 154; Halifax, 93; University of Toronto ground school, 70
Capelle, Eduard von, 48
captive balloons. *See* balloon, observation
Carranza, Venustiano, 29–31, 37–39, 41–42, 50–51
Carrizal, Mexico, 39, 41
Catulle-Mendès, Jane, 177–78
cavalry, 21, 23–24, 61, 65
Central Association of South Carolina, 170
Charleston (WV) Gazette, 149

Christian Commission, 142, 170
Clark, Champ, 60
Cold Harbor, Battle of, 19, 22, 167
Columbus, NM, 37–38
Compston, Robert J. O., 132, 137, 144, 146, 151, 155, 183
Congressional Medal of Honor, 29, 190, 197–98
Cornwell, John J., 60, 65–66, 68–70, 73, 78, 80–82, 84–85, 153, 182–84
Creech, Jesse Orin, 194
Culbertson (wife of J. D. Culbertson), 170, 176
Culbertson, Tingle W., 167
Curtiss Aeroplane Company, 41, 57
Curtiss School, 33, 41

Dallenne, Madeleine, 160, 165, 180, 182
Daniels, Josephus, 55, 68
Davis, John W., 68, 141, 146, 150, 205
Davis, Michael F., 115
Davison, Frederick Trubee, 6, 8–9, 17, 33, 41, 68, 156, 225, 227
Delannoy, Leon, 159–62, 165, 179, 182
Democratic National Convention (DNC), 205, 224
de Ropp, Harold, 44, 46
Detten, G. von, 24
Devera, Anna, 185–86
Dillon, William "Bill," 137, 166–67
Distinguished Flying Cross (DFC), 113, 153–55, 184, 190
Dixon, George "Dixie," 117, 120, 129–33, 153, 155
Don, France, 130, 159, 164
Doolittle, James "Jimmy," 2–3
Douai, France, 123, 131
Douhet, Giulio, 7
Drachen. See balloon, observation
Dredge, Charles, 122, 125–26, 131, 144
Dr. Marvel's Sanitarium, 105, 110, 112, 135
Du Bois, W. E. B., 204
DuPont Corporation, 7, 82–83
Dusch, Bud, 1, 3

election of 1916, 30, 39, 44–45, 49
English Channel, 20, 22, 24, 193
Escadrille Lafayette, 6, 70, 73, 86, 155, 157

Farwell, Johnny, 136
Fere-en-Tardenois, France, 116–17
Field, W. Laurie, 146
First Aero Squadron, 37, 58
Foch, Ferdinand, 23, 108, 110, 115, 117, 137
football, 14, 16, 29, 33, 43–44, 75, 160, 214
Fort Hancock, TX, 42
Fort Washington, 41
Foulois, Benjamin, 37
France, SS, 186
Frantz, Joseph, 24
Frommherz, Hermann, 194
Frost, John and Dora, 109, 135, 143, 146, 156, 176, 179, 216

George V (George Frederick Ernest Albert of Saxe-Coburg and Gotha), 184, 193, 198; and Queen Mary (Mary of Teck, Victoria Mary Augusta Louise Olga Pauline Claudine Agnes), 184, 200
Glenn L. Martin Aeroplane Company, 57
Glen Springs, TX, 38
Gondecourt airfield, 130
Governor's Island, 57, 59
Grand Army of the Republic, 5
Grenzhausen, Germany, 134, 180
Grider, John McGavock, 81, 90, 107
Guggenheim, Daniel, 2

Hadley, Arthur Twining, 15, 28
Haig, Douglas, 99, 115, 119, 155
Harmon Speedster, 33
Hartney, Harold, 59, 70
Harvard University, 15, 26, 28–29, 38, 40, 44, 75; Harvard-Yale Boat Race ("The Race"), 40–41
Hay, James, 35–36
Hays, Cordelia, 75, 143, 147, 150, 181, 195
Hays, Mary, 75, 83, 87, 91, 104, 118, 138, 143, 146–48, 151, 195

Herchenroder, Hans, 165
Herrick, Myron, 24
Hiddessen, Ferdinand von, 24
Hoboken, NJ, 183, 186–87
Hollywood Memorial Association of the Ladies of Richmond, VA, 174
Holtzendorff, Henning von, 48
Horne, Ashley: North Carolina monument to Confederate women, 209
Hoskins, Etta, 158, 171
Hoskins, Stephen Paul, 158, 167
House, Edward M. "Colonel," 45
House Military Affairs Committee, 35
Hubbard, William P., 61
Hughes, Charles Evans, 39
Hull, Cordell, 205

infantry, 41, 53, 56, 60, 99–101, 107–8, 121, 127–28, 133, 147, 184
influenza pandemic, 43, 148–50, 187

Jackson, Thomas J. "Stonewall," 4, 13, 20, 42, 89, 138, 203, 213, 226
Jeanmonod, M., 182, 186
Joffre, Joseph Jacques Césaire "Papa," 22
Johnson, Owen, 17
Jones (wife of R. W. Jones), 183
Jones, J. Sumner, 219
Jordan, David Starr, 62
Jusserand, Elise, 161, 181

Keen, Arthur William, 110, 137
Kennesaw Mountain, Battle of, 19
Kent, William "Tommy," Jr., 32, 72–73, 78, 80, 86
Kerr, Walter, 158
kite balloons. *See* balloon, observation
Knights of Columbus (KofC), 185

La Bassée, France, 130, 132–33, 164
ladies' memorial associations, 202–5, 224; Daughters of the American Revolution (DAR), 203; National Association of Colored Women (NACW), 203–4; Women's Relief Corps (WRC), 203–4

Index   265

See also United Daughters of the Confederacy (UDC)
La Guardia, Fiorello, 106
Lahm, Frank P., 25, 57, 155
Lambert, Albert B., 25, 57
Lambert, Courtney B. *See* West Virginia Flying Corps (West Virginia Aerial Reserve Unit)
Lambert, William "Bill," 114, 121
Landis, Reed, 115, 126, 132–33, 145–46, 153, 155, 226
Lane, Franklin, 55
Lansing, Robert, 37
Laredo, TX, 39
Larrabee, Edward Payne, 183
League of Nations, 47, 187
Lee, Robert E., 13, 193, 209
LeRougetel, Etta, 93, 101, 110, 114, 138, 143, 146–47, 151
Lewis, Cecil, 120
Lewis County, WV, 12–13, 140, 149, 188
Libby, Frederick, 122
Lille, France, 130, 156, 158, 161, 179
Lindbergh, Charles A., 1–4, 9–10, 14, 222, 227, 230
Linsly Institute, 2–3, 210–14, 216, 219–22, 228, 230; Robert C. Hazlett, 213–14, 228; J. J. Holloway, 212–13; George Mecklinburg, 220; Lee C. Paull, 211; Otto Schenk, 221. See also *Aviator, The* (statue)
Lloyd-George, David, 45
London Cenotaph, 10, 190, 192, 197
"Lost Cause," 4, 197, 202–3; and the "Cause Victorious," 197
Louisiana Soldiers' Relief Association, 170
Lovett, Robert "Bob," 24, 41, 52, 227
Lowell, A. Lawrence, 28
Ludendorff, Erich F. W., 98–101, 107–8, 114–15, 121, 127, 133
Lusitania, RMS, 26–27, 30

Manifest Destiny, and similar American Victorian ideas, 171–72, 204; Ambrose Bierce, 172; Horace Bushnell, 171; "Good Death," 170–72; Herman Melville, 172; Protestant doctrine, 61, 171, 174–76, 178; soldier martyrdom, 5, 60, 171, 174, 204, 216, 220; Walt Whitman, 172
Mannock, Edward "Mick," 107, 110, 113, 123, 126, 131, 137
Marblehead, MA, 33, 38–40
Marina, merchantman, 45
Marne, First Battle of, 21–23
Marne, Second Battle of, 108, 115–16
Marquillies, France, 165–66, 180
Marske-by-the-Sea, Great Britain, 101, 103–4, 124
Maxwell, James, 12
McCudden, James, 121, 137
McElroy, George E. H. "McIrish," 114, 118, 120–22, 137, 153
McKinley, Johnson Bennett, 228
McKinley, Johnson C., 12, 51, 53, 56, 58–60, 62, 64–65, 69, 76, 82–83, 87, 92, 105, 111–12, 136, 139–40, 142–43, 148–49, 156, 159, 182, 186, 227
Memorial Day (Decoration Day), 192, 204, 228
Merkelbach, Emil, 133–34, 180–81, 216
Merville, France, 125–26
Meuse-Argonne, Battle of, 137, 223
Mexican Revolution, 29–32, 37–39, 41–43, 48
Meyer, Cord, 33
Miller, James E., 167
Milling, Thomas DeWitt, 183
millionaires' camps. *See* Preparedness Movement
Mitchell, William "Billy," 7, 9, 58, 86, 116, 184, 212, 215, 227
Monash, John, 121
Morrill Act (1862), 36
Mortelecque, Henri, 166
Moundsville, WV, 2, 220

Napier, Ian "Old Naps," 126
National Cemetery System, 173–74, 196, 202; Meuse-Argonne American Cemetery and Memorial, 223

National Defense Act of 1916, 34, 36, 47, 57
National Guard, 26, 28, 34–36, 38–43, 49, 57, 66, 68, 72–73, 76, 81–82, 228; National Aeroplane Fund, 56–57
New York, 1–2, 14, 18–19, 25, 27, 29–30, 33, 37–38, 59–60, 63, 66, 92–93, 110, 142–44, 146, 148–49, 153–54, 182–83, 185–87, 196, 209–10, 219, 225; aviation, 1–2, 25, 44, 56–57, 59, 65–66, 69, 70, 80–82, 84; Bennett social scene, 33, 37, 44, 46, 52; New York, New Haven and Hartford Railroad, 14; *New York Times*, 52, 69; *New York Tribune*, 40, 60; *New York World*, 60; St. Thomas Episcopal Church, 188
Northern Panhandle, WV, 56, 63–64, 140, 220

Offutt, Bertha, 178
Offutt, Jarvis, 24, 32, 38, 86, 115, 136–37, 167, 178
Ohio Valley, 1, 63, 76, 86, 144, 219–20, 223
Oliver Magnetic Car, 44
Oxford Group, 90

Paris, France, 1, 3, 20–22, 24, 99, 108, 146, 156, 160, 182, 186, 188, 196, 209, 219, 223; *Paris Herald*, 207
Parral, Mexico, 38
Patrick, Mason Matthews, 9, 111, 146, 157, 161–62, 184–85, 210–12, 227
Peary, Robert E., 25, 57
Pennsylvania Railroad, 64
Perkins, Elizabeth, 96–98, 100
Pershing, John J., 37–38, 43, 48, 50, 57–58, 100–101, 111, 169, 190–91, 197–98, 225
Pershing Expedition. *See* Punitive Expedition
Petite Hantay, France, 133, 181
Pflieger, Robert Paul, 21, 32
Plancque, Marie Louise, 159, 164–66, 182
Plattsburg Movement. *See* Preparedness Movement

poison gas, 26, 99
Polk, Franklin, 152–53
Preparedness Movement, 7, 9, 25–29, 32, 34, 36, 38, 39, 46, 56, 225
prisoner of war (POW), 136–37, 144, 146
Punitive Expedition, 37–38, 43, 48, 50, 57–58
Purple Cross, 169

Quénault, Louis, 24

Race to the Sea, 22–23
Ralston, Orville A. "Tubby," 96, 106–7, 113, 116–17, 119–20, 136, 183–84
Randolph, Janet, 201
reconnaissance, 22–24, 85, 91, 99, 102, 116–17, 124, 127
Red Cross, 143, 146, 150–52, 156–57, 179
Reid, William, 122, 125–26, 129–31, 144, 146, 152
Reserve Officers Training Corps (ROTC), 36, 47. *See also* National Defense Act of 1916
Richthofen, Manfred von, 100, 115–16; Richtofen Circus, 116
Rickenbacker, Edward "Eddie," 14, 84, 116
Roosevelt, Theodore, 8, 14, 21, 27, 35, 39, 67, 116, 172, 177, 187, 225; Roosevelt Legion, 67, 84; Quentin Roosevelt, 14, 116; Rough Riders, 29, 36, 67
Root, Elihu, 39
Rotterdam, SS, 182
Roy, Indra Lal "Laddie," 113, 153–54
Royal Air Force (RAF). *See* Royal Flying Corps (RFC)
Royal Flying Corps (RFC), 8, 59, 70, 75, 87–92, 94, 100–101, 110, 114, 119, 122, 126, 130–31, 136, 143, 144, 146, 150, 153–55, 166, 183, 193–94, 198–99, 205–7, 218; No. 22 Squadron, 130; No. 24 Squadron, 114; No. 40 Squadron, 106–7, 110, 113–15, 117, 126–27, 130, 132, 137, 145–47, 152–54, 193; No. 56 Squadron, 136, 153; No. 85 Squadron, 107, 110, 113, 117, 120; No. 90

Squadron, 105–6, 140; Nos. 208, 210, 211, 213, 218 Squadrons, 130; Air Ministry, 143, 146, 150, 166, 198–99, 205, 218; "Ak-emma" (*AM*), 122; Central Flying School, Military Wing, Upavon, Wiltshire, 94; Finishing School of Aerial Gunnery at Turnberry, Scotland, 98; Royal Aircraft Factory, 101; Royal Flying Corps (RFC) Memorial Window, 193–210; Shotwick airfield, Chester, Great Britain, 105, 109–10
Ruggles-Brise, Harold, 155

Salmond, John, 126
San Ignacio, TX, 39
Sanitary Commission, 142, 170
Savoy Hotel, 94–95, 97–98, 110
Schlieffen Plan, 20–21; Alfred von Schlieffen, 20
Schmulbach Building, 64, 76, 220
School of Military Aeronautics at Princeton University, 81–82, 84–86, 92
Schrecklichkeit, 21
Second Great Awakening, 171
Sheepshead Bay, NY, 65
Shenandoah, USS, 215; Margaret Lansdowne, 215
Shenandoah Valley, 13, 20
Siebold, George, 194
Signal Officers' Reserve Corps, 85
Snedeker, Dean, 74
Snoke, Ralph, 136
Somme, Battle of the, 22
Spanish Influenza. *See* influenza pandemic
Spirit of St. Louis, 1–2
Springs, Elliot White, 107
Squier, George, 34, 65–66, 70, 75, 85–86
Stafford, Nathaniel H., 186
St. Luke's Preparatory School, PA, 14
Sutherland, Howard, 152, 221

Taft, William Howard, 48–49
Taliaferro Fields, Fort Worth, TX, 90, 92
textile firms, 59

Thaw, William "Bill," 155
Tobyhanna, PA, 27, 41, 43, 225
Touchstone, Grady, 115, 136
Trans-Oceanic Company, 68
Treaty of Versailles, 158, 187
Trenchard, Hugh, 193, 206
trench warfare, 19, 22
Tudhope, John, 106, 109–10, 113
Turner, Frank Browne, 33

United Daughters of the Confederacy (UDC), 183, 202–3, 208–9
unrestricted submarine warfare, 6, 26–27, 30, 45, 48, 51, 61, 93–94, 138
US Air Service (USAS). *See* US Army Air Service (USAAS)
US Army Air Service (USAAS), 7–8, 24–25, 33, 41, 52, 59, 63, 65, 69–70, 72–73, 75, 82, 84–87, 90, 111, 115–16, 132, 155, 157, 183–85, 199, 207, 211, 215, 220, 226; I Corps Observation Group, 115; 1st Pursuit Group, 115; 4th Pursuit Group, 115; 17th Pursuit Squadron, 130, 136, 194; 25th Pursuit Squadron, 115, 132; 95th Pursuit Squadron, 116; 148th Pursuit Squadron, 115, 194; Army Air Corps, 9, 227; Bolling Field, 211, 213; Langin Army Airfield, 2, 220; Simonin, A. E., 220
US Marine Corps, 108, 137, 212, 265
US Military Academy (West Point), 13, 65, 111

Verdun, Battle of, 22, 38, 196
Victoria Cross, 198
Villa, Francisco "Pancho," 37–39, 50

Walmer Castle, SS, 153
Wanamaker, Lewis Rodman, 41, 56, 68
War Department, US Army, 7–8, 35–36, 49, 64–65, 69–70, 76–77, 81–82, 84–85, 168–69, 173–75, 177, 185–86, 211, 226; Army Corps of Engineers, 77, 184, 211–13; Army of Occupation, 185; Newton D. Baker, 8, 36, 43, 49, 55, 64,

War Department, US Army, (*continued*) 68–69, 72, 76, 84–85, 169, 186; Continental Army proposal, 34–36; J. L. Donaldson, 174–75; Lindley M. Garrison, 34–35; General Order 75, 168; Montgomery Meigs, 172; Hugh Scott, 34–35, 39, 225; US Army Graves Registration Service (GRS), Quartermaster Corps, 157–58, 166–69, 172, 174–75; US Army War College, 34–35, 39, 50

Warwood, WV, 64, 76–77, 83

Washington, DC, 3, 34, 44, 46, 56, 68, 70, 72–73, 82, 143, 161, 188, 211–13, 221, 227; *Washington Post*, 207

Wavrin, France, 9, 151, 156–61, 165, 179, 186, 196, 218, 227; German Field Ambulance 25, 179; German field hospital, 159, 165, 179, 181; Memorial Chapel, 10, 159, 162, 165, 179, 181, 184, 218

Wellsburg, WV, 84, 87

Western Front, 7–8, 19, 22, 26, 59, 73, 99–101, 105, 108, 113, 115, 117, 121, 133, 140, 142, 169

Westminster Abbey, 10, 190, 193, 198, 203, 205–8, 224, 227; Burlison and Grylls, 198, 207; Frederick Guest, 206–7; RFC Memorial Window, 193, 195, 199, 205–8, 210; Herbert E. Ryle, 206–7; Tomb of the Unknown Warrior, 190–91, 193, 195, 197, 199, 206–7, 216

Weston, WV, 12–13, 44, 60, 138–39, 144, 160–61, 181–82, 186–88, 218, 221, 227, 229; Edwin Bailey, 221; Louis Bennett League, 188, 221; Louis Bennett Sr. funeral, 138–39; Louis Bennett War Memorial and Public Library, 187–88; Machpelah Cemetery, 186; Mentir Ralston Jr., 221; St. Paul's Episcopal Church, 188; *Weston Democrat*, 13

West Virginia Aircraft Company, 63, 73, 77, 83, 112, 156, 220

West Virginia Aircraft Factory. *See* West Virginia Aircraft Company

West Virginia Flying Corps (West Virginia Aerial Reserve Unit), 6–8, 52–53, 59, 60, 62–65, 68–74, 76–79, 81–86, 199, 205, 212, 220–21, 226, 228; Jack Adams, 73, 221, 228; Dan Burns, 73, 221; William Frey, 70–73, 75, 78–80; investors, 62; E. A. Kelly, 59, 70, 78, 80; Courtney B. Lambert, 73, 79–82

Weyerhaeuser, Frederick, 17, 32–34, 38, 72, 84, 86, 106–7, 119, 155

Wheeling, WV, 1–4, 7, 10, 12, 33, 46, 53, 56, 60–65, 67, 70, 72, 75–77, 80, 82–84, 86–87, 92–93, 112, 136, 144, 154, 187, 207, 210–13, 216, 219–23, 227; William Brice, 152; Independence Day parade, 112; industries and transportation, 63–64; Peninsula Traction Company and Wheeling Traction Company, 64, 76, 80; William J. Steen, 221; *Wheeling Daily News*, 61; Wheeling Hospital, 76, 80; *Wheeling Intelligencer*, 2, 12, 60–61, 215, 219; *Wheeling News Register*, 61, 152, 158, 223

Williams, Alice, 93, 95–96, 109–12, 135, 143, 218; National Federation of Women's Institutes, 135

Williams, O. E., 46

Wilson, Woodrow, 7–8, 10, 21, 25, 27, 29–30, 34–41, 43–51, 54–56, 60–62, 66–69, 78, 141, 168, 172, 186–87

women's suffrage, 141, 201, 223

Wood, Leonard, 28–29, 35, 225

Yale University, 5–6, 8–9, 14–19, 21–22, 24–26, 28–29, 31–33, 36–41, 43–47, 52, 62, 70, 89, 103, 106, 120, 136–37, 154–55, 184, 208–9, 226; Alpha Delta Phi fraternity, 37–38, 43; Lester Page Breckenridge, 25; George Parmly Day, 208; Durfee Hall, 19; Fayerweather Hall, 32; First Yale Unit ("the Millionaires' Unit"), 6, 33, 41, 67–68, 73, 156; Franklin Hall, 46; freshman rush, 14–16, 43; Haughton Hall, 32; "heelers," 15, 28, 172, 208, 227; lacrosse, 16, 26, 37–38; Osborne Hall, 43; "The Race," 40–41; sand, 15, 17–18, 208, 226; Scroll and Key, 15; Sheffield Scientific School, 25; Skull and Bones, 15; *Stover at Yale* (Johnson), 17; Tap Day, 15, 32, 38; Vanderbilt Hall, 43, 53, 208, 210; Whiffenpoofs, 15; Wolf's Head, 15; Woolsey Hall, 28; wrestling, 16, 36–37, 46–47; Yale Battery, 26, 28, 32–33, 37–38, 40–41, 43, 47, 67, 84; *Yale Daily News*, 15

Young, Houston, 64
Young Men's Christian Association (YMCA), 185, 201

zeppelin. *See* airship
Zimmermann, Arthur, 50–51
Zinn, Frederick W., 157, 167

About the Author

Conner Dusch

Dr. Charles D. Dusch is an author and historian who currently serves on the Eberly College of Arts and Sciences Visiting Committee at West Virginia University. He is a founding member of the US Space Force History and Heritage Program and is the former command historian of the United States Air Force Academy.

A recipient of three Department of the Air Force Excellence in History Awards in 2020, 2021, and 2022, Dr. Dusch has been published by the Institute for National Security Studies (INSS), Sorbonne Université Presses, Air University Press, the Naval Institute Press, the *Journal of Military History*, and the *International Encyclopedia of the First World War*, among others.

His teaching assignments include the United States Air Force Academy, Regis University, the University of Colorado Colorado Springs campus, and West Virginia University. He is a retired Air Force weapon systems officer with over two thousand flight hours in RF-4C Phantom II and F-15E Strike Eagle aircraft, including twenty-eight combat missions over Iraq and Bosnia.

A Mitchell Institute Book
Aviation and Air Power
Series Editor: Brian D. Laslie

In his work *Winged Defense*, Brigadier General William "Billy" Mitchell stated, "Air power may be defined as the ability to do something in the air." Since Mitchell made this statement, the definition of air power has been contested and argued about by those on the ground, those in the air, academics, industrialists, and politicians.

Each volume of the Aviation and Air Power series seeks to expand our understanding of Mitchell's broad definition by bringing together leading historians, fliers, and scholars in the fields of military history, aviation, air power history, and other disciplines in the hope of providing a fuller picture of just what air power accomplishes.

This series offers an expansive look at tactical aerial combat, operational air warfare, and strategic air theory. It explores campaigns from the First World War through modern air operations, along with the heritage, technology, culture, and human element particular to the air arm. In addition, this series considers the perspectives of leaders in the US Army, Navy, Marine Corps, and Air Force as well as their counterparts in other nations and their approaches to the history and study of doing something in the air.